Planning and Maintaining a Microsoft® Windows® Server 2003 Network Infrastructure

Exam 70-293

Planning and Maintaining a Microsoft® Windows® Server 2003 Network Infrastructure

Exam 70-293

First Edition

Kenneth C. Laudon, Series Designer
Stacey McBrine, MCSE, MCSA
Simon Sykes-Wright, MCSE

The Azimuth Interactive MCSE/MCSA Team

Carol G. Traver, Series Editor
Kenneth Rosenblatt
Russell Polo
Robin L. Pickering
David Langley
Stacey McBrine, MCSE, MCSA
Richard Watson, MCSE, MCSA
Brien Posey, MCSE
Russell Jones, MCSE
Tim Oliwiak, MCSE, MCT
Nigel Kay, MCSE
David Lundell, MCSE, MCT
L. Ward Ulmer, MCSE, MCT
Wale Soyinka, MCP
David W. Tschanz, MCSE
Mark Maxwell

PEARSON
Prentice
Hall

Upper Saddle River, New Jersey, 07458

Senior Vice President/Publisher: Natalie Anderson
Executive Editor Certification: Steven Elliot
Director of Marketing: Sarah McLean
Marketing Assistant: Barrie Reinhold
Project Manager, Editorial: Laura Burgess
Editorial Assistants: Alana Meyers and Jenille Logan
Media Project Manager: Joan Waxman
Senior Project Manager, Production: Tim Tate
Manufacturing Buyer: Jessica Rivchin
Art Director: Pat Smythe
Design Manager: Maria Lange
Interior Design: Kim Buckley
Cover Designer: Pat Smythe
Cover Photo: Joseph DeSciose/Aurora Photos
Associate Director, Multimedia: Karen Goldsmith
Manager, Multimedia: Christy Mahon
Full Service Composition: Azimuth Interactive, Inc.
Quality Assurance: Digital Content Factory Ltd.
Printer/Binder: Courier Companies, Inc., Kendallville
Cover Printer: Phoenix Color Corporation

10 9 8 7 6 5 4 3 2 1
0-13-189306-8

*To our families,
for their love, patience,
and inspiration.*

Brief Contents

Contents

Welcome to the Prentice Hall Certification Series!

You are about to begin an exciting journey of learning and career skills building that will provide you with access to careers such as Network Administrator, Systems Engineer, Technical Support Engineer, Network Analyst, and Technical Consultant. What you learn in the Prentice Hall Certification Series will provide you with a strong set of networking skills and knowledge that you can use throughout your career as the Microsoft Windows operating system continues to evolve, as new information technology devices appear, and as business applications of computers continues to expand. The Prentice Hall Certification Series aims to provide you with the skills and knowledge that will endure, prepare you for your future career, and make the process of learning fun and enjoyable.

Microsoft Windows and the Networked World

We live in a computer-networked world—more so than many of us realize. The Internet, the world's largest network, now has more than 500 million people who connect to it through an estimated 171 million Internet hosts. The number of local area networks associated with these 171 million Internet hosts is not known. Arguably, the population of local area networks is in the millions. About 60% of local area networks in the United States are using a Windows network operating system. The other networks use Novell NetWare or some version of Unix (Internet Software Consortium, 2003). About 95% of the one billion personal computers in the world use some form of Microsoft operating system, typically some version of Windows. A growing number of handheld personal digital assistants (PDAs) also use versions of the Microsoft operating system called Microsoft CE. Most businesses—large and small—use some kind of client/server local area network to connect their employees to one another, and to the Internet. In the United States, the vast majority of these business networks use a Microsoft network operating system—either earlier versions such as Windows NT and Windows 2000, or the current version, Windows Server 2003.

The Prentice Hall Certification Series prepares you to participate in this computer-networked world and, specifically, for the world of Microsoft Windows 2000 and XP Professional client operating systems, as well as Windows 2000 Server and Server 2003 operating systems.

Prentice Hall Certification Series Objectives

The first objective of the Prentice Hall Certification Series is to help you build a set of skills and a knowledge base that will prepare you for a career in the networking field. There is no doubt that in the next five years, Microsoft will issue several new versions of its network operating system, and new versions of Windows client operating system. In the next five years—and thereafter—there will be a steady stream of new digital devices that will require connecting to networks. Most of what you learn in the Prentice Hall Certification Series will provide a strong foundation for understanding future versions of the operating system.

The second objective of the Prentice Hall Certification Series is to prepare you to pass the MCSE/MCSA certification exams and to receive certification. Why get certified? As businesses increasingly rely on Microsoft networks to operate, employers want to make sure their networking staff has the skills needed to plan for, install, and operate these networks. While job experience is an important source of networking knowledge, employers increasingly rely on certification examinations to ensure their staff has the necessary skills. The MCSE/MCSA curriculum provides networking professionals with a well-balanced and comprehensive body of knowledge necessary to operate and administer Microsoft networks in a business setting.

There is clear evidence that having the MCSE/MCSA certification results in higher salaries and faster promotions for individual employees. Therefore, it is definitely in your interest to obtain certification, even if you have considerable job experience. If you are just starting out in the world of networking, certification can be very important for landing that first job.

The Prentice Hall Certification Series teaches you real-world, job-related skills. About 90% of the work performed by MCSE/MCSAs falls into the following categories, according to a survey researcher (McKillip, 1999):

■ Analyzing the business requirements for a proposed system architecture.
■ Designing system architecture solutions that meet business requirements.

- Deploying, installing, and configuring the components of the system architecture.
- Managing the components of the system architecture on an ongoing basis.
- Monitoring and optimizing the components of the system architecture.
- Diagnosing and troubleshooting problems regarding the components of the system architecture.

These are precisely the skills we had in mind when we wrote this Series. As you work through the hands-on instructions in the text, perform the instructions in the simulated Windows environment on the Interactive Solution CD-ROM, and complete the problem solving cases in the book, you will notice our emphasis on analyzing, designing, diagnosing, and implementing Windows software. By completing the Prentice Hall Certification Series, you will be laying the foundation for a long-term career based on your specialized knowledge of networks and general problem solving skills.

Preparing you for a career involves more than satisfying the official MCSE/MCSA objectives. As you can see from the list of activities performed by MCSE/MCSAs, you will also need a strong set of management skills. The Prentice Hall Certification Series emphasizes management skills along with networking skills. As you advance in your career, you will be expected to participate in and lead teams of networking professionals in their efforts to support the needs of your organization. You will be expected to describe, plan, administer, and maintain computer networks, and to write about networks and give presentations to other business professionals. We make a particular point in this Series of developing managerial skills such as analyzing business requirements, writing reports, and making presentations to other members of your business team.

Who Is the Audience for This Book?

The student body for the Prentice Hall Certification Series is very diverse, and the Series is written with that in mind. For all students, regardless of background, the Series is designed to function as a *learning tool* first, and, second, as a compact reference book that can be readily accessed to refresh skills. Generally, there are two types of software books: books aimed at learning and understanding how a specific software tool works, and comprehensive reference books. This series emphasizes learning and explanation and is student-centered.

The Prentice Hall Certification Series is well suited to beginning students. Many students will just be starting out in the networking field, most in colleges and training institutes. The Series introduces these beginning students to the basic concepts of networking, operating systems, and network operating systems. We take special care in the introductory chapters of each book to provide the background skills and understanding necessary to proceed to more specific MCSE/MCSA skills. We cover many more learning objectives and skills in these introductory lessons than are specifically listed as MCSE/MCSA objectives. Throughout all Lessons, we take care to *explain why things are done*, rather than just list the steps necessary to do them. There is a vast difference between understanding how Windows works and why, versus rote memorization of procedures.

A second group of students will already have some experience working with networking systems and Windows operating systems. This group already has an understanding of the basics, but needs more systematic and in-depth coverage of MCSE/MCSA skills they lack. The Prentice Hall Certification Series is organized so that these more experienced students can quickly discover what they do not know, and can skip through introductory Lessons quickly. Nevertheless, this group will also appreciate our emphasis on explanation and clear illustration throughout the series.

A third group of students will have considerable experience with previous Microsoft operating systems such as Windows NT. These students may be seeking to upgrade their skills and prepare for the Windows 2000/XP/2003 MCSE/MCSA examinations. They may be learning outside of formal training programs as self-paced learners, or in distance learning programs sponsored by their employers. The Prentice Hall Certification Series is designed to help these students quickly identify the new features of new versions of Windows, and to rapidly update their existing skills.

Prentice Hall Series Skills and MCSE/MCSA Objectives

In designing and writing the Prentice Hall Certification Series, we had a choice between organizing the book into lessons composed of MCSE/MCSA domains and objectives, or organizing the book into lessons composed of skills needed to pass the MCSE/MCSA certification examinations (a complete listing of the domains and objectives for the relevant exam will be found inside the front and back covers of the book). We chose to organize the book around skills, beginning with introductory basic skills, and building to more advanced skills. We believe this is a more orderly and effective way to teach students the MCSE/MCSA subject matter and the basic understanding of Windows network operating systems.

Yet we also wanted to make clear exactly how the skills related to the published MCSE/MCSA objectives. In the Prentice Hall Series, skills are organized into Lessons. At the beginning of each Lesson, there is an introduction to the set of skills covered in the Lesson, followed by a table that shows how the skills taught in the Lesson support specific MCSE/MCSA objectives. All MCSE/MCSA objectives for each of the examinations are covered; at the beginning of each skill discussion, the exact MCSE/MCSA objective relating to that skill is identified.

We also recognize that as students approach the certification examinations, they will want learning and preparation materials that are specifically focused on the examinations. Therefore, we have designed the MCSE/MCSA Interactive Solution CD-ROM to follow the MCSE/MCSA domains and objectives more directly. Students can use these tools to practice answering MCSE/MCSA examination questions, and practice implementing these objectives in a realistic simulated Windows environment.

What's Different About the Prentice Hall Series—Main Features and Components

The Prentice Hall Certification Series has three distinguishing features that make it the most effective MCSE/MCSA learning tool available today. These three features are a graphical illustrated 2-page spread approach, a skills-based systematic approach to learning MCSE/MCSA objectives, and an interactive *multi-channel pedagogy*.

Graphical illustrated approach. First, the Prentice Hall Certification Series uses a graphical, illustrated approach in a convenient *two-page spread format* (see illustration below). This makes learning easy, effective, and enjoyable.

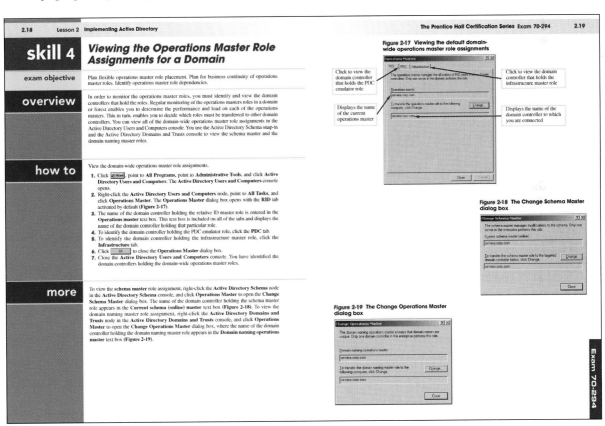

Each two-page spread is devoted to a single skill. On the left-hand side of the two-page spread, you will find a conceptual overview explaining what the skill is, why it is important, and how it is used. Immediately following the conceptual overview is a series of *How To Steps* showing how to perform the skill. On the right hand side of the two-page spread are screen shots that show you exactly how the screen should look as you follow the steps. The pedagogy is easy to follow and understand.

In addition to these main features, each two-page spread contains several *learning aids*:

- *More:* a brief section that provides more information about the skill, alternative ways to perform the skill, and common business applications of the skill.
- *Tips:* hints and suggestions to follow when performing the skill, placed in the left margin opposite the text to which it relates.
- *Caution:* short notes about the pitfalls and problems you may encounter when performing the skill, also placed in the left margin opposite the text to which it relates.

At the end of each Lesson, students can test and practice their skills using three End-of-Lesson features:

- *Test Yourself:* a multiple-choice examination that tests your comprehension and retention of the material in the Lesson.
- *Projects: On Your Own:* short projects that test your ability to perform tasks and skills in Windows without detailed step-by-step instructions.
- *Problem Solving Scenarios:* real-world business scenarios that ask you to analyze or diagnose a networking situation, and then write a report or prepare a presentation that presents your solution to the problem.

Skills-based systematic approach. A second distinguishing feature of the Prentice Hall Certification Series is a *skills-based* systematic approach to MCSE/MCSA certification by using five integrated components:

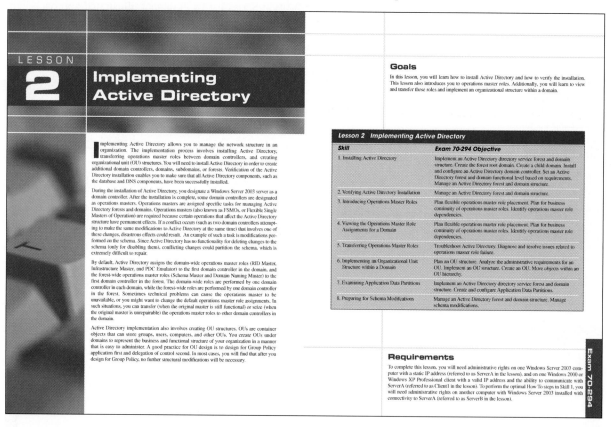

- Main Book—organized by skills.
- Project Lab Manual—for practicing skills in realistic settings.
- Examination Guide—organized by MCSE/MCSA domains and objectives to practice answering questions representative of questions you are likely to encounter in the actual MCSE/MCSA examination.
- Interactive Solution multimedia CD-ROM—organized by MCSE/MCSA domains and objectives—that allows students to practice performing MCSE/MCSA objectives in a simulated Windows environment.
- Powerful Website—provides additional questions, projects, and interactive training.

Within each component, the learning is organized by skills, beginning with the relatively simple skills and progressing rapidly through the more complex skills. Each skill is carefully explained in a series of steps and conceptual overviews describing why the skill is important.

The Interactive Solution CD-ROM is especially useful to students who do not have access to a Windows network on which they can practice skills. It also is useful to all students who want to practice MCSE/MCSA skills efficiently without disturbing an existing network. Together, these five components make the Prentice Hall Certification Series an effective learning tool for students, increasing the speed of comprehension and the retention of knowledge.

Interactive media multi-channel learning. A third distinguishing feature of the Prentice Hall Certification Series is interactive media *multi-channel* learning. Multi-channel learning recognizes that students learn in different ways, and the more different channels used to teach students, the greater the comprehension and retention. Using the Interactive Solution CD-ROM, students can see, hear, read, and actually perform the skills needed in a simulated Windows environment on the CD-ROM. The CD-ROM is based directly on materials in the books, and therefore shares the same high quality and reliability. The CD-ROM and Website for the book provide high levels of real interactive learning—not just rote exam questions—and offer realistic opportunities to interact with the Windows operating system to practice skills in the software environment without having to install a new version of Windows or build a network.

Supplements Available for This Series:

1. Test Bank

The Test Bank is a Word document distributed with the Instructor's Manual (usually on a CD). It is distributed on the Internet to Instructors only. The purpose of the Test Bank is to provide instructors and students with a convenient way for testing comprehension of material presented in the book. The Test Bank contains forty multiple-choice questions and ten true/false questions per Lesson. The questions are based on material presented in the book and are not generic MCSE questions.

2. Instructor's Manual

The Instructor's Manual (IM) is a Word document (distributed to Instructors only) that provides instructional tips, as well as answers to the Test Yourself questions and the Problem Solving Scenarios. The IM also includes an introduction to each Lesson, teaching objectives, and teaching suggestions.

3. PowerPoint Slides

The PowerPoint slides contain images of all the conceptual figures and screenshots in each book. The purpose of the slides is to provide the instructor with a convenient means of reviewing the content of the book in the classroom setting.

4. Companion Website

The Companion Website is a Pearson learning tool that provides students and instructors with online support. On the Prentice Hall Certification Series Companion Website, you will find the Interactive Study Guide, a Web-based interactive quiz composed of fifteen or more questions per Lesson. Written by the authors, there are more than 255 free interactive questions on the Companion Website. The purpose of the Interactive Study Guide is to provide students with a convenient online mechanism for self-testing their comprehension of the book material.

About This Book

Exam 70-293 Planning and Maintaining a Microsoft Windows Server 2003 Network Infrastructure

This book covers the subject matter of Microsoft's Exam 70-293, which focuses on Windows Server 2003. More specifically, you will learn how to plan and maintain a Windows Server 2003 network infrastructure. First, you will examine the network infrastructure planning process, and then plan server roles, plan and optimize network connections, and plan and implement security. You also will learn how to secure remote and wireless access, and then plan remote administration, plan network monitoring, and plan data protection and recovery. Finally, you will learn how to troubleshoot infrastructure problems and to create the master network infrastructure plan.

The following knowledge domains are discussed in this book:

- Planning and Implementing Server Roles and Server Security.
- Planning, Implementing, and Maintaining a Network Infrastructure.
- Planning, Implementing, and Maintaining Routing and Remote Access.
- Planning, Implementing, and Maintaining Server Availability.
- Planning and Maintaining Network Security.
- Planning, Implementing, and Maintaining Security Infrastructure.

How This Book Is Organized

This book is organized into a series of Lessons. Each Lesson focuses on a set of skills you will need to learn in order to master the knowledge domains required by the MCSE/MCSA examinations. The skills are organized in a logical progression from basic knowledge skills to more specific skills. Some skills—usually at the beginning of Lessons—give you the background knowledge you will need in order to understand basic operating system and networking concepts. Most skills, however, give you hands-on experience working with Windows Server 2003 and, in some cases, Windows 2000 Server and Windows XP Professional client computers. You will follow step-by-step instructions to perform tasks using the software.

At the beginning of each Lesson, you will find a table that links the skills covered to specific exam objectives. For each skill presented on a 2-page spread, the MCSE/MCSA objective is listed.

The MCSE/MCSA Certification

The MCSE/MCSA certification is one of the most recognized certifications in the Information Technology world. By following a clear-cut strategy of preparation, you will be able to pass the certification exams. The first thing to remember is that there are no quick and easy routes to certification. No one can guarantee you will receive a certification—no matter what they promise. Real-world MCSE/MCSAs get certified by following a strategy involving self-study, on-the-job experience, and classroom learning, either in colleges or training institutes. Below are answers to frequently asked questions that should help you prepare for the certification exams.

What Is the MCP Program?

The MCP program refers to the Microsoft Certified Professional program that certifies individuals who have passed Microsoft certification examinations. Certification is desirable for both individuals and organizations. For individuals, an MCP certification signifies to employers your expertise and skills in implementing Microsoft software in organizations. For employers, MCP certification makes it easy to identify potential employees with the requisite skills to develop and administer Microsoft tools. In a recent survey reported by Microsoft, 89% of hiring managers said they recommend a Microsoft MCP certification for candidates seeking IT positions.

What Are the MCP Certifications?

Today there are seven different MCP certifications. Some certifications emphasize administrative as well as technical skills, while other certifications focus more on technical skills in developing software applications. Below is a listing of the MCP certifications. The Prentice Hall Certification Series focuses on the first two certifications.

- *MCSA:* Microsoft Certified Systems Administrators (MCSAs) administer network and systems environments based on the Microsoft Windows® platforms.
- *MCSE:* Microsoft Certified Systems Engineers (MCSEs) analyze business requirements to design and implement an infrastructure solution based on the Windows platform and Microsoft Server software.
- *MCDBA:* Microsoft Certified Database Administrators (MCDBAs) design, implement, and administer Microsoft SQL Server™ databases.
- *MCT:* Microsoft Certified Trainers (MCTs) are qualified instructors, certified by Microsoft, who deliver Microsoft training courses to IT professionals and developers.
- *MCAD:* Microsoft Certified Application Developers (MCADs) use Microsoft technologies to develop and maintain department-level applications, components, Web or desktop clients, or back-end data services.
- *MCSD:* Microsoft Certified Solution Developers (MCSDs) design and develop leading-edge enterprise-class applications with Microsoft development tools, technologies, platforms, and the Windows architecture.
- *Microsoft Office Specialist:* Microsoft Office Specialists (Office Specialists) are globally recognized for demonstrating advanced skills with Microsoft desktop software.
- *MCP:* Microsoft Certified Professionals.

What Is the Difference Between MCSA and MCSE Certification?

There are two certifications that focus on the implementation and administration of the Microsoft operating systems and networking tools: MCSA and MCSE. The MCSA credential is designed to train IT professionals who are concerned with the management, support, and troubleshooting of existing systems and networks (see diagram below).

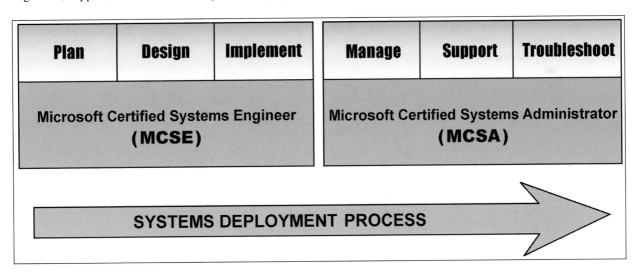

MCSA prepares you for jobs with titles such as Systems Administrator, Network Administrator, Information Systems Administrator, Network Operations Analyst, Network Technician, or Technical Support Specialist. Microsoft recommends that you have six to twelve months experience managing and supporting desktops, servers, and networks in an existing network infrastructure.

The MCSE certification is designed to train IT professionals who are concerned with the planning, designing, and implementation of new systems or major upgrades of existing systems. MCSE prepares you for jobs with titles such as Systems Engineer, Network Engineer, Systems Analyst, Network Analyst, or Technical Consultant. Microsoft recommends that you have at least one year of experience planning, designing, and implementing Microsoft products.

What Does the MCSA on Windows Server 2003 Require?

MCSA candidates are required to pass a total of four exams: three core exams and one elective exam. The list below shows examinations that are included in the MCSA track.

Core Exams (3 Exams Required)

(A) Networking System (2 Exams Required)

- *Exam 70-290:* Managing and Maintaining a Microsoft Windows Server 2003 Environment
  and
- *Exam 70-291:* Implementing, Managing, and Maintaining a Microsoft Windows Server 2003 Network Infrastructure

(B) Client Operating System (1 Exam Required)

- *Exam 70-270:* Installing, Configuring, and Administering Microsoft Windows XP Professional
  or
- *Exam 70-210:* Installing, Configuring, and Administering Microsoft Windows 2000 Professional

Elective Exams (1 Exam Required)

- *Exam 70-086:* Implementing and Supporting Microsoft Systems Management Server 2.0
- *Exam 70-227:* Installing, Configuring, and Administering Microsoft Internet Security and Acceleration (ISA) Server 2000, Enterprise Edition
- *Exam 70-228:* Installing, Configuring, and Administering Microsoft SQL Server 2000 Enterprise Edition
- *Exam 70-284:* Implementing and Managing Microsoft Exchange Server 2003
- *Exam 70-299:* Implementing and Administering Security in a Microsoft Windows Server 2003 Network

As an alternative to the electives listed above, you may substitute the following Microsoft certifications for an MCSA elective:

- MCSA on Microsoft Windows 2000
- MCSE on Microsoft Windows 2000
- MCSE on Microsoft Windows NT 4.0

You may also substitute the following third-party certification combinations for an MCSA elective:

CompTIA Exams: *CompTIA A+* and *CompTIA Network+*
  CompTIA A+ and *CompTIA Server+*
  CompTIA Security+

What Is the MCSE Curriculum for Windows Server 2003?

MCSE candidates are required to pass a total of seven exams: six core exams and one elective exam. The list below shows the examinations that are included in the MCSE track.

Core Exams (6 Exams Required)

(A) Networking System (4 exams required)

- *Exam 70-290:* Managing and Maintaining a Microsoft Windows Server 2003 Environment
- *Exam 70-291:* Implementing, Managing, and Maintaining a Microsoft Windows Server 2003 Network Infrastructure
- *Exam 70-293:* Planning and Maintaining a Microsoft Windows Server 2003 Network Infrastructure
  and
- *Exam 70-294:* Planning, Implementing, and Maintaining a Microsoft Windows Server 2003 Active Directory Infrastructure

(B) Client Operating System (1 Exam Required)

■ *Exam 70-270:* Installing, Configuring, and Administering Microsoft Windows XP Professional
  or
■ *Exam 70-210:* Installing, Configuring, and Administering Microsoft Windows 2000 Professional

(C) Design (1 Exam Required)

■ *Exam 70-297:* Designing a Microsoft Windows Server 2003 Active Directory and Network Infrastructure
  or
■ *Exam 70-298:* Designing Security for a Microsoft Windows Server 2003 Network

Elective Exams (1 Exam Required)

■ *Exam 70-086:* Implementing and Supporting Microsoft Systems Management Server 2.0
■ *Exam 70-227:* Installing, Configuring, and Administering Microsoft Internet Security and Acceleration (ISA) Server 2000 Enterprise Edition
■ *Exam 70-228:* Installing, Configuring, and Administering Microsoft SQL Server™ 2000 Enterprise Edition
■ *Exam 70-229:* Designing and Implementing Databases with Microsoft SQL Server™ 2000 Enterprise Edition
■ *Exam 70-232:* Implementing and Maintaining Highly Available Web Solutions with Microsoft Windows 2000 Server Technologies and Microsoft Application Center 2000
■ *Exam 70-282:* Designing, Deploying, and Managing a Network Solution for a Small- and Medium-Sized Business
■ *Exam 70-284:* Implementing and Managing Microsoft Exchange Server 2003
■ *Exam 70-297:* Designing a Microsoft Windows Server 2003 Active Directory and Network Infrastructure
■ *Exam 70-298:* Designing Security for a Microsoft Windows Server 2003 Network
■ *Exam 70-299:* Implementing and Administering Security in a Microsoft Windows Server 2003 Network

As an alternative to the electives listed above, you may substitute the following Microsoft certifications for an MCSE elective:

■ MCSA on Microsoft Windows 2000
■ MCSE on Microsoft Windows 2000
■ MCSE on Microsoft Windows NT 4.0

You may also substitute the following third-party certification combinations for an MCSE elective:

■ *CompTIA Security+*
■ Unisys UN0-101: Implementing and Supporting Microsoft Windows Server 2003 Solutions in the Data Center

What About Upgrading From a Previous Certification?

Microsoft provides upgrade paths for MCSAs and MCSEs on Windows 2000 so that they can acquire credentials on Windows Server 2003 efficiently and economically. For details on upgrade requirements, visit the following Microsoft Web pages:

http://www.microsoft.com/learning/mcp/mcsa/windows2003/
http://www.microsoft.com/learning/mcp/mcse/windows2003/

Do You Need to Pursue Certification to Benefit from This Book?

No. The Prentice Hall Certification Series is designed to prepare you for the workplace by providing you with networking knowledge and skills regardless of certification programs. While it is desirable to obtain a certification, you can certainly benefit greatly by just reading these books, practicing your skills in the simulated Windows environment found on the MCSE/MCSA Interactive Solution CD-ROM, and using the online interactive study guide.

What Kinds of Questions Are on the Exam?

The MCSE/MCSA exams typically involve a variety of question formats.

(a) Select-and-Place Exam Items (Drag and Drop)

A select-and-place exam item asks candidates to understand a scenario and assemble a solution (graphically on screen) by picking up screen objects and moving them to their appropriate location to assemble the solution. For instance, you might be asked to place routers, clients, and servers on a network and illustrate how they would be connected to the Internet. This type of exam item can measure architectural, design, troubleshooting, and component recognition skills more accurately than traditional exam items can, because the solution—a graphical diagram—is presented in a form that is familiar to the computer professional.

(b) Case Study-Based Multiple-Choice Exam Items

The candidate is presented with a scenario based on typical Windows installations, and then is asked to answer several multiple-choice questions. To make the questions more challenging, several correct answers may be presented, and you will be asked to choose all that are correct. The Prentice Hall Certification Series Test Yourself questions at the end of each Lesson give you experience with these kinds of questions.

(c) Simulations

Simulations test your ability to perform tasks in a simulated Windows environment. A simulation imitates the functionality and interface of Windows operating systems. The simulation usually involves a scenario in which you will be asked to perform several tasks in the simulated environment, including working with dialog boxes and entering information. The Prentice Hall Certification Series Interactive Solution CD-ROM gives you experience working in a simulated Windows environment.

(d) Computer Adaptive Testing

A computer adaptive test (CAT) attempts to adapt the level of question difficulty to the knowledge of each individual examinee. An adaptive exam starts with several easy questions. If you get these right, more difficult questions are pitched. If you fail a question, the next questions will be easier. Eventually the test will discover how much you know and what you can accomplish in a Windows environment.

You can find out more about the exam questions and take sample exams at the Microsoft Web site:
http://www.microsoft.com/learning/mcp/default.asp.

How Long is the Exam?

Exams have fifty to seventy questions and last anywhere from 60 minutes to 240 minutes. The variation in exam length is due to variation in the requirements for specific exams (some exams have many more requirements than others), and because the adaptive exams take much less time than traditional exams. When you register for an exam, you will be told how much time you should expect to spend at the testing center. In some cases, the exams include timed sections that can help for apportioning your time.

What Is the Testing Experience Like?

You are required to bring two forms of identification that include your signature and one photo ID (such as a driver's license or company security ID). You will be required to sign a non-disclosure agreement that obligates you not to share the contents of the exam questions with others, and you will be asked to complete a survey. The rules and procedures of the exam will be explained to you by Testing Center administrators. You will be introduced to the testing equipment and you will be offered an exam tutorial intended to familiarize you with the testing equipment. This is a good idea. You will not be allowed to communicate with other examinees or with outsiders during the exam. You should definitely turn off your cell phone when taking the exam.

How Can You Best Prepare for the Exams?

Prepare for each exam by reading this book, and then practicing your skills in a simulated environment on the Interactive Solution CD-ROM that accompanies this series. If you do not have a real network to practice on (and if you do not build a small network), the next best thing is to work with the CD-ROM. Alternatively, it is very helpful to build a small Windows Server 2003 network with a couple of unused computers. You will also require experience with a real-world Windows Server 2003 network. An MCSE/MCSA candidate should, at a minimum, have at least one year of experience implementing and administering a network operating system in environments with the following characteristics: a minimum of 200 users, five supported physical locations, typical network services and applications including file and print, database, messaging, proxy server or firewall, dial-in server, desktop management, and Web hosting, and connectivity needs, including connecting individual offices and users at remote locations to the corporate network and connecting corporate networks to the Internet.

In addition, an MCSE candidate should have at least one year of experience in the following areas: implementing and administering a desktop operating system, and designing a network infrastructure.

Where Can You Take the Exams?

All MCP exams are administered by Pearson VUE and Prometric. There are 3 convenient ways to schedule your exams with Pearson VUE:
- Online: **www.pearsonvue.com/ms/**
- Toll Free in the US and Canada: call (800) TEST-REG (800-837-8734). Or, find a call center in your part of the world at: **http://www.pearsonvue.com/contact/ms/**
- In person: at your local test center. Pearson VUE has over 3,000 test centers in 130 countries. To find a test center near you, visit: **www.pearsonvue.com**

To take exams at a Prometric testing center, call Prometric at (800) 755-EXAM (755-3926). Outside the United States and Canada, contact your local Prometric Registration Center. To register online with Prometric, visit the Prometric web site, **www.prometric.com**.

How Much Does It Cost to Take the Exams?

In the United States, exams cost $125 USD per exam as of January, 2004. Certification exam prices are subject to change. In some countries/regions, additional taxes may apply. Contact your test registration center for exact pricing.

Are There Any Discounts Available to Students?

Yes. In the US and Canada, as well as other select regions around the globe, full-time students can take a subset of the MCP exams for a significantly reduced fee at Authorized Academic Testing Centers (AATCs). For details on which countries and exams are included in the program, or to schedule your discounted exam, visit **www.pearsonvue.com/aatc**.

Can You Take the Exam More Than Once?

Yes. You may retake an exam at any time if you do not pass on the first attempt. But if you do not pass the second time, you must wait fourteen days. A 14-day waiting period will be imposed for all subsequent exam retakes. If you have passed an exam, you cannot take it again.

Where Can I Get More Information about the Exams?

Microsoft Web sites are a good place to start:

MCP Program (general): **http://www.microsoft.com/learning/mcp/default.asp**

MCSE Certification: **http://www.microsoft.com/learning/mcp/mcse/**

MCSA Certification: **http://www.microsoft.com/learning/mcp/mcsa/**

There are literally thousands of other Web sites with helpful information that you can identify using any Web search engine. Many commercial sites will promise instant success, and some even guarantee you will pass the exams. Be a discriminating consumer. If it was that easy to become an MCP professional, the certification would be meaningless.

Acknowledgments

A great many people have contributed to the Prentice Hall Certification Series. We want to thank Steven Elliot, our editor at Prentice Hall, for his enthusiastic appreciation of the project, his personal support for the Azimuth team, and his deep commitment to the goal of creating a powerful, accurate, and enjoyable learning tool for students. We also want to thank David Alexander of Prentice Hall for his interim leadership and advice as the project developed at Prentice Hall, and Jerome Grant for supporting the development of high-quality certification training books and CDs for colleges and universities worldwide. Finally, we want to thank Susan Hartman Sullivan of Addison Wesley for believing in this project at an early stage and for encouraging us to fulfill our dreams.

The Azimuth Interactive MCSE/MCSA team is a dedicated group of technical experts, computer scientists, networking specialists, and writers with literally decades of experience in computer networking, information technology and systems, and computer technology. We want to thank the members of the team:

Kenneth C. Laudon is the Series Designer. He is Professor of Information Systems at New York University's Stern School of Business. He has written twelve books on information systems and technologies, e-commerce, and management information systems. He has designed, installed, and fixed computer networks since 1982.

Carol G. Traver is the Senior Series Editor. She is General Counsel and Vice President of Business Development at Azimuth Interactive, Inc. A graduate of Yale Law School, she has co-authored several best-selling books on information technology and e-commerce.

Kenneth Rosenblatt is a Senior Author for the Series. He is an experienced technical writer and editor who has co-authored or contributed to over two dozen books on computer and software instruction. In addition, Ken has over five years experience in designing, implementing, and managing Microsoft operating systems and networks. Ken is a co-author of the Prentice Hall Certification Series Exam 70-216, Exam 70-270, and Exam 70-291 textbooks.

Robin L. Pickering is a Senior Author for the Series. She is an experienced technical writer and editor who has co-authored or contributed to over a dozen books on computers and software instruction. Robin has extensive experience as a Network Administrator and consultant for a number of small to medium-sized firms. In addition to this book, Robin is a co-author of the Prentice Hall Certification Series Exam 70-210, Exam 70-215, and Exam 70-270 textbooks.

Russell Polo is the Technical Advisor for the Series. He holds degrees in computer science and electrical engineering. He has designed, implemented, and managed Microsoft, Unix, and Novell networks in a number of business firms since 1995. He currently is the Network Administrator at Azimuth Interactive.

David Langley is an Editor for the Series. David is an experienced technical writer and editor who has co-authored or contributed to over ten books on computers and software instruction. In addition, he has over fifteen years experience as a college professor, five of those in computer software training.

Brian Hill is a Technical Consultant and Editor for the Series. His industry certifications include MCSE 2000 and 2003, MCSA 2000 and 2003, MCSE+I (NT 4.0), CCNP, CCDP, MCT, MCP, Net+, and A+. Brian was formerly Lead Technology Architect and a Bootcamp instructor for Techtrain, Inc. His Windows 2000 experience spans back as far as the first Beta releases. In addition to this book, Brian is also a co-author of the Prentice Hall Certification Series Exam 70-217 and Exam 70-294 textbooks.

L. Ward Ulmer is a former Information Technology Director with eleven years of experience. He began teaching Computer Science in 1996 and has held teaching positions at Patrick Henry Academy and Trident Technical College. He became the Department Chair of Computer Technology Orangeburg-Calhoun Technical College, his current position, in 2000. Ward's certifications include MCSE, MCSA, CCNA, MCP+I, MCT, and CCAI. Ward is a co-author of the Prentice Hall Certification Series Exam 70-217 and Exam 70-294 Project Lab Manuals.

Acknowledgments (cont'd)

Richard Watson has worked in the industry for 10 years, first as a Checkpoint Certified Security Engineer (CCSE), and then as a Lead Engineer for a local Microsoft Certified Solution Provider. Among his many other industry certifications are MCSE on Windows 2000 and NT4, Microsoft Certified Trainer (MCT), Cisco Certified Network Associate (CCNA), and IBM Professional Server Expert (PSE). Richard is currently the President of Client Server Technologies Inc., which provides network installation and support, Web site design, and training in Beaverton, Oregon. Richard is a co-author of the Prentice Hall Certification Series Exam 70-220 and Exam 70-291 textbooks.

Stacey McBrine has spent more than 18 years configuring and supporting DOS and Windows-based personal computers and local area networks, along with several other operating systems. He is certified as an MCSE for Windows NT 4.0, and was one of the first 2000 persons in the world to achieve MCSE certification for Windows 2000. He has brought his real world experience to the classroom for the last 5 years as a Microsoft Certified Trainer. He holds several other certifications for Cisco, Linux, Solaris, and Security. Stacey is a co-author of the Prentice Hall Certification Series Exam 70-293 textbook and Exam 70-270 Lab Manual.

Mark Maxwell is a Technical Consultant and Editor for the Series. He has over fifteen years of industry experience in distributed network environments including TCP/IP, fault-tolerant NFS file service, Kerberos, Wide Area Networks, and Virtual Private Networks. Mark is a co-author of the Prentice Hall Certification Series Exam 70-216 Lab Manual, and has also published articles on network design, upgrades, and security.

Dr. Russell Jones is an Associate Processor and Area Coordinator of Decision Sciences at Arkansas State University and currently holds the Kathy White Endowed Fellowship in MIS. Dr. Jones received his PhD from the University of Texas-Arlington and has been on the ASU faculty for 16 years. He holds certifications from Microsoft, Novell, CompTIA, and Cisco, and is a co-author of the Prentice Hall Certification Series Exam 70-290 Project Lab Manual.

Nigel Kay, MCSE, is a technical writer from London, Ontario, Canada. He has contributed to several published IT certification guides, and is currently the documentation lead for a network security company. Previously, he worked for many years as a Network Administrator. Nigel is a co-author of the Prentice Hall Certification Series Exam 70-293 textbook and Project Lab Manual.

David W. Tschanz, MCSE, MCP+I, A+, iNET+, CIW, is an American who has been living in Saudi Arabia for the past 15 years. There he has worked on a variety of projects related to Web-based information management, training, and applications, as well as computer security issues. He writes extensively on computer topics and is a regular contributor to MCP Magazine. David is a co-author of the Prentice Hall Certification Series Exam 70-220 Lab Manual.

Brien M. Posey, MCSE, has been a freelance technical writer who has written for Microsoft, CNET, ZDNet, Tech Target, MSD2D, Relevant Technologies, and many other technology companies. Brien has also served as the CIO for a nationwide chain of hospitals and was once in charge of IT security for Fort Knox. Most recently, Brien has received Microsoft's MVP award for his work with Windows 2000 Server and IIS. Brien is a co-author of the Prentice Hall Certification Series Exam 70-218 textbook.

Tim Oliwiak, MCSE, MCT, is a network consultant for small- to medium-sized companies. He previously was an instructor at the Institute for Computer Studies, and a Network Engineer for the Success Network. Tim is a resident of Ontario, Canada. Tim is a co-author of the Prentice Hall Certification Series Exam 70-217 Project Lab Manual.

Simon Sykes-Wright, MCSE, has been a technical consultant to a number of leading firms, including NCR Canada Ltd. Simon is a co-author of the Prentice Hall Certification Series Exam 70-293 textbook.

David Lundell is a database administrator and Web developer for The Ryland Group in Scottsdale, Arizona. He holds MCSE, MCDBA, MCSD, MCT, CAN, and CCNA certifications, as well as an MBA from the University of Arizona. David is a co-author of the Prentice Hall Certification Series Exam 70-291 Project Lab Manual.

Wale Soyinka is a systems and network engineering consultant. He holds MCP, CCNA, and CCNP certification. He is the author of a series of lab manuals on Linux, and is a co-author of the Prentice Hall Certification Series Exam 70-218 Lab Manual.

Quality Assurance

The Prentice Hall Certification Series contains literally thousands of software instructions for working with Windows products. We have taken special steps to ensure the accuracy of the statements in this series. The books and CDs are initially written by teams composed of Azimuth Interactive Inc. MCSE/MCSA professionals and writers working directly with the software as they write. Each team then collectively walks through the software instructions and screen shots to ensure accuracy. The resulting manuscripts are then thoroughly tested by an independent quality assurance team of MCSE/MCSA professionals who also perform the software instructions and check to ensure the screen shots and conceptual graphics are correct. The result is a very accurate and comprehensive learning environment for understanding Windows products.

We would like to thank the primary member of the Quality Assurance Team for his critical feedback and unstinting efforts to make sure we got it right. The primary technical editor for this book is Jim Taylor. Jim Taylor is an independent consultant with over 30 years experience in the IT industry, including over 15 years experience with the Microsoft Windows operating systems, in addition to 14 years with the AIX and other Unix-like operating systems. Jim is an instructor and a consultant on various systems and platforms, and also serves as a technical editor of books on Microsoft, Linux, and Unix-related topics.

Conventions Used in This Book

◆ Bold and/or italicized text enclosed within carets, such as *<Server_name>*, indicates a variable item. The carets and bold/italic formatting are solely to alert you to the variable nature of the enclosed text and will not be present in your file structure. If called on to enter the information referred to within the carets, type only the information itself, not the carets, and do not use bold or italics.

◆ Keys on the keyboard are enclosed within square brackets, such as **[Alt]**. A plus sign (**+**) between two key names indicates that you must press those keys at the same time, for example, "press **[Ctrl]+[Alt]+[Del]**."

◆ Folder, file, and program names in the text are shown with initial capitals, although their on-screen appearance may differ. For example, in our text, you may see a reference to a Windows folder, but on your screen this folder may be shown as WINDOWS. Similarly, in our text, you may see a reference to the Iishelp folder, although on screen it may appear as iishelp. When typing folder and file names yourself, you may use upper and/or lower case as you choose unless otherwise instructed.

◆ Command line syntax: Commands to be entered at a command prompt are shown in lower case. Square brackets, carets, and/or bold/italic formatting used in command line syntax statements indicate a variable item. As with material shown within carets, if called on to enter such an item, type only the information referred to within the brackets or carets, not the brackets or carets themselves and do not use bold or italics.

◆ The term *%systemroot%* is used to indicate the folder in the boot partition that contains the Windows Server 2003 system files.

Installing, Configuring, and Administering Microsoft® Windows® 2000 Professional Exam 70-210
ISBN 0-13-142209-X

Installing, Configuring, and Administering Microsoft® Windows® 2000 Server Exam 70-215
ISBN 0-13-142211-1

Implementing and Administering Microsoft® Windows® 2000 Network Infrastructure Exam 70-216
ISBN 0-13-142210-3

Implementing and Administering a Microsoft® Windows® 2000 Directory Services
Infrastructure Exam 70-217   ISBN 0-13-142208-1

Managing a Microsoft® Windows® 2000 Network Environment Exam 70-218
ISBN 0-13-144744-0

Designing Security for a Microsoft® Windows® 2000 Network Exam 70-220   ISBN 0-13-144906-0

Installing, Configuring, and Administering Microsoft® Windows® XP Professional Exam 70-270
ISBN 0-13-144132-9

Managing and Maintaining a Microsoft® Windows® Server 2003 Environment Exam 70-290
ISBN 0-13-144743-2

Implementing, Managing, and Maintaining a Microsoft® Windows® Server 2003 Network
Infrastructure Exam 70-291   ISBN 0-13-145600-8

Planning, Implementing, and Maintaining a Microsoft® Windows® Server 2003 Active Directory
Infrastructure Exam 70-294   ISBN 0-13-189312-2

Designing a Microsoft® Windows® Server 2003 Active Directory and Network Infrastructure
Exam 70-297   ISBN 0-13-189316-5

Designing Security for a Microsoft® Windows® Server 2003 Network Exam 70-298
ISBN 0-13-117670-6

Examining the Network Infrastructure Planning Process

The initial steps in learning any new technology generally involve examining the key features of that technology and learning how to configure and implement it. This lesson assumes you have a basic understanding of the features and functions of Microsoft Windows Server 2003, as well as knowledge of how to configure them. It also assumes that you are aware of the skills required to administer a computer running Microsoft Windows Server 2003. Now it is time to continue to expand and develop your skill set to include the ability to plan and maintain a stable and functional network infrastructure.

Planning and maintaining a network infrastructure will require much more than just technical skills with Microsoft Windows Server 2003. It will be necessary to function as part of a planning team, applying best practices in a structured way to produce detailed plans for each component of a specified design. Each of these individual plans will describe exactly how a solution will need to be implemented and then they will be gathered together to produce one comprehensive Master Project Plan. During any project, there will always be compromises and trade-offs that need to be made in order to complete the solution on time, on budget, and with the required features. As part of the planning team, your roles may include making trade-off decisions, proving or disproving the viability of a particular design, specifying and testing components, working with key stakeholders as well as the customer, and analyzing the risk associated with planning choices.

While there are numerous methodologies to provide structure and discipline to a project, in this lesson we will examine and use the principles embodied in the Microsoft Solutions Framework (MSF). MSF supplies a model designed to improve the quality and success for information technology (IT) projects. It provides best practices with proven results that apply to planning, designing, developing, and deploying a successful solution. MSF provides a framework that will assist in managing a project from its inception to its implementation. The majority of the design work for a project occurs during the envisioning stage of the MSF model. The design team will formulate a solution and then provide it to the planning team so that they can begin to build the detailed plans that will be required to complete the solution.

Goals

In this lesson, you will learn how to apply the principles associated with the Microsoft Solutions Framework to planning and maintaining a Microsoft Windows Server 2003 network infrastructure. You will identify the components that go into producing a completed Master Project Plan and you will learn how to identify the key stakeholders in a network infrastructure project. You will also learn how to manage the scope of the project and the principles associated with controlling project scheduling.

Lesson 1	Examining the Network Infrastructure Planning Process
Skill	**Exam 70-293 Objective**
1. Introducing Structured Planning Using Microsoft Solutions Framework	Basic knowledge
2. Examining Components of a Master Project Plan	Basic knowledge
3. Identifying Key Stakeholders	Basic knowledge
4. Managing Project Scope	Basic knowledge
5. Controlling Project Scheduling	Basic knowledge

Requirements

There are no special requirements for this lesson.

skill 1

Introducing Structured Planning Using Microsoft Solutions Framework

exam objective

Basic knowledge

overview

tip

The Extreme CHAOS report by the Standish Group is available at **www.standishgroup.com /sample_research PDFpages/extreme _chaos.pdf**

tip

More information on MSF can be found at **http://www.microsoft. com/msf**

The **Microsoft Solutions Framework (MSF)** is a set of proven practices that can provide guidance in managing people and processes to plan, build, and deploy successful IT solutions. It was conceived to help businesses achieve their goals and improve the probability of success of their projects. Unfortunately, only a relatively small percentage of projects are successful. In fact, one study by the Standish Group indicated that 23% of all projects failed completely, 49% were not completed on time, within budget, or with required functionality, and only 28% were completed successfully, on time and on budget, with functionality that was the goal of the project. While MSF does not provide step-by-step instructions on project management, it does provide guidance that can be customized to fit your organization. It acts like a compass in that it gives you a sense of direction but you must still choose the path that your organization will follow. MSF is not technology specific and can apply to any IT project. Two main models are used as the foundation of MSF: the **team model** and the **process model**.

Under the MSF team model **(Figure 1-1)**, small multidisciplinary teams are encouraged to share responsibilities as they work together as peers. Within a team, there are six different **role clusters**: Program Management, Development, Test, Release Management, User Experience, and Product Management. You will note that the team model does not define an administrative hierarchy but instead defines roles critical to the success of a project and the corresponding goals that each of those roles must reach. Each role is accountable to the rest of their team to ensure the quality and completion of their goal. The team model enables open and honest communication, thereby avoiding misunderstandings and wasted efforts. This open communication is one of the six cornerstone principles of MSF **(Table 1-1)**. When making key decisions, all roles need to be involved in the process. For this reason, it is important that all team members subscribe to and share a common project vision. This **shared project vision** is based on a clear understanding of the goals and objectives for the project. Another fundamental principle of MSF is that team members must be empowered to be effective. This will ensure they meet the commitments they have made to the customer and other members of their team. **Empowering** team members means providing them with the resources required to achieve their goals, the authority to make decisions necessary to complete their work, and an understanding of their responsibilities within the team.

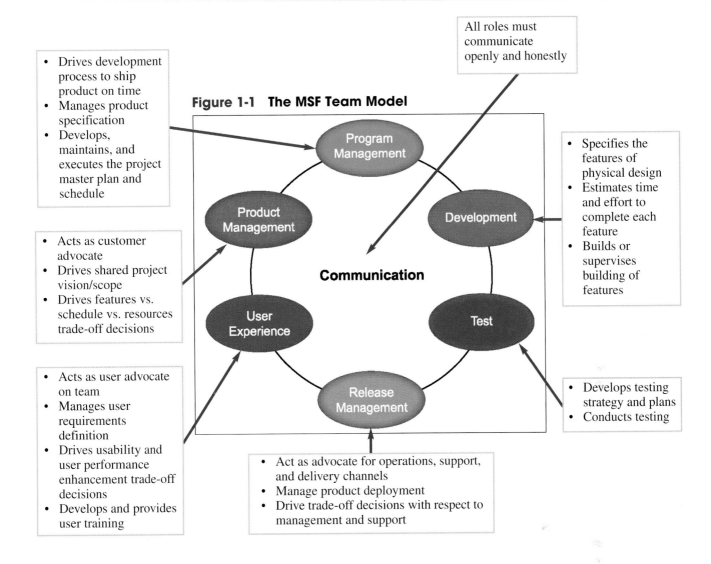

Figure 1-1   The MSF Team Model

- Drives development process to ship product on time
- Manages product specification
- Develops, maintains, and executes the project master plan and schedule

All roles must communicate openly and honestly

- Specifies the features of physical design
- Estimates time and effort to complete each feature
- Builds or supervises building of features

- Acts as customer advocate
- Drives shared project vision/scope
- Drives features vs. schedule vs. resources trade-off decisions

- Acts as user advocate on team
- Manages user requirements definition
- Drives usability and user performance enhancement trade-off decisions
- Develops and provides user training

- Act as advocate for operations, support, and delivery channels
- Manage product deployment
- Drive trade-off decisions with respect to management and support

- Develops testing strategy and plans
- Conducts testing

Table 1-1   The Six Key Principles of the MSF Team Model

Principle	Benefit
Work toward a shared vision	• Provides a clear understanding of what the goals and objectives are for the project. • Focuses the approach of the team.
Focus on business value	• Ensures that key project decisions are based on a solid understanding of the business.
Stay agile, expect change	• As challenges arise, team members can adapt to those changes.
Empower team members	• Builds trust between team members. • Team members are able to deliver on the commitments they have made.
Foster open communications	• Reduces the possibility of misunderstandings. • Ensures that all members of the team can contribute the perspective of their role to any key decisions.
Establish clear accountability with shared responsibility	• Each team member is responsible to the stakeholders, as well as every other team member. • Improves product quality when each role has a complete understanding of the whole project.

skill 1

Introducing Structured Planning Using Microsoft Solutions Framework (cont'd)

exam objective

Basic knowledge

overview

Attitudes of team members will have a profound impact on the success of their project. They must view each other as peers, with no role taking on more importance than any other does. Of course, the focus for each role will change somewhat, depending on the particular project phase involved. In this lesson, we are focusing on the planning phase of the MSF model. **Table 1-2** lists the primary focus and areas of responsibility for each role within the project team during the planning phase. In addition, the project team needs to develop a mindset where their number one priority is satisfying the customer. Open communication with the customer will ensure that they are able to participate in each phase of the project. Another mindset that is important to foster within the team is to be product-focused. While team members may play different roles within the project and may have different job responsibilities, it is important that all remember that their focus is to deliver a completed product to the customer. Developing this mindset will help each member of the team to feel personally responsible for the success of the project. This personal responsibility also leads to a commitment to the quality of the product. It is important that team members develop a zero-defect mindset and ensure their work is of the highest possible quality. The goal is to have a solution ready each day that could be delivered to the customer. If all the components that go into a solution are defect-free, then the final solution will also be of high quality.

Table 1-2 Team Role Focus During Planning

Role	Goal	Focus During Planning
Product Management	Satisfied customers	• Conceptual design • Business requirements analysis • Communications plan
Program Management	Delivering the solution within project constraints	• Conceptual and logical design • Functional specification • Master Project Plan • Master Project Schedule • Budget
Development	Build to specification	• Technology evaluation • Logical and physical design • Development plan/schedule • Development estimates
Test	Ensure all product quality issues are identified and addressed	• Design evaluation • Testing requirements • Test plan/schedule
User Experience	Enhanced user effectiveness	• Usage scenarios/cases • User requirements • Localization/accessibility requirements • User documentation/training • Plan/schedule for usability testing
Release Management	Smooth deployment and ongoing operations	• Design evaluation • Operations requirements • Pilot and deployment plan/schedule

skill 1

Introducing Structured Planning Using Microsoft Solutions Framework (cont'd)

exam objective

Basic knowledge

overview

The MSF process model defines a series of activities that have proven successful when applied to an IT project. Because so many IT projects fail, it is important to improve the probability of your success by applying a proven approach that is flexible enough to fit the needs of your organization. The six key principles (**Table 1-1** on page 1.5) associated with MSF that we examined earlier also apply to the MSF process model. There are also several key concepts associated with the process model that need to be understood (**Table 1-3**). First, it is important to understand the difference between a customer and a user. In most cases, the **customer** is the person or organization that funds the project and derives business benefit from it, and the **user** is the person who will use the solution; however, in some cases, they are the same person or organization. It is also necessary to identify the stakeholders for the project. A **stakeholder** is any person or group that is concerned that certain requirements or features are part of a solution. Another fundamental concept is the use of baselines. A **baseline** is a measurement of a known state of a component related to the solution. Almost all activities and deliverables will be baselined when they are substantially complete. It is recommended that baselines be created as early as possible. Once a baseline has been created for a solution component, any changes to that component need to be handled by change management. Defining the **solution scope** identifies the deliverables that the solution should produce and is a baseline for managing trade-off decisions. Making effective **trade-offs** is one of the primary keys to the success of any project. There is a relationship between the resources required for a project, the delivery schedule, and the features it will deliver. Any change to one of these items will necessitate corresponding adjustments to the other two.

The MSF process model is based on a spiral model with the addition of well-defined major milestones at the end of each project phase and well-defined minor milestones during each project phase (**Figure 1-2**). **Milestones** are predefined points in a project where specified portions of the project are completed. The process model is broken into five different phases that provide guidance for the processes required to complete an IT solution successfully. The five phases cover the life cycle of a project from the creation of the initial concept through to the live deployment of the completed solution. The five phases are as follows:

◆ The envisioning phase
◆ The planning phase
◆ The developing phase
◆ The stabilizing phase
◆ The deploying phase

The MSF process model does not provide guidance on managing the operation of an existing solution. The **Microsoft Operations Framework (MOF)** is a set of best practices that provides guidance for managing an operations environment. MOF is a customization of the practices defined in the **IT Infrastructure Library (ITIL)**, which is an internationally recognized resource for information on IT service management.

tip

You can find more information on MOF at **www.microsoft.com/mof**. Information on ITIL can be found at **www.ogc.gov.uk/index .asp?id=2261**.

Table 1-3   **Key Concepts for the Process Model**

Concept	Explanation
Customer	The individual or organization that funds and derives business benefit from a solution.
Stakeholder	Individual or group whose interests are at stake in a project. Their interest in the project is often different from that of the customer.
Baseline	Recording a measurement of a known state of any component related to a solution. Establishing a baseline allows team members to measure change within the project.
Scope	This can be broken into two different categories: solution scope and project scope. The solution scope specifies what features of the shared vision that the solution will deliver. The project scope defines what work will be required to complete the features defined by the solution scope.
Trade-off	By assigning priorities, balancing resources, schedules, and features, the project can be adjusted so that it will be successfully completed. Any change to one variable will always require compensating changes in the other variables.

Figure 1-2   **The MSF Process Model**

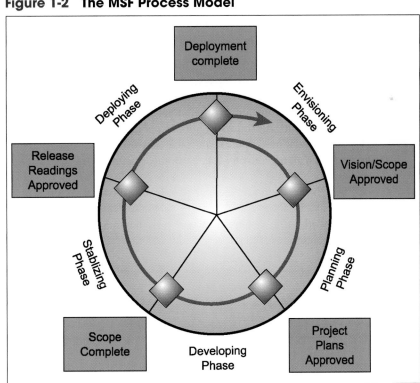

skill 1

Introducing Structured Planning Using Microsoft Solutions Framework (cont'd)

exam objective Basic knowledge

overview

When using the MSF process model, the majority of the design work for an IT solution occurs during the envisioning phase. During the **envisioning phase**, the team will focus primarily on a conceptual model for the solution. The key milestone for the envisioning phase is reached when the vision/scope document is approved. The approval of this document also marks the beginning of the planning phase.

During the **planning phase**, the team continues to build upon the vision/scope document produced during the envisioning phase. They produce the functional specifications, work plans, schedules, and budget estimates for the project. While the work during the envisioning phase focuses on concepts, during the planning phase the team will determine exactly how to build the solution by specifying the technical details required for each component of the solution. Each role holder must then produce a plan for the deliverables for which he or she is responsible. This will result in a set of plans from each of the roles that are then examined by the entire team to identify and manage any dependencies. These individual plans combine to form the **Master Project Plan**. The role holders must also perform risk analysis and produce cost estimates and delivery schedules for the components defined in their plan. All of these schedules combine to form the **Master Project Schedule**. At the end of the planning phase the customer, stakeholders, and the team members must examine the Master Project Plan and Master Project Schedule to ensure that they represent the required deliverables and an acceptable timeline. When all details are agreed upon, the project plans approved milestone has been reached and the **developing phase** can begin.

When we apply MSF to network infrastructure planning, the network infrastructure design document that is produced during the envisioning phase will normally include logical and physical network diagrams. The **logical network diagram (Figure 1-3)** shows the domain architecture, including any trust relationships and server roles within the domain architecture, such as domain controllers or global catalog servers. The **physical network diagram (Figure 1-4)** outlines all of the physical network connections, including both LAN and WAN connections, along with any details for those connections such as their bandwidth. It includes all network-attached devices, such as hubs, switches, routers, modems, CSU/DSUs, and printers. The physical network diagram should also show all servers with their role, domain membership, and IP address. The network diagrams provide a basis for planning and maintaining your network infrastructure. Both network diagrams should be kept up-to-date because they provide a baseline for the network configuration and are invaluable when troubleshooting.

Figure 1-3 Sample logical network diagram

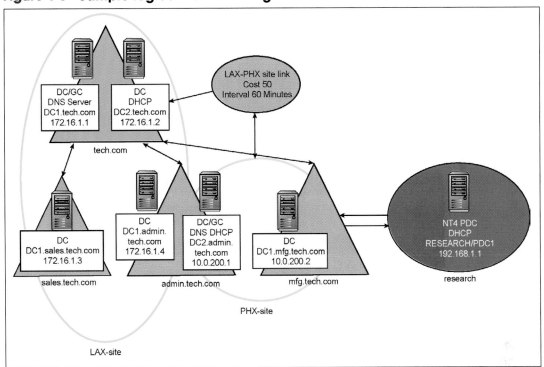

Figure 1-4 Sample physical network diagram

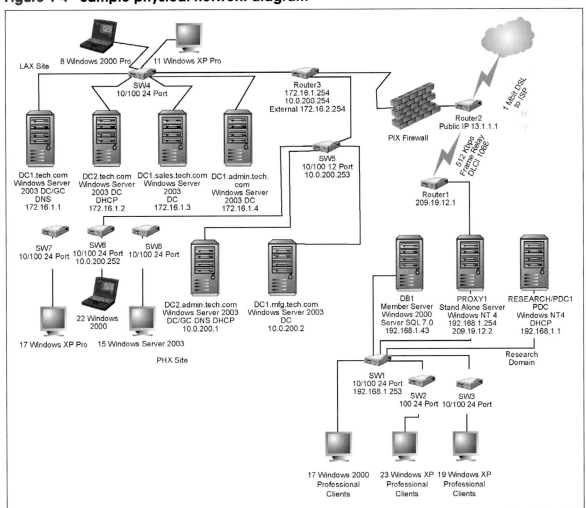

skill 2

Examining Components of a Master Project Plan

exam objective

Basic knowledge

overview

The Master Project Plan (**Figure 1-5**) is not a separate plan of its own but is comprised of all of the individual detailed plans created by the planning team. Normally each team lead will produce a plan related to his or her MSF role (**Table 1-4**). Each of these plans is a description of how each component of the completed solution will be produced. The actual number of individual plans that make up the Master Project Plan will vary depending on the scope of the project. Because the Master Project Plan consists of several individual plans, it allows for concurrent planning by each of the roles. This also ensures accountability and responsibility for the content of each of the individual plans.

As team members examine the vision/scope document provided by the design team, they determine how they will create the necessary components of the solution. Each team lead will produce a plan for his or her role that defines *how* his or her components will be built — not *what* components will be built. To identify exactly what will be built, the teams work together to create the functional specifications for the solution. This may require the validation of the proposed technology to ensure that it provides a viable solution. Once the functional specifications are substantially complete, they are baselined so that changes can be managed.

how to

You are assigned the role of Program Management for the IT infrastructure project within your organization.

1. List the project plans for which you will be responsible.
2. Describe the contents of each of the project plans.
3. Identify any additional documents needed during the planning phase.
4. Perform additional research on MSF at **http://www.microsoft.com/msf** to find the names of the three separate disciplines within MSF.

more

The team lead that holds the program management role will coordinate the other roles to produce a **Work Breakdown Structure (WBS)**. The WBS is an outline of the work that is necessary to produce the required deliverables. As the team plans, they need to ensure that each feature in the solution is traceable to a design requirement. The WBS maps the activities necessary to produce each feature in the solution to a requirement in the functional specification. The WBS is very useful for developing plans, budgets, and schedules because it takes a project and breaks it into the work needed to complete a solution. Once the work to be completed is clearly understood, it is much easier to determine the cost, schedule, and resources required.

Defines the characteristics of the participants and which components will be tested

Lists the hardware, software, and the facilities required to deploy the solution

Identifies the possible risks to the success of the project, specifies the steps that you will take to mitigate selected risks, and lists the risks that you are willing to accept

Estimated project costs from each team are tabulated

Figure 1-5 Components of a Master Project Plan

Specifies what will be tested, by whom, what tools will be needed, and the criteria that will define a successful test

Ensures that existing and new equipment will provide an acceptable level of performance; this involves items such as network bandwidth, storage, processor speed, and RAM

Defines how problems with the solution will be managed; this can include backups, troubleshooting, and help desk functions

While there is shared accountability within the team, the communications plan defines the reporting structure for the team and indicates who is responsible for providing information to the customer

Defines the methods for deployment, the steps to take if there is a problem with the deployment and the tools required to perform it

Identifies the tools that will be used to develop the features outlined in the functional specification

Specifies how and when training will be delivered, what it will include, and who will receive it

Defines which components of the solution will be protected, against what threats, and how

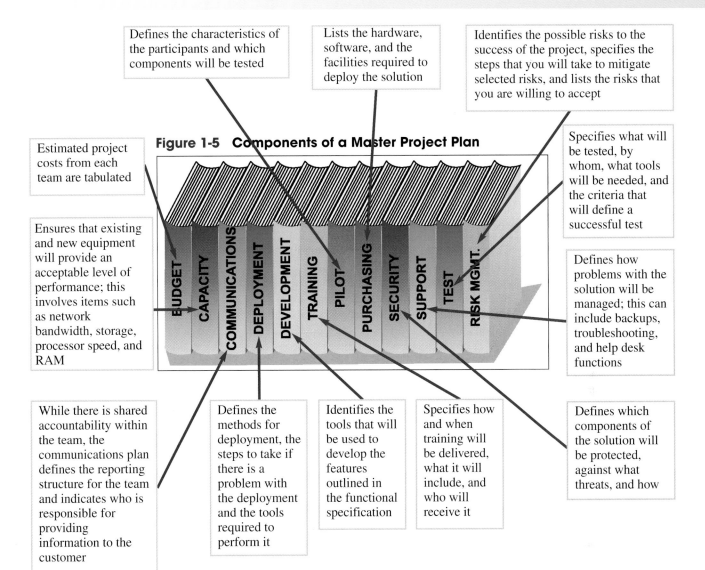

Table 1-4 Team Lead Responsibilities for Individual Plans

Team Lead	Detailed Plan
Program Management	Budget Capacity Risk Management Purchasing
Release Management	Deployment Support Pilot Security
Development Management	Development
Product Management	Communications
User Experience Management	Training
Test Management	Test

skill 3

Identifying Key Stakeholders

exam objective

Basic knowledge

overview

Stakeholders are individuals that will be affected either by the successful outcome of a solution or by the processes leading up to that outcome. Their interest in the project can be quite different from that of the customer and they will each have their own priorities. It is important to be able to identify all the stakeholders early in the project and address their needs.

The product management role is primarily concerned with identifying the stakeholders and managing the relationship with them. In order to locate all stakeholders, members representing each MSF role need to participate as part of the project team that will identify them. It is best to limit the size of that team to no more than eight people if possible. The team should include someone who understands the technical issues of the project, the individual responsible for the project implementation, a person who understands the hierarchy and politics of the company, and someone who understands any external relationships.

Stakeholders are found throughout an organization, and the success of the solution will depend upon their support. This of course means that they must understand and agree with the proposed solution. Then they must be willing to commit whatever resources may be necessary and to maintain that commitment through to the completion of the project. For this reason, any group within the organization that will be affected by the outcome of the project should be identified.

By creating a **stakeholder map**, the political relationships between stakeholders can be identified. This can help to reveal risks to the project due to stakeholder resistance or lack of project sponsorship. It can also show the communication route between each stakeholder. You can categorize stakeholders based on their power within the organization, their goals for the project, and their level of commitment to the project.

A stakeholder map can be presented in different ways. For example, **Figure 1-6** shows a diagram based on a grid with stakeholder interest on the x-axis and stakeholder power on the y-axis. By breaking the grid into quadrants, it becomes clear which stakeholders will require more project involvement and communication. Another type of diagram uses bubbles for each stakeholder connected by lines to indicate the political relationships and communications paths between them **(Figure 1-7)**.

Figure 1-6 Stakeholder map based on interest and power

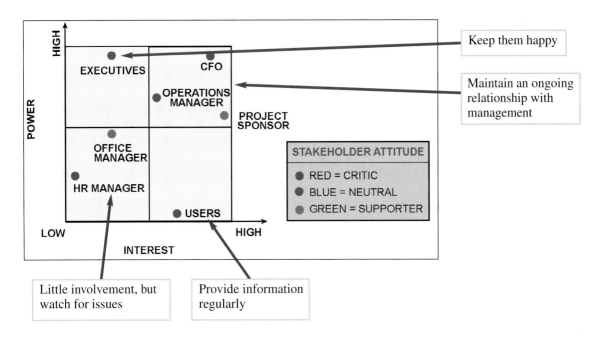

Figure 1-7 Stakeholder map based on project hierarchy

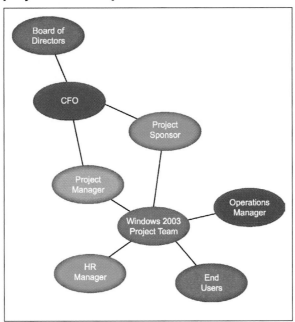

Identifying Key Stakeholders (cont'd)

exam objective   Basic knowledge

overview

A final method is to produce a stakeholder profile by creating a table that lists the stakeholders and their interests in the project (**Table 1-5**).

Although there can be many types of stakeholders, some that are common to many projects are listed below:

◆ Managers whose staff will be affected by the new solution, possibly requiring training, changes in responsibilities, and changes to work schedules.
◆ Managers whose business processes will change because of the solution.
◆ Workers who will support the solution and maintain the operations environment.
◆ Other project teams whose solution may be affected by your project.
◆ Managers who need to supply resources to support the project.
◆ A representative for the interests of the end users.

how to

You are meeting with the rest of the planning team to identify the stakeholders for your current network infrastructure project. Your organization, Fantastic Floss, intends to deploy Microsoft Windows Server 2003 throughout the infrastructure at the head office in Chicago, the manufacturing plant in Detroit, and the sales and marketing office in Los Angeles. Your company, whose main line of business is the production of dental floss, is publicly traded on the New York Stock Exchange. Almost all communication between the offices is done through instant messaging and e-mail. The production line runs a custom business application that will also need to move to a Windows Server 2003 platform. It is critical that the infrastructure project does not affect the preparation for the upcoming Floss World convention. Because of the growth within the organization, the current IT staff regularly work overtime. The operations environment for the organization is distributed, with groups of operations personnel located in each of the offices.

1. Which role is primarily responsible for ensuring that stakeholders are identified?
2. Identify the roles that should be represented when identifying stakeholders for the project.
3. Identify the individuals or groups within your organization that will be stakeholders.
4. Create a stakeholder map that identifies the political and organizational relationships between the stakeholders.

more

It is important that stakeholders have an ongoing involvement throughout the duration of a project. By participating in milestone reviews, stakeholders can ensure that the project is following the desired path and provide input for any necessary changes to the solution. Their approval of the project's deliverables up to the specified milestone is necessary in order for the project to move forward.

An effective approach to keep stakeholders involved is to assign them to act as champions for the project. Often stakeholders hold key positions within an organization that will allow them to influence others and assist in overcoming any opposition that the project may face. The simple fact that a very visible figurehead supports a project can often change the attitudes of others in the organization. Sometimes more will be required, such as conducting short seminars to explain the benefits of the solution to those who will be affected by it. In all cases, the most critical point to remember is that open lines of communication must be maintained between the project team and the stakeholders, as well as between the stakeholders and their organization.

Table 1-5   Sample Stakeholder Profile

Stakeholder	Expected Value	Attitude	Interest
Operations Manager	Reduced operating costs	Concerned that the support staff may not have time to build the necessary skill set	Smooth deployment with little or no issues
Office Manager	Increased user productivity	Excited about possible gains but concerned about time spent re-training users	Would like to move workers to new system in stages
CFO	Return on investment	Happy as long as the solution delivers business benefit	Project funding
Executives	Need to support more client transactions per day	Strong commitment	New system must allow the company to grow
Users	Ease of use	Some resistance due to fear of job loss	No major changes to work routine

skill 4

Managing Project Scope

Basic knowledge

overview

The **project scope** defines the tasks necessary in order to produce the specified solution. Generally, the solution scope is a starting point to define the project scope. There may be adjustments made to the scope as a project progresses because of change requests, limited resources, or a restricted schedule. When these situations occur, a decision can be made to adjust the existing project to accommodate the changes, or to spin off those changes as the next version of the project. Managing and balancing the project scope will require effective trade-offs to be made. For example, if a very tight schedule is imposed, it will be necessary to reduce the deliverables produced by the solution or increase the number of people and resources assigned to the project in order to meet the schedule.

The relationship between these three variables is often shown using a trade-off triangle (**Figure 1-8**). If there is a change to one side of the triangle there will also need to be changes made to the other two sides of the triangle in order to maintain the shape of the triangle. Because one of the principles of MSF is to have a zero-defect mindset, the quality of solution features or deliverables cannot be compromised in order to adjust the other trade-off variables. To assist team members with making wise trade-off decisions, a trade-off matrix (**Figure 1-9**) is often used. This matrix assigns a priority to each of the trade-off variables. One of the variables can be fixed, a preferred value can be chosen for one, and the remaining variable becomes adjustable. A fixed constraint is essentially unchangeable, a chosen constraint is a priority, and an adjustable constraint changes to compensate for the other two constraints. Based on this, the example shown in **Figure 1-9** would read as: "Given fixed resources, we will choose a feature set, and adjust the schedule as necessary." As you can imagine, these trade-off decisions are not easy and must involve all of the team members and the customer.

how to

You have been appointed project manager for the Fantastic Floss Windows Server 2003 project. You have been provided a solution scope document and company management has assigned only one system architect and one technician to the project team due to other IT demands within the organization. Management has been very clear that all components specified in the solution scope must be delivered. Fantastic Floss has done very well financially for the past year and so budget will not be a concern; however, it is important that the project complete within the next four months.

1. Using the trade-off matrix, assign priorities to the project deliverables, resources, and schedule.
2. Based on the project criteria, determine what adjustments will be required to the trade-off triangle to ensure a successful project.
3. Assume that management makes more technical people available for the project. How will that affect your trade-off decisions?
4. Partway through the project, you learn from one of your suppliers that the new routers you ordered to upgrade older ones will not be available for an additional two months. What trade-off decisions may be necessary?

more

When managing the project scope, it is important that the customer and the stakeholders understand the potential compromises required in order to complete the project successfully. Making trade-off decisions is a difficult process but it is necessary to ensure that the project is completed with the specified set of deliverables, on budget, and on schedule. Using the trade-off triangle and the trade-off matrix can assist in helping those involved in a project to understand the relationship among the project deliverables, the required resources, and the schedule.

Figure 1-8 The Trade-Off Triangle

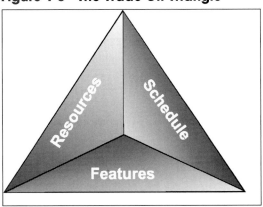

Figure 1-9 The Trade-Off Matrix

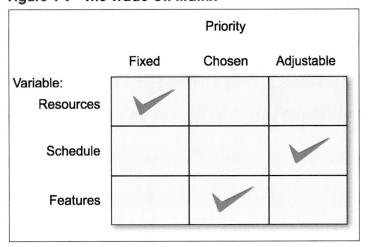

skill 5 | *Controlling Project Scheduling*

exam objective

Basic knowledge

overview

You have learned that the project schedule is one of the constraints when making trade-off decisions. How can you produce an accurate project schedule and what techniques can be used to control your project schedule? The first step is to break up the project deliverables into individual tasks that can be assigned to a specific owner for each task. This is done by creating the Work Breakdown Structure (WBS). The owner for each task will provide a time estimate to complete that task. All of these estimates are gathered together by the team lead and submitted to the program management role holder for inclusion in the Master Project Schedule. This process is called bottom-up estimating. There are many advantages to this technique. For example, because the estimates are created by the people who will actually complete the work, and not by management, they tend to be more accurate. This also creates a sense of accountability and empowerment for the members of the team. After each task is assigned a duration, any dependencies that it has on other tasks are identified and recorded in the WBS. A **Gantt chart (Figure 1-10)** is commonly used to display all project tasks and the duration for each. Four main techniques that can improve scheduling accuracy are listed in **Table 1-6**.

By reviewing previous projects, accuracy of time estimates for specific tasks can improve. It is wise to maintain records for all projects so that future projects can benefit from the experience of past projects. Another excellent approach is to create three-point estimates. A three-point estimate consists of a pessimistic value, a likely value, and an optimistic value. Many project management tools such as Microsoft Project can take these three-point estimates and use them for **Program Evaluation Review Technique (PERT)**. PERT performs statistical analysis on the data to determine the most likely completion date. Other factors in estimating the completion date are the duration and risk for tasks that lie on the critical path for the project. The **critical path** identifies tasks that must be completed before any further progress on the project can continue. Schedule estimates created early in a project are often not as accurate as estimates created later. This is because more uncertainty exists early in a project. For this reason, it is recommended that the schedule be reevaluated at every milestone to improve its accuracy.

how to

1. Using the scenario for Fantastic Floss given in Skill 3, create a simple Work Breakdown Structure for the project.
2. Apply the scheduling techniques in **Table 1-6** to assign pessimistic, expected, and optimistic durations for each task.

more

The Master Project Schedule is not a separate schedule but a composite of the detailed project schedules provided by each of the team leads. The Master Project Schedule defines the release date for the solution based upon the analysis of each of the individual schedules. While this date may change as estimates become more accurate, it is still important to set a release date early because it provides a target for all teams to work towards.

Figure 1-10 A typical Gantt chart

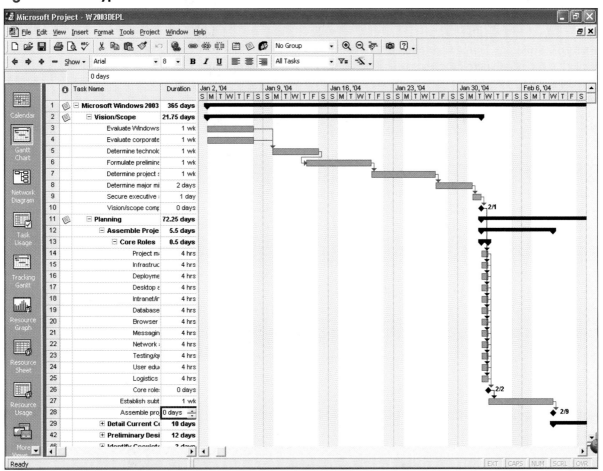

Table 1-6 Key techniques to improve scheduling accuracy

Technique	Explanation
Task Sequencing	For each task to be completed, any dependencies upon the completion of other tasks are identified. The tasks are then ordered so that any task that must complete before other work can continue is scheduled first.
Time-boxing	A reasonable time estimate for the completion of a specific set of deliverables by a team is first established. Time-boxing is used to apply internal motivation for the team to complete the deliverables on schedule. This can help the team to prioritize features and if necessary, eliminate less critical features in order to complete the project on time.
Risk-Driven Scheduling	Once risks to the project's success have been identified, it is best to schedule the highest risk tasks early in the project development so that there will be time to compensate if any of the risks are realized. Risk management is one of three separate disciplines used within MSF.
Buffer Time	Additional time is added to a project schedule to allow for unexpected problems that may arise. By identifying risks early, an appropriate amount of time can be built into the project schedule to accommodate unknown tasks and events. Buffer time should be scheduled as if it is a task of its own and not simply added to the end of each task to provide additional time for that task. This is critical because the buffer time must not be used for planned activities but only for unexpected ones. Once all scheduled buffer time has been used up, any unexpected problem will affect the delivery date for the solution.

Summary

- Microsoft Solutions Framework provides guidance in managing the people and processes necessary to plan, build, and deploy successful IT solutions.
- The MSF team model defines six different role clusters: Program Management, Development, Test, Release Management, User Experience, and Product Management.
- The six key principles of the MSF team model are as follows: Work toward a shared vision; Focus on business value; Stay agile, expect change; Empower team members; Foster open communications; and Establish clear accountability with shared responsibility.
- The MSF process model defines five phases: the envisioning phase, the planning phase, the developing phase, the stabilizing phase, and the deploying phase.
- Key concepts for the MSF process model include the difference between customers and users, the importance of identifying and involving all stakeholders, the use of baselines, defining the solution scope and project scope, and making effective trade-offs.

- The Master Project Plan consists of individual detailed project plans.
- Creating a stakeholder map enables you to identify the political relationships among stakeholders.
- Common types of stakeholders include managers whose staff will be affected, whose business processes will change, or who need to supply resources to support the project; other project teams whose solutions may be affected; workers who will support the solution and maintain the operations environment; and representatives for the interests of end users.
- Project scope must be managed by making trade-offs among the solution deliverables, the available resources, and the schedule.
- Creating an accurate schedule begins with bottom-up estimating using three-point estimates that are based on previous project experience.
- The project schedule should be reevaluated at each project milestone.

Key Terms

Baseline
Critical path
Customer
Developing phase
Empowering
Envisioning phase
Gantt chart
IT Infrastructure Library (ITIL)
Logical network diagram
Master Project Plan

Master Project Schedule
Milestone
Microsoft Operations Framework (MOF)
Microsoft Solutions Framework (MSF)
Program Evaluation Review Technique (PERT)
Physical network diagram
Planning phase
Process model

Project scope
Role clusters
Shared project vision
Solution scope
Stakeholder
Stakeholder map
Team model
Trade-offs
User
Work Breakdown Structure (WBS)

Test Yourself

1. Which of the following are role clusters in the MSF team model? (Choose all that apply.)
   a. Project Management
   b. Release Management
   c. Program Management
   d. Test
   e. Schedule Management

2. Which of the following are key principles of MSF? (Choose all that apply.)
   a. Never directly communicate with other team members.
   b. Work toward a shared vision.
   c. Compromising quality to complete a solution on time is acceptable.
   d. Foster open communication.
   e. Establish clear accountability with shared responsibility.

3. Which of the following is a tool that can help in identifying stakeholders?
   a. Customer matrix
   b. Team model
   c. Stakeholder map

4. What project factors are balanced by a trade-off triangle? (Choose all that apply.)
   a. Resources
   b. Risk
   c. Schedule

   d. Milestones
   e. Features

5. Which of the following techniques is part of creating a Work Breakdown Structure and can improve the accuracy of schedule estimates?
   a. Task sequencing
   b. Baseline
   c. Release Management

Projects: On Your Own

1. Download and read the MSF white papers from **http://www.microsoft.com/msf** by clicking the MSF Resource link on the MSF home page.

2. Download and read the MOF white papers from **http://www.microsoft.com/mof** by clicking the MOF Resource link on the MOF home page.

3. Using Microsoft Project, create a project schedule and a Gantt chart, and perform a critical path analysis and a PERT analysis.

Problem Solving Scenarios

Your company has an existing Windows 2000 forest with two domains within it: **fantasticfloss.com** and **sales.fantasticfloss.com**. There are two domain controllers in each domain. The company plans to add a new domain that will be in a separate site from the other two domains, and will be named **mfg.fantasticfloss.com**. The new site will connect to the existing site with a 512 Kbps leased line. Draw a logical network diagram and a physical network diagram based on the company network. Plan for the creation of the new domain, specifying the required hardware and software. Indicate the placement for DNS servers, global catalog servers, DHCP servers, and routers. Assign IP addresses to the servers. Assume that you will start with a fixed feature set and then choose the resources that will be required and adjust the schedule as necessary. Create a Work Breakdown Structure to list the necessary tasks to add the new domain and then estimate the time required to create the solution.

LESSON

2 Planning Server Roles

As the planning process for a Microsoft Windows Server 2003 infrastructure progresses, the development role will need to begin the infrastructure planning and development process. It is quite possible that there are already various servers in place within the existing network infrastructure. It will be necessary to determine whether any of these will need to be upgraded to a new version of Microsoft Windows in order to provide necessary features or whether additional new servers will be required. Because Microsoft Windows Server 2003 is available in four different editions, it will be necessary to select the appropriate edition of the operating system for the assigned server role within your network. It will require planning to determine what specific server roles will be required to provide fast, reliable services to the network users. Additionally, the placement of each of those servers will need to be identified. For example, where will domain controllers (DCs), and global catalog (GC), Dynamic Host Configuration Protocol (DHCP), Domain Name System (DNS), Windows Internet Naming Service (WINS), and Remote Access Service (RAS) servers reside in the environment? By examining the type of services the server must provide and the load placed upon that server, it is possible to begin to identify system bottlenecks that will limit server performance. By establishing baseline measurements using System Monitor and then comparing subsequent measurements taken when the server is under load, plans can be established to remove the identified bottlenecks. In some cases, even with proper tuning, an existing or proposed server will be inadequate to support the necessary loads. In these cases, capacity planning will help you to specify a properly sized server for the planned role. In situations where the planned loads, or required availability, are more than can be provided by a single server, the decision to utilize either Network Load Balancing or clustering can be made.

Goals

In this lesson, you will learn how to plan Microsoft Windows Server 2003 server roles and server placement. You will learn how to identify and resolve system bottlenecks using System Monitor. And you will learn how to determine when it would be appropriate to use clustering or Network Load Balancing to provide improved availability and support for additional client loads.

Lesson 2   Planning Server Roles

Skill	Exam 70-293 Objective
1. Selecting an Operating System	Evaluate and select the operating system to install on computers in the enterprise.
2. Analyzing Server Placement	Plan and modify a network topology. Plan the physical placement of network resources.
3. Identifying System Bottlenecks	Identify system bottlenecks, including memory, processor, disk, and network related bottlenecks. Identify system bottlenecks by using System Monitor.
4. Planning Server Capacity and Availability	Plan services for high availability. Plan a high availability solution that uses clustering services. Plan a high availability solution that uses Network Load Balancing. Manage Network Load Balancing. Tools might include the Network Load Balancing Monitor Microsoft Management Console (MMC) snap-in and the WLBS cluster control utility. Implement a cluster server. Recover from cluster node failure.

Requirements

To complete this lesson, you will need administrative rights on a Windows Server 2003 computer.

skill 1

Selecting an Operating System

exam objective

Evaluate and select the operating system to install on computers in the enterprise.

overview

Microsoft Windows Server 2003 is available in four different editions **(Table 2-1).** One of the first tasks that you may face when planning a network infrastructure is the selection of the appropriate operating system for each server within the environment. It might seem practical to specify the most capable operating system for all servers so that no matter what changes may be required, they will be able to be adapted to the new circumstances. However, if you recall the trade-off triangle from Lesson 1, you will remember that features are not free. There is additional expense to purchase Enterprise or Datacenter Edition instead of Standard or Web Edition that could easily put a project over budget. For that reason, it is important to select the appropriate operating system for each server role.

Generally, referring to the logical and physical network diagrams will provide the majority of the information required regarding the specific services that a server needs to support. However, more is required. Not only does the intended role need to be considered, but also the projected server load, storage capacity, fault tolerance, and budget must be evaluated **(Figure 2-1)**. These components will be expanded upon in Skills 2, 3, and 4.

The selection of an operating system should focus on the features required. Once the required operating system has been determined, then it will be necessary to identify an appropriate hardware platform for it to run on. Although it is possible to build extremely powerful servers based on the Enterprise and Datacenter Editions of Microsoft Windows Server 2003, it is wise to evaluate whether the same goals can be accomplished using the less expensive Standard or Web Editions. In some cases, this will mean that the necessary services will be distributed across more servers instead of using a single more powerful server, but there can be advantages to distributing services across multiple physical servers. For example, when server maintenance is required, fewer network services are disrupted when they are distributed across more than one physical server. In most cases, the Standard Edition of Windows Server 2003 can support standard network services such as DNS, DHCP, WINS, RAS, and file and printer sharing.

When large application servers, data warehouses and servers supporting Online Transaction Processing (OLTP) are required, the Enterprise and Datacenter Editions, which support more random access memory (RAM) and processors than other editions, are more appropriate. These operating systems can also provide additional fault tolerance because of their support for clustering. For this reason, when reliability and high performance are the primary concerns for your infrastructure, the additional cost of selecting the more expensive operating systems can be justified. In some cases, the projected server load is so high that even a single server running Windows Server 2003 Enterprise or Datacenter Edition would not be able to satisfy that requirement. In these cases, it may be necessary to also utilize clustering or Network Load Balancing to improve network performance.

Once the appropriate operating systems have been selected for the specified server roles, a test environment should be created to measure the server utilization for each service and then project these numbers forward to estimate the loads that will exist in the production environment. This will allow for adjustments to the server selection prior to deploying them in the live environment.

tip

There is also a Small Business Server Edition based on Windows Server 2003 Standard Edition that includes several other Microsoft server products as a package.

how to

Select an operating system and server hardware configuration.

1. Identify required services.
2. Determine the projected server load to estimate the required number of processors and amount of RAM.
3. Estimate the required storage capacity.
4. Specify any availability and reliability requirements.
5. Calculate the system cost and revise the system configuration if there is insufficient budget to deploy the selected systems.

Table 2-1 Microsoft Windows Server 2003 editions and features

Edition	Target	Features
Web	Specified where dedicated Web serving and hosting is required. (Only available to OEMs and System Builders, select licensing customers, and service providers with a service provider licensing agreement.)	• Supports up to 2 processors. • Supports up to 2 GB of RAM. • Can only be used to supply Web pages, Web sites, Web applications, and Web services. • Can not act as a domain controller.
Standard	Designed for departmental servers and standard workloads.	• Supports up to 4 processors. • Supports up to 4 GB of RAM. • Provides file and printer sharing. • Provides secure Internet access and services. • Can provide Active Directory services as a domain controller.
Enterprise	Designed for mission-critical applications such as application servers, Web servers, and infrastructure servers, where high reliability and performance are critical.	• All the features of Standard Edition • Supports up to 8 processors. • Supports up to 32 GB of RAM (64 GB for 64-bit version). • Supports 8-node clustering.
Datacenter	Built for situations where the highest levels of reliability and scalability are chief concerns.	• All the features of Enterprise Edition • Supports up to 32 processors (64 processors for 64-bit version). • Supports up to 64 GB of RAM (512 GB for 64-bit version). • Supports 8-node clustering and load balancing.

Figure 2-1 Operating System Selection Considerations

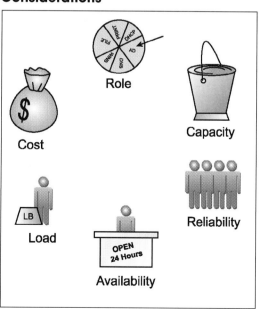

skill 2

Analyzing Server Placement

exam objective

Plan and modify a network topology. Plan the physical placement of network resources.

overview

After selecting the appropriate operating system for each server role, the next step is to examine where each server should reside within the network infrastructure. Once again, the logical and physical network diagrams can provide the information necessary for this planning step. Your design could include many different network services (**Figure 2-2**) and each required service must be available on at least one server within the infrastructure. However, in most cases it will be necessary to implement each service on more than one server in order to meet the needs for the availability and reliability of the service as well as to provide sufficient performance. If your infrastructure includes remote sites, it will be necessary to decide whether each of these network services will exist at the remote location, or whether they will be accessed in some other location through the WAN links connecting the sites. Some services such as those provided by a domain controller are more critical and consequently, particular care should be exercised when planning them. Considerations for planning each network service are described below:

◆ **Domain controllers and global catalog servers: Domain controllers** are perhaps the most fundamental component of a Microsoft Windows Server 2003 network. They host the Active Directory database, allowing it to be searched, and provide Kerberos v5 authentication services. Optionally, a domain controller can also handle the global catalog server role. The **global catalog server** contains the most commonly searched for attributes associated with an object for each object in the entire forest. Each domain should normally contain at least two domain controllers to provide redundancy for Active Directory. It is recommended that a global catalog server be placed in each remote site, if possible. However, if this is not possible, you can enable Universal Group caching on your Windows Server 2003 domain controllers in the remote site to allow for successful universal group lookups in the event that your clients cannot contact a global catalog server. For more information on global catalog servers and Universal Group caching, see the Prentice Hall Certification Series Exam 70-294 textbook.

◆ **Domain Name System (DNS):** One of the most critical network services on a Microsoft Windows Server 2003 network is DNS. **DNS** is a name resolution service that allows IP-based computers to locate other computers and services on a network by using a host name and a domain name. When combined, the host name and domain name become the **Fully Qualified Domain Name (FQDN)**. DNS is a hierarchical database that maintains a mapping between these names and their corresponding IP addresses. Historically, updating DNS entries has been a manual process but Windows Server 2003's DNS service allows for dynamic updates. The DNS servers within your organization can be located almost anywhere, as long as all clients are able to access them by their IP address. One area of consideration related to the placement of DNS servers is security. Any DNS server that contains address mappings for your internal network should not be placed in an exposed location such as a Demilitarized Zone (DMZ) or a perimeter network. Because DNS services are essential for the correct operation of a Microsoft Windows Server 2003 network, it is recommended that more than one server should be configured with the DNS service. Standard DNS design specifies at least one primary server and one secondary server per zone. Using Active Directory-Integrated Zones, the actual DNS database is stored within Active Directory, adding another layer of security. Other factors to consider are the speed of any WAN links, the number of DNS queries performed, and the volume of zone transfer traffic. In situations where very low speed links exist, it may be wise to consider implementing a caching-only DNS server at the remote location. In this way, the number of DNS queries traversing the WAN link will be reduced and zone transfer traffic will be eliminated.

Figure 2-2 Windows Server 2003 network services

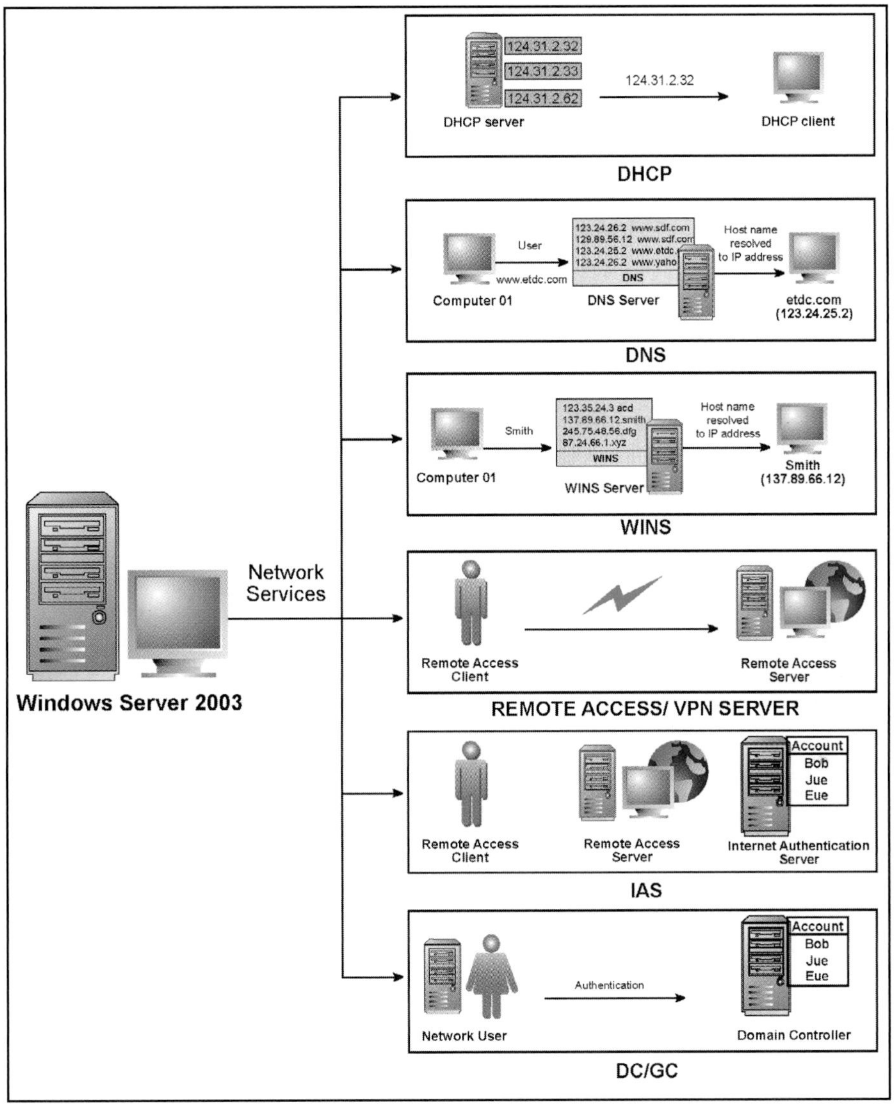

skill 2

Analyzing Server Placement (cont'd)

exam objective

Plan and modify a network topology. Plan the physical placement of network resources.

overview

◆ **Windows Internet Naming Service (WINS):** **WINS** translates NetBIOS names into IP addresses. All Microsoft networks prior to Windows 2000 required the NetBIOS protocol for communication. Computer names were resolved either through broadcasts or by lookup on a WINS server. The use of a WINS server allows NetBIOS name resolution to proceed in situations where broadcasts would not function, such as when multiple networks are interconnected by routers. You may need to implement WINS in your Windows Server 2003 environment to support older Windows operating systems. If you determine that a WINS server is required in your environment, you must consider the placement of network routers and ensure that clients will always be able to access the WINS server. In many cases, this will mean implementing at least one additional WINS server as a replication partner with the original WINS server to ensure redundancy. Because a single WINS server can generally support more than 10,000 WINS clients, in most cases there is no need to add additional WINS servers for server performance considerations. When planning WINS servers, available bandwidth for any WAN links is of utmost concern. The number of client queries and name registration requests along with any replication traffic between WINS replication partners must be considered when determining the locations for WINS servers.

◆ **Dynamic Host Configuration Protocol (DHCP):** The **DHCP Server service** is responsible for assigning an IP address, subnet mask, and optional IP configuration settings to any host that requests them. The DHCP leasing process is comprised of four steps **(Figure 2-3)**. Because the client computer does not have a usable IP address until all four steps are completed, the process uses network broadcasts. It is important to remember this when planning the placement of DHCP servers because by default, routers do not pass broadcast traffic. If your internal network divides into two or more networks separated by routers, you must choose a method to ensure that all dynamically configured clients can receive their IP configuration from a DHCP server. One way to accomplish this would be to place a DHCP server on each network within your infrastructure. However, this approach would complicate administration of your IP addressing configuration because each server needs to be managed independently. Additionally this would require the installation, configuration, and maintenance of the DHCP service in many locations throughout your network infrastructure, which would increase support costs. In situations where low bandwidth network connections would introduce unacceptable delays, the use of separate DHCP servers to provide IP addressing for remote locations is justified. However, in most situations a preferred method would be to configure each of the routers within your infrastructure to act as a DHCP relay agent. A **DHCP relay agent**, sometimes called a BOOTP relay agent, will receive the message broadcast by the client that is requesting an IP address and will send a new request on behalf of the client to the IP address of a DHCP server on another network. The DHCP relay agent will also forward the response of the DHCP server back to the client. In this way, one DHCP server can fulfill client requests for IP addresses on multiple network segments. In order to ensure that the DHCP service is always available, it is wise to configure at least two DHCP servers. Recommended practice dictates that each network address scope should be split such that 80% of the addresses for a scope should be available on one DHCP server with the remaining 20% of the addresses for a scope available on an alternate DHCP server.

tip

RFC1542, available at **www.rfc-editor.org**, defines the behavior of relay agents.

Figure 2-3 DHCP Lease Process

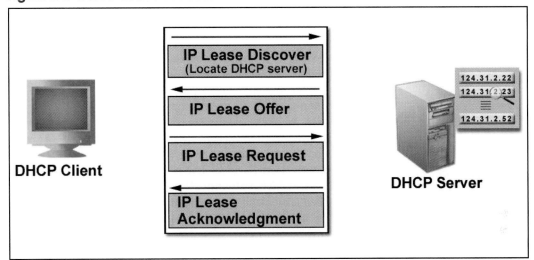

skill 2

Analyzing Server Placement (cont'd)

exam objective

Plan and modify a network topology. Plan the physical placement of network resources.

overview

◆ **Remote Access/Virtual Private Network (VPN) Server:** This server role can provide several functions such as acting as a remote access server, a VPN server, a network router, a Network Address Translation (NAT) router, or several combinations of these functions. The number of remote access or VPN servers to implement will depend on the connectivity needs of your organization. The placement of each server will depend upon its role. For example, a remote access server providing dial-up access to your network will normally be located on your internal private network. On the other hand, a VPN server is commonly placed in the perimeter network. If the server is configured to provide routing or Network Address Translation (NAT), it will typically have two separate network interface cards; one connected to the internal private network and another connected to a perimeter network or another remote network.

◆ **Internet Authentication Service (IAS):** When multiple remote access servers are configured, the **Internet Authentication Service** can be configured to provide a centralized authentication and accounting mechanism. A single server running IAS can support several remote access servers. An IAS server may be placed anywhere on the network. However, for increased security, it is recommended that your IAS server be placed on the internal network whenever possible.

In many cases, the network services listed above are not installed on servers dedicated to providing only a single network service. In many environments, each server must support more than one service. When planning which network services to combine on a single server, it is helpful to remember that certain network services can coexist in a complementary fashion on a single server, while others would compete for the limited resources of that server. **Figure 2-4** provides a compatibility chart that indicates which network services commonly are combined on a server.

more

Always remember that many of the guidelines presented in this lesson are only approximations and your experience within your own production environment will likely vary. For this reason, it is important to test your proposed solutions during the planning phase to validate the chosen technology and its implementation. This cyclical approach to the planning process contributes to a zero defect mindset and will ensure that the solution specified by the planning process can be successfully built during the development phase.

Figure 2-4 Network services compatibility matrix

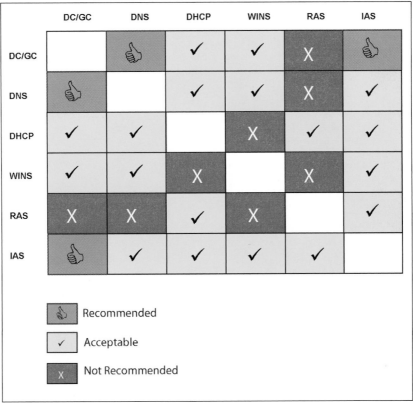

skill 3

Identifying System Bottlenecks

exam objective

Identify system bottlenecks; including memory, processor, disk, and network related bottlenecks. Identify system bottlenecks by using System Monitor.

overview

One of the goals that the network infrastructure planning team should target is the efficient implementation of network services. By ensuring that each network service is operating optimally, the size and number of server class computers can often be reduced, resulting in a cost savings. To optimize each network service, a clear understanding of the various loads imposed by the network service is helpful. For example, while one service may make intensive use of disk resources, another service may use very little disk resources but consume a large amount of system memory (**Figure 2-5**).

Once the resources required to support the desired services are clearly understood, a server computer should be configured with the appropriate hardware and the selected network services should be installed and configured. When the platform has been configured, it is not the end of the system optimization process, it is really just the beginning. At this point, the planning team must now attempt to identify and remove any system bottlenecks. A **bottleneck** normally occurs in one or more computer subsystems and it causes a limiting factor on the overall performance of the system. There are generally four main subsystems to examine for bottlenecks: memory, processor, disk, and network.

After a bottleneck is identified and corrected, the current state of the system must be analyzed. When one bottleneck is removed, there may still be some other factor limiting the peak performance of the system. The elimination of bottlenecks becomes a cyclical procedure that is repeated until the system has been tuned to an acceptable level of performance or until some other factor such as schedule or budget halts the process.

Successfully identifying the effects of the tuning process requires that a baseline performance be established so that subsequent measurements can be compared to it. System activity can be viewed in real-time using either Task Manager or the System Monitor snap-in in the Performance console; however, to create a baseline, record measurements using Performance Logs and Alerts. As you examine each subsystem, the following details can be helpful:

◆ **Memory:** This subsystem should be examined first when trying to identify system bottlenecks. Windows Server 2003 is designed around a virtual memory demand page system. This allows for the use of programs and data larger than the actual physical RAM installed in the computer. The **Virtual Memory Manager (VMM)** swaps the least recently used pages of memory out to the pagefile stored on disk when a program requests additional memory and there is no space left in the physical RAM. If there is insufficient memory installed to support the applications and services hosted on the server, the system memory will become a bottleneck. RAM is much faster than even the fastest fixed disk and as paging to disk increases, system performance drops off rapidly. In some cases, the extra load from paging will make it appear that the bottleneck is in the disk subsystem and not memory. Additionally, processor utilization can also go up dramatically, depending on the type of disk controller in use, as the VMM becomes involved in managing the additional I/O operations to the fixed disk. For this reason, it is critical to eliminate system memory as the source of the bottleneck before proceeding to analyze the rest of the subsystems.

Software that is poorly designed, or that has a memory leak can also make it appear that a bottleneck exists in the memory subsystem. If possible, isolate the processes that use the most RAM and examine them to determine whether their RAM usage is appropriate or not. Task Manager or the Performance console can be used to monitor the memory used by a process. If the amount of memory used by a process continually increases, a memory leak may exist. A process can use one of two types of memory: Paged memory and Non-paged memory. When a process uses **Paged memory**, it will cooperate with other processes and allow pages of its memory to swap out from physical RAM to the page file. Conversely, **Non-paged memory** cannot swap to disk and reduces the overall amount of RAM available to other applications. Watch for both types of memory used by processes, but especially watch for excessive allocations of Non-paged memory.

tip

When a second processor is installed in a system that supports more than one processor, it is necessary to change from the uni-processor Hardware Abstraction Layer (HAL) to a multi-processor HAL through the Computer node in the Device Manager.

tip

Unlike previous version of Windows, both Logical and Physical disk counters are enabled by default in Windows Server 2003.

Figure 2-5 Subsystem loads for network services

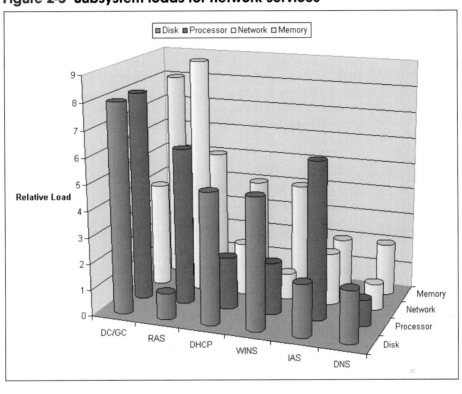

skill 3

Identifying System Bottlenecks (cont'd)

exam objective

Identify system bottlenecks; including memory, processor, disk, and network related bottlenecks. Identify system bottlenecks by using System Monitor.

overview

◆ **Processor:** When a server is not performing as required, some are quick to suggest a processor upgrade, or with a multi-processor system, additional processors. However, the processor is not the bottleneck on most systems. It is true that some applications and services such as Terminal Services, Microsoft Exchange Server, or SQL Server make heavy use of the system processor, but most other network services impose a relatively light load on the processor. In many situations, excessive processor utilization is a symptom of bottlenecks in other subsystems. For example, an IDE controller with fixed disks or CD-ROMs connected to it will generate many interrupts that the system processor has to deal with, causing what seems to be a processor bottleneck. Additionally, runaway processes can use up large amounts of processor time and affect the overall system performance. Identifying such processes and recording appropriate counters over a block of time will indicate where the processor load is coming from.

◆ **Disk:** Prior to examining the disk subsystem for bottlenecks, make sure that there are no memory bottlenecks creating excessive paging activity. Disks should also be defragmented to ensure that performance does not degrade because of the extra head movements required to read fragmented files. After defragmenting the disks and eliminating any memory bottlenecks, disk activity should be compared to your baseline measurements. If you find that disk activity is consistently above your baseline, you should look further to determine whether a disk bottleneck exists. The selection of components for your disk subsystem and the way that you configure the disks can have a significant effect on disk throughput. For example, the type of interface, rotational speed, seek time, and transfer rate of the disks will all affect the disk subsystem's performance. In most cases, SCSI disks perform better in server class computers than IDE disks because the SCSI drives are more intelligent and do not require as much attention from the system processor as IDE drives do. When either software or hardware-based RAID configurations are used, overall disk performance improves. The most common RAID configurations are RAID levels 0, 1, and 5, and when using a hardware RAID controller, level 10. When RAID 0 is used, the data to be read or written is broken into stripes and then distributed across multiple drives, providing excellent read/write performance but no fault tolerance. As more drives are added to a RAID 0 array, throughput will increase until the interface or controller becomes a bottleneck. Raid 0 is generally not used for servers because the loss of one drive will cause a loss of all data stored on the array. Mirroring using RAID 1 can provide a very small performance improvement when reading data and will generally impose a small performance penalty when writing data. By calculating a parity value and writing it in rotated order across each disk along with each data stripe, a RAID 5 array is a fault tolerant disk subsystem that provides excellent read performance. Write performance generally suffers when using RAID 5 because of the overhead associated with the calculation and writing of the parity information. Adding additional drives to a RAID 5 array has a similar effect as it does for a RAID 0 array. RAID 10 is not supported as a software volume set under Windows Server 2003, but is available when using hardware RAID controllers. This RAID level combines disk mirroring (RAID 1) with disk striping (RAID 0). The result is a disk subsystem that provides excellent read/write performance and fault tolerance.

When tuning disk subsystem performance, the type of processes and applications that are in use should be considered and then an appropriate disk configuration should be designed to support those processes. For example, when working with most transactional database systems like Microsoft SQL Server, it is important to understand that while the database file for most systems primarily has random read activity directed at it, the transaction logs typically receive sequential writes. By placing each of these files on separate

Table 2-2 Key performance counters

Subsystem	Counter	Recommendation	Comments
Memory	Page Faults/sec	Displays the average number of page faults each second. It should be less than 5. More indicates a memory bottleneck.	Primary indicator of a memory bottleneck. The usual solution is to add RAM.
	Committed bytes	Should be less than the amount of physical RAM. Committing more memory than physical RAM guarantees paging will occur.	Remember to watch for leaky applications that allocate excessive amounts of memory.
Processor	% Processor Time	If this value is consistently about 80% or higher, further investigation is required to identify any process that may be making excessive use of the processor or to identify other subsystems that are causing unnecessary load. Sometimes unnecessary processes can be stopped to reduce processor load.	If all other subsystems check out, it is probably time for a faster processor.
	Interrupts/sec	The desired baseline for this counter will be different for each system. Generally, a system with no activity will have an interrupt rate around 200-300 per second. These interrupts are mainly caused by the hardware system clock interrupting the processor to look after 'system housekeeping' tasks. As system load increases, there will be a corresponding increase in interrupts. To determine whether the interrupt load is being generated by another subsystem, examine the queue length on the disk system or network interface. If it is longer than 2, this can indicate that the device is a bottleneck and is interrupting the processor excessively.	Using workstation class hardware in a server can cause excessive interrupts. Watch out for NICs, serial interfaces, and disk controllers. Generally, IDE controllers and disks should not be used in a server class computer.
	System: Processor Queue Length	Ideally, this value should not have a sustained value more than 2 per processor, but depending on workload, a value of less than 10 threads per processor may be acceptable. The processor queue length indicates how many threads are waiting to be executed by the CPU. If the queue length grows, it indicates that there is more work to be done than the CPU(s) can handle and could indicate a bottleneck.	This counter is the total queue length even on multiprocessor systems. To determine the maximum acceptable count, multiply the suggested value by the number of processors.
Disk	Physical Disk: Current Disk Queue Length	If a single disk is in use, this value should be less than 2. With multiple disks in an array, the value should be less than 2 more than the number of spindles in the drive set. This value indicates the total number of disk requests currently being serviced plus any requests that are waiting for service.	This is the key indicator of a disk bottleneck if other factors such as excessive paging due to a memory bottleneck have been eliminated.
Network	Network Interface: Bytes Total/sec	Indicates the total number of bytes sent and received by the selected network interface. For example, when using a shared collision domain on an Ethernet network, network utilization should be no more than about 30% of the available bandwidth. However, server network interfaces should be connected to a dedicated port on a network switch. This will allow the use of full-duplex communications and allow network utilization in each direction to exceed 80%.	If system processor utilization increases significantly as network utilization increases, or if it is impossible to achieve high network throughput on a switched network connection, upgrade the NIC to a server class product.

skill 3

Identifying System Bottlenecks (cont'd)

exam objective

Identify system bottlenecks; including memory, processor, disk, and network related bottlenecks. Identify system bottlenecks by using System Monitor.

overview

drive systems, bottlenecks can be eliminated. The database files can be placed on a RAID 5 array with good results, and the transaction logs can be placed on either a mirrored volume (RAID 1), or a RAID 10 array. If the database is being used for Online Transaction Processing (OLTP), there will be significantly more writes than a normal database and therefore performance would increase if a drive configuration that provides better write speed were selected, such as a RAID 10 configuration.

◆ **Network:** Network bottlenecks can be difficult to locate. There are many factors in a network infrastructure that can limit network throughput. In this lesson, we are only considering factors that are directly connected with server hardware. The type of network connection can limit throughput and it is recommended that all servers be connected to a dedicated port on a network switch. The design of the Network Interface Card (NIC) can have a strong influence on throughput, especially when encryption protocols such as IPSec are involved. Some NICs have built-in processors to offload encryption calculations and other housekeeping activities from the system processor. For any server, it is normally worth the additional cost to obtain a server class network adapter.

Table 2-2 on page 2.15 summarizes the key counters used to monitor each subsystem.

how to

Create baseline measurements for a computer by using the Performance Console.

1. Click **Start**, select **Administrative Tools**, and then click **Performance** to open the **Performance** console.
2. Note that **System Monitor** is pre-selected and there are three predefined counters that are already configured (**Figure 2-6**). These counters provide a real time view of the activity of the processor, disks and memory.
3. Click the '+' sign to expand the **Performance Logs and Alerts** node.
4. Select the **Counter Logs** node. Right-click **Counter Logs**, and select **New Log Settings** from the menu. The **New Log Settings** dialog box will open.
5. Type **Bottleneck Measurements** in the **Name** text box (**Figure 2-7**). Click `OK` to open the **Bottleneck Measurements Properties** dialog box. Click `Add Counters...` to open the **Add Counters** dialog box (**Figure 2-8**).
6. The default counter that is highlighted is the **% Processor Time** counter. Click `Explain` to open a dialog box that contains an explanation of the currently selected counter (**Figure 2-9**). Read the explanation for the counter, and then click `Add` to add the **% Processor Time** counter to the Counter Log.
7. Select the **Interrupts/sec** counter from the **Select counters from list** list box. Read the explanation, and then click `Add`.
8. Expand the **Performance Object** list box, and select **System**. Select **Processor Queue Length** from the **Select counters from list** list box, and read the explanation. Click `Add` to add this counter to the counter log.
9. Select **Memory** from the **Performance Object** list box and then select **Page Faults/sec** from the **Select counters from list** list box. Read the explanation for the counter and click `Add`.

tip

To view the counters that have been added to the counter log, drag the Add Counters dialog box out of the way so it does not obscure the Bottleneck Measurements Properties dialog box.

Figure 2-6 System Monitor displaying default counters

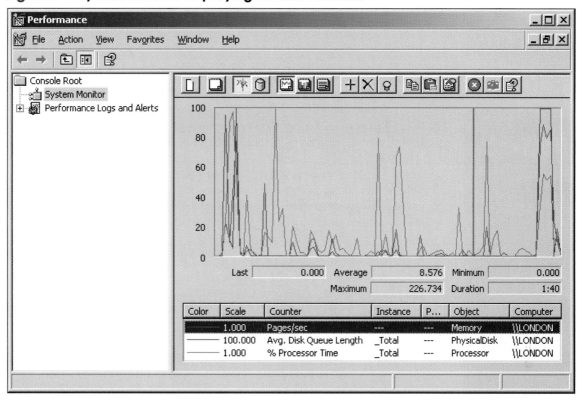

Figure 2-7 Specifying a name for the Counter log

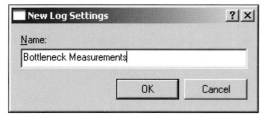

Figure 2-8 Adding counters to a counter log

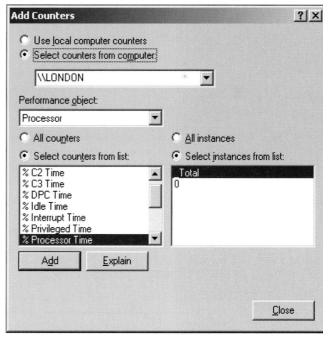

Figure 2-9 Viewing the explanation for a counter

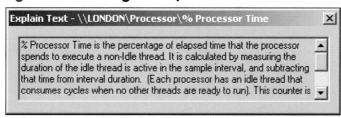

skill 3

Identifying System Bottlenecks (cont'd)

exam objective

Identify system bottlenecks; including memory, processor, disk, and network related bottlenecks. Identify system bottlenecks by using System Monitor.

how to

10. Select **Physical Disk** from the **Performance Object** list box and then select **Current Disk Queue Length** from the **Select counters from list** list box. Read the explanation and click [Add].

11. Expand the **Performance Object** list box and select **Network Interface**. Select **Bytes Total/sec** from the **Select counters from list:** list box. Make sure that the network interface you want to monitor is selected in the **Select instances from list** list box. Read the explanation and then click [Add] to add this counter to the counter log.

12. Once all of the specified counters have been added, click [Close] to return to the **Bottleneck Measurements Properties** log dialog box.

13. All of the counters added will appear in the **Counters** list box **(Figure 2-10)**. Change the value in the **Interval** text box to **5** seconds. This setting will cause the counter log to take a measurement for each of the defined counters every 5 seconds. Click [OK] to save the configuration for this counter log.

14. The default location for the data recorded by each counter log is C:\Perflogs. If this is the first counter log that has been created on the computer and the C:\Perflogs directory does not exist, you will be prompted to create the directory **(Figure 2-11)**. Click [Yes] to create the **C:\Perflogs** directory.

15. The new counter log settings will appear in the Performance console under the **Counter Logs** node **(Figure 2-12)**. After a few seconds, the icon beside the **Bottleneck Measurements** counter log will change color from red to green. This indicates that the log is active and is recording data. Recording can be stopped and restarted by right-clicking a counter log and selecting either **Start** or **Stop** from the menu. By editing the properties of a counter log, it can be scheduled to automatically begin and end recording at specified dates and times.. These settings can be helpful in obtaining baseline measurements for different activity periods of a server (e.g., during a normal workday, during batch processing, or during system backup).

16. Allow the **Bottleneck Measurements** counter log to run for at least 5 minutes. While it is running, go about other 'normal' activities on the computer. For example, you may want to open and close several applications, connect to a Web server using Internet Explorer, edit a file and save it, change some system configuration settings, and copy some files from a network share on another computer to your computer. The goal of this exercise is to create a mixture of activity for all of the different subsystems.

17. After at least 5 minutes has elapsed, right-click the **Bottleneck Measurements** counter log and select **Stop** from the menu.

tip

To learn the function for each icon, briefly hold the mouse pointer over an icon and a tool tip indicating the function for that icon will appear.

Figure 2-10 Viewing counters for the Bottleneck Measurements counter log

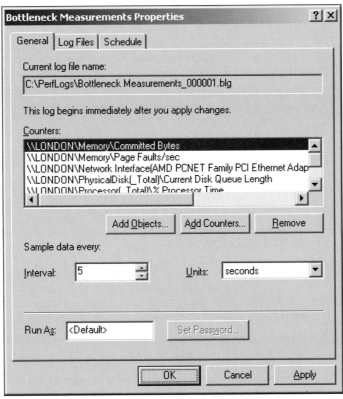

Figure 2-11 Creating the directory to hold counter logs

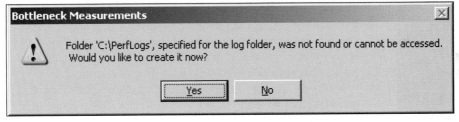

Figure 2-12 Viewing the Bottleneck Measurements counter log

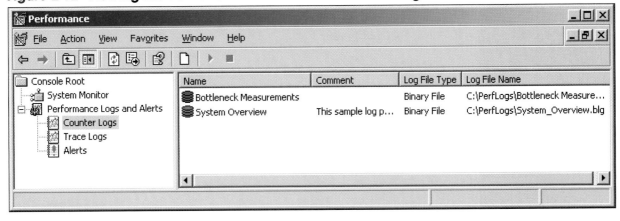

skill 3

Identifying System Bottlenecks (cont'd)

exam objective

Identify system bottlenecks; including memory, processor, disk, and network related bottlenecks. Identify system bottlenecks by using System Monitor.

how to

Open a log file to examine the collected performance data.

18. System Monitor can view counter logs as well as real time counters. Select the **System Monitor** node and then clear the existing counters that are in use by clicking the **New Counter Set** icon in the top left corner of the System Monitor pane.

19. Click the **View Log Data** icon to open the **System Monitor Properties** dialog box.

20. Select the **Log Files** option button, and then click [Add...] to select a log file.

21. The **Select Log File** dialog box will open (**Figure 2-13**). Choose the last log file created, and then click [Open].

22. In the **System Monitor Properties** dialog box (**Figure 2-14**), click [Time Range]. This allows a specific time range to be selected from the counter log for display. Click [OK] to accept the default, which is to display the full time range.

23. To display the counters from the counter log, they must be selected and added to the System Monitor. Click the **Add** icon to open the **Add Counters** dialog box.

24. Notice that the **Performance object** list box contains only the objects selected when the counter log was created. Select **Memory** in the **Performance object** list box. Select **Committed Bytes** in the **Select instances from list** list box, and then click [Add]. Select **Page Faults/sec** in the **Select instances from list** list box and then click [Add] again.

25. Select **Network Interface** in the **Performance object** list box, and add the **Bytes Total/sec** counter by clicking [Add].

26. Continue selecting each of the remaining Performance Objects, and add all of the counters for each of them using the same procedure as for the Memory object and the Network Interface object. After all counters have been added, click [Close] to return to **System Monitor (Figure 2-15)**.

27. Examine the three different data views by clicking the **View Graph**, **View Histogram**, and **View Report** icons. Notice that the values displayed on the histogram and report are the average values for each counter.

28. Save the current counter configuration for System Monitor by clicking the **File** menu and then selecting **Save As** to open the **Save As** dialog box. Type **Baseline Measurements Console** in the **File name** text box and click [Save] to save the console.

29. To open the console later, open System Monitor, click the **File** menu, and select **Open**. Locate the **Baseline Measurements Console.msc** file and click [Open].

30. Close **System Monitor**.

Figure 2-13 Opening a counter log with System Monitor

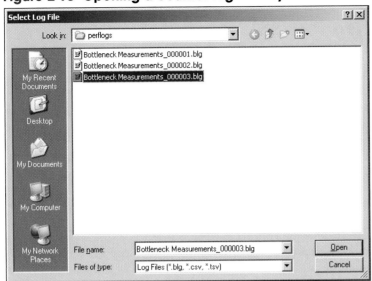

Figure 2-14 Setting a time range for a counter log

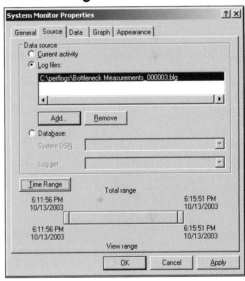

Figure 2-15 Viewing data from a counter log with System Monitor

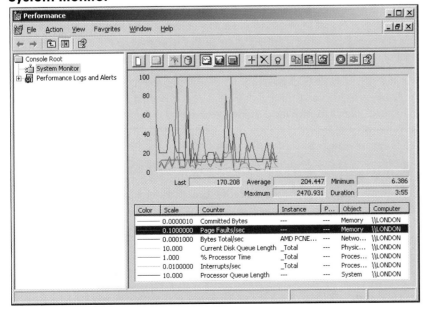

skill 4

Planning Server Capacity and Availability

exam objective

Plan services for high availability. Plan a high availability solution that uses clustering services. Plan a high availability solution that uses Network Load Balancing. Manage Network Load Balancing. Tools might include the Network Load Balancing Monitor Microsoft Management Console (MMC) snap-in and the WLBS cluster control utility. Implement a cluster server. Recover from cluster node failure.

overview

Capacity planning is concerned with providing the right services, at the right time, in the right quantity, and at the right price. When planning a network infrastructure, it is important to determine accurately the specific server resources required to support each server role within the environment. The chosen hardware configurations for each server will have an impact on the overall project budget. In order for a project to be judged a success, it must not only provide the desired solution but it also must complete on time and on budget. This means that server configurations should not be unnecessarily costly yet still provide the required levels of reliability, availability, and performance specified for the project.

Determining an appropriate hardware configuration for a system is not always easy. One environment is always a little different from another. Because of this, the only accurate way to determine the loads that the server will have to handle is to measure them after deploying the server. Of course, this approach does not help with the planning process. However, you may be able to utilize measurements taken within your existing environment to produce close estimates for new servers that will be deployed. For this reason, it is strongly recommended that baseline measurements be taken at regular intervals within any environment to forecast increasing server loads and collect data for future planning purposes.

If it is determined that the required availability, reliability, and performance for a network service cannot be achieved using a single server, it may be necessary to consider the use of Network Load Balancing or clustering. **Network Load Balancing (NLB)** is a Windows Server 2003 service that allows a group of up 32 computers, referred to as a **server farm**, to provide services to clients by accepting incoming network requests and distributing them to one server within the group. As additional requests arrive, they distribute in a balanced manner across all servers in the group. This improves availability because even if one server in the group is down, the other members of the group will still respond to network requests, thus ensuring continuous availability of the network service. If a server fails, any processes running on it will be lost, but the client will reconnect to a functional server so that work can continue. Performance also improves because total throughput for the server farm becomes the sum of the throughput for each server. NLB most often supports Web-based applications but is not limited to that role. Network Load Balancing Manager is the recommended tool for creation and management of all nodes in a Network Load Balancing cluster (**Figure 2-16**). After configuring a cluster, you can use either Network Load Balancing Manager or the command line tool **Nlb.exe** to control its operation.

When using Windows Server 2003 **clustering**, up to eight computers connect together and operate as a single system. All nodes in the cluster share a common disk subsystem and use either SCSI or Fiber Channel to provide a shared storage bus (**Figure 2-17**). Clustering is applicable where more system processing power is required than could be provided by a single computer or for mission critical systems where high availability is a key concern. If a node in a cluster fails, its processes will move to another node in the cluster to ensure uninterrupted service. Database and e-mail servers such as Microsoft SQL Server and Exchange Server often run on server clusters. Both Cluster Administrator (**Figure 2-18**) and the **Cluster.exe** command line tool allow creation and management of server clusters.

tip

Third party products can help with capacity planning. PATROL, for Windows servers (available from **www.bmc.com**) has versions that record performance measurements and predict future capacity needs.

Figure 2-16 Network Load Balancing Manager

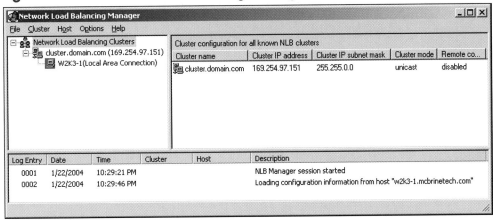

Figure 2-17 Typical server cluster configuration

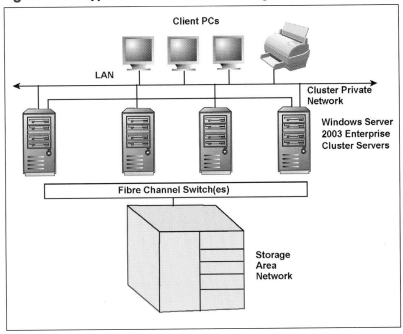

Figure 2-18 Cluster Administrator

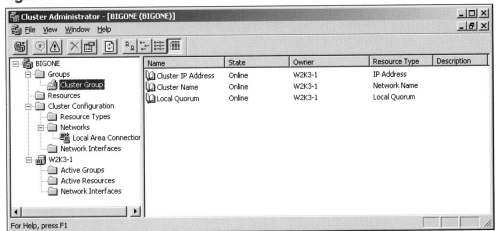

skill 4

Planning Server Capacity and Availability (cont'd)

exam objective

Plan services for high availability. Plan a high availability solution that uses clustering services. Plan a high availability solution that uses Network Load Balancing. Manage Network Load Balancing. Tools might include the Network Load Balancing Monitor Microsoft Management Console (MMC) snap-in and the WLBS cluster control utility. Implement a cluster server. Recover from cluster node failure.

overview

Various industry benchmarks and configurations can provide some guidance in planning server loads and selecting appropriate hardware to support those loads. Some rough suggestions for the hardware resources required for each network service are listed below:

◆ **Domain controllers and global catalog servers:** While domain controllers host Active Directory, allowing it to be searched, and provide authentication services, a domain controller is primarily a database server. Many techniques that will improve the performance of any database server apply to domain controllers. There must be sufficient storage capacity to hold the Active Directory database. The amount of memory and number of processors required to support the infrastructure must also be determined. Remember that even if only one domain controller is required to provide sufficient capacity, it is recommended that at least two domain controllers per domain are deployed to provide fault-tolerance and disaster recovery. Microsoft has provided some guidance in properly sizing domain controllers. **Table 2-3** lists some of the suggested values based on the number of users in a domain. All of these numbers are based on Pentium III 850 MHz processors or higher. The disk space allocation does not take into account space required by the operating system, so at least an additional 2 GB should be added to the planned storage. In a single domain environment, when a domain controller is also a global catalog server, there is no additional space required. When there is more than one domain in the forest, additional space must be available on each domain controller that will also hold the global catalog. The additional space required is approximately half of the size of the database for the other domains. For example, domain Alpha has a database that is 3 GB and domain Beta has a database that is 4 GB. If a global catalog server is configured in the Alpha domain, the total space required would be 3 GB + (4 GB / 2) = 5 GB.

◆ **DNS:** DNS is a critical service for a Windows Server 2003-based network. To ensure availability, there must always be at least two DNS servers for a network infrastructure and the actual physical network layout must be considered to ensure that a broken wide area network (WAN) link or defective router will not prevent access to a DNS server. DNS is a very efficient service and even very modest server hardware can support a large number of clients. For example, in one Microsoft test, a Pentium III 733 MHz with 256 MB of RAM was able to perform 9500 queries per second and 1300 updates per second with only 75% processor utilization. On a DNS server hosting a large zone or several zones, performance improvements can be made by adding RAM. This is effective because when a DNS server starts, all zone records are loaded into memory. Calculate the amount of memory required by multiplying the number of records by 100 bytes, which is the size of a single record.

◆ **WINS:** One Microsoft benchmark suggests that even a single WINS server with a Pentium II 350MHz processor, 128 MB of RAM and a single IDE hard disk can support more than 300 registrations and 350 queries each second. This translates into supporting up to 10,000 clients on a single dedicated server configured as indicated above. To squeeze more performance out of a server, adding a second processor can increase performance by approximately 25%. Because WINS causes heavy disk activity, adding a dedicated, high-speed drive or RAID array for the WINS database will also improve throughput. WINS is a service based on the Microsoft Jet database engine and performance tuning techniques that apply to most databases will improve WINS performance. Network traffic considerations are generally of little concern because WINS records are small and Unicast network packets are utilized. The heaviest system load for a typical WINS server occurs when all client computers register their addresses at the start of a workday. To ensure availability of the WINS service, at least two WINS servers are normally configured as replication partners. If the highest level of fault tolerance is required, create a Windows Server 2003 cluster and install WINS on it. The advantages of clustering compared

Table 2-3   Domain controller capacity planning

Number of users	Active Directory database size	Additional space for Sysvol and Logs	Number of servers	Memory required per server	Processors per server
< 500	200 MB	512 MB + 512 MB	1	512 MB	1
< 1000	400 MB	512 MB + 512 MB	1	1 GB	2
< 3000	1.2 GB	512 MB + 512 MB	2	2 GB	2
< 10000	4 GB	512 MB + 512 MB	2	2 GB	4
> 10000	4 GB + 400 MB for every 1000 users	512 MB + 512 MB	2 + 1 for every 5000 users	2 GB	4

skill 4

Planning Server Capacity and Availability (cont'd)

exam objective

Plan services for high availability. Plan a high availability solution that uses clustering services. Plan a high availability solution that uses Network Load Balancing. Manage Network Load Balancing. Tools might include the Network Load Balancing Monitor Microsoft Management Console (MMC) snap-in and the WLBS cluster control utility. Implement a cluster server. Recover from cluster node failure.

overview

with simply configuring replication partners are that the WINS database is shared and not replicated, and when a failure occurs, there is less interruption in client activity.

◆ **DHCP:** Under the hood, a DHCP server is really just another database server running the Microsoft Jet database engine. When client computers boot up at the beginning of a workday, the DHCP server will see a peak load. Generally, after that, lease renewals are naturally distributed over a wider time range. When performing capacity planning for a DHCP server, the main concern is whether it will be able to provide acceptable response time during the peak load condition. The main keys to DHCP performance are fast disk drives and sufficient RAM. One Microsoft benchmark used a server with two Pentium III 500 MHz processors and 256 MB of RAM to produce approximately 16 lease assignments per second. Adjusting the DHCP lease duration can have a dramatic effect on the number of clients that can be supported because it will reduce the number of lease assignments required. Sufficient space must be available to store the DHCP database, audit logs, backups, and temporary directory. Each lease uses 600 bytes and each lease transaction in the audit logs will use another 500 bytes. The audit logs are kept for 7 days so with a default lease duration of 8 days, there will normally be two transactions for each lease in the audit logs at the end of a week. If the lease duration is shorter than 8 days, then the number of transactions in the audit logs will increase and more disk space must be available. Another 1200 bytes are used for backup and the temporary directory. To calculate required disk space, multiply the number of leases by 1800 (Lease = 600 + Backup =1200) and add the result to the number of leases multiplied by 1000 (Two sets of transactions = 500 + 500). For example, if a DHCP server provides addresses for 10,000 hosts, the database size would be calculated as follows: 10,000 * 1800 + 10,000 * 1000 = 28,000,000 bytes or approximately 28 MB. By configuring two DHCP servers, each with a portion of the address scope for the network, availability can improve. The normal process involves allocating 80% of the addresses for a scope to one server and 20% to the other and reversing those numbers for a second scope. If DHCP performance and availability must meet the highest standards, a Windows Server 2003 cluster can be configured to provide fault-tolerance for the DHCP service.

◆ **Remote Access / VPN Server:** From a hardware perspective, the most important factor for a remote access server that is providing dial-up connections by means of modems or serial interfaces is to ensure that intelligent communications adapters offload processing from the system processor. For VPN servers, it is important to use a network interface that supports IPSec so that the NIC can handle the encryption processing. A remote access or VPN server must be able to support a high level of network throughput. Network connections should be in full-duplex operation and be connected to a dedicated network switch port. For up to 1000 concurrent connections, approximately 512 MB of RAM should be sufficient. Add at least an additional 256 MB of RAM for every 1000 additional connections. It is best to use Network Load Balancing to ensure availability for remote access and VPN servers. If one of the servers fails, the client connections to that server will drop and they will reconnect to another server. The user will be prompted to logon to open a new session.

◆ **Internet Authentication Service (IAS):** If performance is the only consideration, one IAS server will likely handle all of the remote access and VPN authentications that are required for an organization. However, to ensure continued accessibility, it is recommended to deploy IAS servers in pairs and then configure RADIUS proxies to balance the authentication load across both the Primary and Backup IAS server **(Figure 2-19)**. To improve performance, IAS should be installed on a domain controller that is also a global catalog server. If certificate based authentication is used, the volume of traffic created is much larger than password-based authentication. Consider this additional load when planning your IAS configuration.

Figure 2-19 IAS configuration using a RADIUS proxy

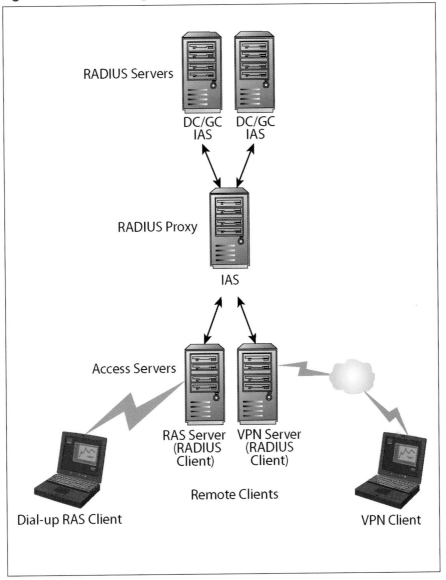

RADIUS Servers

DC/GC   DC/GC
IAS   IAS

RADIUS Proxy

IAS

Access Servers

RAS Server   VPN Server
(RADIUS   (RADIUS
Client)   Client)

Remote Clients

Dial-up RAS Client   VPN Client

Summary

- There are four different editions of Microsoft Windows Server 2003: Web, Standard, Enterprise, and Datacenter
- Selecting the appropriate operating system for each server within the environment is one of the first tasks in planning a network infrastructure.
- Selection of an operating system should focus on the features required.
- Windows Server 2003 Standard Edition supports standard network services such as DNS, DHCP, WINS, RAS, and file and printer sharing.
- Windows Server 2003 Enterprise and Datacenter Editions are more appropriate when larger application servers, data warehouses, and servers supporting OLTP are required, since they support additional RAM and processors and provide additional fault tolerance due to their support for Network Load Balancing and clustering.
- Determining where each server should reside within the network infrastructure is the next step after selecting the appropriate operating system for each server role.
- There should be a minimum of two domain controllers per domain.
- There should be a minimum of one global catalog server per site.
- A DNS server must be available to locate Active Directory resources.
- WINS servers can provide NetBIOS name resolution across WAN links.
- A DHCP relay agent must be configured to allow DHCP clients on one subnet to obtain IP addresses from a DHCP server on another subnet.
- Remote access can be configured to provide dial-up and VPN network connections as well as route packets between networks and perform Network Address Translation.
- IAS provides centralized authentication and accounting for remote access connections.
- Always validate a planned server configuration through testing.
- Bottlenecks are performance-related blockages in computer subsystems that limit the overall performance of a system.
- Baseline measurements should be made to provide a basis for judging the success of any tuning or configuration change.
- Insufficient memory can make other subsystems slow down. Remove any memory bottlenecks prior to investigating other bottlenecks.
- Low-performance disk subsystems can cause additional system processor load.
- SCSI disk systems are much more efficient for servers than IDE systems.
- RAID drive configurations can provide improved performance and fault tolerance.
- Intelligent network adapters offload work from the system processor.
- System Monitor can help locate system bottlenecks.
- Network Load Balancing or clustering can be used when a single server cannot provide required levels of performance and availability.
- Network Load Balancing distributes network requests evenly across a group of up to 32 independent computers.
- Clustering combines up to eight computers into a single logical system. All computers in the cluster share a common mass storage system.

Key Terms

Bottleneck
Clustering
Cluster.exe
DHCP relay agent
DHCP Server service
Domain Name System (DNS)
Domain controller (DC)

Fully Qualified Domain Name (FQDN)
Global catalog (GC) server
Internet Authentication Service (IAS)
Network Load Balancing (NLB)
Nlb.exe
Non-paged memory

Paged memory
Remote access server
Server farm
Virtual Memory Manager (VMM)
Virtual Private Network (VPN) server
Windows Internet Naming Service (WINS)

Test Yourself

1. Which Windows Server 2003 operating system would be appropriate to support a domain controller that authenticates 5000 users?
   a. Web Edition
   b. Standard Edition
   c. Enterprise Edition
   d. Datacenter Edition

2. You have a remote office that you decide to configure as a separate Active Directory site. All computers at the remote site are on the same subnet and you use dynamic IP addresses. It connects to the head office via a 256 Kbps WAN link. What services would you configure at the remote site? (Choose all that apply.)
   a. Domain controller
   b. Global catalog server
   c. DNS server
   d. WINS server
   e. DHCP server
   f. All of the above

3. Which System Monitor counter can help identify a memory bottleneck?
   a. Interrupts/sec
   b. Current Disk Queue Length
   c. Page Faults/sec
   d. Processor Queue Length

4. Which network service commonly uses Network Load Balancing to provide additional performance and availability?
   a. DHCP
   b. VPN

   c. DNS
   d. IAS

5. A Remote Access/Virtual Private Network (VPN) server can also function as a network router and/or as an NAT router.
   a. True
   b. False

6. When trying to find a bottleneck, you generally should examine all of the following except:
   a. Memory.
   b. Printers.
   c. Processors.
   d. Disks.

7. Which of the following best describes the function of capacity planning?
   a. Providing the right peripherals to the right personnel.
   b. Determining how many computers can fit in a given building or other facility.
   c. Providing the right services at the right time in the right quantity.
   d. Determining the amount of memory per computer and per network.

8. All of the following services can be combined on a single domain controller except:
   a. DHCP.
   b. DNS.
   c. WINS.
   d. RAS.

Projects: On Your Own

1. Examine the selection of operating systems and placement of servers within your organization or that of your training center. Determine whether you would make the same planning decisions. What changes would you make to the infrastructure to provide improved availability?

2. Using System Monitor, analyze a computer system and recommend configuration changes to eliminate the most serious bottlenecks.
3. Write a short paper explaining what conditions would need to exist before you would feel that the use of server clustering would be justified. Include a description of the reasons for and against the decision.

Problem Solving Scenarios

1. Fantastic Floss wants to build a Windows Server 2003 forest made up of three domains and two sites. Two of the domains exist in both sites and have 1000 users each, and one domain exists only in one site and has 2000 users. The sites will be connected with a 512 Kbps leased line. You have chosen to build your own routers instead of purchasing dedicated hardware based routers. You plan to use dynamic IP addressing and need to be able to resolve NetBIOS names in all sites from anywhere in the infrastructure. Your budget for the hardware portion of the project is $100,000. Each single processor server costs $7,000 and each quad processor server costs $20,000 with Windows Server 2003, Standard Edition installed. Determine how many servers of each type are required and the services that each will support. Within the budget for this project, can the availability of the infrastructure be improved?

Planning and Optimizing Network Communications

After identifying the required services and determining their placement within your network infrastructure, begin planning the network communications between them. You must identify the network protocols required to support the chosen services. While other optional network protocols may be chosen, TCP/IP is the default for a Windows Server 2003 network.

Planning for TCP/IP includes identifying the number of interconnected networks, selecting an appropriate address range for the overall infrastructure, and determining how to divide that address into subnets to supply addresses to hosts on each network. It will also be necessary to determine whether the IP addresses will be configured manually using static addressing, or dynamically using a DHCP server.

To move packets between each subnet, a router is required. Routers can use static routing but this can require a lot of administrative effort and will not adapt to changes to the infrastructure such as when a link between two routers fails. Instead, routing protocols enable routers to exchange information about network routes dynamically, allowing the routers to reconfigure their routing tables to accommodate network changes automatically.

By measuring and monitoring the network, you can evaluate the choices made during the planning phase. As network traffic patterns change, it may be necessary to reconfigure or replace routers and switches to optimize the network. There are many tools available to measure network load and utilization. Microsoft provides software like the Performance console that can monitor network throughput. Microsoft also provides a protocol analyzer that can examine the contents of network packets. SNMP can be used along with network management software to monitor devices in your network. There are also third party software tools, hardware-based network protocol analyzers, and diagnostic tools that can be helpful in assessing your network.

Most networks today have connections to the Internet. There are several different approaches and questions to consider when planning your network communications. For example, will the connection be dedicated or dial-up? Will the private network's addressing scheme be isolated from the public network? Will there be servers placed in a perimeter network? Will a proxy server be used to track and control user's access to the Internet? These and many more issues will need to be addressed.

Many companies today have a large mobile workforce that must occasionally connect to the corporate network while traveling or from home. There are different ways to provide access but one method is to allow dial-up connections via remote access servers. In some cases, small offices also connect to a central office using the same technology. Network planning must include a thorough examination of these connections.

Goals

In this lesson, you will examine the "plumbing" that transports network packets within your infrastructure. You will learn how to select appropriate network and routing protocols, define and manage a network address scheme, and monitor and improve network performance. You will also learn how to specify devices and technologies that will interconnect your entire network infrastructure.

Lesson 3 Planning and Optimizing Network Communications

Skill	Exam 70-293 Objective
1. Selecting Network Protocols	Plan and modify a network topology. Identify which network protocols to use. Specify the required ports and protocols for specified services.
2. Planning TCP/IP Addressing	Plan a TCP/IP network infrastructure strategy. Analyze IP addressing requirements. Create an IP subnet scheme.
3. Planning a DHCP Solution	Plan a TCP/IP network infrastructure strategy. Analyze IP addressing requirements. Plan and modify a network topology. Plan the physical placement of network resources.
4. Optimizing a DHCP Solution	Plan and modify a network topology. Plan the physical placement of network resources.
5. Selecting Routing and Switching Devices	Plan a TCP/IP network infrastructure strategy. Plan an IP routing solution. Plan and modify a network topology. Plan the physical placement of network resources.
6. Selecting a Routing Protocol	Plan a routing strategy. Identify routing protocols to use in a specified environment. Plan a TCP/IP network infrastructure strategy. Plan an IP routing solution.
7. Optimizing Network Performance	Plan network traffic monitoring. Tools might include Network Monitor and System Monitor.
8. Planning Internet Connectivity	Plan an Internet connectivity strategy.
9. Planning for IP Multicast Routing	Plan a routing strategy. Identify routing protocols to use in a specified environment. Plan routing for IP multicast traffic.

Requirements

To complete this lesson, you will need administrative rights on a Windows Server 2003 computer.

skill 1

Selecting Network Protocols

exam objective

Plan and modify a network topology. Identify network protocols to be used. Specify the required ports and protocols for specified services.

overview

Computers use network protocols to communicate with each other. **Protocols** are well-defined rules that specify exactly how one computer can send information to another. You will need to plan which protocols your network will use to ensure efficient communications and support the planned infrastructure, including non-Microsoft servers and services. Windows Server 2003 supports the following protocols:

tip

Neither Windows Server 2003 nor Windows XP support NetBEUI.

tip

See **www.rfc-editor.org** to find the RFCs mentioned in the text.

◆ **Transmission Control Protocol/Internet Protocol (TCP/IP):** TCP/IP is actually an entire suite of protocols that includes TCP, UDP, IP, ICMP, ARP, and other protocols. The TCP/IP protocol suite is the default for Windows Server 2003. It is also the current protocol standard for the Internet. Internet Protocol (IP) is a routable Network Layer protocol that carries packets between networks to a destination host. Dotted decimal notation represents the 32-bit IP addresses and a subnet mask defines how many bits in the address identify the network and how many identify the host. RFC 791 defines the IP protocol specifications.

◆ **IP version 6 (IPv6):** IPv6 uses a 128-bit address space. All devices in a network communicating using IPv6 must support the protocol. A larger address space is not the only benefit IPv6 provides. IPv6 addresses create an efficient, hierarchical structure that reduces the size of routing tables on backbone routers. It can automatically configure link-local addresses to allow hosts on a subnet to communicate if a DHCP server is unavailable. Internet Protocol Security (IPSec) provides network security and is an integral part of the IPv6 protocol suite. There is better support for Quality of Service (QoS) that allows routers to identify and prioritize traffic flow. IPv6 is also extensible, allowing the addition of extension headers, which support additional features. Organizations should begin planning for IPv6 now to ensure their infrastructure is ready to support it. RFC 2460 is a draft standard that defines the IPv6 specifications. RFC 3513 is a proposed standard that specifies the IPv6 addressing architecture and RFC 2893 explains the co-existence of IPv6 and IPv4 addresses in the same network.

◆ **NWLink:** The NWLink protocol allows Microsoft Windows clients to access resources on Novell Netware operating systems. NWLink is Microsoft's implementation of the Internet Packet Exchange/Sequenced Packet Exchange (IPX/SPX) protocol. Because IPX/SPX is a Novell Netware proprietary protocol, it is only used in environments with Novell Netware servers. If your network has any Netware servers, and your Windows clients need to access them, you must plan to install NWLink.

◆ **AppleTalk:** AppleTalk is a protocol suite used for network communications between older Apple Macintosh computers. AppleTalk can run on various network media including LocalTalk, Ethernet, and Token Ring. If your environment includes Macintosh computers running AppleTalk that will require access to your Windows Server 2003 servers, you must plan to implement AppleTalk. To configure Windows to support these Macintosh clients, you must install File Services for Macintosh and Print Services for Macintosh along with the AppleTalk protocol.

◆ **Reliable Multicast Protocol:** This implementation of the Pragmatic General Multicast Protocol (PGM) adds reliability to multicast applications. It is described in RFC 3208. Unlike the rest of the protocols discussed here, PGM is a Transport Layer protocol that directly uses IP for the delivery of its packets. Reliability is managed by each PGM-enabled receiver, which sends a Negative Acknowledgement (NACK) packet when a packet is lost. The missing packets are retransmitted by either a PGM-enabled router or the PGM sender. Plan to use Reliable Multicast Protocol if your infrastructure includes multicast applications that require reliable communications.

Each protocol supported by Windows Server 2003 is used for specific purposes. Each protocol also has advantages and disadvantages that you should consider when selecting protocols for use within your network. **Table 3-1** lists the primary considerations for each protocol.

Table 3-1   Windows Server 2003 network protocol selection criteria

Protocol	Advantages	Disadvantages	Recommendations
TCP/IP	• Native protocol for Windows Server 2003, Windows 2000 and XP, Unix, and Netware 5 and 6 • Internet standard	• Requires proper address design to support multiple subnets • 32-bit address space is limited • More overhead than NWLink	Use as the standard protocol in most Windows Server 2003 networks.
IPv6	• Supports large 128-bit hierarchical address space • Encryption and Quality of Service are built in	• Requires IPv6-compatible equipment • Requires proper address design to support multiple subnets • Larger headers than IPv4	Use when planning for future growth and compatibility.
NWLink	• Easy to configure • Low overhead	• Proprietary	Use when connecting to Netware servers.
AppleTalk	• Easy to configure	• Proprietary	Use when providing file and print services for Macintosh computers or when connecting to them.
Reliable Multicast Protocol	• Adds reliability to multicast communications	• To work efficiently in larger environments with multiple subnets, routers must be PGM-enabled	Use when providing reliable multicast communications.

skill 1

Selecting Network Protocols (cont'd)

exam objective

Plan and modify a network topology. Identify network protocols to be used. Specify the required ports and protocols for specified services.

how to

Install a network protocol.

1. Click [*Start*] and select **Control Panel**.
2. Right-click **Network Connections** and select **Open**.
3. Right-click a LAN connection and select **Properties** from the menu. The **Local Area Network Properties** dialog box will open.
4. Click [Install...] to open the **Select Network Component Type** dialog box (**Figure 3-1**).
5. Highlight **Protocol** in the list box and click [Add]. The **Select Network Protocol** dialog box will open (**Figure 3-2**).
6. Select **Microsoft TCP/IP version 6** and click [OK]. After a few seconds, the **Select Network Protocol** dialog box will close and the selected protocol will appear in the **Local Area Connection Properties** dialog box (**Figure 3-3**).
7. Click [Close] to close the **Local Area Connection Properties** dialog box.
8. Close the **Network Connections** window.

Figure 3-1 The Select Network Component Type dialog box

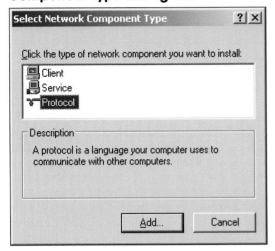

Figure 3-2 Adding a network protocol

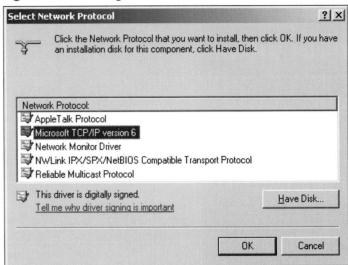

Figure 3-3 Viewing installed network protocols

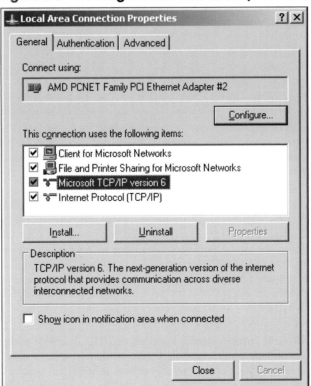

skill 2

Planning TCP/IP Addressing

exam objective

Plan a TCP/IP network infrastructure strategy. Analyze IP addressing requirements. Create an IP subnet scheme.

overview

Understanding TCP/IP addressing is fundamental knowledge necessary to plan a Windows Server 2003 network. There are numerous factors to consider as part of your decision-making process.

Start with the physical layout of the network, considering the number of sites, number of hosts in each site, network bandwidth requirements, and network utilization estimates for each site. Using this information, determine the number of subnets that will be required for your network. There will normally be a subnet for each physical site; but for performance reasons, more than one subnet can be created at each location to segment broadcast domains and isolate network traffic. Often, additional broadcast domains are created by defining a **Virtual LAN (VLAN)** on network switches. Each VLAN will require a subnet for its hosts. You should also reserve additional subnets to support future growth. The number of hosts that must be supported determines the size of each subnet. Each device that requires an IP address counts as a host. Do not forget to include remote access and VPN clients when calculating the number of required host addresses.

Next, select the address range that will support your environment. Will you be connecting your network to an existing network and therefore need to conform to its existing address scheme? If so, ensure that the existing address space will support the correct number and size of subnets that are required. It may also be possible to further subnet an existing subnet in the address space to support your network. This technique uses **Variable Length Subnet Masks (VLSM)** for each different portion of a network. If a single subnet mask is used for an entire network, each subnet will support the same number of hosts. However, if some subnets in your environment have few hosts while others have many, this will waste many network addresses. VLSM allows the creation of subnets of different sizes to accurately reflect the number of hosts required for each. The use of VLSM will require routing protocols that support classless routing as discussed later in this lesson.

Most organizations use private addresses selected from one of the ranges reserved by the **Internet Assigned Numbers Authority (IANA)** for their internal address space (**Table 3-2**). However, if your network will connect to the Internet, at least one public IP address will be required. These addresses are generally obtained from your Internet Service Provider (ISP). Each Internet-accessible device will usually be assigned a public address, although sometimes a single public address is used with individual TCP or UDP ports mapped to servers behind a device that performs Network Address Translation (NAT). A **proxy server** such as Microsoft ISA server allows hosts on a private network to connect to the Internet through a single public IP address.

After selecting an appropriate address space, you must decide whether to use class-based or classless addressing. **Class-based addressing** divides the address space up into five blocks, of which the first three can be used for host addresses. Class-based addressing allows the subnet mask associated with an address to be implicitly determined by examining the first few bits in the address (**Table 3-3**). This simplifies routing protocols, as there is no need to provide subnet mask information when sending a network route to a neighboring router. However, class-based addressing often wastes numerous host addresses because a network can only have 254 hosts for Class C, 65,534 hosts for Class B, or 16,777,214 hosts for Class A. When dealing with a private address space, these limitations may not be a problem.

Classless Inter-Domain Routing (CIDR) does not make any assumptions regarding the subnet mask that is associated with an address. Instead of representing the network portion of the address with a fixed number of bits defined by the address class, **classless routing** can use any number of contiguous left justified bits to identify the network. When a CIDR address is written, it is followed by a slash and the number of bits in the network portion of the address (**Figure 3-4**). This means that the division between the network and host portions of the address can occur anywhere within the address, not just on an octet boundary, allowing for efficient and flexible network design. The formula 2^n-2 calculates the number of host addresses on a subnet, where n is the number of bits used to represent the host portion of the

tip

See RFC 1878 for information on VLSM.

tip

While not defined as one of the private address ranges in RFC 1918, 169.254.0.0/16 is allocated in RFC 3330 for auto-configured link local addresses. See RFC 3300 for more information on private addresses and a complete list of all special IPv4 addresses.

Table 3-2 Private address ranges

Block	Address range	Default subnet mask	Number of addresses	Available bits
192.168.0.0/16	192.168.0.0 – 192.168.255.255	255.255.0.0	65,536	16
172.16.0.0/12	172.16.0.0 – 172.31.255.255	255.240.0.0	1,048,576	20
10.0.0.0/8	10.0.0.0 – 10.255.255.255	255.0.0.0	16,777,216	24

Table 3-3 Address classes

Class	Leftmost bits	Address range	Default mask	Number of networks	Number of hosts/network
A	0xxxxxxx	1.x.x.x – 126.x.x.x	255.0.0.0	126	16,777,214
B	10xxxxxx	128.x.x.x – 191.x.x.x	255.255.0.0	16384	65,534
C	110xxxxx	192.x.x.x – 223.x.x.x	255.255.255.0	2097152	254
D	1110xxxx	224.x.x.x – 239.x.x.x	n/a	n/a	n/a
E	1111xxxx	240.x.x.x – 255.x.x.x	n/a	n/a	n/a

Figure 3-4 Classless addressing

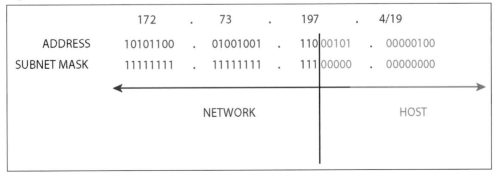

skill 2

Planning TCP/IP Addressing (cont'd)

exam objective

Plan a TCP/IP network infrastructure strategy. Analyze IP addressing requirements. Create an IP subnet scheme.

overview

address. Therefore, when using CIDR, a subnet can contain a more representative number of host addresses such as 2, 6, 14, 30, 62, 126, 254, and so on. Another benefit is that a technique called **supernetting** can aggregate multiple subnets together into a single router table entry, thereby reducing the amount of memory required by backbone routers. When planning the use of classless routing, ensure that all routers in your network support it. Select routing protocols such as Routing Information Protocol (RIP) version 2 or Open Shortest Path First (OSPF) that are able to send the subnet mask along with each network route when updating neighboring routers.

After all these decisions have been made, a subnet mask for each subnet must be identified that will support the network design, then the network address for each subnet must be identified. For example, assume your network has 45 subnets and each has a varying number of hosts from 4 to 300. You need to plan for potential growth and you will choose a private address range.

1. Calculate the number of bits required to represent 45 subnets. One method to do this is to convert the decimal number 45 into binary and count the number of right-most bits. An easier method is to find the power of two that is larger than the desired number. The exponent indicates the number of bits required (**Figure 3-5**). Using either method, you will find that 6 bits will support 45 subnets. In fact, because the formula to calculate the number of available subnets is given by 2^n, you will find that 6 bits will support a maximum number of 64 subnets when the zero subnet and all-ones subnet are used.

2. Calculate the number of bits to represent the maximum number of host addresses required. Again, the methods used above can be used to identify the number of bits required, except that you must take into account the fact a host address cannot be all binary zeros or all binary ones. If the host portion of an address is all binary zeros, the address is not a host address but is the network address for the subnet. If the host portion of an address is all binary ones, the address is the broadcast address for that subnet. To account for these two addresses, use the formula 2^n-2 to determine the number of bits required. For this exercise, the largest number of hosts on a subnet is 300. To represent 300, you will require 9 bits, because $2^9-2 = 510$. This number of bits will allow for sufficient growth if it occurs so no further work is necessary.

3. Six bits are required to represent the subnets and nine bits for the hosts. This gives a total of 15 bits and so your selection of an address range must provide a minimum of 15 bits that are unassigned. Reviewing the private address ranges in **Table 3-2** shows that the 10.0.0.0/8 block has 24 bits available and the 172.16.0.0/12 block has 20 bits available. You will select the 172.16.0.0/12 range. As there are 20 bits available, instead of the 15 that you require, you must decide where you will use the extra bits. In this scenario, you have decided that, for performance reasons, there will never be more than 500 hosts on a subnet and so you will assign the extra bits to the network portion of the subnet mask. The resulting 11 bits that represent the network portion of the subnet mask can represent 2^{11} or 2048 subnets. Remember that the network portion of the chosen address block is 12 bits and, while you cannot touch that portion of the address, the remaining 20 bits can be manipulated to represent the subnets and hosts specified by the design.

4. Now that the number of bits for the network portion of the address has been determined, the subnet mask can be specified. When using CIDR, the number of left-justified consecutive binary ones in the subnet mask is placed after the network address to indicate the subnet mask. For this network, this would be the 12 bits in the private address block and the 11 bits needed to represent the subnets or 172.16.0.0/23. While this is the standard format for CIDR addresses, it is necessary to convert the subnet mask into dotted decimal notation in order to enter it into the Windows interface. If the bits in the subnet mask are all ones for an entire octet, the decimal representation is 255. Therefore, for 172.16.0.0/23, the first two octets of the subnet mask are 255.255. The third octet is only 7 bits so you must convert it to decimal. The easiest way to do this is to write the powers of two from 2^7 to 2^0 on a piece of paper as shown in **Figure 3-6** and place the

tip

RIP version 1 and Cisco's IGRP are both class-based routing protocols that do not propagate subnet masks along with network routes. RIP version 2, Cisco's EIGRP, and OSPF are all classless routing protocols that send the subnet mask along with each network route.

tip

RFC 950 suggests that the zero subnet and all-ones subnet should not be used. More recent RFCs, such as RFC 1878, allow for their use. Microsoft follows the more recent RFCs, but it is also critical that all routers within your infrastructure are configured to support the zero subnet and all-ones subnet.

Figure 3-5 Finding the number of bits to allow a specified number of subnets

1st value greater than 45 has an exponent of 6
VALUE 128 64 32 16 8 4 2 1
POWER 2^7 2^6 2^5 2^4 2^3 2^2 2^1 2^0
45 = 1 0 1 1 0 1
6 BITS

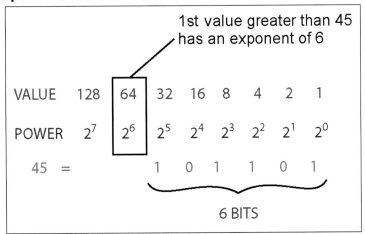

Figure 3-6 Converting the number of bits in a subnet mask to decimal

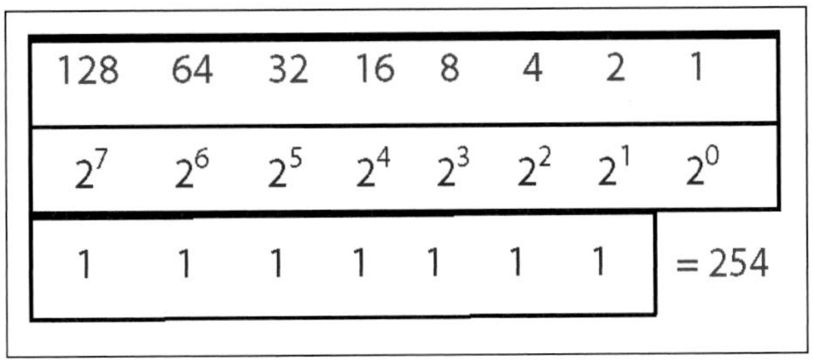

128 64 32 16 8 4 2 1
2^7 2^6 2^5 2^4 2^3 2^2 2^1 2^0
1 1 1 1 1 1 1
= 254

skill 2

Planning TCP/IP Addressing (cont'd)

exam objective

Plan a TCP/IP network infrastructure strategy. Analyze IP addressing requirements. Create an IP subnet scheme.

overview

number of binary ones that remain in the subnet mask under each value. Add the decimal values for each place where a bit in the subnet mask is set to one. For this example, this would be $128 + 64 + 32 + 16 + 8 + 4 + 2 = 254$ and so the third octet of the subnet mask is 254. The rest of the bits in the subnet mask are binary zeros representing the host portion of the address and so the last octet in the subnet mask is a zero. The completed subnet mask is therefore 255.255.254.0.

5. After specifying the subnet mask, determine the network address for each subnet by finding the subnet increment value. Subtracting the last non-zero value in the subnet mask from 256 produces the subnet increment value. In this case, $256-254 = 2$. This value determines the network address for each subnet. The subnet mask ends in the third octet so you will add the increment value of 2 to the value of the third octet to find each network address. The assigned network portion of your selected address range is 172.16.0.0 and this is the first usable network address when the zero-subnet is enabled. **Table 3-4** lists the network address for each consecutive subnet. The second subnet in this example is 172.16.2.0. Note that the each network address has all the host bits set to binary zero.

6. To determine the broadcast address for each subnet, subtract one from the network address of the next subnet. Remember that the broadcast address is the network address of the subnet with all the host bits set to binary ones. The binary representation of the broadcast address in this example is **10101100.00010000.00000001.11111111**. The nine right-most bits are all set to one for each broadcast address because you have chosen a subnet mask that defines nine bits for host addresses. To calculate this in decimal, remember that the largest value an octet can contain is 255. If 1 is added to an octet containing 255, it becomes a 0 and the next octet to the left is incremented by 1. This is the same as when you carry a one when adding base 10 numbers. When subtracting, the reverse is true. Subtracting 1 from an octet that contains a 0 sets that octet to 255 and subtracts 1 from the octet on its left. Therefore, the decimal representation of the broadcast address for the first subnet in this example is 172.16.1.255.

7. The final task is to list the first and last valid host addresses on each subnet. This is a simple task if the network address and broadcast address for each subnet have been determined. The first valid host on each subnet is 1 more than the network address and the last valid host on each subnet is 1 less than the broadcast address. For your first subnet, the first valid host is 172.16.0.0 plus 1 or 172.16.0.1 and the last valid host is 172.16.1.255 minus 1 or 172.16.1.254.

Table 3-4 Subnetting a network

Assigned network address   172.16.0.0
Subnet mask   255.255.254.0
Subnet increment value   2

	Subnet network address	First host address	Last host address	Broadcast address
1st subnet	172.16.0.0 10101100.00010000.0000000 0.00000000	172.16.0.1 10101100.00010000.0000000 0.00000001	172.16.1.254 10101100.00010000.0000000 1.11111110	172.16.1.255 10101100.00010000.0000000 1.11111111
2nd subnet	172.16.2.0 10101100.00010000.0000001 0.00000000	172.16.2.1 10101100.00010000.0000001 0.00000001	172.16.3.254 10101100.00010000.0000001 1.11111110	172.16.3.255 10101100.00010000.0000001 1.11111111
3rd subnet	172.16.4.0 10101100.00010000.0000010 0.00000000	172.16.4.1 10101100.00010000.0000010 0.00000001	172.16.5.254 10101100.00010000.0000010 1.11111110	172.16.5.255 10101100.00010000.0000010 1.11111111
4th subnet	172.16.6.0 10101100.00010000.0000011 0.00000000	172.16.6.1 10101100.00010000.0000011 0.00000001	172.16.7.254 10101100.00010000.0000011 1.11111110	172.16.7.255 10101100.00010000.0000011 1.11111111
5th subnet	172.16.8.0 10101100.00010000.0000100 0.00000000	172.16.8.1 10101100.00010000.0000100 0.00000001	172.16.9.254 10101100.00010000.0000100 1.11111110	172.16.9.255 10101100.00010000.0000100 1.11111111
. . .	. . .	. . .	. . .	. . .
Last subnet	172.16.254.0 10101100.00010000.1111111 0.00000000	172.16.254.1 10101100.00010000.1111111 0.00000001	172.16.255.254 10101100. 00010000.1111111 1.11111110	172.16.255.255 10101100. 00010000.1111111 1.11111111

skill 2

Planning TCP/IP Addressing (cont'd)

exam objective

Plan a TCP/IP network infrastructure strategy. Analyze IP addressing requirements. Create an IP subnet scheme.

how to

Your network has 5 locations with plans to add 2 more locations. Each site will have no more than 10 hosts. You will choose a private address range and assign a single subnet mask for the entire network.

1. Calculate the number of bits that will be required to represent the subnets, allowing for future growth.
2. Calculate the number of bits that will be required to represent the number of hosts for each subnet.
3. Select a private address range that will provide enough bits to support the number of subnets and hosts.
4. Specify the subnet mask.
5. Determine the subnet increment value and identify the network address for each subnet.
6. Identify the broadcast address for each subnet.
7. List the first and last valid host address on each subnet.

more

Because the size of many of the sites in the given scenario is widely different, it would make sense to plan to use VLSM to further subnet at least one of the subnets to support the smaller sites. Once the previous seven steps have been completed, start over again, treating the number of bits in the resulting subnet mask as the assigned portion and therefore as untouchable, that is 172.16.0.0/23. Use additional bits from the host portion of the mask to create additional smaller subnets that support fewer hosts on each, as shown in **Figure 3-7**.

Figure 3-7 Using Variable Length Subnet Masks

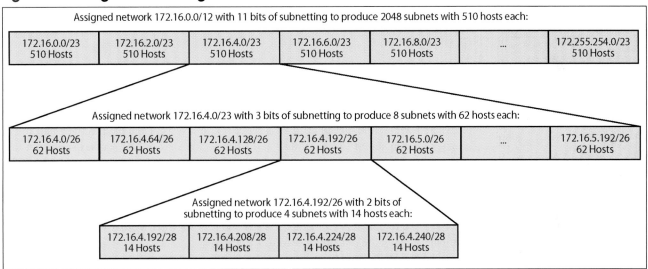

skill 3

Planning a DHCP Solution

exam objective

Plan a TCP/IP network infrastructure strategy. Analyze IP addressing requirements. Plan and modify a network topology. Plan the physical placement of network resources.

overview

After planning TCP/IP addressing and defining each subnet address, the next requirement is to assign IP addresses to each host. There are several methods that can be used. Static addresses can be assigned manually, but **Dynamic Host Control Protocol (DHCP)** is used to assign addresses in most environments. If client computers running Windows 2000, XP, or Server 2003 try to obtain addresses dynamically and they cannot contact a DHCP server, they will use **Automatic Private IP Addressing (APIPA)** to assign a unique address to themselves within the 169.254.0.0/16 address block.

While DHCP requires less administrative overhead than static addressing and is therefore less prone to configuration errors, the ability to assign additional options along with the IP address is a key advantage. The greatest planning consideration for DHCP is ensuring that client computers will always be able to contact a DHCP server each time an address is requested or renewed. When planning to support continuous availability for DHCP servers, there are two main approaches to determine server placement. DHCP servers can be centralized, distributed, or a combination of both.

When your network consists of more than one subnet, a DHCP server can be placed on each subnet to supply dynamic addressing to client computers. However, unless each subnet has two DHCP servers, there is no guarantee of availability. When two DHCP servers provide service for a local subnet, each server usually supplies 50% of the addresses for that subnet. A typical setup will define the same address scope on both servers and then exclude half of the addresses on one server and the other half of the addresses on the second server. In this configuration, when one server fails, the other can continue to supply address leases until the failed server is repaired. The problem with a distributed DHCP configuration is that it requires at least two servers per subnet, and an administrator must configure and manage the address scopes on all of those servers. Higher availability can be achieved by using the Windows Cluster service to cluster two or more DHCP servers together so that if one fails, its load redistributes among the remaining server(s).

A centralized DHCP configuration places a DHCP server with multiple scopes defined on one subnet and clients from all subnets obtain their address leases from it. Because the DHCP lease process utilizes broadcasts, and routers normally block broadcast traffic, the routers connecting the subnets must act as DHCP/BOOTP relay agents as defined in RFC 1542. To ensure availability, there must be at least two DHCP servers.

A combined plan is often used when more than one subnet has a DHCP server but not all subnets do. Using this approach requires that routers must be configured to act as DHCP relay agents. A common practice is to configure a DHCP server that is local to a subnet with 80% of the address scope for that subnet and then, to ensure availability, configure a DHCP server on another subnet with 20% of the same address scope (**Figure 3-8**). This provides good performance because most address assignments are handled on the local subnet. This also allows address assignment to take place if the local DHCP server is down by accessing one on another subnet. When planning, it is wise to place a DHCP server as near as possible to the bulk of the clients that it will service. This is especially important when configuring a remote location connected by a low speed link. Because the speed of the link and its reliability may affect the DHCP process, it is recommended that a DHCP server be placed in each of these locations.

Once DHCP server placement has been determined, they must be configured with the appropriate address scopes, address reservations, and scope options. Besides splitting an address scope between two servers using the 50/50 or 80/20 rules, there is often the need to reserve specific addresses so that a device will always have the same address. Reservations

Figure 3-8 A combined DHCP solution using a relay agent

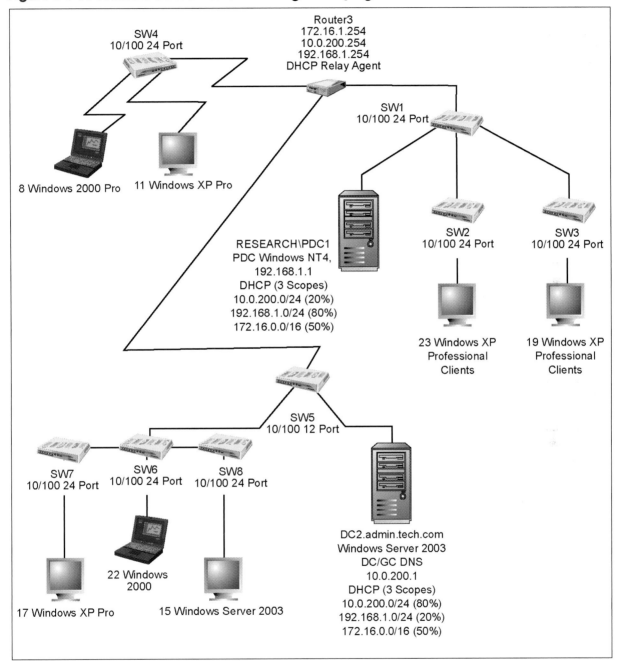

skill 3

Planning a DHCP Solution (cont'd)

exam objective

Plan a TCP/IP network infrastructure strategy. Analyze IP addressing requirements. Plan and modify a network topology. Plan the physical placement of network resources.

overview

are common for printers but have other applications as well. Address reservations are based on the MAC address of the device and this reservation must be entered on all DHCP servers that will service the address scope containing the reserved address.

A major strength of DHCP is its ability to assign configuration options beyond an IP address and subnet mask. These options can be configured at four different levels, as shown in **Table 3-5**. The options configured at each level can be overridden by options configured at each of the more specific levels as indicated in the table. The most commonly configured options are listed in **Table 3-6**.

DHCP in Windows Server 2003 provides two types of option classes that can assign specific settings to a defined group of devices. Vendor option classes allow assignment of specific IP configurations to groups of devices based on the operating system used. The DHCP client must identify itself by sending its class ID when it requests an address from the DHCP server. If there is a matching class ID configured on the server, its settings are applied to the client device. There are three pre-configured vendor classes available for use: Microsoft Windows 2000 Options, Microsoft Windows 98 Options, and Microsoft Options. Additionally, there is a default vendor class, DHCP Standard Options, used when no other vendor class applies. Additional vendor classes can be created and specific options assigned to those classes. Customized vendor classes commonly support groups of printers from a specific manufacturer.

User-defined option classes are used to group DHCP clients by type. For example, there are two default user classes: Default Routing and Remote Access Class and Default BOOTP Class. Additional user-defined classes can be created to group client devices based on any characteristic. To participate in an option class, each device must send the correct class ID when it requests an address from the DHCP server.

how to

Configure DHCP with an address scope, set scope options, create a user-defined class, and configure a client computer with the correct class ID.

1. Click **Start**. Select **Manage Your Server**. The **Manage Your Server** window will open.
2. If **DHCP Server** is not listed under **Your server has been configured with the following roles**, click **Add or remove a role** to start the **Configure Your Server Wizard**. Skip to step 7 if **DHCP Server** is already installed.
3. Read the **Preliminary Steps** screen and click [Next>]. The **Server Role** screen will open.
4. Highlight **DHCP Server** in the **Server Role** list box and click [Next>] to open the **Summary of Selections** screen (**Figure 3-9**).
5. Confirm that you have selected **Install DHCP server** and click [Next>] to proceed.
6. After installing the DHCP server, the system will start the **New Scope Wizard**. Click [Cancel] to stop the wizard, as you will configure the scope manually. A **Cannot Complete** warning dialog box will appear. Click [Finish].
7. Click **Start**, point to **Administrative Tools**, and then click **DHCP** to open the **DHCP** management console.
8. Right-click the server icon and select **New Scope** on the shortcut menu. The **New Scope Wizard** will open.
9. Click [Next>]. The **Scope Name** window will open.
10. Type **Tucson Subnet** in the **Name** text box and click [Next>].

caution

If you already have a DHCP server operating on your network, make sure that you do not activate your new scope in this exercise.

Table 3-5   DHCP options precedence

Option	Description
Server	Affects all client computers unless overridden by a scope, class, or reserved client option.
Scope	Affects client computers that have obtained an address from a specific scope unless overridden by a class or reserved client option.
Class	Affects client computers that supply a DHCP class ID when obtaining a lease that matches the defined class ID unless overridden by a reserved client option.
Reserved client	Affects the client computer that matches the reservation. Overrides all other options.

Table 3-6   Commonly used DHCP options

Option	Number	Value	Description
Router	003	IP address	Supplies the IP address for the default gateway.
DNS server	006	IP addresses	Provides the IP addresses of the DNS servers used for name resolution.
DNS domain	015	Domain name (e.g., microsoft.com)	Sets the domain name for a client.
WINS server	044	IP addresses	Provides the IP addresses for the WINS servers used to resolve NetBIOS names.
WINS node type	046	0x1 (B-node): Only broadcasts are used to resolve NetBIOS names. 0x2 (P-node): Point-to-Point mode only uses WINS to resolve NetBIOS names. 0x4 (M-node): Mixed mode uses a broadcast first and on failure uses WINS to resolve NetBIOS names. 0x8 (H-node): Hybrid mode uses WINS first and on failure uses a broadcast to resolve NetBIOS names.	Defines NetBIOS name resolution behavior. Using this option an administrator can control whether NetBIOS names will be resolved using broadcasts or lookups on WINS servers and in what order those resolution steps will occur.

Figure 3-9   Installing the DHCP service

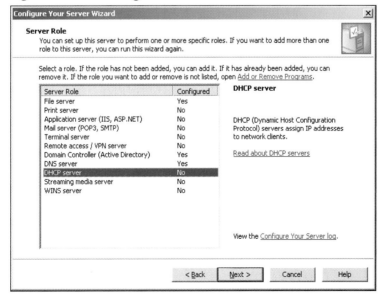

skill 3

Planning a DHCP Solution (cont'd)

exam objective

Plan a TCP/IP network infrastructure strategy. Analyze IP addressing requirements. Plan and modify a network topology. Plan the physical placement of network resources.

how to

11. The **IP Address Range** screen will open. Type **172.16.2.1** in the **Start IP address** text box. Type **172.16.3.254** in the **End IP address** text box. Type **23** in the **Length** text box. Notice that the **Subnet Mask** changes to reflect the number of bits entered in the **Length** box. Click [Next>].

12. The **Add Exclusions** screen will open. If any addresses within the defined IP address range are statically allocated to a device, such as a network-attached printer, they must be excluded here. Click [Next>] to continue.

13. The **Lease Duration** screen will open. The default duration of 8 days is generally acceptable; however, further examination of the lease duration will be made in Skill 4. Click [Next>].

14. Select **No, I will configure these options later** on the **Configure DHCP Options** screen and click [Next>].

15. Click [Finish] to complete the **New Scope Wizard**.

16. Right-click the server icon and select **Define User Classes** on the shortcut menu. The **DHCP User Classes** dialog box will display a list of available classes.

17. Click [Add] to open the **New Class** dialog box (**Figure 3-10**).

18. Type **Notebook Computers** in the **Display name** and **Description** text boxes.

19. Click in the **ID** box directly under the **ASCII** heading and type **NBComp1** as the user class ID. Notice that as the ASCII text string is entered, a binary representation is also entered. Click [OK].

20. Click [Close] to close the **DHCP User Classes** dialog box.

21. Expand the newly created scope by clicking the ⊞ sign beside it. Right-click **Scope Options** and select **Configure Options** on the menu.

22. Place a checkmark by **003 Router** by clicking the square beside it. Type **172.16.2.1** in the **IP Address** text box and click [Add] to define the address for the default gateway for this scope (**Figure 3-11**). This is a good example of an address that should be excluded from the address range. Other options can be configured in a similar manner.

23. Click the **Advanced** tab.

24. Select **Notebook Computers** in the **User Class** drop-down list.

25. Place a checkmark by **003 Router** by clicking the square beside it. Type **172.16.2.2** in the **IP address** input box and click [Add] to define the address for the default gateway for this user class (**Figure 3-12**). This default gateway assignment will override the assignment made at the scope level for all computers that send **NBComp1** as their class ID when they request an address.

26. Click [OK] to close the **Scope Options** dialog box.

27. Close the **DHCP** management console.

28. Go to a computer configured to obtain its IP address dynamically.

29. Open a command prompt window by clicking [Start] and then **Run**. The **Run** dialog box will open. Type **cmd** in the **Open** text box and click [OK].

30. At the command prompt, type **ipconfig /setclassid "Local Area Connection" NBComp1** and then press **[Enter]**. This command permanently stores the assigned class ID in the computer's Registry. Each time this client computer attempts to request or renew an address, it will send the class ID to the DHCP server.

31. Type **ipconfig /all** and press **[Enter]** to confirm that the class ID has been set (**Figure 3-13**).

32. Type **exit** and press **[Enter]** to close the command prompt.

tip

If your network connection has another name, substitute it for "Local Area Connection".

Figure 3-10 Configuring scope options

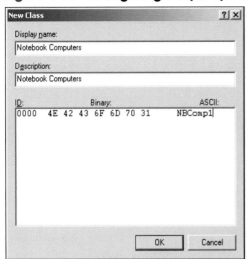

Figure 3-11 Creating a user-defined class

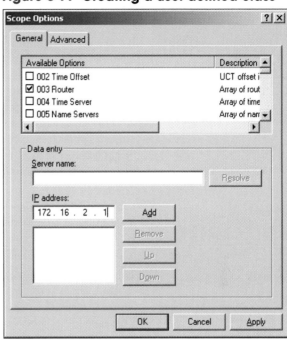

Figure 3-12 Setting user-defined class options

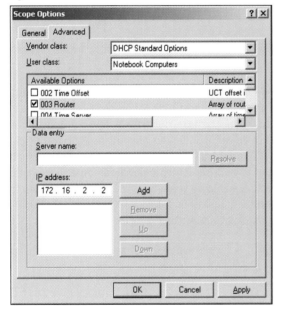

Figure 3-13 Confirming a client computer's class ID

skill 4

Optimizing a DHCP Solution

exam objective

Plan and modify a network topology. Plan the physical placement of network resources.

overview

If client devices within your infrastructure take an excessively long time to obtain a lease from a DHCP server, three main areas may be improved. First, confirm that the server hosting the DHCP Server service is not overloaded with other activities. DHCP by itself will not usually load a server to the point where performance suffers. The key areas of utilization to observe are the CPU, available memory, and the amount of disk I/O. Apply the skills learned in Lesson 2, Skill 3 to determine where the system bottleneck resides. If a server is heavily loaded and upgrades or performance tuning are not options, you may need to move the DHCP Server service to another server. If there are many clients that must renew their leases at the same time of day, you may need to install additional DHCP servers to handle the load.

The second area to observe is the infrastructure and the placement of the DHCP servers. If a number of client devices must obtain their addresses across slow links, place a DHCP server local to those computers. Remember that while the actual volume of traffic generated by DHCP is relatively small, other network activity that consumes available bandwidth can result in poor DHCP performance.

The third area is the lease duration assigned to an address scope. Optimizing the lease duration has two effects that interact. Increasing the lease duration reduces the number of address renewals; however, the leased addresses are assigned for longer periods. Consequently, a larger address pool may be required in environments where there are many hosts that connect infrequently for short periods. Each host will obtain and hold an address lease for its full duration even if the host connects only once for a few minutes. This relationship can be tuned to provide the best trade-off of address availability and performance. Recall from Lesson 3, Skill 3 that user option classes can be created. A common use for such classes is creating groups of devices that will have different lease durations. In a more static environment, longer lease durations may be acceptable. If you have a large number of remote access or VPN users, it is best to assign short lease durations for both performance and security. **Table 3-7** lists the effects that changes in lease duration can have on the network.

how to

Reduce the lease duration for remote access clients.

1. Click **Start**, point to **Administrative Tools**, and then click **DHCP** to open the **DHCP** management console.
2. Expand a scope by clicking the ⊞ sign beside it. Right-click **Scope Options** and select **Configure Options** from the menu.
3. Click the **Advanced** tab.
4. Select **Default Routing and Remote Access class** in the **User Class** drop-down list.
5. Scroll down the list of available options to locate option **051 Lease**. Select it by clicking the square beside it. Type **1800** in the **Data entry** text box to set the lease duration to 1800 seconds (30 minutes) and click ▭ OK ▭ to close the **Scope Options** dialog box **(Figure 3-14)**.
6. Close the **DHCP** management console.

tip

The lease duration is stored internally as a hexadecimal number. When you enter the seconds in the Data entry text box as a decimal number, it automatically converts to hexadecimal when you click OK to close the Scope Options dialog box. You also can enter hexadecimal values directly by prefacing the value with 0x, such as 0x708, which is the hexadecimal equivalent of 1800 seconds.

Table 3-7   Effects of changes in lease duration

Indicators	Action	Results
Few changes to network infrastructure	Use longer lease durations.	• DHCP traffic is reduced. • If many new hosts are added, available addresses could be exhausted quickly.
Devices move between subnets often Remote access/VPN users Limited address scope	Use shorter lease durations.	• DHCP traffic increases. • Addresses are available for reuse sooner.

Figure 3-14 Setting lease duration for remote access clients

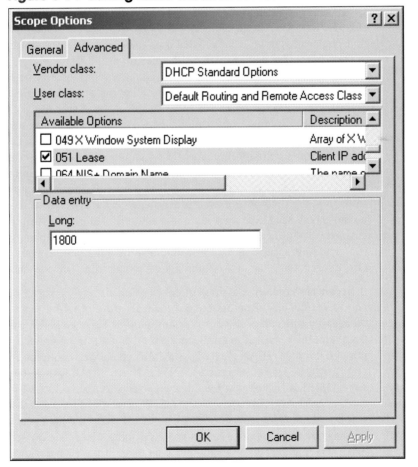

skill 5

Selecting Routing and Switching Devices

exam objective

Plan a TCP/IP network infrastructure strategy. Plan an IP routing solution. Plan and modify a network topology. Plan the physical placement of network resources.

overview

When planning the network infrastructure for an organization, you will normally be provided with some design guidelines and perhaps even some preliminary network diagrams. Your job will be to determine what devices are required to support the planned network and allow for growth. It is important to select devices that will provide specified levels of performance within the assigned project budget. The types of devices that can be selected are listed in **Table 3-8**. Each of these devices helps to solve a specific network problem. To specify each device properly, understanding the concepts of broadcast and collision domains is necessary.

Planning a network is much like building a freeway system. Your goal is to move packets efficiently from their source to their destination while avoiding traffic congestion and collisions. As the number of cars on a road increase, the speed at which any single car travels reduces and the possibility of a collision increases. Each network topology has defined a cable access method to try to reduce or eliminate collisions and to provide a fair chance for each device on the network that needs to transmit data. While some protocols, like Token Ring, eliminate collisions by only allowing a device that possesses the token to transmit, the overall throughput of a device is still affected by the volume of traffic from other devices. Most networks today use Ethernet that uses **Carrier Sense Multiple Access/Collision Detection (CSMA/CD)** to arbitrate cable access. CSMA/CD specifies that multiple devices can attach to a single network segment and that each must listen before transmitting to ensure the cable is free. If another device happens to transmit at the same instant, a collision occurs. The device detects the collision and then waits a random interval before restarting the whole process. A **collision domain** is any group of devices whose transmissions have the potential to collide. If you are driving, the best way to reduce the chance of a collision with another car is to ensure that you are the only car on the road or that there are few others. This is also the goal of network planning. All devices listed on **Table 3-8**, other than a hub, will divide a network into additional collision domains. Most commonly, switches create individual collision domains for each attached device. When all devices in a network infrastructure are attached to their own switched port, it is called **micro-segmentation**. This configuration removes collisions from the environment. Because a single device exists in each collision domain, there is no longer any need to listen prior to transmitting. Additionally, **full-duplex** communication is enabled when using typical Unshielded Twisted Pair (UTP) cabling because one pair of wires can be used to receive at the same time that the other pair of wires is used to transmit. This effectively doubles the network throughput to and from a device, and eliminates collisions.

A **broadcast domain** is a group of devices that all receive a broadcast frame transmitted by one of the devices. Routers block broadcast traffic. All Layer 2 and lower devices pass broadcast traffic unless a switch contains multiple VLANs. In this case, each VLAN becomes a separate broadcast domain because they cannot communicate with each other except through a router. VLANs are very flexible and easy to configure. For example, a group of ports can be assigned a specific VLAN or a device's MAC address can be assigned to a VLAN so regardless of which port the device connects to, the correct VLAN is assigned. In either case, each VLAN will require a separate IP network address and the devices on each VLAN will be able to communicate with each other directly. Communication between their VLAN and any other will require a router. When planning VLANs or any separate broadcast domain, make sure that the bulk of communication to and from each device is local. Ideally, no more than 20% of all communication should have to cross a router. Segmenting broadcast domains can become important if there are a large number of clients in a broadcast domain and broadcast traffic is affecting the performance of unicast transmissions. While inserting switches into a network can be done without extensive planning, the use of routers requires careful planning. Each interface connected to a router must be, by definition, a separate network.

Table 3-8   Network device selection

Device	OSI Layer	Function	Use
Hub connect	Layer 1 Physical	Attaches additional network devices to a single network segment. All devices exist in a single collision domain. Acts as a signal repeater. Does not create additional network segments.	Provides inexpensive method to connect small groups of computers. Because all bandwidth is shared, performance is limited.
Switch	Layer 2 Data Link	Divides a network into multiple segments. Each port is a separate collision domain. Listens to transmissions and learns the location of each device. Builds a table of MAC addresses used for switching decisions. Switching is normally performed using special purpose hardware.	Used to segment a network into multiple collision domains, thereby reducing the probability of a collision and increasing network throughput. If VLANs are configured, separate broadcast domains are created.
Bridge	Layer 2 Data Link	Functions like a switch but usually has fewer ports and switching is performed by software running on general-purpose hardware.	Because switches have become so inexpensive, monolithic bridges are not common. Today bridging is often an integrated function of another device such as a router.
Layer 3 Switch; Brouter	Layer 2 and 3 Data Link and Network	Functions as a switch but also has an integrated router that enables communication between VLANs on the switch.	Many enterprise switches have Layer 3 capabilities. Without a Layer 3 switch, either an external router or a VLAN-aware NIC must be used to enable communication between VLANs. Brouter is an older term for a Layer 3 switch.
Router	Layer 3 Network	Divides a network into multiple broadcast domains. Makes routing decisions based on Layer 3 addresses provided by protocols such as IP, IPX, and AppleTalk.	Connects separate networks together. Improves network performance by limiting the size of broadcast domains.

skill 5

Selecting Routing and Switching Devices (cont'd)

exam objective

Plan a TCP/IP network infrastructure strategy. Plan an IP routing solution. Plan and modify a network topology. Plan the physical placement of network resources.

overview

Imagine the work required to reconfigure an existing network containing hundreds of hosts. Careful planning beforehand can produce an IP addressing scheme that will accommodate a router by changing only the subnet mask.

You must also plan for routers to support WAN connections to your network. If your infrastructure will include dissimilar network systems, routers will be required to interconnect them. When selecting routers, make sure they support the Layer 3 protocols that you plan to use and that they are configured with the appropriate hardware interfaces to connect to your networks.

how to

Improve the network design shown in **Figure 3-15** to eliminate collisions, allow full-duplex communications and reduce the number of network routing and switching devices required. Assume that each computer icon represents 15 computers.

1. Connect to the Internet and select appropriate products from **http://www.cisco.com/en/US/products/index.html**
2. Can a single device support the entire infrastructure?
3. If broadcast domain one and two were geographically separated, what devices would you select?

more

A further consideration when selecting network devices is the method that will be used to manage them. Devices can be managed in-band or out-of-band. **In-band management** uses the network connections supplied by the device to manage it. **Out-of-band management** uses a separate port that cannot be accessed through the network. For example, a Cisco router can be managed through the console port which provides out-of-band management or through a Telnet connection which provides in-band management. Many devices today provide an in-band administrative Web interface, while others utilize Simple Network Management Protocol (SNMP). In some cases, devices that only support out-of-band management can be managed by connecting their management ports to a multi-port access server that will allow network-based access to each device.

Figure 3-15 Collision and broadcast domain segmentation

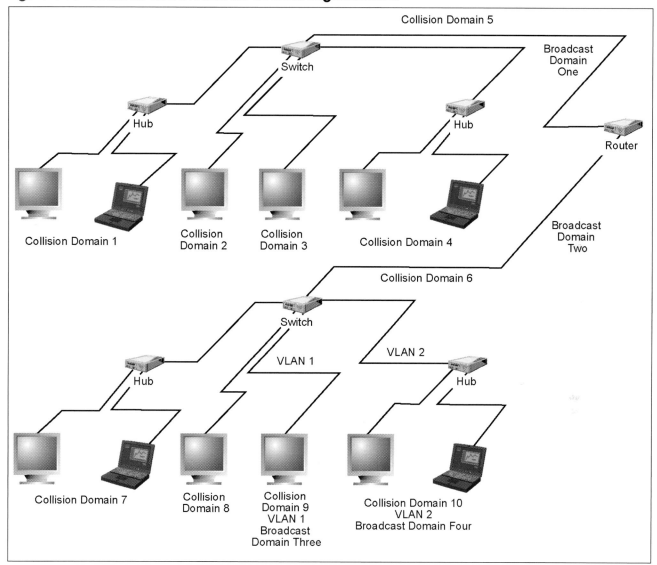

skill 6

Selecting a Routing Protocol

Plan a routing strategy. Identify routing protocols to use in a specified environment. Plan a TCP/IP network infrastructure strategy. Plan an IP routing solution.

overview

Routers are always aware of the networks to which they are directly connected. In order for a router to forward packets to a more distant network, a routing table entry must be available that indicates how to reach that network. These routing table entries are stored in the memory of each router. The routing table can be populated manually or dynamically.

To build a routing table manually, an administrator enters static routes for each of the networks that do not have direct connections to one of the router's interfaces. If any changes to the infrastructure occur, the routing tables must be updated manually to reflect the current state. Because of the administrative overhead associated with static routes, they do not scale well to large environments. In some cases, they may still be used, such as when defining demand-dial connections or to enforce the best possible security. **Table 3-9** lists the pros and cons of static routes.

Dynamic routing protocols can build a routing table automatically and adapt to changes in the infrastructure. Routing protocols are different from routed or routable protocols. While **routed protocols** like IP carry actual network communications, **routing protocols** do not. They are only concerned with sending network route updates to neighboring routers. Windows Server 2003 Routing and Remote Access Service supports two routing protocols, RIP version 1 & 2 and OSPF. Dedicated routers such as Cisco routers support other routing protocols as well, such as Interior Gateway Routing Protocol (IGRP), Enhanced Interior Gateway Routing Protocol (EIGRP), Border Gateway Protocol (BGP) and Intermediate System-Intermediate System (IS-IS). Each of these routing protocols can be broadly classified as either distance vector protocols or link state protocols.

Distance vector protocols are simple protocols that learn of routes to distant networks through neighboring routers that learned of the routes through their neighbors and so on. This is often referred to as routing by rumor. Distance vector protocols are often slow to converge when there are changes in the infrastructure. Convergence occurs when all routers have a correct, unified view of the network. Distance vector protocols are also inherently noisy because they send a complete copy of a router's routing table out from all interfaces at regular intervals. RIP sends updates every 30 seconds by default and Cisco's IGRP sends updates every 90 seconds by default. Finally, the metric used to select a preferred route is often very simple and therefore not flexible. For example, RIP uses only the hop count as its routing metric to select a preferred route and does not take into account the available bandwidth or any other property. For these reasons, distance vector protocols do not scale well to large inter-networks.

Link state protocols overcome many of the weaknesses associated with distance vector protocols. Instead of learning routes by rumor, link state protocols send Link State Advertisements (LSAs) when an interface on a router changes state. Link state routers use these LSAs to create a map of the network. This results in fast convergence and an accurate view of the network. Routers using OSPF maintain a map of the network in a link state database and maintain a separate routing table. As a result, OSPF is highly scalable, highly flexible, and uses minimal bandwidth. However, OSPF does consume greater memory and processor resources on each router than RIP.

tip

Routing and Remote Access Service can also act as a DHCP relay agent and an IGMP router and proxy.

Table 3-9 Routing protocol selection

Protocol	Type	Pros	Cons	Comments
Static routes	n/a	• Secure • No bandwidth overhead	• Administrative overhead • Does not scale well • Does not adjust to changes	Used for small networks, networks without redundant paths, and demand-dial connections.
RIP version 1	Distance-vector	• Easy to configure • Wide compatibility	• Susceptible to introduction of false routes • Class-based only • Does not support VLSM or CIDR • High bandwidth consumption • Inflexible metric • Slow convergence	Use only if your network contains redundant paths and routers do not support any other routing protocol.
RIP version 2	Distance-vector	• Easy to configure • Wide compatibility • Supports VLSM and CIDR • Inflexible metric • Slow convergence	• Susceptible to introduction of false routes • High bandwidth consumption	Use if your network has redundant routes and OSPF is not supported. Most routers support RIP version 2.
OSPF	Link-state	• Fast convergence • Scales well • Supports VLSM and CIDR • Low bandwidth usage	• More difficult to configure • Higher routing resource consumption	Use for large networks especially where there are frequent changes to its structure.

skill 6

Selecting a Routing Protocol *(cont'd)*

exam objective

Plan a routing strategy. Identify routing protocols to use in a specified environment. Plan a TCP/IP network infrastructure strategy. Plan an IP routing solution.

how to

Configure a remote access/VPN server.

1. Click [*Start*] and then click **Manage Your Server**.
2. If **Remote Access/VPN Server** is not listed under **Your server has been configured with the following roles**, click **Add or remove a role**. If it is listed, skip ahead to step 11.
3. The **Preliminary Steps** screen will open. Click [Next >].
4. On the **Server Role** screen, select **Remote Access/VPN Server** and click [Next >]. The **Summary of Selections** screen will open.
5. Click [Next >]. The **Routing and Remote Access Server Setup Wizard** will start.
6. The **Configuration** screen will open. Select **Custom configuration** and click [Next >].
7. The **Custom Configuration** screen will open (**Figure 3-16**). Select the **LAN routing** check box and click [Next >]. The **Completing the Routing and Remote Access Server Setup Wizard** screen will open.
8. Click [Finish] to complete installation of the Routing and Remote Access Server.
9. You will be prompted if you want to start the service. Click [Yes].
10. A dialog box will open, declaring that **This Server is Now a Remote Access/VPN Server**. Click [Finish].
11. The **Remote Access/VPN Server** will now appear in the **Manage Your Server** window. Click **Manage this Remote Access/VPN server**.
12. The **Routing and Remote Access** console opens. Expand the node that represents your server and expand the **IP Routing** node.
13. Under the **IP Routing** node, right-click **General** and select **New Routing Protocol** on the menu. The **New Routing Protocol** dialog box will open (**Figure 3-17**).
14. Select **RIP Version 2 for Internet Protocol** and click [OK].
15. A new **RIP** node will appear under **IP Routing**. Right-click **RIP** and select **New Interface** on the menu.
16. The **New Interface for RIP Version 2 for Internet Protocol** dialog box will open. Select **Local Area Connection** and click [OK]. If your system has more than one interface, the routing protocol will need to be associated with each interface that will be involved in sending or receiving routing table updates.
17. The **RIP Properties – Local Area Connection Properties** dialog box will open (**Figure 3-18**). Examine the contents of each tab.
18. Try to find where the RIP interval is set.
19. Click [OK] to close the **RIP Properties – Local Area Connection Properties** dialog box.
20. Close the **Routing and Remote Access** console.
21. Close **Manage Your Server**.

Figure 3-16 Configuring basic RRAS functionality

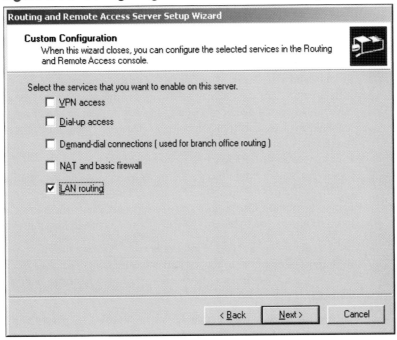

Figure 3-17 Selecting a Routing Protocol

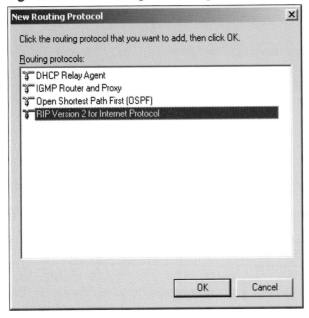

Figure 3-18 Viewing RIP properties

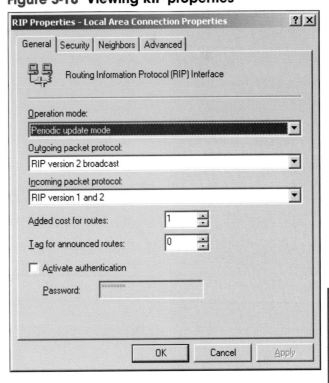

skill 7 *Optimizing Network Performance*

exam objective

Plan network traffic monitoring. Tools might include Network Monitor and System Monitor.

overview

Optimizing network performance means ensuring that each host is able to communicate as quickly and efficiently as possible. To do so, you must design and select an appropriate infrastructure and then manage network bandwidth to reduce or eliminate bottlenecks. We have already examined how routers and switches can be used to segment networks and create smaller broadcast and collision domains. However, the tuning process involves more than just the physical network components and interfaces. The protocols you select can have a significant impact on the efficiency of network communications. Optimizing network performance requires planning, monitoring, and measuring. One fundamental principal of the Microsoft Solutions Framework that you are already familiar with is the creation of a baseline for any part of a solution that requires measurement. Comparing subsequent measurements to the baseline allows you to identify whether or not a change has improved network performance.

Before examining the tools Windows Server 2003 provides to analyze the network, you must first understanding what the various measurements indicate. Because the vast majority of networks today use Ethernet architecture, we will focus on understanding Ethernet network statistics.

Traffic on an Ethernet network can be likened to trucks traveling on a road system **(Figure 3-19)**. Imagine that a road represents the network. The road has the ability to carry a maximum number of trucks each hour traveling at the posted speed limit. Each truck can carry an amount of cargo up to the maximum capacity of the truck. In some cases, there may be delays on the road system due to stoplights or collisions. All of these factors taken together determine the actual amount of cargo that can be moved within a given time frame.

The overall performance of Ethernet networks depends upon similar factors. Ethernet has a theoretical maximum number of bits per second that can be transmitted called the **line speed** or **media speed**. This peak speed does not really represent the amount of cargo, or data sent each second. Another measurement, called **bandwidth**, indicates the maximum amount of data that can be delivered each second. This represents the number of bits of data sent per second using the maximum possible number of trucks, or network frames, carrying the maximum amount of data per frame, sent without any delays. Many times, the trucks are not full and the frame does not carry the maximum amount of data. This reduces the **efficiency** of the network because each truck, or frame, on the network uses a fixed number of bits for headers and trailers regardless of the amount of data that a frame carries. The relationship between the amount of data a frame contains and the total frame size represents the efficiency **(Table 3-10)**. The maximum frame size of an Ethernet frame is 1518 bytes. To achieve 100% efficiency, there would be no header or trailer, just data; however, there is always overhead as indicated in **Figure 3-20**. The header contains the destination and source MAC addresses and the type field identifying the Layer 3 protocol that the frame carries. The trailer consists of the **frame check sequence (FCS)**, which is a **cyclical redundancy check (CRC)** used to verify the integrity of the frame. Together the header and trailer add 18 bytes of overhead to each frame and so the maximum amount of Layer 3 data or **maximum transmission unit (MTU)** an Ethernet frame can carry is 1500 bytes. There is also a minimum frame size of 64 bytes, which will carry up to 46 bytes of data. When Layer 3 and 4 headers (which average 40 bytes) are also considered, application data efficiency drops even more quickly as the frame size decreases.

Some texts base efficiency calculations on these values and omit the fact that 8 bytes are consumed by the preamble and start frame delimiter (SFD). Additionally, an inter-packet gap (IPG) is inserted between frames, which are measured as 96 bit times in length, the equivalent

Figure 3-19 Ethernet compared to a road system

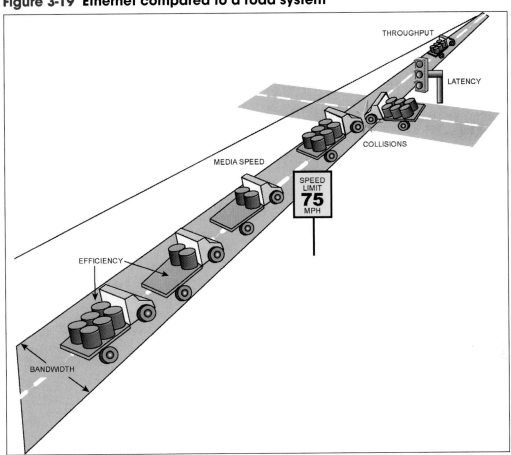

Table 3-10 Determining network efficiency

Data Bytes	Frame Size	Frame Size, IPG, Preamble, and SFD	Calculation	Frame Efficiency	Average Transport Layer Data Bytes	Application Efficiency
1500	1518	1538	1500 / 1538	97.5%	1460	94.9%
732	750	770	732 / 770	95.0%	692	89.9%
357	375	395	357 / 395	90.0%	317	80.3%
132	150	170	132 / 170	77.6%	92	54.1%
46	64	84	46 / 84	54.7%	6	7.1%

Figure 3-20 Frame overhead

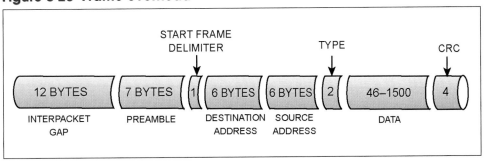

skill 7

Optimizing Network Performance
(cont'd)

Plan network traffic monitoring. Tools might include Network Monitor and System Monitor.

overview

tip
You can download
complete Ethernet
specifications from
**http://standards.ieee.org
/getieee802/802.3.html**

caution
The maximum average
utilization values
suggested here are not
fixed rules but rough
guidelines. The number of
hosts on a network
segment will strongly
influence acceptable
utilization values. Always
monitor your network to
determine acceptable
levels.

of 12 bytes, for a total additional overhead of 20 bytes per frame. When this overhead is considered, it becomes clear that larger packets are much more efficient than are smaller ones. An interesting fact is that when monitoring a typical network, the distribution of frame size is bimodal in nature. That is, frames tend to be either the minimum size of 64 bytes or the maximum size of 1518 bytes with few frames between those sizes.

Other factors can also reduce the amount of data that can be transmitted each second. There are often delays in a network that slow the transit of a frame from source to destination. These delays are like stop lights on a road system and they introduce latency into the network. Picture a stream of trucks traveling down a road. They may travel at the rated road speed until they reach a traffic signal, where each truck must stop for a moment, reducing the number of trucks that can deliver their cargo. Occasionally there will be an accident and until the trucks involved are cleared from the road, no other trucks can pass. Additionally, the cargo on the damaged trucks cannot be delivered and must be reshipped by the sender using new trucks. With an Ethernet network using shared media, collisions can occur when two hosts attempt to transmit at the same time. This introduces delays, as each host will wait a random amount of time before attempting to retransmit its data.

If your truck is the only one on the road, the chance of a collision is low and the same principal is true of Ethernet. The possibility of a collision increases with the volume of network traffic. It can be difficult to pull a truck out into heavy traffic, as there are few gaps large enough to avoid the risk of a collision. Similarly, as the utilization of an Ethernet network increases, it becomes more difficult for a host to transmit because there are fewer opportunities when the cable is free. **Utilization** is the percentage of time that the media is busy transferring frames. If network utilization is high, performance for each host will suffer because they will have to wait for the media to become available each time that they need to transmit. When using shared Ethernet, average utilization should be kept below 30% to provide reasonable performance. With switched Ethernet, 85% average utilization is acceptable and when using switched full-duplex Ethernet, average utilization in each direction can be 95% or a total utilization of 190%, because there is no possibility of a collision. Using full-duplex communications on any switched network will result in a significant performance increase.

All of these factors, taken together, can be used to predict the network **throughput**. The formula to determine throughput is as follows:

$$\text{Throughput} = (\text{Utilization} - \text{Collisions}) * \text{Line Speed} * \text{Efficiency}$$

For example, assume that your 100 Mbps shared media Ethernet network is averaging 30% utilization, 2% collisions, and an average frame size of 750 bytes. Referring to **Table 3-10**, the efficiency for a 750-byte frame is 95.0%. Therefore the throughput for this network is:

$$\text{Throughput} = (.30 - .02) * 100 \text{ Mbps} * .95$$
$$\text{Throughput} = 26.6 \text{ Mbps}$$

It might seem from these calculations that higher utilization rates result in higher throughput. However, as utilization on shared media with many hosts increases, the number of collisions increases at a higher rate. If a small number of hosts are on a network segment, the chance of a collision is lower than if there are a large number of hosts, regardless of the current utilization. Combining a large number of hosts in a single collision domain with high utilization is a certain recipe for increased collisions.

If subjective network performance is inadequate and monitoring confirms these observations, there are several standard approaches to optimize the network. **Table 3-11** lists some possible optimization techniques.

Table 3-11   Network optimization techniques

Technique	Description	Pros	Cons
Increase network bandwidth	Replace 10 Mbit interfaces with 100 Mbit or 100 Mbit with Gigabit.	Increases network capacity by a factor of 10 or more. Most current devices support 100 Mbit.	May be an expensive upgrade if replacing NICs, hubs, and switches is necessary. Could require rewiring using CAT5 cabling.
Segment network	Create multiple collision domains using switches.	Reduces possibility of collisions. Reduces network utilization on each network segment.	Cost of switches. Some latency introduced by each switch.
Segment network	Create multiple broadcast domains using VLANs.	Eliminates unnecessary broadcast traffic. Can improve network security.	Requires switches that support VLANs. To allow inter-VLAN communication, either a router or a Layer 3 switch is required.
Micro-segmentation	Provide a dedicated switched port for each network host.	Allows high utilization for each connection without impact on others. Provides option to configure full-duplex communication.	Cost of switches. Many switch ports required.
Full-duplex	With only one device connected to a switched port, enable concurrent bi-directional communication.	Virtually doubles throughput. Eliminates collisions. Reduces latency because CSMA/CD is no longer required to arbitrate cable access.	Requires a dedicated switch port for each full-duplex device.

skill 7

Optimizing Network Performance
(cont'd)

exam objective

Plan network traffic monitoring. Tools might include Network Monitor and System Monitor.

overview

Now let's examine some of the tools Windows Server 2003 provides that enable you to monitor and measure network activity: Task Manager, the Performance console, and Network Monitor.

Task Manager provides real time quantitative feedback on network utilization, the number of unicasts and non-unicasts sent, and the media speed for each network adapter (**Figure 3-21**). Additional columns can be selected using the Select Columns dialog box (**Figure 3-22**) which can be accessed by selecting **View** on the Menu bar and then choosing **Select Columns**. These measurements provide a quick assessment of current network loads and activity.

The **Performance console** captures similar information and many additional measurements. It can also record measurements in log files so that a baseline can be established and trends can be examined over time. The Network Interface object can be used to examine statistics related to your network interfaces. Some of the commonly used counters for this object include:

- **Bytes Total/Sec**: This counter simply shows statistics on the total number of bytes (sent and received) per second. It can be used to see peak traffic periods during the day, and the bandwidth used during those periods. Remember, this is listed in bytes, not bits. This means that the maximum total speed for a 10 Mb half-duplex Ethernet connection would be 1.25 MB (10 megabits divided by 8 to find megabytes). Also, on a half-duplex connection, the most you should ever see is around half of the total maximum possible bandwidth.
- **Packets Received Errors**: This tells you how many packets were received and then discarded due to errors. A large number of errors could mean that a large number of collisions are occurring, or it could be a sign of a malfunctioning application.
- **Packets Received Non-Unicast/Sec**: By comparing this counter to the Packets Received/Sec counter, you can determine the percentage of unicast to non-unicast packets on your network. Non-unicast traffic includes both broadcast and multicasted traffic.
- **Packets Received/Sec**: This counter displays the total number of packets received per second.
- **Packets Sent Non-Unicast/Sec**: By comparing this counter to the Packets Sent/Sec counter, you can determine the percentage of unicast to non-unicast packets being sent from this computer.
- **Packets Sent/Sec**: This counter displays the total number of packets sent per second.

While **Network Monitor** also captures basic utilization statistics (see the More section on Page 3.38), its primary purpose is the examination of the protocols and data that are used. Network Monitor captures frames and breaks down the contents of each into the network and transport layer headers and data that are carried by each protocol. By analyzing the contents of network frames, it is possible to determine what each frame carries, such as an initial transmission of data, or retransmission of data due to timeouts or errors.

Figure 3-21 Using Task Manager to view network utilization

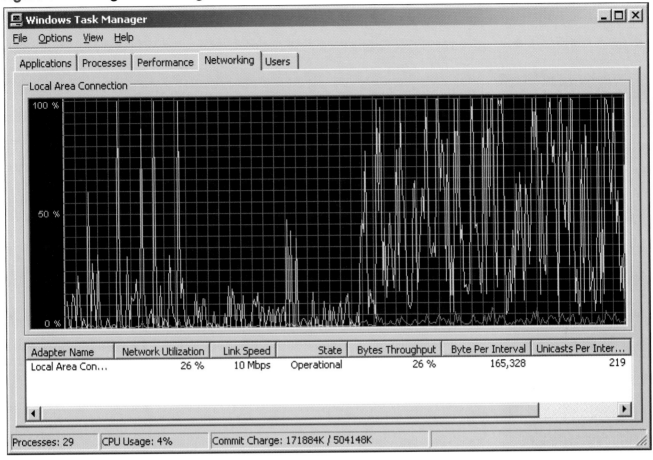

Figure 3-22 Selecting columns to display in Task Manager

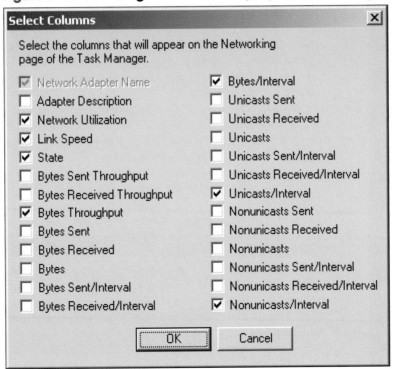

skill 7

Optimizing Network Performance
(cont'd)

Plan network traffic monitoring. Tools might include Network Monitor and System Monitor.

how to

Create a baseline for network performance using Performance Logs and Alerts.

1. Click **Start**, point to **Administrative Tools**, and select **Performance**.
2. Expand the **Performance Logs and Alerts** node.
3. Right-click **Counter Logs** and select **New Log Settings** on the shortcut menu.
4. The **New Log Settings** dialog box will open. Type **Network Baseline** in the **Name** text box **(Figure 3-23)**.
5. The **Network Baseline** dialog box will appear. Click **Add Objects** to open the **Add Objects** dialog box **(Figure 3-24)**.
6. Select **Network Interface** in the **Performance Objects** list box and click **Add** and then **Close**.
7. Click **OK** to save the Performance log configuration and begin recording network activity. Performance logs should be recorded over periods of typical network activity for future comparison.
8. To stop recording, right-click **Network Baseline (Figure 3-25)** and select **Stop** on the shortcut menu. View the performance log using System Monitor.
9. Close the Performance console.

more

While each network will have its own challenges and problems, some common items to look for using Network Monitor are:

◆ **% Network Utilization:** On Ethernet networks, this number is extremely important. As noted on Page 3.34, with half-duplex, unswitched Ethernet, this number should remain below 30%. Values over 30% will result in a significant number of collisions. With switched Ethernet, utilization of greater than 85% is cause for concern. In either case, the solution to high network utilization is typically to simply increase the bandwidth of the link by upgrading hubs, switches, network adapters, and possibly, cabling. However, you should examine your traffic further to determine which protocols are causing the majority of the traffic, and optimize those applications if possible. For instance, if you notice a high amount of DNS SOA record transfers, increasing your DNS refresh interval can reduce this traffic significantly.

◆ **# Broadcasts:** This number is important because broadcasts can saturate your switches and cause some processing overhead on client computers. If broadcasts constitute more than 25% of all traffic, you should typically take steps to reduce the total number of broadcasts. This will require that you analyze your broadcast traffic further to determine the most prevalent type of broadcast traffic. For instance, if you see a large number of NetBIOS name request broadcasts, installing and configuring a WINS server can significantly reduce this traffic. Alternately, you can install more routers or create new VLANs to segment your network further.

◆ **CRC Errors:** While not common, CRC errors do occur occasionally. A CRC error will occur when a frame's FCS does not compute properly. CRC errors can be caused by many factors, including improper frame type settings (primarily in IPX/SPX) and corrupted NIC drivers. If you notice many CRC errors, examine the source computer associated with the errors. If a single computer is causing the errors, examine that computer's configuration settings and ensure that the correct drivers are installed. If the malformed packets are coming from many sources, examine your cabling and network devices for problems.

Figure 3-23 Entering a performance log name

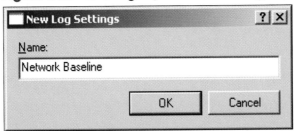

Figure 3-24 Selecting a network object for logging

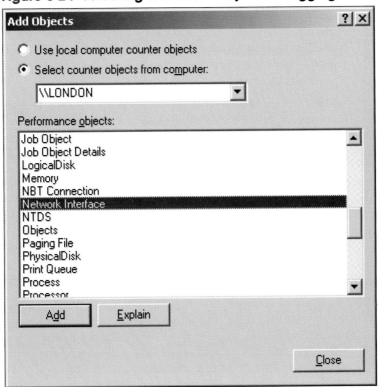

Figure 3-25 Stopping a performance log

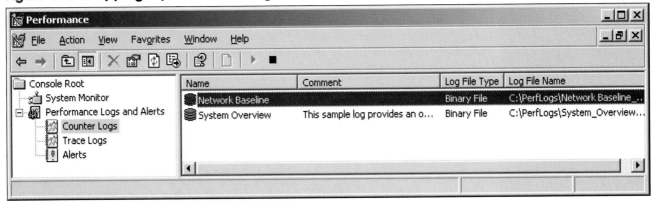

skill 8 *Planning Internet Connectivity*

exam objective

Plan an Internet connectivity strategy.

overview

Most organizations include Internet connectivity in their network plans. Users need access to resources on the Internet and e-mail communications. Many companies host their own Web and mail servers to provide services to their intranet, extranet, and Internet users. Regardless of the specific usage, many questions must be answered when planning to provide Internet connectivity.

For example, what internal addressing scheme is in use? If your organization has selected one of the private address ranges reserved by IANA, a device to translate outbound requests into an address that is routable on the Internet is required. If a public address range has been selected, your organization must reserve its exclusive use, and additional security planning should be considered.

Will there be any hosts with an Internet-accessible address, perhaps a Web or e-mail server? If so, depending on the placement of these servers, it might be necessary to obtain a separate IP address from your ISP for each externally accessible host. The number of external addresses required is also dependent on the number of internal users that will access the Internet. If a private address range is used, every session established by a user with an Internet resource will require an available port on the Internet access device to map to its internal address. Because there are a finite number of ports, each public address will only support a fixed number of concurrent sessions. The number of internal users accessing the Internet and the number of external users accessing services provided by your organization will affect the bandwidth required to provide acceptable response times. If Internet access is critical to your organization, it might be necessary to plan for redundant connections to the Internet to provide fault-tolerance.

One of the most important issues related to Internet connectivity is security. What are your organization's security requirements? How will the Internet connection be protected and secured? Is a firewall required, or will a properly configured router provide adequate security? Where will firewalls be positioned? How will inbound and outbound access be controlled? Will all users have direct outbound access or will Internet access be controlled and recorded based on user account? Which ports and protocols will be approved for use? Will content filtering, virus scanning, and user access reporting be required? Every organization must consider these questions and the answers should be a key part of the organization's security policy. Depending on these decisions, hardware and software that support the required functionality will need to be specified.

There really are four basic solutions to provide Internet connectivity for an organization **(Figure 3-26)**. Combining these solutions with a firewall or packet filtering router provides additional security (see the More section on Page 3.44).

The first solution is to create a direct connection to the Internet for a single host. The connection can be anything from a 56 Kbps dial-up to a ISDN or DSL line, cable modem, or satellite link. This approach can work in small environments where the number of users that require Internet access is limited. Some organizations believe that this is a successful way to completely control and monitor all Internet activity. However, most organizations have found that this model is too restrictive.

A second approach is to configure all hosts with live Internet addresses. Several years ago, when an organization had many hosts that provided Internet services, this type of configuration was common. Security concerns and the expense involved with leasing a large number of IP addresses from an ISP has reduced its popularity. As a result, this approach is typically only used when an organization already has a large block of public IP addresses

Figure 3-26 Four Internet connectivity solutions

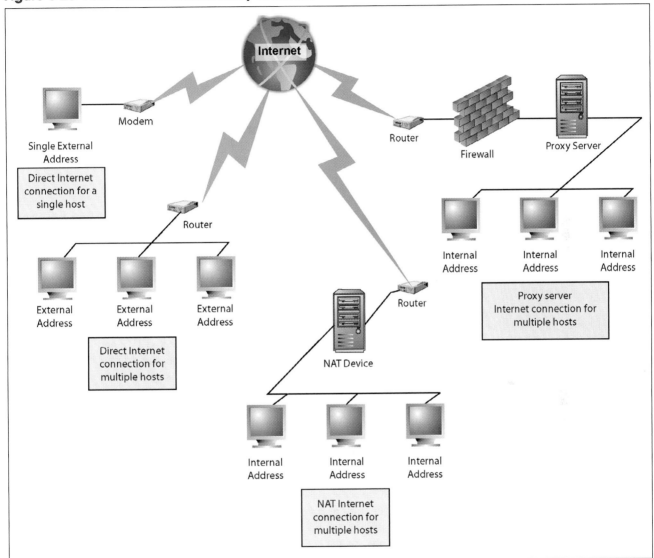

skill 8

Planning Internet Connectivity (cont'd)

exam objective

Plan an Internet connectivity strategy.

overview

assigned to it. In this configuration, the hosts would provide their own security. Most organizations use a layered security model to reduce risk of intrusion by blocking unauthorized access at the router and firewall, as well as hardening Internet-accessible hosts.

Network Address Translation (NAT), the third Internet connectivity solution, is a function that a host, router, or firewall performs. It hides the internal addressing scheme of an organization and allows as few as one live Internet address to be shared by a number of internal hosts. Two different Windows Server 2003 features can provide NAT. In small environments, **Internet Connection Sharing (ICS)** allows a single host to share its Internet connection with other hosts on its local subnet. ICS is limited in its application because the internal NIC on the host that provides the service uses the IP address 192.168.0.1, and all other hosts on the subnet are dynamically assigned addresses in the same range by the ICS host.

A more flexible option for NAT is **Routing and Remote Access Services**. True NAT maps a single external IP address to a corresponding internal IP address **(Figure 3-27)**. While this occurs in some cases, especially when locating Internet-accessible resources behind the NAT device, in most cases another approach, called **Port Address Translation (PAT)**, is used. PAT allows one or more external addresses to represent internal hosts by mapping specified ports on the external interface of the NAT device to a port on an internal host **(Figure 3-28)**. As each Internet application attempts a connection, the NAT device builds a translation table using the internal host's IP address and port, and then maps them to an available port on its external address. As a packet passes through the NAT device, the TCP and IP headers of the packet are modified so that all packets seem to originate from the external IP address of the NAT device. Any packets received in response to sent packets return to the external interface of the NAT device where their headers will be edited based on the translation table. Once the headers are correct, delivery to the originating host takes place. Because NAT works at the Network Layer, user account information is not available. Consequently, controlling or recording an individual user's Internet access is not possible. Filtering of traffic is done only by source address and port or destination address and port.

The fourth solution that provides Internet access is a **proxy server**, such as the Microsoft Internet Security and Acceleration (ISA) server. At first glance, a proxy server seems to perform the same function as a NAT device. While a proxy server translates an external address space into an internal one, the process involved is very different. A NAT device simply edits the network packet headers and routes the packet through to the proper destination. A proxy server goes much further, receiving a request from a client, de-encapsulating that request by stripping off all headers added by each protocol and then rebuilding a new packet, encapsulating the received data with new headers for each protocol used on the destination network.

A proxy server is a true application gateway and has access to information at every layer of the network protocol stack. This means that a proxy server must perform a lot more work than a simple router or NAT device but this overhead enables significant additional functionality. For example, a proxy server can filter and record access based on user account information. Packets can be examined for malicious payloads, such as known types of TCP/IP attacks, viruses, and even forbidden Application Layer protocol commands. Third party add-ons are available to provide anti-virus, content scanning, site blocking, and many other functions. Most proxy servers integrate additional features such as content caching to increase user access speed.

tip

More information on ISA server and its add-ons is available at **http://www.microsoft .com/isaserver** and **http://www.isaserver.org**

Figure 3-27 True Network Address Translation

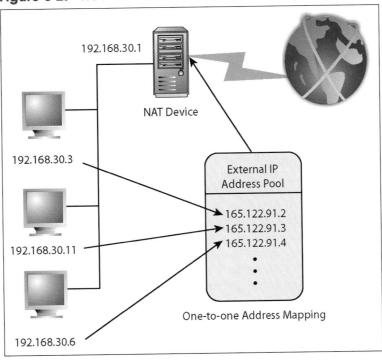

Figure 3-28 Port Address Translation

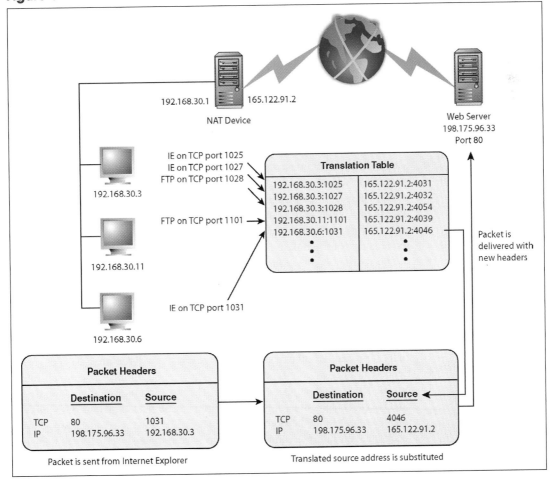

skill 8

Planning Internet Connectivity (cont'd)

exam objective

Plan an Internet connectivity strategy.

how to

Configure NAT using Routing and Remote Access Services. (Two NICs on separate subnets are required to perform this configuration. It is assumed that Routing and Remote Access Services has not been configured.)

1. Click `⊞ Start`, point to **Administrative Tools**, and click **Routing and Remote Access** to open the **Routing and Remote Access** console.
2. Right-click the name of your server, and select **Configure and Enable Routing and Remote Access** on the menu (**Figure 3-29**).
3. The **Routing and Remote Access Setup Wizard** will open. Click `Next >`.
4. The **Configuration** screen will present configuration options for Routing and Remote Access. Select **Network Address Translation (NAT)** and click `Next >`.
5. The **NAT Internet Connection** screen will appear. In the **Use this public interface to connect to the Internet** list box, select the interface that will connect to the public network (**Figure 3-30**). To secure the NAT interface against unauthorized access from the public network, ensure that there is a check mark in the **Enable security on the select interface by setting up Basic Firewall**. Click `Next >`.
6. The **Completing the Routing and Remote Access Server Setup Wizard** screen will open. Click `Finish` to complete the NAT configuration. A message indicating that the Routing and Remote Access service is starting will appear.
7. Examine the NAT configuration by clicking **NAT/Basic Firewall** under the **IP Routing** node in the RRAS console. Next, right-click the name of the public interface in the right hand pane, and select **Properties** on the menu.
8. Examine all of the tabs in the Properties dialog box for the NAT interface (**Figure 3-31**). Click `Cancel` when done.
9. Close the Routing and Remote Access console.

more

Once you have determined your address allocation method, you need to determine the Internet connectivity topology. This is where you will choose the number and speed of your connections to the Internet. The most common options for this decision are:

◆ Single Internet connection for the organization: In this scenario, a single Internet connection services all users in the organization, regardless of the site at which the user is located. This is one of the more common scenarios in use, as it is simple and cost effective. In this scenario, private WAN connections to the remote sites provide access to the Internet link at the primary site. The primary disadvantage in this scenario is lack of redundancy for the link to the Internet.

◆ Single Internet connection for each site: In this scenario, each site has its own Internet connectivity. In this scenario, VPNs are typically employed to connect all sites together. When using VPNs to connect the sites, this option becomes cost effective, as Internet links are typically cheaper than dedicated WAN links. Also, failure of a single Internet link in this scenario does not affect the entire network, as each location has its own Internet connection. However, this option can be much more complex to configure and support, especially if private IP addresses are used, as each site will require a NAT device.

◆ Redundant Internet connections for the organization: In this scenario, all Internet access is provided by a small number of locations. The most common configuration for this option has dual Internet connections at the headquarters location, and private WAN links to connect all other locations to the headquarters (**Figure 3-32**). However, you can also have two or more locations with Internet connectivity, and have remote sites distribute their Internet access between the connected sites (**Figure 3-33**). This scenario is the most complex of all, as

Figure 3-29 Configuring Routing and Remote Access

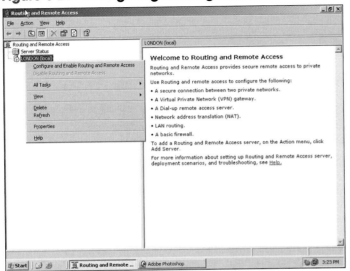

Figure 3-30 Selecting public NAT interface and firewall options

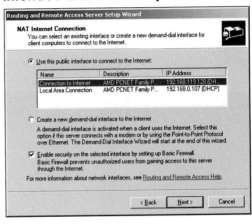

Figure 3-31 NAT interface properties

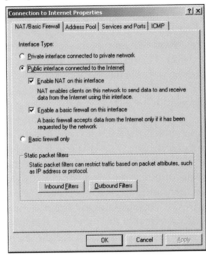

Figure 3-32 Redundant Internet connections for a primary site

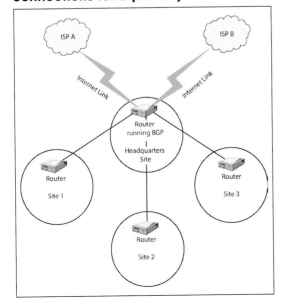

Figure 3-33 Redundant Internet connections split between two sites

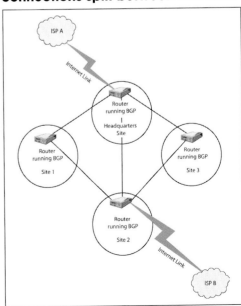

skill 8

Planning Internet Connectivity (cont'd)

exam objective

Plan an Internet connectivity strategy.

more

Border Gateway Protocol (BGP) must be installed and configured on one or more routers. The use of BGP is necessary anytime you wish to provide redundant Internet connectivity. Since BGP is a rather complex protocol, configuration of this option is rather daunting. Additionally, due to the size of BGP routing tables (usually 60,000+ routes), the routers that will host BGP must have large amounts of memory, increasing costs. However, this is the only way to truly provide for redundancy in connectivity to the Internet.

Finally, after deciding on your topology, you should consider your security requirements. Since protecting the organization from improper access from Internet hosts is extremely important, this is perhaps the most important decision you will make. In this regard, you have four primary options for each site that contains an Internet connection:

♦ Single firewall, no Demilitarized Zone (DMZ): In this scenario, you simply configure a single firewall to protect all resources. This option is typically only valid when your organization does not have any publicly accessible servers in the location for which you are configuring Internet access. For instance, if your organization has no public servers in the enterprise, then you may configure a single firewall to protect the entire organization **(Figure 3-34)**. The disadvantage to this scenario is that you are placing all of your security chores on a single device, which is less difficult to circumvent than the other options. However, the advantage is ease of configuration and support.

♦ Single firewall with a DMZ: In this scenario, you have a single firewall protecting each site with Internet access that contains three interfaces. One interface is used to connect to the Internet, one is used for the private network, and one is used for the DMZ, also known as a screened subnet. The DMZ is where you will place all publicly accessed servers, such as public Web, e-mail, and FTP servers. By configuring a DMZ, you can configure the firewall to be extremely restrictive regarding access to the internal network, while allowing the public to have the necessary access to the public resources on the DMZ **(Figure 3-35)**. The advantages of this scenario include reduced costs and ease of configuration. However, like the previous scenario, this bases all of your security on a single firewall product, which reduces overall security.

♦ Dual firewalls with a DMZ: In this scenario, dual firewalls protect the internal network. A single firewall is placed between the DMZ and the Internet, while another firewall is placed between the DMZ and the internal network **(Figure 3-36)**. Done properly, this scenario is significantly more secure than either of the previous scenarios, as the would-be intruder must circumvent two separate firewall devices to gain improper access. However, the disadvantages to this layout include increase configuration and support costs, as well as increased purchase costs.

♦ Triple firewalls with two DMZs: In this scenario, three firewalls are used to protect the internal network, and the DMZ is split into two sections: internal and external **(Figure 3-37)**. The external DMZ is where most of your publicly accessible servers will reside, and the outside firewall will be configured to allow access to those servers from the Internet. The mid-ground firewall is then configured to only allow access to the internal DMZ from servers residing on the external DMZ. The internal DMZ would be where you place support servers for the public servers. For instance, your SQL server containing the databases for your public Web applications would be contained on the internal DMZ. Since the mid-ground firewall does not allow direct access to the internal DMZ from the Internet, this provides the same level of security for the SQL server as placing it on the Internal network in the previous scenario. However, a final firewall is configured to restrict most, if not all, access from the Internet and protects your internal network from the Internet. This scenario is the most secure of all proposed designs, however, it is much more costly than any of the previous designs.

Figure 3-34 A single firewall without a DMZ

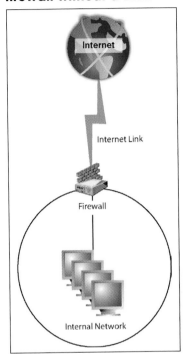

Figure 3-35 A single firewall with a DMZ

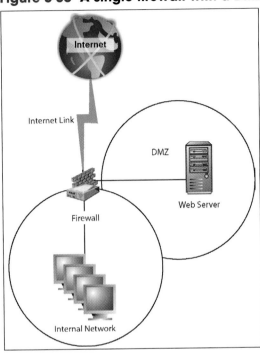

Figure 3-36 A dual firewall DMZ

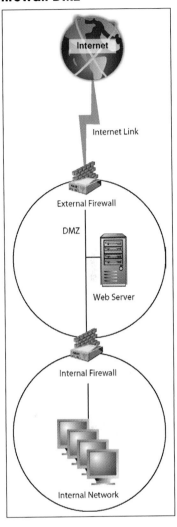

Figure 3-37 A triple firewall DMZ

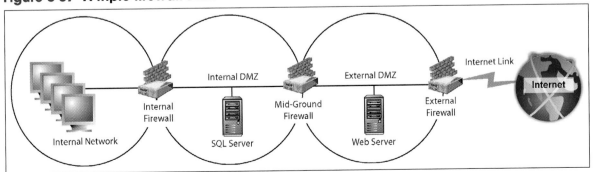

skill 9

Planning for IP Multicast Routing

exam objective

Plan a routing strategy. Identify routing protocols to use in a specified environment. Plan routing for IP multicast traffic.

overview

tip

For more information about IP multicast see RFC 1112 at **www.rfc-editor.org**

Multicast routing is more complicated than unicast routing, and is a subject that is often confusing to a great many network administrators, as it operates on principles that are completely different from that of most network traffic. Unlike unicast transmissions where there is a single destination host on a single network, with **multicast** transmission, the destination can be an ever-changing group of hosts located on multiple networks. Planning to support multicast routing requires an understanding of how multicast transmission works, how hosts become members of multicast groups, and how routers learn which networks contain destination hosts.

To understand multicasting, you first must understand why it is needed. In the network shown in **Figure 3-38**, there is a multimedia server offing a video stream that you want your clients in the remote offices to receive. In this example, 50 of the clients in each office should receive the video, while the other clients in each office should not receive the video. When unicasting, a single flow of packets for each client must be sent directly to the client address. This means that if the video stream used 128 KB of bandwidth per second, you would need 6.4 MB per second of bandwidth available on the WAN links to each office (128 KB x 50). Broadcasting, on the other hand, would only send two streams, one for each office. However, there are a few problems with broadcasting in this case. First, routers separate the offices, and routers, by definition, deny broadcasts. Second, most WAN links are Non-Broadcast Multi-Access (NBMA) media, which means that broadcasts are not even supported on the links. Finally, you only want the video stream to reach 50 of the clients at each remote site, not all 200, but a broadcast, by definition, is sent to all hosts. This is where multicasting comes in.

When a multicast transmission is sent, any hosts that have joined the multicast group defined for that multicast server (MCS) receive it. The actual IP address of the multicast group will fall in the class D address range that is from 224.0.0.0 through 239.255.255.255. The address may be one of the reserved multicast addresses listed at **http://www.iana.org /assignments/multicast-addresses**, or it could be one of the available addresses within the Class D range **(Table 3-12)**. Each host is assigned the correct multicast address when registering itself with a multicast application running on a multicast server. The multicast server receives its multicast address, which defines its multicast group, from a Multicast Address Dynamic Client Allocation Protocol (MADCAP) server. The Windows Server 2003 DHCP Server service provides the facility to define multicast scopes and can act as a MADCAP server.

tip

For more information about IGMP v3, see RFC 3376 at **www.rfc-editor.org**.

Each IP multicast address is mapped to a corresponding MAC multicast address **(Figure 3-39)**. Because MAC addresses are 48 bits and IP addresses are only 32 bits, the first 25 bits of the MAC address are always fixed. The remaining 23 bits correspond to the bits in the IP address. The MAC address range of 01-00-5E-00-00-00 to 01-00-5E-7F-FF-FF has been reserved for multicast addresses. Notice that for all MAC multicast addresses the last bit in the first byte is set to a value of 1. This bit is called the multicast bit and it is set for all

Figure 3-38 An example of a scenario where multicasting could save bandwidth

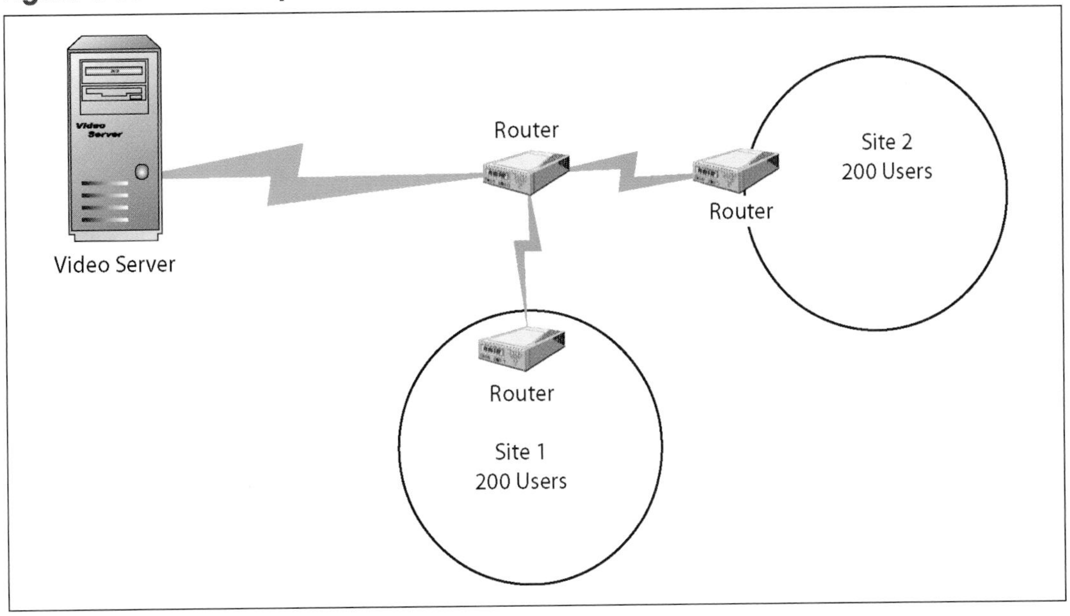

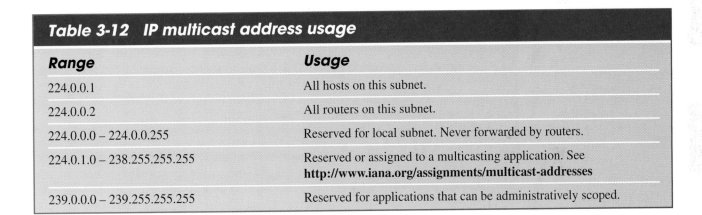

Range	Usage
Table 3-12 IP multicast address usage	
Range	Usage
224.0.0.1	All hosts on this subnet.
224.0.0.2	All routers on this subnet.
224.0.0.0 – 224.0.0.255	Reserved for local subnet. Never forwarded by routers.
224.0.1.0 – 238.255.255.255	Reserved or assigned to a multicasting application. See **http://www.iana.org/assignments/multicast-addresses**
239.0.0.0 – 239.255.255.255	Reserved for applications that can be administratively scoped.

Figure 3-39 Mapping an IP multicast address to a MAC address

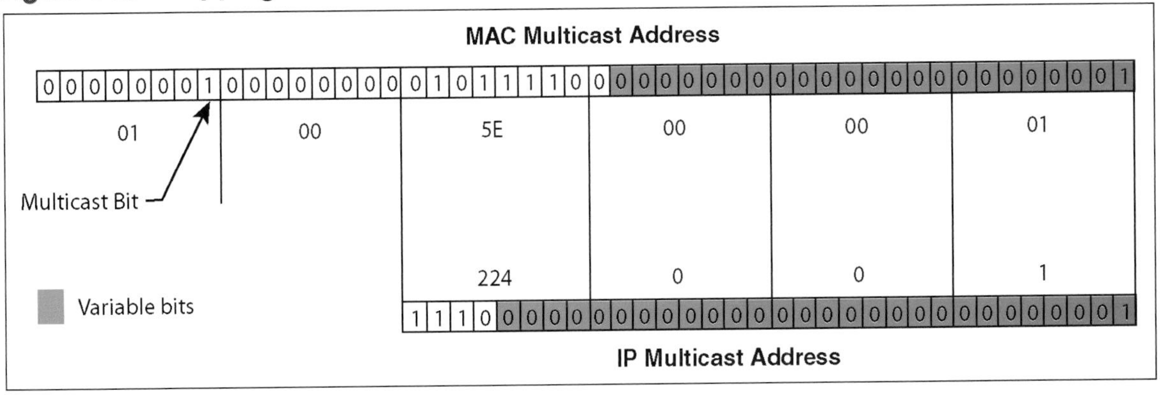

skill 9 *Planning for IP Multicast Routing*
(cont'd)

exam objective

Plan a routing strategy. Identify routing protocols to use in a specified environment. Plan routing for IP multicast traffic.

overview

multicast and broadcast frames. If the NIC in a host goes into multicast promiscuous mode, the network stack will process any frames that have the multicast bit set.

When a host connects to a multicast server on the same subnet, there is no further configuration or planning required. However, if the multicast server is on another subnet, additional planning will be required. All the routers between the client and the multicast server must be multicast-enabled so that they can receive and forward the multicast traffic. In addition, they must learn which networks contain multicast clients so that multicast traffic forwards only when required. Hosts use the **Internet Group Management Protocol (IGMP)** to notify the router servicing their subnet that it contains clients that belong to a multicast group. Routing and Remote Access Services in Windows Server 2003 supports all three versions of IGMP. Each subsequent version adds additional features to improve the efficiency of hosts joining and leaving multicast groups. Multicast routing protocols such as Distance Vector Multicast Routing Protocol (DVMRP), Multicast Open Shortest Path First (MOSPF), or Protocol Independent Multicast (PIM) are used to communicate multicast group membership between routers.

Windows Server 2003 Routing and Remote Access Services does not support any multicast routing protocols. However, it can act as an IGMP proxy so that it can connect a subnet containing multicast group members to a multicast-enabled network **(Figure 3-40)**. When a RRAS interface is configured as an IGMP proxy, it behaves like a multicast host, joining multicast groups on behalf of the multicast group members that connect to the RRAS server's other interfaces. The interface configured as an IGMP proxy always connects to the network that will be the source of the multicast transmissions.

An additional feature of Windows Server 2003 is the ability to use IP-in-IP tunnel to tunnel multicast traffic across non-IGMP routers. For instance, in **Figure 3-41**, there are four non-multicast routers separating the multicast sites. Since these routers do not support multicasts, a packet with a Class D IP address sent to these routers will simply be discarded and will not be forwarded. To resolve this problem, you would configure an IP-in-IP tunnel to connect the two ends of the multicast path across the four routers **(Figure 3-42)**. The IP-in-IP tunnel will take the multicast packets and insert them into a standard unicast packet destined for the remote end of the tunnel. When the packet reaches the far side, the multicast packet will then be removed from the unicast packet and sent along normally.

A final feature of Windows Server 2003 that is useful in certain multicasting situations is multicast boundaries. Multicast boundaries are used to prevent a specific group of computers or location from receiving a multicast stream, even if the clients join the correct IGMP group. This is useful in situations where you want to ensure the privacy of a multicast stream.

Using these multicasting features in your network design can considerably improve your quality of service in regards to high-volume traffic, but be aware that Windows Server 2003 is but a small component in the entire multicast design. Appropriate multicast server software and true multicast routers will also be needed to fully implement multicasting.

Figure 3-40 RRAS configured as an IGMP proxy

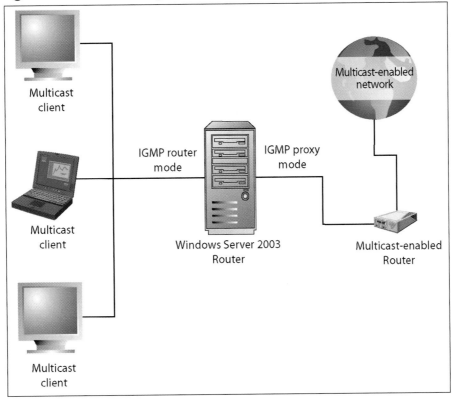

Figure 3-41 An example of a network that could use an IP-in-IP tunnel

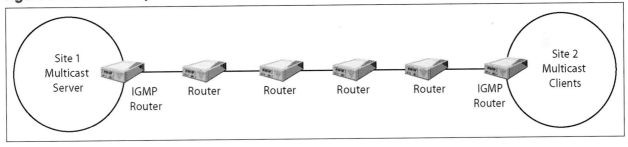

Figure 3-42 An IP-in-IP tunnel

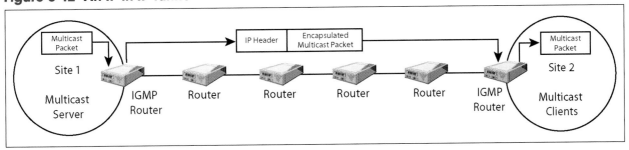

skill 9

Planning for IP Multicast Routing
(cont'd)

exam objective

Plan a routing strategy. Identify routing protocols to use in a specified environment. Plan routing for IP multicast traffic.

how to

Examine IGMP settings. (This exercise assumes that you completed the exercise in Skill 8, and have installed and configured RRAS to provide NAT.)

1. Open the **Routing and Remote Access** console. Click the "+" beside the name of your server to expand the contents of the node.
2. Expand the **IP Routing** node.
3. Select **IGMP (Figure 3-43)**. Notice that the two interfaces have already been configured with the NAT Configuration Wizard during Skill 8.
4. Right-click the **Local Area Connection** and select **Properties**.
5. The **Local Area Connection Properties** dialog box will open to the **General** tab **(Figure 3-44)**. Notice that this interface is configured to act as an IGMP router using IGMP version 3.
6. Click the **Router** tab **(Figure 3-45)**. You can use these values to optimize the latency involved when IGMP is used to join or leave a multicast group.
7. Click [Cancel] to close the Local Area Connection Properties dialog box.
8. Right-click the **Connection to Internet** icon and select **Properties**.
9. The **Connection to Internet Properties** dialog box will open to the **General** tab **(Figure 3-46)**. Notice that this interface is configured to act as an IGMP proxy.
10. Click the **Router** tab. There are no configurable router options for an IGMP proxy interface.
11. Click [Cancel] to close the Connection to Internet Properties dialog box.
12. Close the Routing and Remote Access console.

Figure 3-43 Viewing IGMP configuration

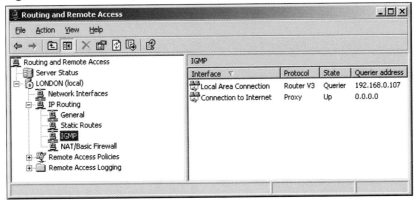

Figure 3-44 IGMP router mode interface configuration

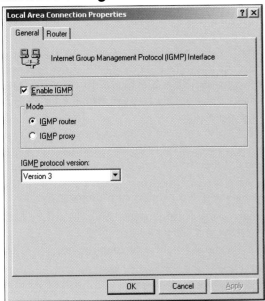

Figure 3-45 IGMP router options

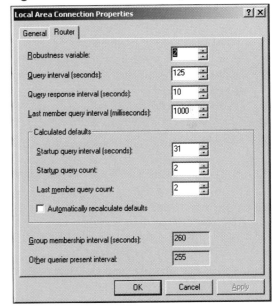

Figure 3-46 IGMP proxy mode interface configuration

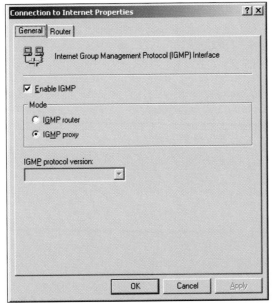

Summary

◆ Windows Server 2003 supports the following Network Layer protocols:

- TCP/IP with IPv4
- IP version 6
- NWLink
- AppleTalk

◆ TCP/IP is the default protocol for Windows Server 2003. Planning should include IPv6 for future growth. Use NWLink and AppleTalk only when required for compatibility with Novell and Apple networks.

◆ Determining an appropriate IP addressing scheme begins with collecting information about the required infrastructure. Identify how many sites, VLANs, and hosts will be necessary. Will the network use a registered address space or a private range?

◆ Create a subnet mask that provides flexibility and growth. Use VLSM, if supported by your routers, to create appropriately sized subnets and conserve IP addresses.

◆ Subnetting an address involves seven steps:

1. Calculate the number of bits that will be required to represent the subnets, allowing for future growth.
2. Calculate the number of bits that will be required to represent the number of hosts for each subnet.
3. Select a private address range that will provide enough bits to support the number of subnets and hosts.
4. Specify the subnet mask.
5. Determine the subnet increment value and identify the network address for each subnet.
6. Identify the broadcast address for each subnet.
7. List the first and last valid host address on each subnet.

◆ Use DHCP to simplify address assignment. Add redundancy by configuring portions of the same scope of addresses on more than one DHCP server using the 50/50 or 80/20 rule. Configure DHCP relay agents on remote subnets so their hosts can obtain DHCP assigned addresses from centralized DHCP servers.

◆ Use DHCP option classes to manage devices that have differing requirements. For example, create one class for mobile systems with short lease durations and another for permanently connected hosts with longer lease durations.

◆ Optimize your network by creating multiple collision and broadcast domains. Micro-segmentation improves network throughput by providing a dedicated switch port for each host. Be sure to enable full-duplex communication on as many hosts as possible, especially servers, to improve throughput.

◆ VLANs segment the network into separate broadcast domains and are effective to enforce communication patterns, security, and reduce unnecessary broadcast traffic.

◆ Routers can use static or dynamic routing. Routing protocols are divided into two main categories: Link State and Distance Vector. Windows Server 2003 supports RIP versions 1 and 2 and OSPF. The goal of all routing protocols is to propagate an accurate view of the network to all routers. When this is achieved, the network has reached convergence.

◆ The first step in optimizing a network is to create a baseline so that the effect of changes is easily measured. Windows Server 2003 provides Task Manager, the Performance console, and Network Monitor to measure network performance.

◆ Throughput is the actual amount of data delivered by a network once overhead, collisions, and line speed are considered. Large frames are more efficient than small ones.

◆ The throughput of a network can be improved by:

- Increasing network bandwidth
- Segmenting the network
- Utilizing full-duplex communications

◆ Internet access for an organization is most commonly provided by one of the following:

- Direct routed connection using live Internet addresses
- A NAT device translates a private address space into a live Internet address.
- A proxy server acts as a gateway between a private address space and a live Internet address.

◆ All routers between a multicast server and the members of a multicast group must support multicast routing. Routers rely on multicast routing protocols to notify other routers of multicast group memberships. Multicast clients use IGMP to notify the router on their subnet of their participation in a multicast group.

Key Terms

AppleTalk
Bandwidth
Broadcast domain
Classless Inter-Domain Routing
  (CIDR)
Class-based addressing
Classless routing
Collision domain
Cyclic Redundancy Checking (CRC)
Carrier Sense Multiple
  Access/Collision Detect
  (CSMA/CD)
Distance vector protocol
Dynamic Host Configuration Protocol
  (DHCP)
Efficiency
Frame Check Sequence (FCS)
Full-duplex

In-band management
Internet Assigned Number Authority
  (IANA)
Internet Connection Sharing (ICS)
Internet Group Management Protocol
  (IGMP)
Internet Protocol version 6 (Ipv6)
Line speed
Link state protocol
Micro-segmentation
Maximum transmission unit (MTU)
Multicast
Network Address Translation (NAT)
Network Monitor
NWLink
Out-of-band management
Performance console
Port Address Translation (PAT)

Protocol
Proxy server
Reliable Multicast Protocol
Routed protocol
Routing protocol
Routing and Remote Access Services
  (RRAS)
Supernetting
Task Manager
Transmission Control
  Protocol/Internet Protocol (TCP/IP)
Throughput
Utilization
Virtual LAN (VLAN)
Variable Length Subnet Mask
  (VLSM)

Test Yourself

1. Which network protocol includes encryption as an integral component of the protocol suite?
   a. TCP/IP
   b. IPv6
   c. NWLink
   d. AppleTalk

2. Which of the factors in network planning listed below can be used to help determine the total number of required subnets? (Choose all that apply.)
   a. Number of hosts
   b. Number of remote locations
   c. Number of VLANs
   d. Number of switches

3. Which of the following routing protocols support VLSM?
   a. OSPF
   b. RIP version 1
   c. RIP version 2

4. Which of the following are valid host addresses?
   a. 192.168.1.72/29
   b. 192.168.1.79/29
   c. 192.168.1.78/29
   d. 192.168.1.81/29

5. A router examines the first octet of the destination address for a packet and finds that it is equal to the binary value 11010100. What class is this destination address?
   a. Class A
   b. Class B
   c. Class C
   d. Class D

6. In a network with multiple subnets and DHCP relay agents configured for all routers, how many DHCP servers are recommended and how are they configured?
   a. One DHCP server with a separate scope for each subnet.
   b. One DHCP server with one scope for the entire network.
   c. Two DHCP servers, each configured with a separate scope for exactly half of the subnets.
   d. Two DHCP servers, each configured with parallel scopes for each subnet but with opposite halves of each scope excluded.

7. Reducing the number of collision domains on a network improves throughput.
   a. True
   b. False

8. What is the maximum amount of Layer 3 data that an Ethernet frame can carry and how many bytes of overhead are involved?
   a. 1500 bytes data, 38 bytes overhead
   b. 1460 bytes data, 40 bytes overhead
   c. 1500 bytes data, 18 bytes overhead
   d. 1518 bytes data, 20 bytes overhead

9. Which of the following Internet connection methods support user based control and content filtering?
   a. A router configured with the NAT protocol
   b. A proxy server
   c. Windows Server 2003 configured with ICS
   d. A direct dial-up connection

10. What protocol does a host use to notify the router on its subnet that it is a member of a multicast group?
   a. IGMP
   b. MADCAP
   c. MCS
   d. PIM

Projects: On Your Own

1. Build a small inter-network consisting of 3 subnets. This will require a minimum of four computers, two configured with two NICs each to act as routers and two to act as hosts on each stub network.
   a. Use 192.168.80.0/24 as the assigned network address.
   b. Define a subnet mask that will support the required subnets and still allow room for growth.
   c. Install the DHCP Server service on one of the router computers and configure it with address scopes for each subnet. For each subnet, create a router scope option that points to the correct interface on the corresponding router computer.
   d. Configure the other router computer to act as a DHCP relay agent.
   e. Configure the two host computers to obtain their IP configuration dynamically.
   f. Configure Routing and Remote Access Services to the RIP version 2 protocol.
   g. Confirm correct routing by using Tracert to test the connection from a host on one stub network to a host on the other stub network.

Problem Solving Scenarios

You are responsible for the overall network performance on the network at your organization's head office. You have compared current network activity to a baseline recorded six months ago and have found that there is a heavy spike in network load between 1 PM and 5 PM. The current network infrastructure consists of 6 locations connected by T1 lines to the head office in a hub/spoke configuration. There are 700 hosts on the LAN, each connected to a dedicated switch port. Each of the 16 servers connects to a dedicated switch port on the same network as the hosts. By analyzing network activity at each server, you have found that the majority of the additional network traffic is flowing between 5 of the servers and very little additional load is being generated by the network hosts. It is determined that a new business critical application that runs on the servers is generating the additional inter-server network traffic. What possible solutions can optimize the network, improve host response time, and reduce latency?

4 Planning and Optimizing Name Resolution

On a Windows Server 2003 TCP/IP network, hosts use IP addresses to connect and communicate with each other. On a small network, it is easy to remember the assigned IP address of a certain host, but on a large network with hundreds of hosts, it would be extremely difficult to recall the IP address of a particular host without having to record it somewhere where you can easily look it up. It is much easier to refer to a host by an alphanumeric host name, such as *server1*. To realize the potential of this method, there must be a fast and reliable service to resolve this host name into an identifiable IP address.

In Windows Server 2003, there are various methods to resolve names to IP addresses, including broadcast, LMHOSTS file, NetBIOS name cache, NetBIOS name server (WINS), HOSTS file, and Domain Name System (DNS). The most efficient and popular of these methods for resolving host names is DNS, which is the naming standard for the Internet. DNS is an integral part of the Windows Server 2003 operating system. In addition to using DNS to resolve names, Windows uses it to locate different services on the network. Active Directory and many other system functions of Windows Server 2003 depend heavily on the DNS model.

Before the proliferation of the Internet, most organizations with DOS, Windows, or OS/2-based networks typically used the NetBEUI protocol to communicate on the network. NetBEUI does not support routing, and is best suited for small networks that do not need to route network traffic externally. NetBEUI is based on the NetBIOS naming scheme, which is used to assign names to hosts on a network. With the arrival of the Internet and larger in-house networks, however, the NetBEUI protocol became unworkable because of its limitations. TCP/IP became the preferred communication protocol suite. TCP/IP uses IP addresses to identify and communicate with computers on internal and external networks. WINS (Windows Internet Naming Service) is used to resolve Windows NetBIOS names to IP addresses on a TCP/IP network.

Goals

In this lesson, you will learn how to plan the implementation of Windows Server 2003 naming services such as DNS and WINS, as well as how to optimize these services.

Lesson 4 Planning and Optimizing Name Resolution

Skill	Exam 70-293 Objective
1. Planning a DNS Namespace	Plan a DNS namespace design.
2. Planning a DNS Infrastructure	Plan a hostname resolution strategy. Examine the interoperability of DNS with third-party DNS solutions.
3. Planning DNS Zones	Plan zone replication requirements.
4. Configuring DNS Zone Replication	Plan zone replication requirements.
5. Implementing DNS Forwarding	Plan a forwarding configuration.
6. Optimizing DNS	Diagnose and resolve issues related to DNS services. Troubleshoot host name resolution.
7. Planning WINS Servers	Plan a NetBIOS name resolution strategy. Plan NetBIOS name resolution by using the LMHOSTS file.
8. Planning WINS replication	Plan a WINS replication strategy.
9. Optimizing WINS	Basic knowledge

Requirements

To complete this lesson, you will need administrative rights on a Microsoft Windows Server 2003 computer with DNS and WINS installed.

skill 1

Planning a DNS Namespace

exam objective

Plan a DNS namespace design.

overview

Domain Name System (DNS) is the main name resolution service for Windows Server 2003. DNS is fully integrated with Windows Server 2003, and allows users to locate hosts and services on the local network in the same way that they locate them on the Internet. **DNS servers** (also referred to as **DNS name servers**) perform the task of name resolution by resolving host names to IP addresses. The DNS server maintains a database containing IP addresses mapped to their corresponding names. To access a computer on the network, users need only specify its name.

The **DNS** namespace consists of a hierarchical structure of named nodes called **domains** (**Figure 4-1**). As you add more domains to the DNS hierarchy, the name of the parent domain is added to the sub-domain (child domain). For example, in the domain name *sales.company.com*, *sales* represents a sub-domain of the *company.com* domain, and *company* is a sub-domain of the *com* domain.

The domain at the top of the DNS namespace is called the **root domain** and is represented by a period (.). The sub-domain of the root domain is called a **top-level domain**, and the sub-domain of a top-level domain is called a **second-level domain**. Common top-level domains include *com*, *edu*, *net*, *gov*, *org*, *tv*, *mil*, *info*, and the various country codes such as *uk* and *ca* (United Kingdom and Canada). Second-level domains have two parts: a top-level name and a second-level name. You can use second-level domains to create a distinct place for your organization such as *company.com*. A **host name** is at the bottom of the DNS hierarchy, and it designates a particular computer, on either the Internet or a private network (**Table 4-1**). To identify a host name in the DNS hierarchy, you must use a **Fully Qualified Domain Name (FQDN)**. An FQDN includes a domain name in addition to the host name. *Server1* may be the alias for a computer on a TCP/IP network, whereas *server1.company.com* is the FQDN for the computer (**Figure 4-2**).

If you plan to have an Internet presence, you must register your domain name with an Internet naming authority such as Network Solutions. The domain name you register is generally a second-level domain under a top-level domain. You typically have the authority to maintain domains that you register.

If you plan to implement DNS only on your intranet, you are not required to register the domain name with a naming authority, but it is recommended. If the internal name you have chosen has already been registered by another organization, internal clients will not be able to distinguish between the internal name and the publicly registered DNS name. Your Active Directory domain name should be based on a domain that you have under your control.

tip

You should not use unregistered suffixes, for example, *company.xyz*. Although unregistered suffixes can work internally, they can become an issue in the future as your organization expands.

how to

Plan your DNS namespace.

1. Decide on your primary domain name, such as *company.com*.
2. Decide if you will use sub-domains of your main domain name, such as *sales.company.com*.
3. Determine if you only want to use the domain name locally, or across the Internet.
4. Register your domain name with an Internet naming authority, if required.

Figure 4-1 DNS Namespace Hierarchy

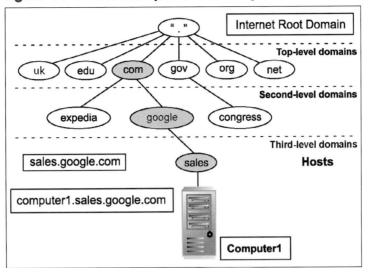

Table 4-1   The DNS Namespace

Domain hierarchy	Description
Root domain	The primary domain in the DNS namespace. The root domain is represented by a period (.)
Top-level domains	These domains are located below the root domain in the DNS namespace. They define the organization type or geographic location. On the Internet, top-level domains include com, used for commercial organizations; gov, used for government entities; net, used for networking organizations; and org, used for non-profit organizations, among others. You can see a list of the current top-level domains and the organizations that operate them at **http://www.iana.org/gtld/gtld.htm**. For a list of the two-character country codes, visit **http://www.iana.org/cctld/cctld-whois.htm**.
Second-level domain	These are placed below the top-level domains in the DNS namespace. For example, the .com top-level domain assigns and registers second-level domains to individuals and organizations such as Microsoft, Yahoo, Apple, etc.
Host name	The host name is the leftmost portion of a FQDN and is located below the second-level domains and sub-domains, sometimes several layers down in the naming hierarchy. The host name designates a particular computer, either on the Internet or a private network.

Figure 4-2 Host names and FQDN structure

HOST NAME	FULLY QUALIFIED DOMAIN NAME (FQDN)	IP ADDRESS
Server1	Server1.bcg.com	192.68.100.1
Sarah	Sarah.bcg.com	192.68.100.2
Tower	Tower.bcg.com	192.68.100.3
Backuppc	Backuppc.bcg.com	192.68.100.4
Laserjet4600	Laserjet4600.bcg.com	192.68.100.10
Dslmodem	Dslmodem.bcg.com	192.68.100.21

skill 2

Planning a DNS Infrastructure

exam objective

Plan a hostname resolution strategy. Examine the interoperability of DNS with third-party DNS solutions.

overview

Once you have planned your DNS namespace, and determined the number of domains and sub-domains you will use, you must next plan and design your DNS infrastructure. Various factors will affect the DNS infrastructure. For instance, the size of your network is an important consideration because key implementation issues will vary for small, mid-sized, and large networks.

On a small network, the main factor to consider is DNS availability. This refers to the ability of DNS servers to continue operating when individual components fail. To ensure DNS services are always available, you should have at least one primary and one secondary DNS server for a domain.

When implementing DNS on a mid- to large-sized network, a number of other factors come into play, including administrative efficiency. To begin, you will need to determine the number and type of DNS servers that you will need to ensure that DNS name resolution proceeds quickly and efficiently, and whether it is necessary to divide administrative control and DNS functions into zones. **Zones** are distinct, contiguous segments of the DNS namespace that make a large domain more manageable by enabling different administrators to manage different segments of the namespace. For example, if the resources in domain1.com are related to marketing and finance, the domain can be divided into the zones marketing.domain1.com and finance.domain1.com, respectively. The part of the DNS namespace for which a zone is responsible is known as the **zone of authority**. Servers in each zone store all records about the resources in that zone in a separate file called a **zone database file** (or sometimes, just a **zone file**). The zone database file contains various types of **resource records** that DNS uses to resolve host names to IP addresses. All resources in a domain must have a separate resource record in its domain zone database file that provides information about the type of resource and its role. **Table 4-2** provides a brief description of some of the different types of resource records that a zone database file can contain.

When multiple DNS servers are created in a standard DNS zone, there are two kinds of DNS database files: primary and secondary. One DNS server in the zone (called the **primary DNS server** or the **primary name server**) will store the **primary zone database file**, and the other DNS servers (known as **secondary DNS servers** or **secondary name servers**) will store copies of it, called the **secondary zone database file**. Modifications and updates can only be made to the primary zone database file. **Zone transfers** occur to replicate any changes to the primary zone database file to the secondary zone database files. The server where the primary zone database file is stored is also called the **authoritative server** because it has authority over the other DNS servers in the zone. The purpose of the secondary DNS servers is to reduce the traffic and query load on the primary name server. Secondary DNS servers also provide resolution redundancy, so if the authoritative (primary) server is down, the secondary servers can process name resolution requests (**Figure 4-3**).

You can also implement a caching-only DNS server. **Caching-only DNS servers** (also known as **caching-only name servers**) use caching to store information collected during name resolution. Caching is a method of storing frequently requested information in memory so that clients can quickly access it when required. A caching-only DNS server has no database files. It simply forwards requests to a designated DNS server and caches the resolved result. The next client to request resolution for that record will be answered from the cache, which reduces the load on the real DNS server and can reduce excessive network traffic caused by name resolution. Caching-only name servers are not authoritative for any zone. They are used when you need to provide DNS services locally, but do not want to create a separate zone for

tip

The zone database files are stored with the file extension .dns in the *%systemroot%\WINDOWS \system32\dns* folder on the DNS server.

Figure 4-3 The DNS namespace subdivided into zones

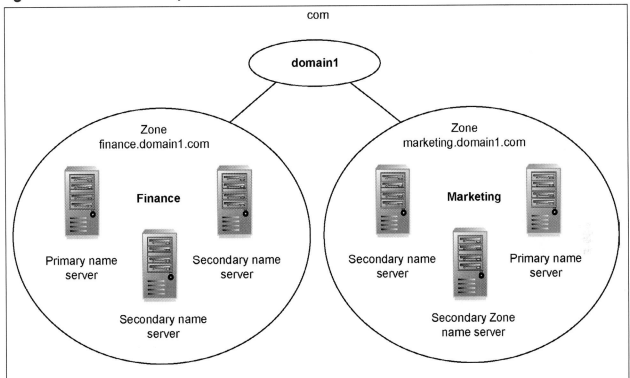

skill 2

Planning a DNS Infrastructure (cont'd)

exam objective

Plan a hostname resolution strategy. Examine the interoperability of DNS with third-party DNS solutions.

overview

this location. This situation may arise when the number of hosts that require DNS services at a location is small, or you do not want to increase administrative overhead by maintaining another zone. Zone traffic is another reason a caching-only name server is implemented rather than a primary or secondary name server. Unlike primary and secondary name servers, caching-only name servers do not participate in zone transfers. This could be a critical design consideration when deciding to implement DNS at a remote location connected to your central intranet via slow WAN links. If you configure a primary DNS server at the central location and a secondary DNS server at the remote location, it may result in excessive zone transfer traffic.

If there is already an existing DNS solution within your organization, such as BIND on a Unix system, there may be issues with integrating this solution with Windows Server 2003 Active Directory DNS requirements. Older versions of certain DNS systems do not support SRV (service) resource records or dynamic updates. SRV records, in particular, are required as they allow DNS support in Active Directory. Windows Server 2003 DNS also supports fast zone transfers, which allows multiple records, rather than just one record, to be sent at a time. You can either upgrade older systems to a version that supports these specifications, or for full support for Active Directory, migrate your existing DNS zones to the Windows Server 2003 DNS system. It is recommended that third-party servers become secondary servers and Windows 2003 DNS servers be configured as the primary. If the third-party DNS servers do not support fast zone transfer, you must disable them by selecting the BIND Secondaries option in the server's Properties dialog box.

Another important issue is whether you will use DNS on an intranet, the Internet, or both. If you plan to use DNS to serve both the intranet and Internet requirements of your organization, you must decide whether you want to use the same domain name on your intranet and the Internet. If you implement the same namespace, users will be able to access resources on both the intranet and the Internet using a single domain name **(Figure 4-4)**. If you are going to use the same namespace for both internal and external resources, you should create two primary DNS zones on two separate and unrelated servers to secure your intranet. One zone will allow Internet clients to access public resources and will not be configured to resolve internal resources. Since this DNS zone will not be configured to resolve internal resources, internal clients will not be able to access publicly available resources. You can overcome this problem by duplicating part of the content of the zone you created for Internet clients and then configuring hosts on your network to use this zone so that internal clients can resolve external resources. This will solve the problem of security, but it will lead to more administrative overhead because you will have to manage two database files separately.

Another alternative is to use different domain names for the intranet and the Internet (company.local, or company.net), or to use a sub-domain of the Internet name (corp.company.com). The advantages of using different namespaces for internal and external resources are that you have added security if the internal namespace is not published externally, and you also have a clear demarcation between internal and external resources. To create separate internal and external DNS zones, you would create two separate primary DNS servers. One DNS server will service external clients, and the other would service internal clients. For the external server, you would only provide support for the external namespace. However, the internal server would have to support both namespaces. For this support, you would need to create a zone for both the internal and external namespaces on the internal server. The external zone on the internal server, however, must be kept completely separate from the external zone on the external server. This requires that you have two separate primary zones for the external namespace (one on the internal server and one on the external server), and that you update each zone separately.

Table 4-2 Types of resource records in a zone database file

Record type	Represented in file as	Description
Start of authority	SOA	First record in the DNS database file. Defines the general parameters for the DNS zone, including the name of the primary DNS server for the zone.
Name server	NS	Lists additional name servers in the zone.
Address (host name)	A	Associates a host name with its corresponding 32-bit IPv4 address.
IPv6 address	AAAA	Associates a host name with its corresponding 128-bit IPv6 address.
Canonical name (Alias)	CNAME	States the host name or the server name as a reference name, or alias, that can be referred to in place of the corresponding A record.
Pointer record	PTR	Associates an IP address to a host name. Used in reverse lookup zones.
Mail exchange	MX	Specifies the mail exchanger host (e-mail server) for mail sent to the domain name that you have specified.
Service record	SRV	Associates the location of a Windows Server 2003 computer that offers a particular service such as HTTP, FTP, or LDAP with information about how to contact the service.

Figure 4-4 Same internal and external DNS namespace

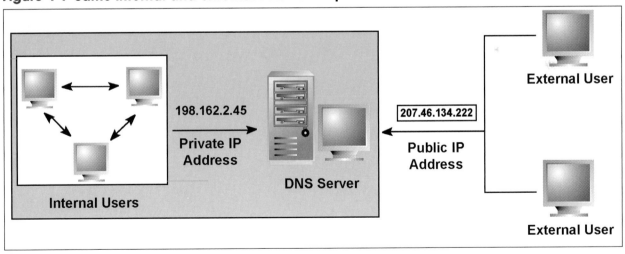

skill 2

Planning a DNS Infrastructure (cont'd)

exam objective

Plan a hostname resolution strategy. Examine the interoperability of DNS with third-party DNS solutions.

overview

Finally, you will need to ensure that your DNS implementation is reliable and fault tolerant. It is recommended that you implement at least two DNS servers, either one primary and one secondary or two Active Directory-integrated. Having multiple DNS servers will enhance reliability because if any one DNS server is unavailable, the other DNS server can handle client requests. Active Directory-integrated zones improve fault tolerance by allowing zone changes to occur on any available Active Directory-integrated DNS server, as opposed to the standard primary architecture, in which changes can only be made on the primary name server. The different types of DNS zones are discussed further in Skill 3.

Table 4-3 summarizes the various factors that you should consider when planning your DNS infrastructure.

how to

Design a DNS infrastructure.

1. Consider the size of your network.
2. Determine how many zones you will need.
3. Determine how many DNS servers you will need and their assigned roles (primary, secondary, caching-only).
4. Specify any requirements for fault tolerance, Active Directory integration, zone file transfers across WAN links, and so on.

Table 4-3   *Factors to consider when planning DNS infrastructure*

Factor	Considerations	Actions
Size of the network: small, medium, or large	Small: DNS availability	Install at least one primary and one secondary DNS server.
	Medium to large: DNS availability, administrative efficiency	Determine number and types of DNS servers and whether to implement zones.
Existing DNS solution	Integration of existing solution with Windows Server 2003 Active Directory DNS requirements	Upgrade older systems, or migrate DNS zones to Windows Server 2003 DNS.
Use DNS on intranet, Internet, or both?	Same domain name or different domain names for intranet and Internet	Same namespace: Create two primary DNS zones on two separate and unrelated servers.
		Separate internal and external DNS zones: Create two separate primary DNS servers.
Reliability and fault tolerance		Implement at least two DNS servers, one primary and one secondary, or two Active Directory-integrated.

skill 3

Planning DNS Zones

exam objective

Plan zone replication requirements.

overview

When planning your DNS infrastructure, you must decide what types of zones you need and which zone type role to assign to each DNS server on the network.

There are three kinds of DNS zones (**Table 4-4**):

◆ **Root zone:** A zone authoritative for the root domain. A root zone is either an Internet root, or an internal root (also known as a "fake root" or "empty root"). An internal root zone is rarely implemented.

◆ **Forward lookup zone:** Used to resolve host names to IP addresses.

◆ **Reverse lookup zone:** Used to resolve IP addresses to host names.

If you require an internal root zone, this file must contain the names of DNS servers that are authoritative for the root domain on your network to allow the resolution of local DNS intranet names to take place. The root name server is a DNS server that has authority for the top-most root domain in the DNS namespace hierarchy.

You configure a DNS server in the role of an internal root name server by creating the root zone. The internal root zone can either be an Active Directory-integrated or standard primary zone. The root zone contains the Start of Authority (SOA) record for the root domain. The SOA record is the first record in the zone and indicates the root name server for that particular zone.

The forward lookup and reverse lookup zone categories support four different zone type roles:

Standard primary zone: This is the first zone that must be created. It maintains the original copy of all information about the part of the DNS namespace for which it is responsible in a zone database file (referred to as the primary zone database file) and stores it locally on the hard disk of the DNS server (called the primary DNS server or primary name server).

Standard secondary zone: Secondary zones are created after the primary zone to provide redundancy for the primary DNS server. The DNS server that maintains the secondary zone is called the secondary DNS server or secondary name server. The secondary DNS server contains a read-only copy of the primary zone database file so that client requests can be answered when the primary name server is not available.

Stub zone: Stub zones are a new feature of Windows Server 2003 DNS, and are an enhancement to delegated sub-domains. A delegated sub-domain is created when a parent domain (*company.com*) delegates a specific sub-domain of its namespace (such as *sales.company.com*) to another server or group of servers. Delegated sub-domains are required because when someone in a sub-domain such as *marketing.company.com* queries for *sales.company.com*, the *marketing.company.com* DNS servers would forward that query to the parent servers (*company.com*). The parent DNS servers in *company.com* would then need to contain either the zone information for *sales.company.com*, or a delegation pointing to the DNS servers that contain that information. The problem with a basic delegated sub-domain is that the servers in the parent zone are never updated when new DNS servers for the child domain are added, meaning that the parent zone's list of servers that have been delegated control for the child domains can become outdated. Stub zones resolve this problem by replicating the SOA, NS, and core A records from the delegated child domain to the parent domain. When a new secondary DNS server is added to the child domain, the parent domain is already aware of it.

Active Directory-integrated zone: The zone information for a primary and secondary zone is stored in a text file. When you create an Active Directory-integrated zone, information about the zone is stored in Active Directory. An Active Directory-integrated zone inherits all security features of Active Directory, allowing for the secure storage and transfer of zone information. One of the advantages of creating and maintaining an Active Directory-integrated zone rather than a standard DNS zone is the automatic management of zone transfers.

tip

It is a relatively common practice to point all clients and other DNS servers to the secondary zones, rather than the primary name server. The main advantage is that it helps secure the database against unauthorized additions.

tip

You can create an Active Directory-integrated zone only if the DNS server is a domain controller.

Table 4-4 DNS Zones

Root	Zone that is authoritative for the root domain. A root zone is either the Internet root, or an internal root. An internal root is rarely implemented by corporate customers.
Forward lookup	Zone in which forward lookup queries are performed. Forward lookup queries are searches that begin with the DNS name of a host as it is stored in an address (A) resource record. The resource data returned will be an IP address.
Reverse lookup	Zone in which reverse lookup queries are performed. Reverse lookup queries start with a known IP address and search for a host name based on its address. Since DNS was not designed to support reverse lookup queries, the only way to do this would be to search in all domains in the DNS namespace, which would be time exhaustive. This is why the in-addr.arpa domain was defined in the DNS standards. in-addr.arpa is set aside in the Internet DNS namespace to provide a practical and dependable way to perform reverse queries. Sub-domains within the in-addr.arpa domain are created by reversing the order of the IP address octets so that the octet representing the individual host name will be read first. When read from left to right, the IP host address (which normally would be contained in the last octets) will be read first, and the IP network address (which normally would be contained in the first octets) will be read last. IPv6 networks use the ip6.int domain to create reverse lookup zones.

skill 3

Planning for DNS Zones (cont'd)

exam objective

Plan zone replication requirements.

overview

Table 4-5 provides you with a summary of the different zone type roles.

how to

Plan your DNS zones and DNS server roles.

1. Determine how many DNS zones and what types are required, such as root, forward, and reverse lookup zones, and which zone types (primary, secondary, stub, or Active Directory-integrated) you will use.
2. For each zone, determine the number and types of DNS servers required, keeping in mind redundancy and load balancing.
3. Plan how to integrate your DNS servers into your Active Directory structure.

Table 4-5   Zone types

Zone Type	Description
Standard primary zone	This zone type maintains the original copy of zone data in a standard text file and stores it locally on the server. This is the only copy that can be edited (read-write).
Standard secondary zone Secondary zones	This zone type maintains a read-only copy of the primary zone database file. It is created after the primary zone has been configured on the server. provide fault tolerance and redundancy to ease the strain on a primary name server.
Active Directory-integrated zone	This zone type uses Active Directory to store and replicate zone database files. It provides integrated storage and secure updates of all zone database files.
Stub zone	Enhancement to delegated sub-domains: When you use basic delegated sub-domains, servers in the parent zone are not updated when new DNS servers for the child domain are added. Thus the parent zone's list of servers that have been delegated control for the child domains can become outdated. Stub zones resolve this problem by replicating the SOA, NS, and core A records from the delegated child domain to the parent domain. This way, when a new secondary DNS server is added to the child domain, the parent domain is already aware of it.

skill 4

Configuring DNS Zone Replication

exam objective

Plan zone replication requirements.

overview

In DNS architecture, there could be multiple zones representing the same portion of a namespace. As you have learned, the primary zone is one in which all updates for the records that belong to that zone are made. A secondary zone is represented by a read-only copy of the primary zone. The changes made to the primary zone file are replicated to the secondary zone file.

A name server can host multiple zones, and can therefore be primary for one zone and secondary for another zone. The process of replicating a zone file to multiple name servers is called zone transfer. A zone transfer occurs by copying the zone file information from the master primary server to the secondary server.

A **master server** is the source of the zone information, and can be a primary or secondary server. If the master is primary, then the zone transfer comes directly from the source. If the master server is secondary, the file received from the master server by means of a zone transfer is a copy of the read-only zone file (**Figure 4-5**).

A zone transfer is initiated in one of the following ways:

◆   The master server sends a notification to the slave server(s) of a change in the zone.
◆   When the slave server's DNS service starts or the slave server's refresh interval has expired, it will query the master server for the changes.

When you use standard DNS zones, zone transfers can be performed in one of two ways: completely or incrementally. **Complete zone transfers (AFXR)** copy the entire database whenever a change occurs. If your database contained 50,000 records, and a single record changed, AFXR would transfer all 50,000 records. AFXR is typically reserved for backwards compatibility with older DNS servers, but it is also used when there are severe database errors and when a secondary server is first brought online and requires a full copy of the database. **Incremental zone transfers (IFXR)** only transfer the record that has changed, which is much more efficient. Standard primary and secondary DNS servers are limited to using AFXR or IFXR, but Active Directory-integrated DNS servers improve upon IFXR by inserting the DNS database into Active Directory and using attribute level Active Directory replication techniques. When you create Active Directory-integrated zones, the zone appears as an object in Active Directory, and the information is updated and replicated automatically across the domain as part of the Active Directory replication cycle.

DNS zones can be stored in Active Directory in the domain directory partition, or an application directory partition. The **domain directory partition** is where data pertaining to a particular Active Directory domain is stored, such as data about objects like users and computers. Data stored in the domain directory partition is replicated to all domain controllers in an Active Directory domain, but it cannot be replicated to domain controllers in other Active Directory domains. If they are not DNS servers, all domain controllers in the domain will receive copies of the zone. Unnecessary Active Directory synchronization will occur and network traffic will be increased, but you will always have a valid copy of the DNS database as long as you have at least one domain controller running, even if all of your DNS servers fail.

tip

If you store an Active Directory-integrated zone on a Windows 2000 Server computer, you must store the zone in the domain directory partition, since application directory partitions are available only on a Windows Server 2003 computer.

Figure 4-5 Master DNS servers

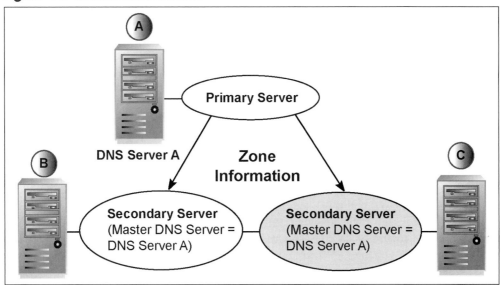

skill 4

Configuring DNS Zone Replication
(cont'd)

exam objective

Plan zone replication requirements.

overview

Application directory partitions are implemented to improve replication efficiency in situations where only a subset of the domain controllers needs a copy of the application data. You can use them to store data in Active Directory that will only be replicated to a specific group of domain controllers. Domain controllers where an application directory partition is stored do not have to be in the same Active Directory domain, but they must be in the same Active Directory forest. Data can be replicated to any domain controller in the same Active Directory forest. In an application directory partition, you can store DNS zones on all DNS servers in the Active Directory forest, on all DNS servers in the Active Directory domain, or on all servers designated in a scope that you create for the partition. Synchronization will only occur between servers which actually use the DNS data, unlike using a domain directory partition.

With Windows Server 2003, you have four options for replicating the application directory partition (**Table 4-6**). You can replicate to all DNS servers in the forest (**Figure 4-6**), to all DNS servers in the domain (**Figure 4-7**), to all domain controllers in the domain, or to all domain controllers specified in a custom scope. While most of these choices are self-explanatory, the last option, "all domain controllers in a custom scope," is a bit complicated. It gives advanced administrators more flexibility in scope than the default application data partitions allow. When choosing a scope, keep in mind that in general, the wider the scope, the larger the quantity of traffic generated for DNS replication.

Table 4-6 Active Directory Zone Replication Scopes

Zone Replication Scope	Description
All DNS servers in the Active Directory forest	Replicates zone data to all DNS servers running on domain controllers in the Active Directory forest. Usually, this is the broadest scope of replication.
All DNS servers in the Active Directory domain	Replicates zone data to all DNS servers running on domain controllers in the Active Directory domain. This option is the default setting for Active Directory-integrated DNS zone replication in the Windows Server 2003 family.
All domain controllers in the Active Directory domain	Replicates zone data to all domain controllers in the Active Directory domain. If you want Windows 2000 DNS servers to load an Active Directory zone, this setting must be selected for that zone.
All domain controllers in a specified application directory partition	Replicates zone data according to the replication scope of the specified application directory partition. For a zone to be stored in the specified application directory partition, the DNS server hosting the zone must be enlisted in the specified application directory partition.

Figure 4-6 Creating an application directory partition for a forest

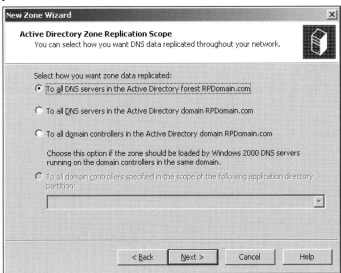

Figure 4-7 Creating an application directory partition for a domain

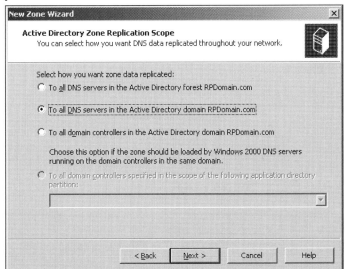

skill 5

Implementing DNS Forwarding

exam objective

Plan a forwarding configuration.

overview

DNS forwarding is used to resolve queries that cannot be resolved on the local DNS server. The process involves having a DNS server communicate directly with other outside DNS servers. An advantage of forwarding is that forwarded queries are cached, allowing for cache information to be distributed between DNS servers.

Prior to Windows Server 2003, you could identify multiple servers to which all unresolved queries could be forwarded. If one server was unavailable, the requests would be sent to the next server on the list. This is called standard forwarding in Windows Server 2003.

Conditional forwarding defines where DNS queries on specific domains are forwarded. This is a new feature available in Windows Server 2003 DNS, and is designed to work with multiple DNS zone environments in which systems in one namespace need to communicate with systems in another namespace.

By configuring settings on the **Forwarders** tab (**Figure 4-8**), you can specify a DNS server (or servers) to handle DNS requests that the local DNS server is either unable to resolve, or that you do not want the local DNS server to resolve.

To add a domain to the DNS domain list, click the **New** button on the Forwarders tab. The **New Forwarder** dialog box will open (**Figure 4-9**). Type the domain for which you want DNS queries to be forwarded in the **DNS domain** text box, and then click **OK**. The domain you selected will now appear in the **DNS domain** list box on the **Forwarders** tab (**Figure 4-10**), where you can select the domain and assign a forwarder to it.

By default, recursion on a Windows Server 2003 DNS server is enabled, which means that if the designated forwarder fails to resolve a DNS query, the local DNS server will then contact other name servers repeatedly until it finds one that can resolve the request for the original client. Recursion, therefore, can serve as a measure of fault tolerance. However, if the forwarder failed to resolve the query through no fault of its own, the local server will likely be unable to resolve the requested host name on its own. In this case, recursion merely delays the arrival of an additional error message. To eliminate this redundancy of failures, you can disable recursion by selecting the **Do not use recursion for this domain** check box near the bottom of the Forwarders tab.

Similar in function to forwarding is the concept of root hints. The Internet contains several top-level DNS name servers that resolve requests for host names on the Internet. If you click on the properties of a DNS server from your DNS console, you can view the list of root servers on the **Root Hints** tab. The DNS server needs these root hints to help locate the root DNS servers. These root DNS servers help resolve queries of Internet host names that cannot be derived from local DNS servers.

Figure 4-8 The Forwarders tab

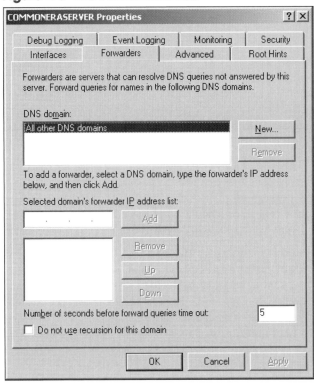

Figure 4-9 The New Forwarder dialog box

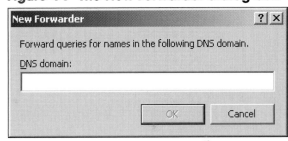

Figure 4-10 Adding a new forwarder domain

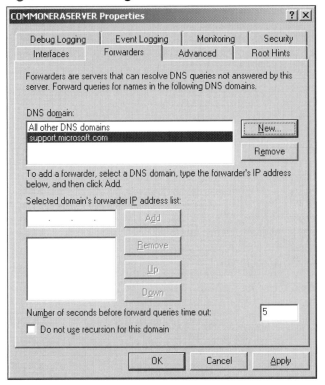

skill 6

Optimizing DNS

exam objective

Diagnose and resolve issues related to DNS services. Troubleshoot host name resolution.

overview

Once you have implemented and tested DNS, you need to monitor the performance of the DNS server. Monitoring the performance of a DNS server provides you with information that you can use to diagnose problems and optimize performance.

You will initially need to establish a baseline for your DNS performance. After you establish a baseline, you can compare it with the performance data that you collect over time to determine performance trends. If there is degradation in the performance of your DNS server, the data that you collect helps to identify where you will be able to optimize the performance of the DNS server.

To monitor different aspects of DNS, Windows Server 2003 provides you with various types of DNS server performance counters (**Table 4-7**) that can be used with the System Monitor and Performance Logs and Alerts tools available in the Performance console. The **System Monitor** depicts data collected by performance counters in the form of graphs, bar charts, and text reports. You use **Performance Logs and Alerts** to maintain records of data collected by performance counters and to set alerts, which can be used to initiate actions such as sending a message and/or executing a program when a particular condition is true. If you want to monitor and analyze data collected using performance counters for a short period, use System Monitor. If you wish to collect and analyze data over a longer period, Performance Logs and Alerts are a better choice.

Monitoring the performance of a DNS server is not limited to the Performance console. You can also use the following Windows Server 2003 features to keep your DNS server running efficiently:

Event Viewer: You can use the Event Viewer to look for events concerning the DNS service. In the Event Viewer console, click **DNS Server** to view errors, warnings, and other information about routine events, such as the startup of service. You can configure which events are logged on the **Event Logging** tab in the **Properties** dialog box for the DNS server. You can further configure the DNS events log by using the DNS console. Right-click **DNS Events** under the Event Viewer node and click **Properties** to open the **DNS Events Properties** dialog box. The **DNS Events Properties** dialog box contains a **General** tab and a **Filter** tab. On the **General** tab, you can control settings such as the file name of the DNS Events log, its storage location, and maximum size. On the **Filter** tab, you can control the content of the DNS Events log file by using filter parameters such as event ID, event source, event type, event date, and so on.

DNS debug log: The **Properties** dialog box for a DNS server also contains a **Debug Logging** tab. The options on this tab enable you to keep a log of the packets that a DNS server sends and receives. You can filter which packets are logged by criteria including:

◆ Packet direction (outgoing and/or incoming)
◆ Transport protocol (UDP and/or TCP)
◆ Packet contents (queries/transfers, updates, and/or notifications)
◆ Packet type (request or response)

You can access the DNS debug log file in Windows Explorer by navigating to %*systemroot*%\WINDOWS\system32\Dns\Dns.log. You must stop the DNS Server service in order to view the debug log, and you should not leave debugging active unless you are troubleshooting as it can use significant system resources. For instance, if left running for a long period, debug logging will create a large log file.

Table 4-7 DNS server performance counters

Counter type	Counter name	Description
All zone transfer (AFXR)	AFXR Request Received AFXR Request Sent AFXR Response Received AFXR Success Received AFXR Success Sent	Tracks the number of full zone transfer requests and responses processed by the DNS server.
Incremental zone transfer (IFXR)	IFXR Request Received IFXR Request Sent IFXR Response Received IFXR Success Received IFXR Success Sent IFXR TCP Success Received IFXR UDP Success Received	Tracks the number of incremental zone transfer requests and responses processed by the DNS server.
Zone transfer	Zone Transfer Failure Zone Transfer Request Received Zone Transfer SOA Request Sent Zone Transfer Success	Tracks the number of requests and responses processed by the DNS server during the process of copying the DNS database between DNS servers.
DNS server memory	Caching Memory Database Node Memory Nbtstat Memory Record Flow Memory	Tracks the amount of memory used by the DNS server.
Dynamic update	Dynamic Update NoOperation Dynamic Update NoOperation/sec Dynamic Update Queued Dynamic Update Received Dynamic Update Received/sec Dynamic Update Rejected Dynamic Update TimeOuts Dynamic Update Written to Database Dynamic Update Written to Database/sec	Tracks the requests and responses processed by the DNS server during dynamic updating of DNS.
Secure dynamic update	Secure Update Failure Secure Update Received Secure Update Received/sec	Tracks the number of secure dynamic updates sent and received by the DNS server.
Notification	Notify Sent Notify Received	Tracks the number of notifies sent by the master DNS server and the number of notifies received by the secondary DNS server.
Recursion	Recursive Queries Recursive Queries/sec Recursive Query Failure Recursive Query Failure/sec Recursive TimeOuts Recursive TimeOuts/sec	Tracks data related to recursive queries used by a DNS server.
TCP	TCP Message Memory TCP Query Received TCP Query Received/sec TCP Response Sent TCP Response Sent/sec	Tracks the number of requests and responses processed by the DNS server using TCP.
UDP	UDP Message Memory UDP Query Received UDP Query Received/sec UDP Response Sent UDP Response Sent/sec	Tracks the number of requests and responses processed by the DNS server using UDP.
Total	Total Query Received Total Query Received/sec Total Response Set Total Response Set/sec	Tracks the total number of requests and responses processed by the DNS.
WINS lookup	WINS Lookup Received WINS Lookup Received/sec WINS Response Sent WINS Response Sent/sec WINS Reverse Lookup Received WINS Reverse Lookup Received/sec WINS Reverse Response Sent WINS Reverse Response Sent/sec	Tracks the number of requests and responses sent to the WINS server by the DNS server when DNS is used for WINS lookup.

skill 6

Optimizing DNS (cont'd)

exam objective

Diagnose and resolve issues related to DNS services. Troubleshoot host name resolution.

overview

Replication Monitor: Replication Monitor enables you to monitor the replication of DNS activity in Active Directory-integrated zones. In order to use Replication Monitor, you must install Windows Support Tools from your Windows Server 2003 CD-ROM.

Once installed, you can access Replication Monitor by entering **replmon** in the Run dialog box. You can use Replication Monitor to do the following:

◆ Identify a domain controller that has failed to replicate DNS data.
◆ Force the replication of DNS data.
◆ Log the success and failure rates of replication nodes.
◆ Check the operational standing of domain controllers responsible for replication across forests.
◆ Display a graphical representation of DNS replication topology.

how to

Monitor the performance of a DNS server.

1. Click [Start], point to **Programs**, point to **Administrative Tools**, and then click **Performance** to open the **Performance** console (**Figure 4-11**). The left pane of the window lists the two performance tools that are available in the console, System Monitor and Performance Logs and Alerts. System Monitor is selected by default. In the right pane, System Monitor immediately begins charting values for the default counters in real time. The default counters, which you can see at the bottom of the right pane, are **Pages/sec**, **Avg. Disk Queue Length**, and **% Processor Time**. Actual values for the counter that is selected appear between the graphical display and the list of active counters.
2. Click [+] on the Performance console toolbar above the graphical display area to open the **Add Counters** dialog box.
3. Click **DNS** in the **Performance object** list box (**Figure 4-12**). The performance counters related to DNS display in the **Select counters from list** box.
4. Select the counter that you want to monitor in the Select counters from list box, such as **Total Query Received**.
5. Click [Add] to add the selected performance counter to the list of performance counters that are being monitored. Choose more counters from the **Add Counters** dialog box to monitor other DNS functions.
6. Click [Close] to close the Add Counters dialog box. You will now see the counter you selected in the list of active counters near the bottom of the Performance console. The counters are color-coded so that you can identify them in the graphical display.
7. Close the Performance console.

more

Monitoring the DNS server helps you to identify potential bottlenecks that would require troubleshooting the DNS service. These bottlenecks might be related to DNS servers, clients, and/or zones. If a DNS server is unable to resolve queries from a DNS client, troubleshooting the DNS server is necessary; otherwise, name resolution failures will likely bring the general functioning of the network to a grinding halt. It is also important to troubleshoot problems related to DNS zones because all DNS queries in a zone are resolved using the zone file. Any problem in a zone invariably results in a problem resolving DNS queries. You must identify and correct zone problems to ensure smooth functioning of the DNS environment

Figure 4-11 The Performance console

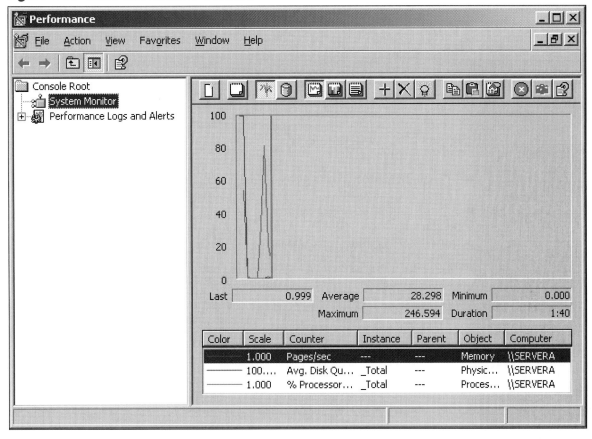

Figure 4-12 The Add Counters dialog box

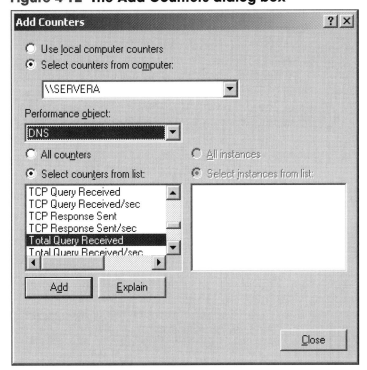

skill 7

Planning WINS Servers

Plan a NetBIOS name resolution strategy. Plan NetBIOS name resolution by using the LMHOSTS file.

overview

Windows Internet Naming Service (WINS) resolves Windows NetBIOS names to IP addresses on a TCP/IP network. Before the proliferation of the Internet, most organizations with DOS, Windows, or OS/2-based networks typically used the **NetBEUI** (NetBIOS Extended User Interface) protocol to communicate on the network. NetBEUI does not support routing, and is best suited for small networks that do not need to route network traffic externally.

The NetBEUI protocol implements the **NetBIOS** naming scheme, which uses NetBIOS names to identify and communicate with computers on a network. These names typically take the form of a single word, such as *server1*, or *pc12*. With the arrival of the Internet and larger in-house networks, TCP/IP became the preferred communication protocol. TCP/IP uses IP addresses to identify and communicate with computers on internal and external networks.

NetBEUI has been gradually phased out, and there is no support for it in the default installation of Windows Server 2003. Many legacy operating systems and applications, however, still require that NetBIOS names be resolved to IP addresses, and this is the purpose of WINS.

WINS clients use the following methods to resolve NetBIOS names to IP addresses:

1. **NetBIOS name cache:** The client checks its own NetBIOS name cache for the name and address of the destination. These names have been previously resolved and stored in the client's cache. This is always the first method to be used.
2. **WINS server:** The client tries to resolve the host name by querying the primary WINS server for the IP address of a specific NetBIOS name. If the query is unsuccessful for any reason, the client will send the query to any additional configured WINS servers (up to 12 in Windows 2003 Server).
3. **Broadcast:** The client tries a basic network broadcast to query all hosts on a subnet. When the destination host receives the broadcast, it sends its IP address to the client **(Figure 4-13)**. These broadcasts do not cross routers, and therefore this method is not suitable for large networks with many subnets.
4. **LMHOSTS file:** An LMHOSTS file is a text file that is stored on the local computer. The LMHOSTS file contains a list of mappings of NetBIOS names to IP addresses for the network. If an entry for the destination NetBIOS resource exists, the NetBIOS name is resolved **(Figure 4-14)**. The **LMHOSTS** file can be edited with a text editor such as Notepad. The LMHOSTS file is stored in the *%systemroot%*\system32\drivers\etc folder. This file is not installed by default, but a sample version of an LMHOSTS file called lmhosts.sam can be used to create the file. To create an LMHOSTS file, edit lmhosts.sam as required, and then save it as lmhosts with no file extension.

The resolution method and the order in which the above methods will be used after the NetBIOS name cache is checked depend on the NetBIOS node type of the client **(Table 4-8)**.

To enable WINS support in a Windows Server 2003 infrastructure, you will need to install the service on a Windows Server 2003, Windows 2000 Server, or Windows NT Server system. The **WINS server** is a NetBIOS Name Server (NBNS), which is server software dedicated to resolving NetBIOS names to IP addresses. An NBNS contains a database file that can accept dynamic NetBIOS name-to-IP address registrations and answer queries for NetBIOS name resolutions. As an NBNS, a WINS server hosts a WINS database for registration and resolution of client NetBIOS name-to-IP address queries.

tip

The LMHOSTS file is read from top to bottom. Place frequently accessed resources at the top of the file.

Figure 4-13 NetBIOS name resolution using broadcast

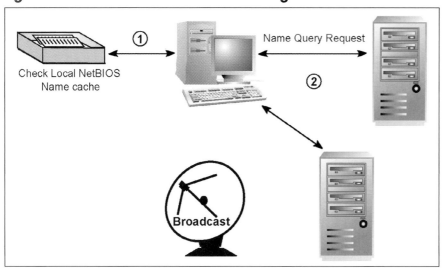

Figure 4-14 NetBIOS name resolution using LMHOSTS file

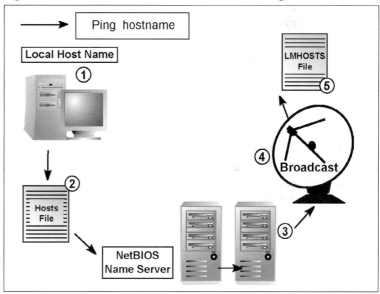

Table 4-8 Node types	
Type	**Description**
B-node	Broadcast node clients simply broadcast the name query, and do not use WINS. This is the default node type for clients that are not configured to use WINS.
P-node	Peer-to-Peer or Point-to-Point node clients query a WINS server for name resolution and do not use broadcasts.
M-node	Mixed node clients will use broadcast name queries and if they do not receive a response, they will query a WINS server.
H-node	Hybrid node clients first query a WINS server, and if unable to resolve the query, then use B-node methods (i.e., broadcast and LMHOSTS file). This is the default node type for WINS-enabled clients.

skill 7

Planning WINS Servers *(cont'd)*

exam objective

Plan a NetBIOS name resolution strategy. Plan NetBIOS name resolution by using the LMHOSTS file.

overview

After installing a WINS server, you need to configure **WINS clients** to use the WINS server for NetBIOS name resolution. To configure a WINS client, you assign the client the IP address of the WINS server to which the client can send its name resolution queries.

A WINS client uses two processes during the implementation of WINS:

◆ **Dynamic registration:** When a WINS client first starts, it sends a name registration request to the WINS server **(Figure 4-15)**. Upon receiving the name registration request, the WINS server checks its database for an existing entry for that name. If the name does not exist in the database, the WINS server registers the NetBIOS name. If the name does exist, the server attempts to contact the previously registered client at the listed address. If the contact is successful, the client attempting to register the name is denied. If the contact is unsuccessful, the previous entry is removed and the client is allowed to register the name.

◆ **NetBIOS name resolution:** The process of resolving a NetBIOS name to an IP address begins with the client checking its local NetBIOS name cache for a matching entry. If the name is not found, the process continues with the WINS client sending a request to the WINS server for a NetBIOS name resolution. **(Figure 4-16)**. The WINS server searches its database for the IP address that corresponds to the NetBIOS name of the computer. If there is a match in its database, the WINS server returns the IP address to the requesting WINS client.

When planning to install and integrate WINS services into a Windows Server 2003 infrastructure, you must:

◆ Determine the number of WINS servers that you need.
◆ Plan the replication partnerships.
◆ Assess the impact of WINS communication traffic on slower WAN links.
◆ Assess the level of WINS network fault tolerance.
◆ Test your planned WINS installation.

A Windows Server 2003 infrastructure should include at least two WINS servers if compatibility with down-level operating systems or applications is required. To ensure efficient NetBIOS name resolution and provide redundancy, you should deploy multiple WINS servers. Having multiple WINS servers creates redundancy so that if one WINS server fails, other servers will be able to continue to resolve NetBIOS to IP addresses for WINS clients. Your network should contain at least one WINS server and a backup WINS server for every 10,000 WINS clients to service name registrations and name queries effectively. A WINS server can typically register 1500 names and field 4500 name queries in about 60 seconds.

For networks with multiple sites, you will need to install at least one WINS server at each site. If WINS clients from a remote site try to register or query a primary WINS server over a slow, WAN link, the request may time out, or cause bandwidth issues if too many remote clients are sending WINS requests. You will be able to utilize replication to copy the WINS database from one WINS server to another to ensure that WINS clients are registered on all WINS servers. Replication is discussed in Skill 8.

Figure 4-15 NetBIOS name registration process

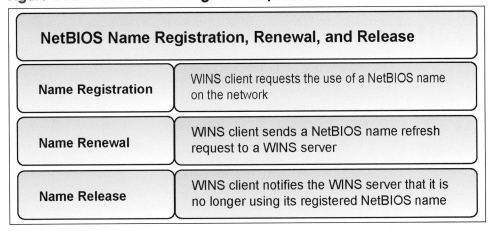

NetBIOS Name Registration, Renewal, and Release	
Name Registration	WINS client requests the use of a NetBIOS name on the network
Name Renewal	WINS client sends a NetBIOS name refresh request to a WINS server
Name Release	WINS client notifies the WINS server that it is no longer using its registered NetBIOS name

Figure 4-16 NetBIOS name resolution process using WINS

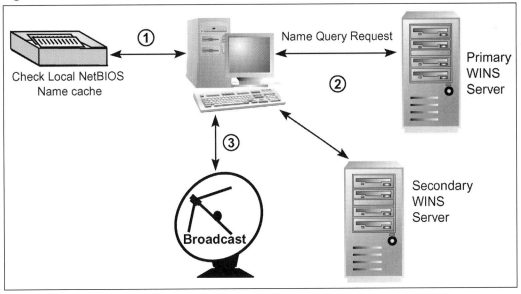

skill 8   *Planning WINS replication*

exam objective

Plan a WINS replication strategy.

overview

To maintain consistency among the multiple WINS servers on a network, you need to implement replication so that the servers can share information with each other. **WINS replication** enables a WINS server to resolve NetBIOS names of computers that are registered with another WINS server.

When planning your Windows Server 2003 infrastructure, you also need to take into account any networks that will be communicating over slow WAN links. For efficiency and redundancy, the WINS database can be replicated from one server to another. However, you need to ensure that the intervals at which the database replicates are not too frequent, as this excess may cause bandwidth issues between network sites. For example, *Client1* is registered with *WINSserver1*. *Client1* needs to access an application or service located on *Client2*, which is registered with *WINSserver2*. To allow *Client1* to query its WINS server and receive a successful NetBIOS name resolution for *Client2*, replication of the databases on the two WINS servers must take place.

During the process of WINS database replication, entries are either pushed to or pulled from the WINS server's configured replication partner. A **push partner** is a WINS server that sends replication data to its partner after a specific number of changes. For instance, if the interval for push replication is set to 10, the push partner pushes replication data every time 10 or more changes occurred. A **pull partner** is a WINS server that requests to receive changes from its partner after a specific period of time has elapsed. If the pull interval is set to 10, the pull partner attempts to retrieve changes every 10 minutes, regardless of whether any changes have actually occurred (**Figure 4-18**).

For pull replication to work properly, its partner must be set to push to create a push-pull relationship. A push-push or pull-pull relationship will not work. To create an effective WINS replication relationship, you must configure each server to be a push or pull partner of the other server. An interval time can be set to trigger the replication, such as once an hour.

When configuring WINS replication, two main topologies can be used. In the first case, you can simply enable all WINS servers on a network to replicate with each other by adding all servers as replication partners. This ensures that new changes to the WINS database are quickly replicated to all servers. The disadvantage of this method is that it creates a large load of replication traffic on the network, and this excess load can cause some bandwidth issues with slow WAN link connections.

In the second case, one WINS server acts as a central primary hub, while all other WINS servers connect to and replicate with the single central WINS server. This topology is scalable and bandwidth efficient, and is typically used by having multiple WINS sites connect to a central network site for WINS replication. The disadvantage of this type of strategy is that the central WINS server becomes a single point of failure for the topology, and if it fails, the other WINS servers have no way of replicating with each other. The time it takes for new changes to replicate to all servers is also much longer. **Table 4-9** lists the different configuration methods that can be used to initiate replication of a WINS database.

tip

With the **Use persistent connection for replication** check box selected, the WINS server will not disconnect from replication partners once replication is complete. This will allow the server to begin sending records to partners for replication without having to establish a connection each time.

how to

Plan WINS replication.

1. Determine the replication partners for each WINS server.
2. Create the WINS replication topology with either a central server, or have all WINS servers replicate with each other.
3. Configure the replication partners as either a push or pull partner.
4. Determine the interval frequency of replication between the partners.

Figure 4-17 WINS Replication

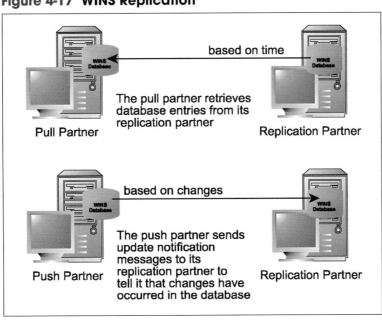

based on time

The pull partner retrieves database entries from its replication partner

Pull Partner

Replication Partner

based on changes

The push partner sends update notification messages to its replication partner to tell it that changes have occurred in the database

Push Partner

Replication Partner

Table 4-9   Methods for initiating replication of a WINS database

Configure the WINS service to start replication at system startup. This enables a WINS server to pull or push database entries automatically each time WINS is started.

Configure the WINS service to start replication at a specific interval (such as every three hours, every five hours, every eight hours).

Configure the WINS service to start replication when a WINS server performs a specific number of registrations and modifications to its WINS database. When the specified number is reached, the WINS server informs its pull partners; the pull partners then request the new entries.

Use the WINS console to force replication rather than wait for it to occur according to configuration settings.

skill 9

Optimizing WINS

exam objective

Basic knowledge

overview

After installing and configuring the WINS service, you can use the WINS console to perform administrative tasks required to optimize WINS, such as compacting the WINS database, checking entries in the WINS database for consistency, backing up and restoring the database, and backing up the WINS Registry settings **(Figure 4-18)**.

The size of a WINS database grows as entries are added. When a WINS server releases an entry, the server does not release the space that was used by that entry. To recover the unused disk space in the WINS database, you will need to compact it offline (by stopping the WINS process) on a routine basis. WINS performs online compaction as an automatic background process, but this online compaction does not recover the space used by released entries as efficiently as offline compaction. This results in the database slowly growing in size over time.

Over time, a WINS database may become inconsistent and unsynchronized with the other WINS databases. Checking the consistency of the database entries ensures that updated mapping entries are available to all WINS servers. During a consistency check, a WINS server verifies its database and compares its entries with entries on other WINS servers. All records of the other WINS servers are compared with records in the local database. If a record in the local database is identical to the corresponding record of the other WINS server, the timestamp of the local record is updated. If the record in the other database has a higher version ID, the record is added to the local database, and the existing local record is stamped for deletion.

WINS server performance should be continuously monitored to ensure WINS is working correctly and efficiently. You can monitor the performance of the WINS server through the **WINS Server Statistics** dialog box **(Figure 4-19)**. The dialog box **(Figure 4-20)** displays information such as the number of successful and failed registration attempts and the number of successful and failed WINS queries made to the server. Such statistical information enables you to narrow down the source of a problem and administer the WINS service accordingly.

WINS server performance can also be measured via the System Monitor, which contains special performance counters specifically for WINS.

how to

View WINS statistical information.

1. Open the **WINS** console.
2. Click the name of the WINS server in the console tree to select the server, open the **Action** menu, and then click **Display Server Statistics**. Alternatively, you can right-click the server and then click **Display Server Statistics** on the shortcut menu.
3. The **WINS Server Statistics** dialog box opens. Click [Reset] to clear the previous statistics and begin recording statistical information from the current time.
4. Click [Close] to close the **WINS Server Statistics** dialog box.
5. Close the WINS console.

Figure 4-18 Administering WINS

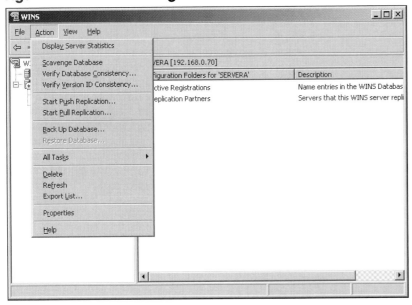

Figure 4-19 Displaying server statistics

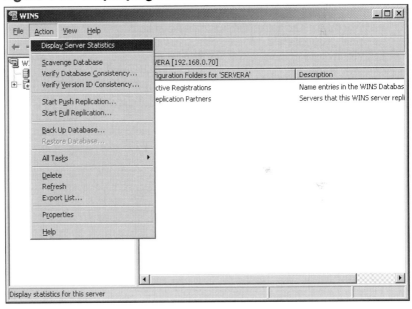

Figure 4-20 The WINS Server Statistics dialog box

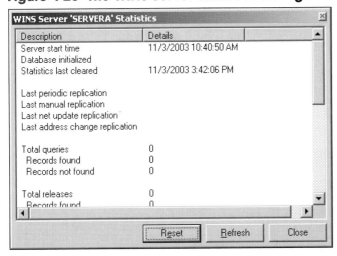

Summary

- Domain Name System (DNS) is the main name resolution service for Windows Server 2003. DNS translates host names to IP addresses.

- The DNS namespace consists of a hierarchical structure of named nodes called domains. The domain at the top of the DNS namespace is called the root domain and is represented by a (.). The sub-domain of the root domain is called a top-level domain. The sub-domain of a top-level domain is called a second-level domain. A host name is at the bottom of the DNS hierarchy and it designates a particular computer, on either the Internet or a private network.

- To identify a host name in the DNS hierarchy, you must use a Fully Qualified Domain Name (FQDN), which consists of a domain name in addition to the host name.

- If you plan to have an Internet presence, you must register your domain name with an Internet naming authority. If you plan to implement DNS only on an intranet, you are not required to register the domain name, but it is still recommended.

- The size of a network is an important consideration in planning a DNS infrastructure. On a small network, the main factor to consider is DNS availability. When implementing DNS on a mid- to large-sized network, you will need to determine the number and type of DNS servers that will be needed to ensure that DNS name resolution proceeds quickly and efficiently, and whether it is necessary to divide administrative control and DNS functions into zones.

- If there is an existing DNS solution being used by the organization, such as BIND on a Unix system, there may be issues with integrating this solution with Windows Server 2003 Active Directory DNS requirements.

- Another important issue is whether you will use DNS on an intranet, the Internet, or both. If you plan to use DNS to serve both the intranet and Internet requirements of the organization, you must decide whether to use a single domain name or different domain name.

- You also need to ensure that your DNS implementation is reliable and fault tolerant.

- There are three kinds of DNS zones: root zone, forward lookup zone, and reverse lookup zone.

- Forward lookup and reverse lookup zones support four different zone type roles: standard primary zones, standard secondary zones, stub zones, and Active Directory-integrated zones.

- The process of replicating a zone file to multiple name servers is called zone transfer.

- When you use standard DNS zones, there are two ways zone transfers can be performed: a complete zone transfer (AFXR) copies the entire database whenever a change occurs, while an incremental zone transfer (IFXR) only transfers the record that has changed.

- DNS zones can be stored in Active Directory in the domain directory partition, or in an application directory partition. The domain directory partition is where data pertaining to a particular Active Directory domain is stored. An application directory partition stores data in Active Directory that will only be replicated to a specific group of domain controllers.

- DNS forwarding is sued to resolve queries that cannot be resolved on the local DNS server.

- Once you have implemented and tested DNS, you need to monitor the performance of the DNS server. Tools you can use to do so include the System Monitor, Performance Logs and Alerts, the Event Viewer, the DNS debug log, and the Replication Monitor.

- Windows Internet Naming Service (WINS) resolves Windows NetBIOS names to IP addresses on a TCP/IP network.

- Name resolution methods used by WINS clients include the NetBIOS name cache, WINS server, broadcast, and LMHOSTS file. The NetBIOS name cache is always checked first. The order in which the other methods will be used depends on the NetBIOS node type of the client.

- WINS replication enables a WINS server to resolve NetBIOS names of computers that are registered with another WINS server.

- A push partner is a WINS server that sends replication data to its partner after a specific number of changes.

- A pull partner is a WINS server that requests to receive changes from its partner after a specific period of time has elapsed.

- There are two topologies that can be used when configuring WINS replication:
  - Enable all WINS servers on a network to replicate with each other by adding all servers as replication partners.
  - One WINS server acts as a central primary hub, while all other WINS servers connect to and replicate with the single central WINS servers.

- You use the WINS console to perform tasks required to optimize WINS, such as compacting the WINS database, checking entries in the WINS database for consistency, backing and restoring the database, and backing up the WINS Registry settings.

Key Terms

Active Directory-integrated zone
Application directory partition
Authoritative server
Caching-only DNS server
Complete zone transfer (AFXR)

DNS forwarding
DNS server
Domain
Domain directory partition
Domain Name System (DNS)

Forward lookup zone
Fully Qualified Domain Name
  (FQDN)
Host name
Incremental zone transfer (IFXR)

LMHOSTS
Master server
Namespace
NetBEUI
NetBIOS
Primary DNS server
Primary zone database file
Push partner
Pull partner
Resource record

Reverse lookup zone
Root domain
Root zone
Second-level domain
Secondary DNS server
Secondary zone database file
Standard primary zone
Standard secondary zone
Top-level domain
Stub zone

Windows Internet Naming Service
  (WINS)
WINS client
WINS replication
WINS server
Zone
Zone database file
Zone of authority
Zone transfer

Test Yourself

1. Which of the following services is used to resolve domain names to IP addresses?
  a. WINS
  b. NetBIOS
  c. NetBEUI
  d. DNS

2. Which of the following services is used to resolve NetBIOS names to IP addresses?
  a. NetBEUI
  b. WINS
  c. DNS
  d. TCP/IP

3. A distinct, contiguous segment of a DNS namespace is referred to as:
  a. A record.
  b. FQDN.
  c. Zone.
  d. Host.

4. In the FQDN *sales.company.com*, what is the term used to describe "com"?
  a. Top-level domain
  b. Sub-domain
  c. Zone
  d. Root domain

5. What type of DNS zone is used to resolve IP addresses to host names?
  a. Reverse lookup zone
  b. Forward lookup zone
  c. Root zone
  d. Transfer zone

6. Which of the following DNS zone types replicate critical records from a delegated child domain to a parent domain?
  a. Primary zone
  b. Stub zone
  c. Secondary zone
  d. Zone transfer

7. Which zone transfer method only transfers DNS records that have changed since the last update?
  a. Root zone transfer
  b. Complete zone transfer
  c. Stub zone transfer
  d. Incremental zone transfer

8. What DNS function is used to query other DNS servers when a local DNS server cannot resolve the host name?
  a. Zone resolution
  b. Zone transfer
  c. Zone forwarding
  d. Zone replication

9. What WINS functionality is used to ensure that all WINS databases are synchronized?
  a. Replication
  b. Push and Pull
  c. Host name transfer
  d. Zone transfer

10. What WINS optimization method ensures that expired records are removed from the database?
  a. Replication
  b. Consistency check
  c. Defragmentation
  d. Expiration

Projects: On Your Own

1. Make a flow chart diagram of a DNS structure for a company, including various sub-domains for the parent domain. Include a process flow of how your DNS zone transfers will occur.

2. Install the DNS service on a server.
   a. Log on as an **Administrator**.
   b. Click **Start**, select **Control Panel**, and then click **Add or Remove Programs**.
   c. Click the **Add/Remove Windows Components** button to open the **Windows Components Wizard**.
   d. Scroll down the **Components** list and double-click **Networking Services**.
   e. Select **Domain Name System (DNS)** on the **Subcomponents of Networking Services** list.
   f. Click **OK** to close the Networking Services dialog box.
   g. Click **Next** to open the **Configuring Components** screen where the setup utility configures the components.
   h. After the components are configured, the **Completing the Windows Components Wizard** screen opens. Click **Finish**.
   i. Close the Add or Remove Programs window.

3. Install the WINS service on your server.
   a. Click **Start**, select **Control Panel**, and click **Add or Remove Programs**.
   b. Click the **Add/Remove Windows Components** button to open the **Windows Components Wizard**.
   c. Scroll down the **Components** list and double-click **Networking Services**.
   d. Select the **Windows Internet Name Service (WINS)** check box to select the WINS service for installation, and then click **OK** to close the Networking Services dialog box.
   e. Click **Next** to open the **Configuring Components** screen where the setup utility configures the components.
   f. When the Wizard has finished configuring the WINS service, the **Completing the Windows Components Wizard** screen will open. Click **Finish** to close the Wizard.
   g. Close the Add or Remove Programs window.

Problem Solving Scenarios

You are the network administrator at the head office for the company *ourcompany.com*. The company has two smaller remote offices that require DNS and WINS servers installed. The remote offices connect to the head office via a slow 64K ISDN line. The remote offices will be part of your DNS structure as sub-domains (*sales* and *development*) of your parent domain, *ourcompany.com*. You must plan your DNS and WINS infrastructure to include these two sites, keeping in mind that bandwidth is limited for DNS zone transfers and WINS replication.

5

Planning and Implementing Security

As part of the planning and design process for a Microsoft Windows Server 2003 implementation, you must plan for the security of your infrastructure. A security framework needs to be created that will take into account the security risks to your environment, and the security requirements of your organization. You will need to plan for internal security as well, to ensure that certain sensitive data, such as employee and payroll information, can be accessed only by authorized users.

Part of your security framework will include creating a baseline for server security. This will be the default system policy that should be applied to all systems on your network. This security baseline will include items such as user account policies, file and directory permissions, auditing policies, and security parameters specific to certain server roles, such as domain controllers, or Web servers. The domain controller requires greater security considerations because it contains all the user account and security policies for your network, and therefore requires higher security than a typical member server such as a print server. Specific network services such as DNS and DHCP must also be secured to prevent tampering and interruption to these critical components of the network infrastructure.

Implementing security throughout your enterprise can be a daunting task, especially when different servers require different settings. Trying to implement and maintain security manually is an almost impossible task, especially for large environments. Windows Server 2003 allows you to use group security policies and security templates to ease the administrative burden so that you can make broad changes to your security settings by simply updating and deploying a small set of security policies.

Another critical aspect of network security is keeping it up to date, and monitoring your environment for attacks that can indicate weaknesses in your security infrastructure. You must create an audit policy that allows you to have detailed information on what is happening in your network. These logs must be checked regularly so that security issues can be quickly identified and resolved. As new security risks and threats arise, you must make sure that your operating system and application software are up-to-date with the latest security updates and patches. This ensures that any security issues within the software itself have been patched before malicious hackers can attempt to exploit them. Microsoft provides some excellent tools to help you keep your system up to date. The Microsoft Baseline Security Analyzer checks your system and compares it with the latest software service packs and updates, and reports which aspects of the system require updating. To efficiently retrieve and roll out these security updates, Microsoft also provides Software Update Services, which can be configured to automatically obtain these updates and roll them out to the servers and client computers on your network.

Goals

In this lesson, you will learn how to plan a security framework for a Windows Server 2003 infrastructure. By analyzing Windows Server 2003's default security settings, you will be able to design a security baseline for your environment, and create specific security requirements for each of your server roles. Utilizing Group Policy Objects and security templates, you will learn how to efficiently roll out this security policy to all systems in your enterprise. To protect critical network services, you will learn how to secure your DNS and DHCP services. Finally, you must maintain this secure infrastructure through monitoring, and updating security as required.

Lesson 5 — Planning and Implementing Security

Skill	Exam 70-293 Objective
1. Planning a Change and Configuration Management Framework for Security	Plan a framework for planning and implementing security. Plan for security monitoring. Plan a change and configuration management framework for security.
2. Planning Baseline Server Security	Plan a secure baseline installation. Plan a strategy to enforce system default security settings on new systems. Identify client operating system default security settings. Identify all server operating system default security settings. Identify the minimum configuration to satisfy security requirements.
3. Configuring Server Security	Configure security for servers that are assigned specific roles. Plan security for servers that are assigned specific roles. Roles might include domain controllers, Web servers, database servers, and mail servers. Deploy the security configuration for servers that are assigned specific roles. Create custom security templates based on server roles.
4. Planning for DNS Security	Plan for DNS security.
5. Securing a DHCP System	Basic knowledge
6. Planning for Security Monitoring	Plan a framework for planning and implementing security. Plan for security monitoring.
7. Maintaining a Secure Infrastructure	Plan a security update infrastructure. Tools might include Microsoft Baseline Security Analyzer and Microsoft Software Update Services.

Requirements

To complete this lesson, you will need administrative rights on a Windows Server 2003 computer.

skill 1

Planning a Change and Configuration Management Framework for Security

exam objective

Plan a framework for planning and implementing security. Plan for security monitoring. Plan a change and configuration management framework for security.

overview

When planning a Windows Server 2003 infrastructure, you should address security issues during the network design stage to ensure that your overall infrastructure is created with full security in mind. Your framework for network security includes the following areas:

◆ Identifying security risks.
◆ Defining site-specific security requirements.
◆ Planning and implementing security policies.

To fully understand the security risks facing your organization, create a team that includes members from all departments of the organization. Each department will have its own specific security requirements. For example, the HR department may require stringent measures to protect the company's accounting, financial, and personnel data from both external and internal risks. All departments need to identify the resources that need to be protected. The technical side of the security team, which typically consists of network administrators and other technical personnel, will identify risks from a technological and infrastructure perspective, such as the network and server architecture. Together, the security team should be able to identify all of the resources that need protection, which resources are most at risk, and what specific security features are required to protect them. The final results will be the outline for a security framework (**Figure 5-1**).

Security planning typically includes the following basic requirements (**Figure 5-2**):

◆ **Authentication:** Verifying the identity of users before they can access the network. At a basic level, this includes logins and passwords, but a more secure foundation includes encryption, digital certificates, and hardware tokens such as smart cards.
◆ **Authorization:** Once authenticated to the network, users must be authorized to use certain resources. For example, most company users would be restricted from accessing sensitive payroll information. A framework of security permission policies must be created and implemented.
◆ **Auditing:** Network administrators must continually monitor the network for security issues, by keeping and examining audit logs, and using real-time monitoring applications.

As part of maintaining your secure infrastructure, you must create a plan for a change and configuration management framework for security. Once your security infrastructure is implemented, you will face the task of keeping it current, from both external security threats and internal changes in your company's policies and physical network architecture. The security policies that you have planned, designed, and implemented must be regularly reviewed and changed as required to meet ongoing security needs. The changes to these overall policies must be efficiently filtered throughout the organization. In a very large organization, it would be next to impossible to keep all individual server and client systems up to date manually. Windows Server 2003 makes this task much easier with Group Policies, which are automatically communicated to domains, servers, and clients throughout the organization. Software patches and security updates can also be easily added to systems throughout the enterprise via automated tools such Microsoft Software Update Services. However, before deploying any type of security update or policy, the proposed change should be thoroughly tested in a lab environment to ensure that it will not negatively impact your organization's production environment, and that all applications and systems will continue to work properly after the change is applied. Your change and configuration management framework also should include the mechanism for how software updates and policy security changes are rolled out throughout the organization.

tip

Make sure that you include both external and internal security risks in your overall security framework.

Figure 5-1 Planning a security framework

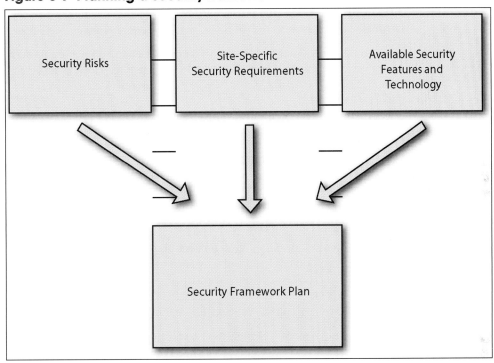

Figure 5-2 Basic security requirements

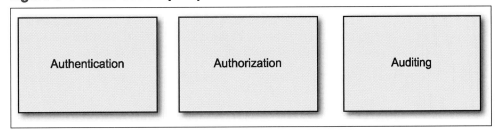

skill 2

Planning Baseline Server Security

exam objective

Plan a secure baseline installation. Plan a strategy to enforce system default security settings on new systems. Identify client operating system default security settings. Identify all server operating system default security settings. Identify the minimum configuration to satisfy security requirements.

overview

Windows Server 2003 installs with a very secure default security configuration, but the default settings may not be appropriate for your environment. Depending on the information resulting from your security planning framework, there may be certain security risks in your environment that are not covered by the default security policies.

You should create your own custom security baseline and deploy it to all servers in your enterprise. This ensures that the default security settings have been augmented to deal with your organizations security issues. You create a baseline security policy using a Group Policy Object (GPO).

During initial installation, a default security configuration is applied to your server or client system. Although Windows Server 2003 comes preconfigured with a very secure default installation, you may want to modify the default values to suit your particular security requirements. As part of your security baseline, you must be aware of the default security configuration and how it affects your overall security framework.

File system: The default file system settings applied when you format a drive with the NTFS file system include the following:

◆ The Administrators Group has full control over the entire drive.
◆ The Users group has Read and Execute permissions for the entire drive.
◆ Members of the Users group cannot modify or delete file or folders except in their own home directory.
◆ The Everyone group can execute, list, and read all files and directories.

For file shares, Windows Server 2003 creates only the basic administrative shares during installation. These hidden shares are named with a drive letter and a dollar sign (**$**), such as **\\server\C$**, and cannot be deleted or modified. When a new file share is created, the Everyone group receives Read permissions only (**Figure 5-3**).

Registry: The Windows system Registry, which contains critical configuration data for the operating system and applications, must be protected from manual modifications. If a user were to play around in the Registry, he or she may render the system unusable. The default Registry permissions allow full access to the Administrators group, while the Everyone group has only the Read permission for the HKEY_LOCAL_MACHINE and HKEY_USERS keys. It is unlikely that you would change these secure default settings.

Active Directory permissions: Active Directory has its own permissions that allow only certain users access to modify and manage objects in the database. The default permissions are as follows:

◆ Enterprise Admins: Full control over the entire forest.
◆ Domain Admins and Administrators: Full control over their domain, but no permissions in other domains.
◆ Authenticated Users: Read permission for the entire domain, plus the Modify permission to change their own account values such as their password.

Account policies: Several account policies (**Figure 5-4**) are enabled by default in Windows Server 2003, such as the following:

◆ Password policies: maximum and minimum age, minimum length, password histories, complexity requirements, and encrypted password storage.
◆ Account lockout policies: lockout threshold duration and logon restrictions.
◆ Kerberos policies: session ticket distribution parameters.

Figure 5-3 Default network share permissions

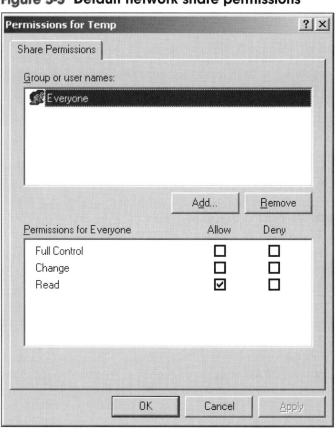

Figure 5-4 GPO Account Policies

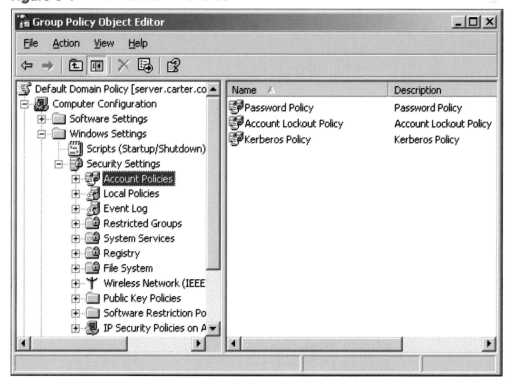

skill 2

Planning Baseline Server Security
(cont'd)

exam objective

Plan a secure baseline installation. Plan a strategy to enforce system default security settings on new systems. Identify client operating system default security settings. Identify all server operating system default security settings. Identify the minimum configuration to satisfy security requirements.

overview

Audit policies: Audit policies enabled by default in Windows Server 2003 include the following (**Figure 5-5**):

- System events
- Logon events
- Policy change
- Account logon events
- Account management
- Directory service access

The default audit setting is to audit successes only. For security purposes, it is recommended that you audit failures as well, to identify unauthorized attempts at hacking into user accounts.

Event log: The system event log requires policies that control its maximum size, permissions to access the log, and log data retention methods. You must balance the amount of information you want to collect with the size of the log and how many days of information you want to retain.

System services: You can control which system services are started at boot time, which ones can be started manually, and the services that should be disabled (**Figure 5-6**). Unneeded services should be disabled, to prevent unauthorized users from trying to hack open system ports on the server. All of these settings can be configured manually for each server, but it is much more efficient to configure these parameters as part of the GPO and apply it to a container of similar systems.

Security options: The **Security Options** container (**Figure 5-7**) consists of several security policies that can be applied to protect system services. These security settings refer to specific functions from a wide range of services, including the following:

- Allowing the system to be shut down without logging on.
- Digitally signing SMB client and server communications.
- Restricting access to CD-ROM and floppy drives.
- Remote access to the Registry.
- Backup and restore privileges.
- Specifying an alternate name for the guest account.
- Ability to disable the local administrator account.

how to

Create a new baseline GPO. (In this exercise, you will change one of the Security Options from the default settings.)

1. Click **Start**, point to **Administrative Tools**, and then click **Active Directory Users and Computers**.
2. Select your domain.
3. Click **Action** on the Menu bar and then click **Properties**.
4. The **Properties** dialog box opens. Click the **Group Policy** tab, and then click **New**.
5. Enter a name for the new policy, such as **MyBaseline**, and press **[Enter]** (**Figure 5-8**).
6. Click **Edit...** to start the **Group Policy Object Editor** console.
7. In the **Computer Configuration** container, select **Windows Settings**, **Security Settings**, and then the **Local Policies** container.
8. Click the **Security Options** container.
9. From the list of policies in the right-hand pane, select **Accounts: Rename Guest Account** (**Figure 5-9**). Select **Enable**, and enter a new name.
10. Click **OK** to exit.

Figure 5-5 GPO Audit Policies

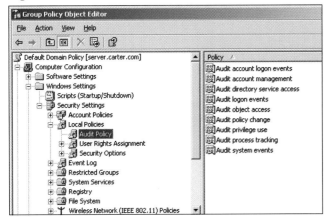

Figure 5-6 GPO System Services

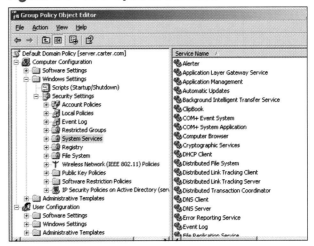

Figure 5-7 GPO Security Options

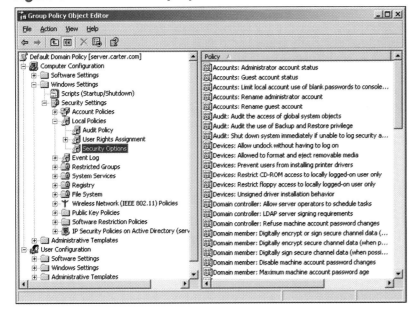

Figure 5-8 Creating your own baseline policy

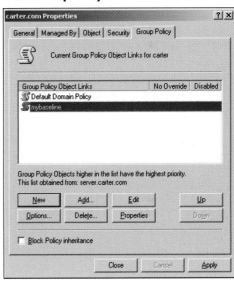

Figure 5-9 Security Options

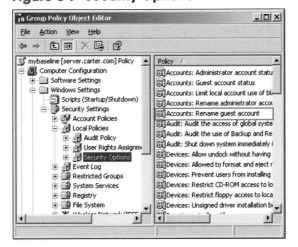

skill 3

Configuring Server Security

exam objective

Configure security for servers that are assigned specific roles. Plan security for servers that are assigned specific roles. Roles might include domain controllers, Web servers, database servers, and mail servers. Deploy the security configuration for servers that are assigned specific roles. Create custom security templates based on server roles.

overview

When you have configured general security baselines for your infrastructure, you must move on to the next security level by determining security requirements for various types of server roles. Domain controllers, in particular, require more stringent security measures than, for example, a network print server. Any servers running Internet Information Service (IIS) for HTTP or FTP purposes are especially vulnerable to attack because of the types of services they offer to external users. Depending on the type of server role, you must plan for the types of security risks and requirements that effect each server type.

Role-specific group policies: Windows Server 2003 allows you to assign role-specific GPOs that can be applied to several servers grouped into a similar role. The following describes the server roles and their specific security requirements.

tip
The default domain controller GPO enables many audit policies, but tracks only audit successes. You may want to modify the default configuration to record failures.

♦ **Domain controllers:** These servers provide the vital function of network authentication and authorization. It is especially important to fully secure these servers when using Active Directory, as it will contain all critical authentication and security policy information. Domain controllers should have all non-essential services disabled, and only network administrators should have any type of access, whether physical or through the network, to the system. The domain controller GPO **(Figure 5-10)** should be examined to see if the default settings need additional configuration or the addition of more detailed audit policies. Other access permissions such as Log on locally, shutting down the system, and the ability to add a workstation to the domain should also be reviewed to ensure that only the correct users and groups are allowed to perform these functions.

♦ **Network infrastructure services:** These types of servers include required network services such as DNS and DHCP. As a critical part of your infrastructure, these services must be locked down to prevent any type of tampering or attacks. DNS servers should be integrated with Active Directory to provide additional security, because the zone database itself will be part of the Active Directory database. If DNS is not integrated with Active Directory, the zone databases are stored in basic text files in the \%systemroot% \system32\DNS directory. Access permissions to this directory should be reviewed to ensure that only the administrative users can access these zone files. DHCP is used to automatically configure clients with network address information when they access the network. If this system is attacked, your clients will not be able to connect to the network to access its resources. You can authorize only certain clients to be able to obtain addresses from a DHCP server by adding their MAC address to a list of known clients.

♦ **File and print servers:** To protect user data files on file servers, you typically use NTFS permissions to control access. The default NTFS setting is that the Full Control permission is assigned to the Everyone group. This, of course, is inadequate for security purposes, and you must design a file and directory permission structure that will filter the directory tree to allow only certain users access to specific data. You can specify NTFS permissions in the GPO via the File System container in the Group Policy Object Editor console.

♦ **Application servers:** Application servers can include a variety of servers such as IIS, SQL, and other third-party applications used by the organization. It is difficult to create a general security policy to cover all of them, and each service must be analyzed individually to understand and implement its security requirements.

Figure 5-10 Domain Controller GPO

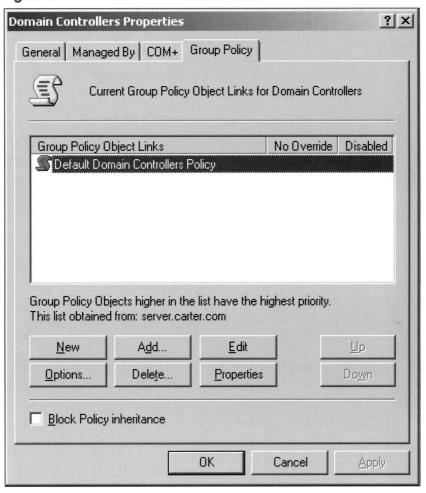

skill 3

Configuring Server Security *(cont'd)*

exam objective

Configure security for servers that are assigned specific roles. Plan security for servers that are assigned specific roles. Roles might include domain controllers, Web servers, database servers, and mail servers. Deploy the security configuration for servers that are assigned specific roles. Create custom security templates based on server roles.

overview

Security templates: Another way to apply security settings to multiple systems is through the use of security templates. **Security templates** are simple configuration text files and have a .inf extension. These files can be modified, saved, and deployed to multiple systems as required. Security templates can be associated with a particular Active Directory object, which becomes part of the object's GPO.

Security templates can be used to configure a variety of security policies, such as user account policies for password restrictions, permissions for system startup services, file system permissions, and local audit policies. There are a number of predefined default templates that can be used as is, or modified as required. The default templates include (**Figure 5-11**):

- ◆ **Compatws.inf:** Enables members of the Users group to run all applications, including non-Windows compliant applications, without giving them Power User capabilities.
- ◆ **DC Security.inf:** The default file system and Registry permissions for domain controllers.
- ◆ **Hisecdc.inf:** High security settings for domain controllers, requiring digital signatures and encrypted communications.
- ◆ **Hisecws.inf:** High security workstation settings. Removes all users from the Power Users group, and makes Domain Admins and the local Administrator account the only members of the local Administrator group.
- ◆ **Rootsec.inf:** Default permissions for the system drive.
- ◆ **Securews.inf:** Secures workstations with higher security restrictions than the default template, such as account and auditing policies.
- ◆ **Securedc.inf:** Secures domain controllers with higher security restrictions than the default template, such as stricter account policies and limitations on the anonymous users.
- ◆ **Setup Security.inf:** The default security template used when Windows Server 2003 is installed.

tip

You must first create the Security Templates console from the Microsoft Management Console (MMC) by running mmc.exe and then adding the Security Templates snap-in.

how to

Create the Security Templates console.

1. Log on as an **Administrator**.
2. Click ⟦*Start*⟧, and then click **Run**.
3. Enter **mmc** in the **Open** text box in the **Run** dialog box and then click ⟦ OK ⟧.
4. Click **File** on the menu bar, and then click **Add/Remove Snap-in**.
5. The **Add/Remove Snap-in** dialog box opens. Click ⟦ Add... ⟧, and then click **Security Templates**.
6. Click ⟦ Close ⟧, and then click ⟦ OK ⟧.
7. An entry for Security Templates will appear in the console window.
8. Click **File** on the Menu bar, and then click **Save As**. Enter **SecurityTemplates.msc** in the **File name** text box and click ⟦ Save ⟧.

Modify an existing template.

1. In the Security Templates console, expand the **Securews** template and then expand the **Account Policies** container (**Figure 5-12**).
2. Click **Password Policy (Figure 5-13)**.
3. Double-click **Maximum Password Age** and enter a new value, such as **15** days.
4. Click ⟦ OK ⟧.
5. Click **Action** on the Menu bar, select **Save As**, and save this template with a new name, such as **MaxPasswordAge.inf**.

Figure 5-11 Default Security Templates

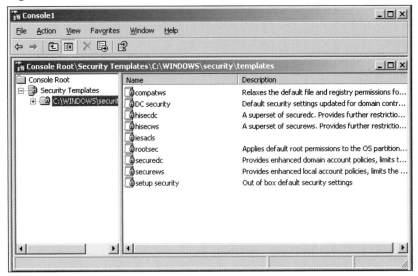

Figure 5-12 Securews Account Policies

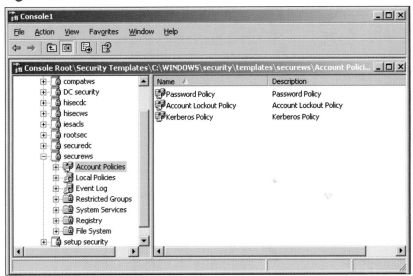

Figure 5-13 Maximum Password Age

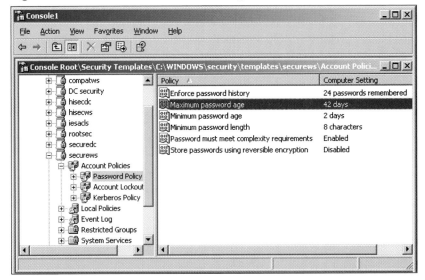

skill 4 *Planning for DNS Security*

exam objective

Plan for DNS security.

overview

Because DNS was designed to be an open protocol, DNS data can be vulnerable to security attacks. In Windows Server 2003, DNS provides the foundation for Active Directory and can provide a tremendous amount of information about your network infrastructure. For instance, "A" resource records contain information about the hosts on your network, NS resource records identify the DNS servers on the network, and SRV records provide information on computers providing Kerberos, LDAP, and global catalog services. If a hacker is able to initiate an unauthorized zone transfer, he or she will be able to learn a lot about your internal network structure (this is sometimes referred to as "footprinting"). If the hacker is able to change these resource records, he or she might be able to redirect e-mail to a different server than intended, or set up a fake Web server that masquerades as your own (sometimes referred to as a "redirection" attack).

Windows Server 2003 DNS provides some improved security features to decrease this vulnerability. To help prevent unauthorized zone transfers, configure the properties of the DNS server to restrict zone transfers only to specifically authorized servers (**Figure 5-14**). You can further secure your DNS data by encrypting any zone replication traffic that travels over a public network such as the Internet. Also consider using Active Directory replication to replicate zone data rather than a file-based zone transfer. Active Directory replication traffic is automatically encrypted and the domain controllers that perform replication are mutually authenticated, thereby reducing security risks.

Securing the cache against pollution is another method of protecting the integrity of resource records. This option (also known as **cache pollution protection**), which is enabled by default in Windows Server 2003, tells the DNS server to disregard DNS resource records that originate from DNS servers that are not authoritative for those resource records (**Figure 5-15**). While leaving cache pollution protection enabled can increase the number of DNS queries, this is a small price to pay in return for the enhanced security which this option provides.

The **Only secure dynamic updates** feature is another Windows Server 2003 feature available to enhance DNS security. Dynamic updates are a major advancement in how DNS records are handled in Windows Server 2003. In the original implementations of DNS, each record had to be created and when changes occurred, manually updated. With the implementation of Dynamic DNS (DDNS), clients can automatically update their records. Domain controllers can also take advantage of DDNS by automatically entering all of their SRV records as well. By configuring the DNS zone to allow dynamic updates, both the DHCP server and Windows clients can update their records in DNS automatically. However, with this type of zone configuration change comes a security vulnerability that could allow an attacker to add a rogue system's records to the DNS database. To protect against this type of attack, you must change your standard zone files to integrate with Active Directory. Standard forward and reverse lookup zones store their information in standard text files on the DNS servers. Active Directory-integrated zone information is stored as an object in Active Directory. By making this conversion, you will be able to use the Only secure dynamic updates feature (**Figure 5-16**). Secure dynamic update allows you to restrict DNS zone file updates to authenticated computers that are part of the same Active Directory domain as is the DNS server.

tip

By using Active Directory-integrated zones, you introduce fault tolerance into your zone data. Every domain controller hosts a writable copy of the zone, which is stored as an object in Active Directory.

Figure 5-14 Restricting zone transfers via DNS Zone Properties

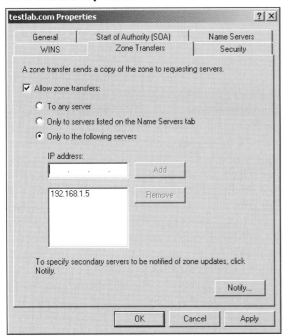

Figure 5-15 Securing the cache from data pollution

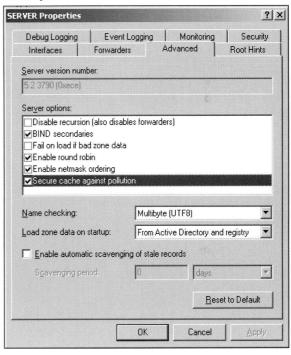

Figure 5-16 Enabling Secure Dynamic Updates

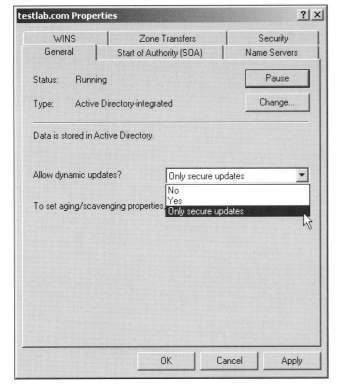

skill 4

Planning for DNS Security (cont'd)

exam objective

Plan for DNS security.

overview

Finally, another method to protect your internal network is to install two DNS servers: one for internal name resolution and the other for external name resolution. This is sometimes referred to as "split-brain" DNS (**Figure 5-17**). Split-brain DNS provides separate internal and external views of your network. The internal DNS servers send queries they cannot resolve to external DNS servers. The external DNS server provide name resolution for hosts such as Web servers, FTP servers, and any other IP addresses you want to make accessible to those on the outside. When users on the internal network need to resolve a Fully Qualified Domain Name (FQDN) to an IP address, they will query the internal DNS server, which will provide an IP address to them even if it has to query other DNS servers to obtain it. The external name server will answer external users that request name resolution. The external name server resolves names for only the Web servers, FTP servers, and any other IP addresses you want to make accessible. It does not have records of the internal systems on the private side of your network.

Figure 5-17 Split-Brain DNS

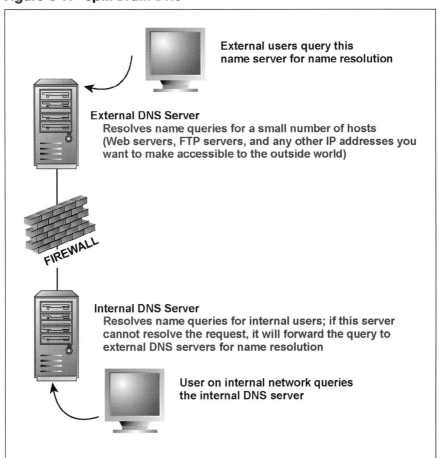

External users query this
name server for name resolution

External DNS Server
Resolves name queries for a small number of hosts
(Web servers, FTP servers, and any other IP addresses you
want to make accessible to the outside world)

FIREWALL

Internal DNS Server
Resolves name queries for internal users; if this server
cannot resolve the request, it will forward the query to
external DNS servers for name resolution

User on internal network queries
the internal DNS server

skill 5

Securing a DHCP System

exam objective

Basic knowledge

overview

Dynamic Host Configuration Protocol (DHCP) provides an excellent method of automating assignment of IP addresses to DHCP-enabled clients, but it can introduce a number of security risks that must be minimized.

Rogue DHCP servers are unauthorized servers on a network that are handing out IP addresses to DHCP-enabled clients. In Windows Server 2003, DHCP servers that are part of an Active Directory domain must be authorized before they can issue IP addresses to clients **(Figure 5-18)**. To determine if there is a rogue DHCP server on the network, use the **ipconfig /all** command to review the DHCP configuration information on a client. The DHCP server's IP address will be included in the output. You can also run a port scan of the network and look for all computers listening on port 67, which is the port used by DHCP. Compare the list with your list of known and valid DHCP servers.

A similar problem is that of unauthorized clients receiving automatic network configuration from a DHCP server. To prevent this from happening, you must reserve your IP addresses in your scope for only clients that match certain MAC addresses, which is the hardware address of their network card.

The Windows Server 2003 DHCP Server service can be configured to perform dynamic DNS updates and secure dynamic DNS updates for DHCP clients, which eliminates the need for administrators to update DNS records manually when a client's IP address changes. By itself, dynamic update is not secure; any client can modify DNS records. When **only secure updates** is configured on the DNS server, the authoritative name server accepts updates only from clients and servers that are authorized to make dynamic updates to the appropriate objects in Active Directory. As noted in Skill 4, secure dynamic update is available only on Active Directory–integrated zones. When using multiple DHCP servers and secure dynamic updates, add each of the DHCP servers as members of the **DnsUpdateProxy** global security group so that any DHCP server can perform a secure dynamic update for any record **(Figure 5-19)**. Otherwise, when a DHCP server performs a secure dynamic update for a record, that DHCP server is the only computer that can update the record.

tip

Only members of the Enterprise Admins group can authorize a DHCP server. This permission can be delegated to other groups/users.

tip

If DHCP will perform DNS dynamic updates, do not install it on a domain controller. Instead, install DHCP on a member server.

how to

Configure dynamic update for DHCP clients and servers.

1. Log on as an **Administrator**.
2. Open the **DHCP** console, then select and right-click the DHCP server you want to configure.
3. Click **Properties** to open the *<server_name>* **Properties** dialog box.
4. Click the **DNS** tab and select the **Enable DNS dynamic updates according to the settings below** check box.
5. Then select **Dynamically update DNS A and PTR records only if requested by the DHCP clients (Figure 5-20)**.
6. Close the Properties dialog box and the DHCP console window.

Figure 5-18 Authorizing a DHCP server in Active Directory

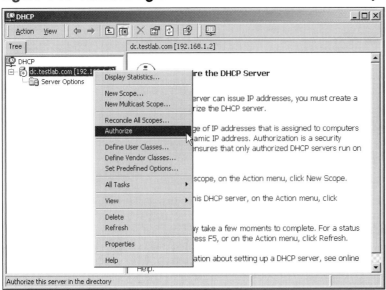

Figure 5-19 DnsUpdateProxy Global Security Group

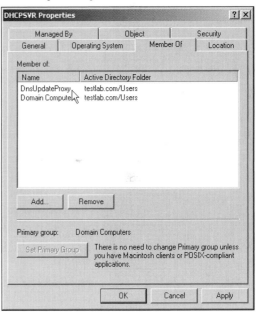

Figure 5-20 Configuring DHCP Dynamic DNS Updates

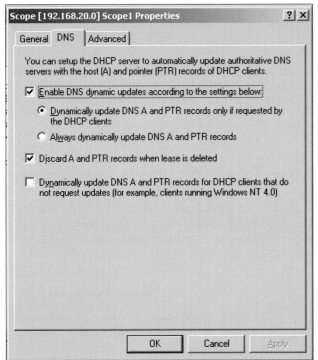

skill 6 | *Planning for Security Monitoring*

exam objective | Plan a framework for planning and implementing security. Plan for security monitoring.

overview

Once your security plan has been implemented, you must carefully monitor your systems to ensure that the security you have installed is working properly. Security monitoring includes monitoring both individual systems and the communications network that connects them for indications of a possible security breach.

For server systems, you must regularly check the system logs for unusual behavior, such as a large amount of failed logins for a particular account (especially the Administrator account), file and directory security permission violations, and unusual application usage. Poor performance of a server may be the result of a Denial of Service (DoS) attack. For example, a Web server that is suddenly very slow or completely unresponsive to Web page requests may actually be under attack.

For networks, you must carefully monitor the border router and firewall that provide your first line of defense against network attacks. You must routinely inspect the device logs for suspicious behavior or indications of an attack or security breach.

Security monitoring tools fall into two categories, passive and active. Passive security tools are those that can detect and log security issues, but do not take any active involvement in their resolution. Active security monitoring tools, such as advanced intrusion detection systems can detect the security breach and take automatic steps to close it, such as shutting TCP/IP ports under attack.

Passive tools, such as the various logs described below, are effective only when an administrator actually views those logs, or configures the security application to contact him or her by e-mail or pager if a critical event is detected. Even then, by the time the administrator is able to reach the affected system, the attacker may have already come and gone and damaged the system. Active monitoring tools are more effective at taking action during an attack rather than after it has happened.

The following are some Windows Server 2003 tools that can be used to monitor security:

Event Viewer: The Event Viewer can be used to review various log events. It provides the following logs (**Figure 5-21**):

◆ **System log:** Records information, warning and error messages related to system events that occur with respect to various services, such as the DHCP, DNS, and remote access services.

◆ **Application log:** Records information, warning and error messages generated by various applications used on the system.

◆ **Security log** (sometimes called the **security event log**): Enables an administrator to record various events, such as valid and invalid logon attempts, account management activities, object access attempts, privilege uses, etc. You can choose from a variety of events, and you can choose to audit the success and/or failure of these events. However, tracking all events will consume a lot of resources so you need to carefully decide what to audit or else your event logs will be become too large. Auditing the Registry is an important aspect of auditing because the Registry contains important system configurations. Noting any changes that take place in the Registry is crucial for maintaining the integrity, confidentiality, and availability of your systems. You can audit changes made to specific Registry keys. If someone manages to gain physical access to a domain controller or if there are many administrators in a corporation, it is highly recommended to implement Registry auditing as a security control to determine who made the modifications. Registry auditing is set up in the Registry Editor utility (regedt32.exe).

tip

The System and Application Logs can be viewed by anyone. Only systems administrators or users with the Manage Auditing and Security Log user right can view the Security Log.

tip

You can log to a CD-ROM to prevent logs from being deleted by a hacker.

Figure 5-21 Event Viewer logs

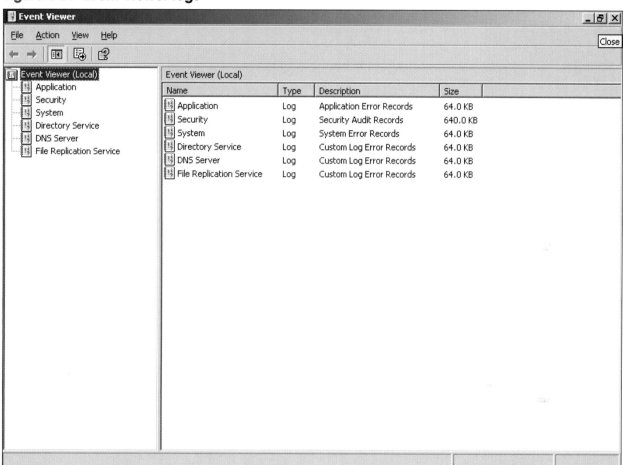

skill 6

Planning for Security Monitoring
(cont'd)

exam objective

Plan a framework for planning and implementing security. Plan for security monitoring.

overview

Note that creating an audit policy and recording events in the security log is just the beginning of the security monitoring process. It is also important that systems administrators actually review the log and follow up on any unusual events.

In addition, the logs themselves must also be secured. If they are not, a hacker might be able to delete logs to prevent any unauthorized activities from being detected. Log files can be found in the *%systemroot%\System32\CONFIG* directory. The best way to protect log files is to create an auditor group that has access to these files, and then remove access from all other groups. The people assigned to the auditor group will be responsible for maintaining the data within the logs.

Performance console: You can monitor the resources on your server by using the Performance console. Although the Performance console is typically used to track objects such as processors, memory, cache, threads, processes, and services running on a Windows Server 2003 computer, it can also be used to monitor selected security-related events. The information can be viewed in a variety of formats, such as a chart or report.

The Performance console consists of the System Monitor and the Performance Logs and Alerts tool. The **System Monitor** is used to view a graphical real-time representation of the performance of the resources on the system **(Figure 5-22)**. The **Performance Logs and Alerts** tool is used to record the performance of resources in counter logs and trace logs and to configure alerts, which are activated based on threshold values that you set, to perform specific actions. Alerts help administrators perform real-time security monitoring. For instance, instead of reviewing a security log at the end of each day and finding a security problem after the fact, an alert can be configured to warn about a potential security violation as it occurs.

Network Monitor: You can use to capture, display, and analyze statistics on network traffic using the Network Monitor tool **(Figure 5-23)**. Network Monitor is also useful for security, as you will be able to monitor network problems that may indicate attacks such a Denial of Service attack.

Because Network Monitor can disclose important data about your network, it is important to prevent its unauthorized use. To protect a network from unauthorized use of Network Monitor, make sure that you use its password protection features. Network Monitor can also detect other installations of Network Monitor on a network and provide the information about them, such as the name of the computer, user, adapter address, and whether the utility is running, capturing, or transmitting information. However, it cannot detect third-party monitoring and/or capturing (sometimes called "sniffing") software and/or equipment.

Figure 5-22 System Monitor

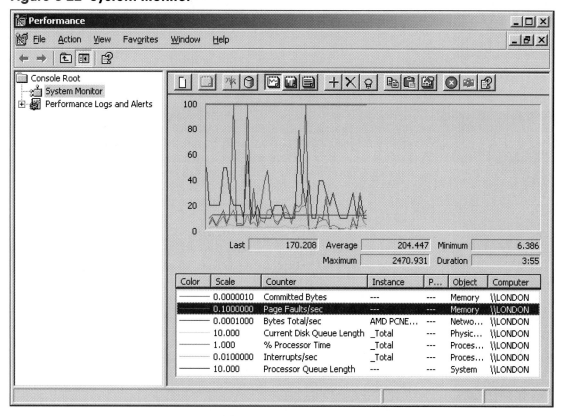

Figure 5-23 Viewing network statistics with Network Monitor

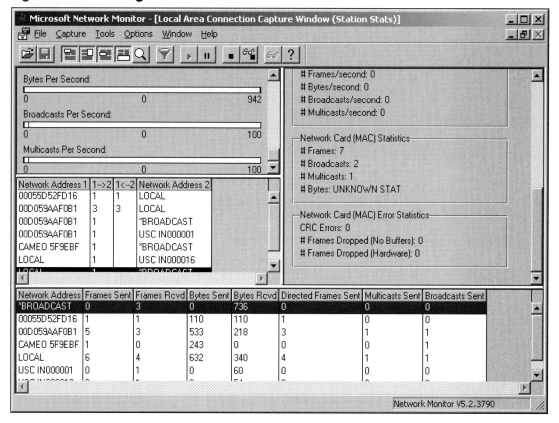

skill 7

Maintaining a Secure Infrastructure

exam objective

Plan a security update infrastructure. Tools might include Microsoft Baseline Security Analyzer and Microsoft Software Update Services.

overview

Security is an ongoing concern, and once you have all your planned security measures in place, you must ensure that it is constantly monitored and updated to be able to deal with new threats. Over time, attackers are able to discover weaknesses in existing operating systems and software applications. These weaknesses can be easily exploited once they become well known. Microsoft regularly releases patches and updates to deal with new security issues discovered in its software. But the existence of these updates will not protect your system until you actively obtain and install them.

To address these concerns, Microsoft provides the Microsoft Baseline Security Analyzer (MBSA), which you can use to examine your system for security weaknesses, and Software Update Services (SUS), which offers you an efficient and proactive way to keep your operating system and application software up to date.

You can use **Microsoft Baseline Security Analyzer (MBSA)** to check your Windows Server 2003 system to make sure that the way you have configured the operating system and supporting services such as IIS, SQL, and desktop applications do not raise any security issues **(Figure 5-24)**. MBSA can scan a single computer, or multiple computers (up to 10,000 computers at a time). MBSA generates a security report that lists each issue found and offers suggestions as to how to fix the problem, and saves it on the computer on which MBSA is running **(Figure 5-25)**. Specifically, MBSA examines security issues related to:

◆   **Operating system configuration**, such as
  •   whether the computer being scanned is a domain controller (if so, a higher level of security is required)
  •   whether the Guest account is enabled (possible vulnerability)
  •   whether NTFS, Windows' most secure file system, is being used (recommended)
  •   whether there are any shared folders and if so, listing them
  •   the types of passwords being used (blank, simple, and non-expiring passwords all present security issues)
  •   whether auditing is enabled (recommended as a useful tool for administrators)
  •   whether any unnecessary network services or protocols are enabled
  •   whether Auto Logon is enabled, and if the logon password is stored in plaintext (presents a security vulnerability)
  •   whether Automatic Updates is enabled (recommended) and if so, how it is configured
  •   whether Internet Connection Firewall is enabled (recommended)
  •   identifying and listing the individual user accounts that belong to the local Administrators group (membership in the Administrators group should be restricted to a limited number)

◆   **Internet Information Server**, such as
  •   whether IIS is being run on a domain controller (considered a high level of vulnerability)
  •   whether IIS logging is enabled, and whether the IIS Lockdown tool (which helps an administrator configure and secure IIS servers) is being used
  •   whether certain virtual directories that may raise potential security issues are present on the computer

◆   **Microsoft SQL Server**, such as
  •   the type of authentication mode being used on the SQL server (Windows Authentication mode recommended)
  •   whether SQL is running on a domain controller (not recommended)
  •   SA account password status
  •   SQL service account memberships

◆   **Security updates**, such as
  •   Whether the latest security packs and updates have been installed for a variety of Microsoft software products

tip

In a multi-domain environment, where a firewall or filtering router separates the two networks (two separate Active Directory domains), TCP ports 139 and 445 and UDP ports 137 and 138 must be open in order for MBSA to connect and authenticate to the remote network being scanned.

Figure 5-24 Microsoft Baseline Security Analyzer

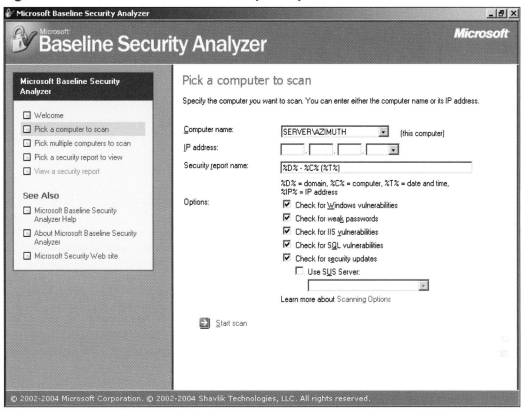

Figure 5-25 Microsoft Baseline Security Analyzer Report

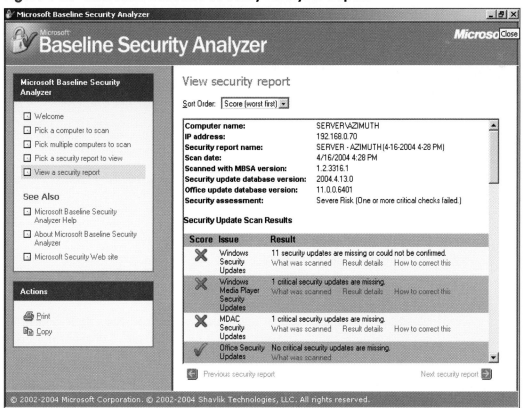

skill 7

Maintaining a Secure Infrastructure
(cont'd)

exam objective

Plan a security update infrastructure. Tools might include Microsoft Baseline Security Analyzer and Microsoft Software Update Services.

overview

◆   **Software Applications settings**, such as
   *   the settings being used for various Internet Explorer security zones on the local computer
   *   the macro protection settings for various Office applications

Microsoft Software Updates Services (SUS) gives you the ability to download, control, and deploy updates, service packs, and patches to the operating system and its components automatically, using an internal server **(Figure 5-26)**. SUS is designed to give administrators a high degree of control over the bandwidth used by Windows Update and the service packs and updates applied to client computers using the Automatic Updates service. By storing the content locally, clients can download their updates locally, rather than each client tying up WAN bandwidth retrieving each update from Microsoft. By allowing the administrator to approve each package before it is made available to the clients, Software Update Services gives the administrator the ability to approve only those updates that will not affect system stability or the stability of custom applications. Additionally, new Group Policy features included with Software Update Services allow the administrator to define the configuration of the Automatic Updates feature on client computers on as large or as small a scale as necessary.

Software Update Services consist of two components. The first component is a client-side service, known as the Automatic Updates service, which retrieves updates from a Software Update Services (SUS) server or the Internet and installs them. The Automatic Updates service is included with Windows Server 2003, and is available as a free download for the following operating systems:

◆   Windows 2000 Professional (SP2)
◆   Windows 2000 Server (SP2)
◆   Windows 2000 Advanced Server (SP2)
◆   Windows XP Home
◆   Windows XP Professional

Administrators have several options when configuring Automatic Updates, depending on the level of control he or she desires over the downloading and installation of updates. For instance:

◆   Updates can be downloaded automatically and the administrator notified when they are ready to be installed (the default setting, which requires that the administrator approve the update before it is installed),
◆   Updates can be automatically downloaded and installed on a schedule that the administrator specifies,
◆   The administrator can require that he or she be notified before an update starts downloading any updates (which allows for precise control over not only which updates are installed, but also which updates are downloaded).

The second component of Software Update Services is a server-side service that can be the central point for distributing updates to clients. While Software Updates Services do not require a SUS server, dedicating a server for this purpose can significantly reduce update bandwidth requirements.

Another tool similar to Software Update Services is **Systems Management Server (SMS)**. SMS provides a comprehensive solution for change and configuration management for the Microsoft platform, enabling organizations to provide relevant software and updates to users quickly and cost-effectively. Although SMS can be used to update systems and security patches, it goes beyond security and also offers application deployment, asset management, and advanced system and remote management capabilities.

Figure 5-26 Microsoft Software Updates Services

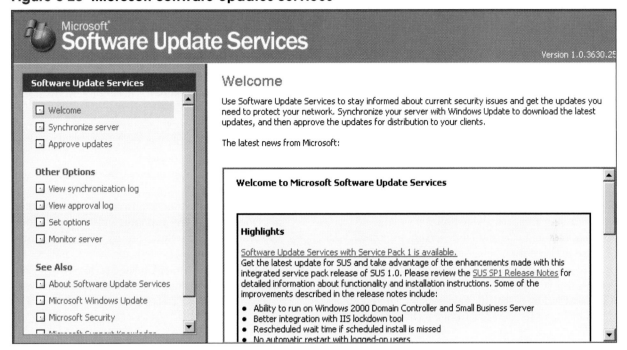

Summary

◆ Create a security framework by identifying risks, defining site-specific security requirements, and by planning and implementing security policies.

◆ Security planning must cover authentication, authorization, and auditing.

◆ Modify the default Windows Server 2003 security settings to create your own security baseline.

◆ Use Group Policy Objects to roll out your defined security policies to multiple systems.

◆ Use different security policies for specific server roles, such as domain controllers, infrastructure services such as DNS and DHCP, file and print servers, and application servers.

◆ Use security templates to apply security configuration settings to multiple systems.

◆ Security templates are text files with a .inf extension, and are associated with a particular Active Directory object.

◆ Threats to DNS infrastructure include footprinting, unauthorized zone transfers, and redirection attacks.

◆ Use internal and external DNS servers to protect your internal network from being seen by external clients.

◆ Ensure your network does not contain rogue DHCP servers that are handing out false IP address information.

◆ Use MAC address lists to prevent unauthorized clients from obtaining IP addresses from the DHCP server.

◆ When using multiple DHCP servers and secure dynamic updates, add each of the DHCP servers as members of the DnsUpdateProxy global security group.

◆ Monitor event logs regularly for security issues, especially the security log.

◆ Monitor networks, especially the border router and firewall for signs of attacks or security weaknesses.

◆ Active monitoring tools take steps to resolve a security issue without administrator intervention. Passive tools just monitor and send alerts to administrators.

◆ Use the System Monitor to check for performance issues related to security.

◆ The Performance Logs and Alerts tool in the Performance Console can send alerts to administrators when certain events occur.

◆ Network Monitor can analyze network traffic for security issues.

◆ Make sure that other unauthorized Network Monitors are not monitoring and/or capturing traffic on your network.

◆ Use Microsoft Baseline Security Analyzer (MBSA) to analyze your current systems for security issues.

◆ Use Microsoft Software Update Services (SUS) to ensure all security patches and updates have been applied.

Key Terms

Application log
Auditing
Authentication
Authorization
Cache pollution protection
Event Viewer

Microsoft Baseline Security Analyzer (MBSA)
Microsoft Software Update Services (SUS)
Network Monitor
Performance console
Performance Logs and Alerts

Rogue DHCP server
Security log
Security template
System log
System Management Server (SMS)
System Monitor

Test Yourself

1. What type of policy covers user password options such as minimum password length?
   a. Audit Policy
   b. Account Policy
   c. File System Policy
   d. Services Policy

2. What are the system services security policies typically used for?
   a. DNS and DHCP security
   b. Security policy service startup
   c. Enabling unneeded services
   d. Disabling unneeded services

3. Which of the following servers require stricter security policies?
   a. FTP server
   b. Remote access server
   c. Domain controller
   d. Print server

4. What should be enabled to ensure client updates of DNS tables are secure?
   a. Secondary zone server
   b. Active Directory replication
   c. Secure zone transfer
   d. Secure dynamic update

5. What should be used to prevent unauthorized clients from receiving information from a DHCP server?
   a. MAC address list
   b. Small DHCP scope

   c. Short lease duration
   d. Long lease duration

6. Which of the following Event Viewer logs would show file and directory auditing events?
   a. System log
   b. Security log
   c. Application log
   d. Audit log

7. Which of the following tools can be used to find out if there are any unused open TCP/IP ports on your server?
   a. Microsoft Update
   b. Microsoft Software Update Services
   c. Microsoft Baseline Security Analyzer
   d. Microsoft Service Pack

Projects: On Your Own

1. Examine your System, Security, and Application logs for security issues. What items should you be auditing to provide you with more information in the logs? List the minimum types of auditing that you require for your environment.

2. Examine your DNS and DHCP security structure and identify areas where security can be increased, such as

encryption, authorized zone transfers, secure dynamic updates, and Active Directory replication options.

3. Run the Microsoft Security Baseline Analyzer on your system to test its security settings and software patch levels.

Problem Solving Scenarios

1. Your company is rolling out a new HR and Accounting application service across the enterprise. Each company office will require its own server to act as the database and front end for the application. The data contains personal employee data and company financial information. Create a security framework to protect the applications and data from unauthorized use, both internal and external. List the security risks, and security requirements for this type of data. Create a security policy or template that can be applied to all servers for maximum security.

2. In an effort to increase corporate security for a growing company, you have been asked to create a full company-wide security framework for all networks, servers, and clients, with particular attention to account and audit policies. Management wants to ensure that user access is very restricted, and that file and directory access is carefully audited. Create a security policy that includes stronger account and audit policies than are provided by default. Create different types of policies to cover your different server roles, such as the domain controllers, file servers, and application servers.

Securing Remote and Wireless Access

As companies increasingly rely on non-traditional methods of corporate network access such as VPNs over public networks and wireless LANs, there is also an increased risk in security, because if these methods are not secured, it may be very easy for an unauthorized user to gain access to corporate network resources. Remote access methods that include direct dial-up to a corporate LAN, or a VPN created over a public network such as the Internet, need to be protected from unauthorized access. Without proper authentication, an unauthorized remote dial-in user can access a corporate LAN utilizing a simple modem and phone line. Similarly, when a VPN solution is used over the Internet, an unauthorized user may be able to access a corporate LAN if there are not adequate authentication and encryption security measures in place. Once authenticated, there must also be security policies that govern what the user can do with that connection. Additional security should be in place to ensure that the authenticated user has only certain access rights to the network.

Authentication and encryption methods for remote access include the use of Public Key Infrastructure (PKI) technologies and certificates, authentication services such as RADIUS, and encryption technologies such as IPSec to encrypt VPN communications.

Wireless LANs, in particular, must be planned with high security in mind. A wireless LAN does not have the same type of boundaries as a normal wired LAN. To gain access to a wired LAN, an unauthorized user must be plugged into the network in some way, either locally, or remotely via dial-up or VPN. A wireless LAN may even extend beyond the boundaries of the company's physical perimeter, allowing someone physically near the location to be able to access the wireless LAN with a laptop and wireless network adapter. As a result, wireless LANs must be secured with strict authentication and encryption methods.

Goals

In this lesson, you will learn how to plan the security for remote and wireless network access. You will learn how to identify and implement authentication and encryption for remote access using technologies such as PKI, certificates, and IPSec. You will also learn how to secure a wireless network from unauthorized access.

Lesson 6   Securing Remote and Wireless Access

Skill	Exam 70-293 Objective
1. Analyzing Security Requirements for Remote Access Users	Plan security for remote access users. Plan remote access policies.
2. Selecting Authentication Methods for Remote Access Users	Plan security for remote access users. Analyze protocol security requirements. Plan authentication methods for remote access clients.
3. Planning a Public Key Infrastructure	Configure Active Directory directory service for certificate publication. Plan a public key infrastructure (PKI) that uses Certificate Services. Identify the appropriate type of certificate authority to support certificate issuance requirements. Plan the enrollment and distribution of certificates. Plan for the use of smart cards for authentication.
4. Selecting a Virtual Private Network Solution	Implement secure access between private networks.
5. Implementing IPSec Policy	Implement secure access between private networks. Create and implement an IPSec policy. Configure network protocol security. Configure protocol security by using IPSec policies. Configure security for data transmission. Configure IPSec policy settings. Plan for network protocol security. Plan an IPSec policy for secure network communications. Plan security for data transmission. Secure data transmission by using IPSec. Configure protocol security in a heterogeneous client computer environment. Secure data transmission between client computers to meet security requirements.
6. Planning Security for Wireless Networks	Plan secure network administration methods. Plan security for wireless networks.

Requirements

To complete this lesson, you will need administrative rights on a Windows Server 2003 computer and a Windows XP client computer.

skill 1

Analyzing Security Requirements for Remote Access Users

exam objective

Plan security for remote access users. Plan remote access policies.

overview

With the additional requirements for remote connectivity to corporate network resources, administrators must consider the following basic security requirements: the need to validate users, authorize their access to resources, protect user data in transit from being viewed or manipulated, and audit and log their access.

Through the implementation of **Routing and Remote Access Services (RRAS)**, Windows Server 2003 supports dial-up and VPN access methods for remote users. Whether you implement dial-up or virtual private networks as your remote access solution, you must consider the risks introduced into your network. The risks that must be addressed fall into three main categories:

◆ Authentication of remote users
◆ Authorization of remote users
◆ Protection of data while in transit between the remote user and the remote access server

Authentication of remote users: Authentication is the process of verifying the credentials used during the connection attempt. If a weak authentication method is used, malicious hackers can obtain user names and passwords to penetrate the corporate network. Windows Server 2003 uses authentication protocols to send a user's credentials safely to the remote access server when a connection is attempted.

Authorization of remote users: After a user has been authenticated, he or she must still be authorized. Authorization is the process of verifying that the connection attempt is allowed. This is accomplished by checking the user's dial-in properties **(Figure 6-1)** as well as matching the connection to a remote access policy. **Remote access policies** can be used to restrict access to certain users, groups, times, or specific client configurations. Remote access policies are discussed further below. RRAS also offers additional security by providing caller ID and callback features. The caller ID specifies a number the remote user must call in from. If he or she does not call in from that number, the connection is refused. The callback feature can also be used to secure the remote connection by disconnecting the user and then calling the user back at a predefined number. This occurs after the authentication and authorization of the connection attempt has been made.

Protection of data while in transit: Information that is transmitted between the corporate network and a remote user may contain sensitive data. If malicious hackers capture the information in transit by using a "sniffer program," they could possibly view confidential information, modify it or even, in some cases, corrupt the information. Where data confidentiality is critical, the remote access server can be configured to require encryption. Once configured, it will deny any attempts to connect that are not encrypted.

Remote access policies: When the number of remote access servers increases, you must consider how to incorporate remote access policies distributed across multiple servers. Remote access policies are used to control what connection attempts will be rejected or accepted by the RRAS server. You create them to determine which users can access the network and to prevent unauthorized access. A remote access policy consists of a set of rules and conditions that must be met by a connection before a user can gain access. The criteria, which can include parameters such as the time, groups, and connection type, are evaluated one by one when a user connects to the RRAS server. Remote access policies are either stored locally on the RRAS server or they can be stored and managed using RADIUS. They are not stored in Active Directory. There are actually three components of a remote access policy: conditions, permissions, and a profile.

A **condition** is a set of criteria that the user must match in order for the policy to apply to them. Conditions include specifications such as time of day, day of the week, number dialed, and Windows group membership **(Figure 6-2)**. If the user does not match all of the conditions

Figure 6-1 Protecting remote access connections

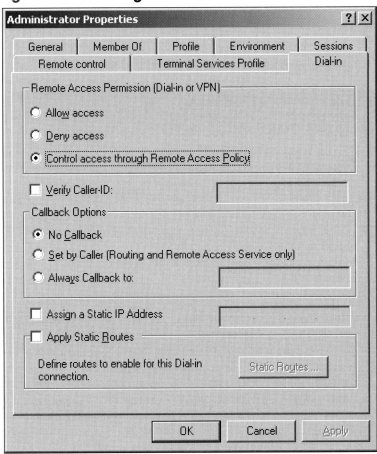

Figure 6-2 The Select Attribute dialog box

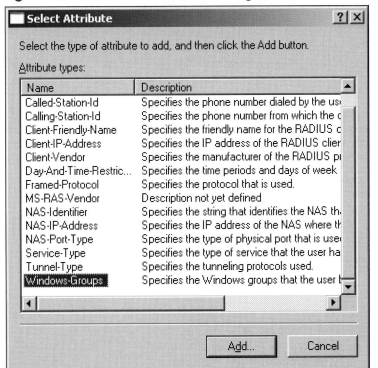

skill 1

Analyzing Security Requirements for Remote Access Users (cont'd)

exam objective

Plan security for remote access users. Plan remote access policies.

overview

in a given policy, then a match is attempted against the next policy. If the user doesn't match any policies, they are disconnected.

When a user matches all of the conditions in a given policy, the **Remote Access Permissions** section of the user account is consulted. Remote access permissions are located on the Dial-in tab in the user account Properties dialog box. There are three settings: Allow access, Deny access, and Control access through Remote Access Policy (**Figure 6-3**). If the user account permission is set to Deny access, the call is disconnected. If it is set to Allow access, the permissions section in the remote access policy is skipped, and the remote access profile is applied. If the user account dial-in permission is set to Control access through Remote Access Policy, the permissions configured in the remote access policy are checked. If it is set to Grant remote access permission, the profile is applied. If it is set to Deny remote access permission, the caller is disconnected.

Regardless of whether the caller is allowed to connect through the user account permissions or through remote access policy permissions, the last thing to apply is the profile. The **remote access profile** is a list of settings that are offered to the client. These settings include allowed dial-in days and times, connection limits, allowed dial-in media and phone numbers, authentication settings, encryption settings, and so forth. The settings in the profile are offered to the client, and if the client cannot support the offered settings, the client is disconnected. For example, if the profile offers EAP as the only authentication method and the client does not support EAP, the client will be disconnected. You configure a remote access profile in the Edit Dial-in Profile dialog box, which contains the following tabs:

◆ **Dial-in Constraints:** This tab is used to specify the dial-in number and the type of media to be used for connection. For example, you can specify that a dial-in connection can use only a modem to connect to the RRAS server. You can also set day and time restrictions for connections and the idle time period that will be permitted. When the maximum idle time has been reached, the user will be disconnected (**Figure 6-4**).

◆ **IP:** This tab is used to set the IP properties for a connection. You can specify the method a client will use to obtain an IP address. For example, you can specify either that the RRAS server must provide the IP address or that a client can request a specific IP address. You can also enhance security by defining IP packet filters. Using IP packet filters, you can control which TCP and UDP ports a client can use, the allowed upper-layer protocols, and the remote IP addresses with which they may communicate. There are two kinds of IP packet filters: input and output (**Figure 6-5**). You use input filters to filter packets sent to your server and output filters to control packets your server sends to the RAS client. Input filters are more commonly used for the RRAS server in order to control the types of connections users can establish (**Figure 6-6**).

Figure 6-3 **The Dial-in tab in the Properties dialog box for a user**

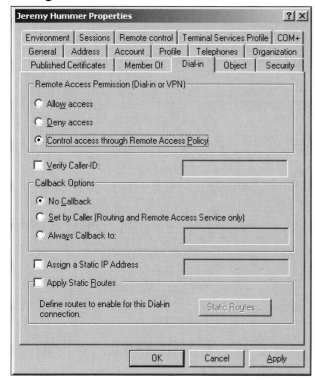

Figure 6-4 **The Dial-in Constraints tab on the Edit Dial-in Profile dialog box**

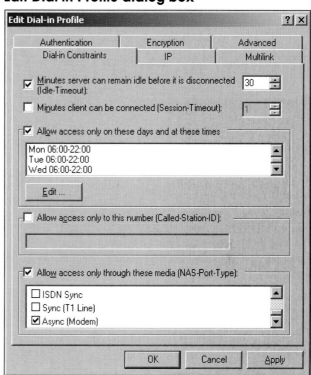

Figure 6-5 **The Inbound Filters dialog box**

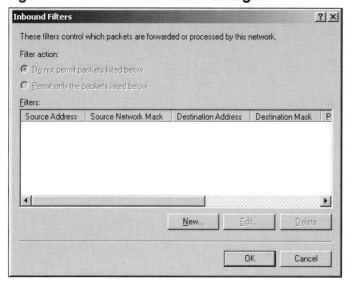

Figure 6-6 **The Add IP Filter dialog box**

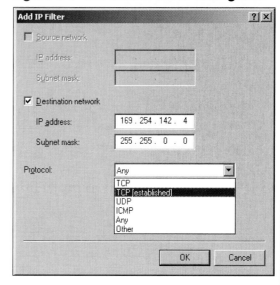

skill 1

Analyzing Security Requirements for Remote Access Users (cont'd)

exam objective

Plan security for remote access users. Plan remote access policies.

overview

◆ **Multilink:** This tab is used to configure the RRAS server to handle multilink calls and to specify the number of ports that a single remote client may use at one time. You can also specify Bandwidth Allocation Protocol (BAP) settings. BAP settings are used to specify the actions to be taken if the bandwidth usage by remote clients drops below a set threshold. For example, you can drop a multilink line if the client no longer needs the increased bandwidth so that you use only as much bandwidth as is required for the current network traffic **(Figure 6-7)**.

◆ **Authentication:** This tab is used to set the authentication protocols that can be used, such as PAP, SPAP, CHAP, MS-CHAP, MS-CHAP v2, and EAP (discussed further in Skill 2). If multiple protocols are selected, they will all be attempted in order from most secure (the top of the list) to least secure (the bottom of the list) until a match is found. If no match is found, the caller will be disconnected.

◆ **Encryption:** This tab is used to specify the type of encryption for your remote access clients: no encryption, basic, strong, or strongest. Like authentication, if multiple levels of encryption are selected, they will all be tried in order, from most secure to least secure, until a match is found.

   • **No encryption** allows clients to connect without using data encryption.
   • **Basic** allows clients to connect using 40-bit encryption key **MPPE (Microsoft Point-to-Point Encryption)** for dial-up or PPTP connections, or 56-bit DES encryption for L2TP/IPSec connections. MPPE, which is included in Windows operating systems, is a point-to-point encryption technique that uses encryption keys between 40 and 128 bits.
   • **Strong** allows clients to connect using 56-bit encryption key MPPE for dial-up or PPTP connections or 56 bit DES for L2TP/IPSec connections.
   • **Strongest** allows clients to connect using 128-bit encryption key MPPE for dial-up or PPTP connections, or Triple DES (3DES), which uses three 56-bit keys, for L2TP/IPSec connections.

◆ **Advanced:** This tab is used to configure connection attributes such as RADIUS (Remote Authentication Dial In Service), frame types, AppleTalk zones, special filters, Ascend attributes, and many more. In order to use IPSec encryption, you have to configure IPSec as a TCP/IP property of the RRAS server in the Network and Dial-up Connections window. In order to use MPPE, the client must have MS-CHAP, MS-CHAP v2, or EAP authentication support.

tip

RADIUS is described in RFC 3579.

Figure 6-7 The Multilink tab

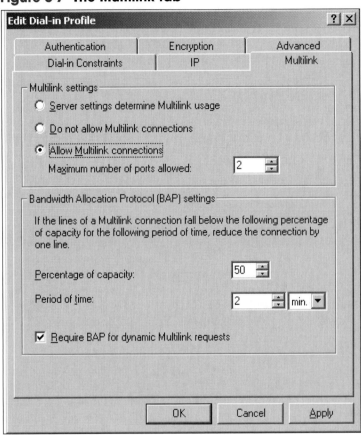

skill 2

Selecting Authentication Methods for Remote Access Users

exam objective

Plan security for remote access users. Analyze protocol security requirements. Plan authentication methods for remote access clients.

overview

Remote clients connect to the private network by connecting to a network access server. This server can be configured as a router to perform the role of a gateway that provides users with access to their company's private network. It can also be configured to provide users with access only to resources on the network access server itself.

Users typically access the server via a dial-up connection or a VPN. This functionality is implemented on the server using RRAS.

In each of these access methods, authentication protocols can be implemented to validate the user and encryption protocols to protect data while in transit (**Table 6-1**).

◆ **Password Authentication Protocol (PAP):** PAP is the least secure authentication protocol used with Point-to-Point Protocol (PPP) connections. It uses plain text passwords for authentication. However, PAP is used when a more secure authentication method cannot be used, and this protocol may be necessary for creating dial-up connections with non-Windows networks that do not encrypt passwords. Finally, you may choose to use PAP when attempting to troubleshoot connection problems, as PAP is the most compatible of all authentication protocols.

◆ **Shiva Password Authentication Protocol (SPAP):** SPAP is an authentication protocol that is used if you are connecting to a Shiva server. This protocol is more secure than PAP but less secure than CHAP or MS-CHAP. Data encryption is not supported with SPAP.

◆ **Challenge Handshake Authentication Protocol (CHAP):** CHAP is a protocol that provides authentication on the basis of a one-way hash created by seeding the Message Digest 5 (MD5) encryption algorithm with the password. Essentially, the user sends his or her user name to the RAS server in plain text form, but does not send the password. The server then creates a challenge message and sends this challenge to the client. The client computer then uses the MD-5 algorithm, seeded with the user's password, to encrypt the challenge. When the client sends this challenge to the server, it will compare the client's hash to the hash it expected to receive (based on the password it has listed for the client). If the values match, the client is allowed to connect, and if not, the client is disconnected. It is important to note that for CHAP to function properly, the password that CHAP uses must be in plain text. In Windows Server 2003, this requires that you store domain passwords in a reversibly encrypted format. This means that the password's encryption can be quickly and easily reversed, which is a major security consideration. For this reason, the use of CHAP is not generally recommended.

◆ **Microsoft CHAP (MS-CHAP):** MS-CHAP is Microsoft's version of CHAP. The challenge message is specifically designed for Windows operating systems and one-way encryption is used. MS-CHAP is used with Windows 9.x and Windows NT and only the client is authenticated. In the extended version, MS-CHAP2, both the client and the server are authenticated. Windows 9.x clients can now be modernized so that they are compatible with MS-CHAP2 by downloading the patch for Dial-up networking that upgrades it to version 1.3. MS-CHAP2 also uses different encryption keys for transmitting and receiving data. MS-CHAP v1 CPW and MS-CHAP v2 CPW are updated versions of these protocols in which the user can change an expired password. Both versions of MS-CHAP support data encryption using the MPPE algorithm, but only MS-CHAP 2 supports mutual authentication.

tip

Authentication itself does not guarantee you will be connected. You must also be authorized via your dial-up user properties and/or remote access policies as well.

tip

CHAP is described in RFC 1994, updated by RFC 2484.

tip

MS-CHAP is described in RFC 2433. MS-CHAP2 is described in RFC 2759.

Table 6-1   Authentication Protocols

Name	Description
PAP	The least secure of all authentication protocols because it sends all information in a clear text format. PAP has no provision for authenticating the client and the server to each other. Therefore, PAP is used only when minimal security is required.
SPAP	Provides more security than the PAP protocol. SPAP is an authentication protocol that is used if you are connecting to servers manufactured by Shiva.
CHAP	Considered a more secure protocol than PAP or SPAP. Used by Unix-based and other non-Microsoft clients to communicate with a RRAS server. CHAP provides authentication on the basis of a value that is calculated using an algorithm. When the client dials in, CHAP sends a challenge message to the client when the client dials in. The client applies an algorithm to the message to calculate a hash value (a fixed-length number), and sends the value to the server. The server also calculates a value and compares this value to the value sent by the client. If the value matches, the connection is established and the user can access shared resources on the server.
MS-CHAP	Microsoft's version of CHAP. There are two versions: MS-CHAP version 1 and MS-CHAP version 2. MS-CHAP version 1, also known commonly as MS-CHAP, supports only a one-way authentication process. MS-CHAP version 2 supports a two-way authentication process known as mutual authentication.
EAP	An extension to the Point-to-Point Protocol (PPP). EAP provides support for authentication mechanisms such as smart cards, token cards, and certificates to validate remote access server connections. Using EAP, a RAS client and a RAS server negotiate and agree upon an authentication method that both of them support. For example, when a RAS client uses a generic token card, the RAS server separately sends queries to the remote access client to obtain information about the user. As each query is asked and answered, the remote access client passes through another level of authentication. After all questions have been answered, the RAS client is authenticated.

skill 2

Selecting Authentication Methods for Remote Access Users (cont'd)

exam objective

Plan security for remote access users. Analyze protocol security requirements. Plan authentication methods for remote access clients.

overview

tip

EAP is described in RFC 2284, updated by RFC 2484.

◆ **Extensible Authentication Protocol (EAP):** EAP is the strongest authentication protocol available, but in Windows Server 2003, it is used only when using smart cards. EAP supports encryption and mutual authentication and can be used to customize your method of remote access authentication for PPP connections. It supports authentication using either TLS (Transport Layer Security) or MD5-CHAP. TLS supports smart cards and certificates. It is composed of two layers: the TLS Record protocol, which uses symmetric data encryption to ensure that connections are private, and the TLS Handshake protocol, which negotiates an encryption algorithm and cryptographic key before the application protocol can transmit or receive any data. EAP MD5-CHAP uses the same challenge handshake protocol as CHAP, but the challenge and response messages are sent as EAP messages.

how to

Configure authentication protocol settings on a Windows Server 2003 remote access server.

1. Open the **Routing and Remote Access** console, right-click the server name, and click **Properties**.
2. Click the **Security** tab and then click **Authentication Methods**.
3. Check the authentication methods you want to use as shown in **Figure 6-8**.

Configure authentication protocol settings on a Windows XP remote access client.

1. Right-click the dial-up connection and then click **Properties**.
2. Click the **Security** tab and then click the **Advanced (custom settings)** option button.
3. Click Settings... . The **Authentication – Type** dialog box opens (**Figure 6-9**). Here, you can configure or modify the existing authentication protocol settings.

Figure 6-8 Selecting the Authentication Protocols-Server

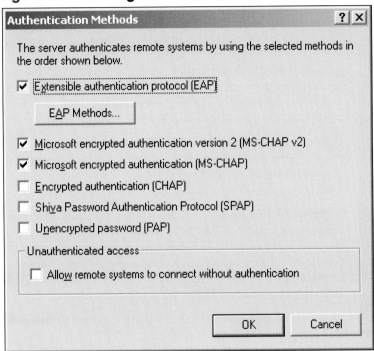

Figure 6-9 Selecting the Authentication Protocols-Client

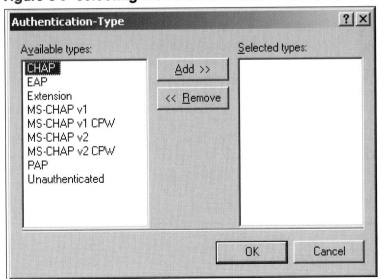

skill 3

Planning a Public Key Infrastructure

exam objective

Configure Active Directory service for certificate publication. Plan a public key infrastructure (PKI) that uses Certificate Services. Identify the appropriate type of certificate authority to support certificate issuance requirements. Plan the enrollment and distribution of certificates. Plan for the use of smart cards for authentication.

overview

A **Public Key Infrastructure (PKI)** is a combination of protocols, standards, and technologies that provide both authentication and encryption services for networks using public key cryptography. The components of PKI include public/private keys, digital certificates, and Certification Authorities.

Public key cryptography uses a pair of mathematically related keys: one public, and one private. When one of these keys is used to encrypt a message, the other key can be used to decrypt it (**Figure 6-10**). The public key is widely disseminated, while the private key is issued to only an authorized user and must be kept secure.

A **digital certificate** is a digitally signed document that verifies the identity of a user, computer, or service. A **Certification Authority (CA)** signs the certificate to confirm that the private key linked to the public key in the certificate is owned by the subject named in the certificate (**Figure 6-11**). The CA is responsible for authenticating the public keys and certificate information. The CA acts as the center of trust, and if the CA is considered trusted, all certificates issued by the CA are automatically trusted.

There are two types of CAs: **Enterprise CAs** and **Standalone CAs**. **Table 6-2** provides characteristics of each type.

Both Standalone and Enterprise CAs self-sign their own digital certificates. Unlike Standalone CAs, an Enterprise CA requires that Active Directory be implemented on the network. You can use Enterprise CAs to take advantage of several features that Active Directory provides, such as smart card authentication and predefined certificate templates. An Enterprise CA uses information in Active Directory to automatically identify the requester of a certificate. Enterprise CAs use Group Policy to enter their certificates in the trusted root store of all users/computers in the domain.

For each category, a Root CA or Subordinate CA is implemented. A **Root CA** signs its own certificate during the installation process and is considered the point of trust for a PKI hierarchy. A Root CA can issue certificates to computers and users but is designed to issue certificates only to other CAs, known as Subordinate CAs. **Subordinate CAs** issue certificates to users and computers.

tip

Standalone CAs may or may not be members of the domain. A Standalone CA does not require Active Directory to function, but will use it, if it is present, to publish certificates and certificate revocation lists.

Figure 6-10 Public key cryptography

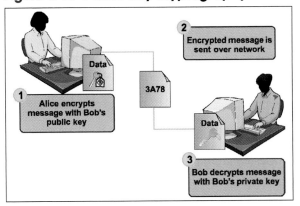

Figure 6-11 Creating a certificate

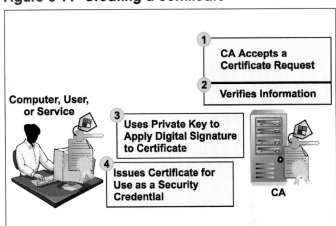

Table 6-2 Standalone versus Enterprise Certification Authorities	
Standalone Certification Authority	**Enterprise Certification Authority**
Can be removed from the network and placed in a secure physical location.	Cannot be removed from the network due to its dependency upon Active Directory.
When a small number of certificates are required, the manual approval process required is manageable.	Provides for auto-enrollment and approval of certificate requests by using information stored in Active Directory. No manual intervention is required.
Clients cannot take advantage of Active Directory.	Clients can take advantage of integration with Active Directory.
Certificate enrollment is only accessible via the Microsoft Certificate Services Web Enrollment Support pages.	Certificate enrollment can be handled via the Web Enrollment Support pages or using the Certificates Support snap-in via a Microsoft Management Console (MMC).
Users must manually enter information to identify themselves when requesting a certificate.	User's information is automatically retrieved from Active Directory and entered, regardless of method used to enroll.
Certificates are manually approved or denied.	Certificates are approved manually, or automatically through Active Directory.
Can be installed on a domain controller, member server, or standalone server. (Note: Microsoft recommends not installing a CA on a domain controller due to security reasons).	Can be installed on a domain controller or member server. Since it is registered as a resource in the forest, it must not be installed on a standalone server.

skill 3

Planning a Public Key Infrastructure
(cont'd)

exam objective

Configure Active Directory service for certificate publication. Plan a public key infrastructure (PKI) that uses Certificate Services. Identify the appropriate type of certificate authority to support certificate issuance requirements. Plan the enrollment and distribution of certificates. Plan for the use of smart cards for authentication.

overview

By installing Certificate Services on a Windows Server 2003 computer, you can configure your own Certification Authority. In addition to issuing certificates, CAs also manage the certificates to maintain the integrity of the PKI. Some networks will have only one CA, while others will have multiple CAs configured in what is known as a certification hierarchy. Certificate Services are managed by using the Certification Authority tool that can be added into a Microsoft Management Console or accessed via the Start-Programs-Administrative Tools menus.

Certificates are obtained by using the Microsoft Certificate Services Web Enrollment Support pages or by using the Certification Request Wizard. Although Enterprise CAs offer both options, a Standalone CA allows certificate enrollment only by using Web Enrollment Support pages.

how to

Install an Enterprise Root CA.

1. Click **Start**, point to **Control Panel**, and click **Add or Remove Programs**.
2. Click **Add/Remove Windows Components** and then select the **Certificate Services** check box. Click in the message box that informs you that you will not be able to change the computer name or domain membership.
3. Click **Next >** on the **Windows Components** screen.
4. For the CA type, select **Enterprise root CA (Figure 6-12)** and then click **Next >**.
5. Type **Enterprise root** in the **Common name for this CA** text box and then click **Next >**.
6. Leave the default locations for the certificate database, database log, and configuration information and click **Next >**.
7. Click **Yes** when you receive the message indicating that Certificate Services must temporarily stop Internet Information Services.
8. Click **Finish** to close the Windows Component Wizard.
9. Select **Start**, point to **Administrative Tools**, and click **Certification Authority** to confirm the installation. You should see a green check mark next to the CA's name as shown in **Figure 6-13**.

Figure 6-12 Configuring an Enterprise root CA

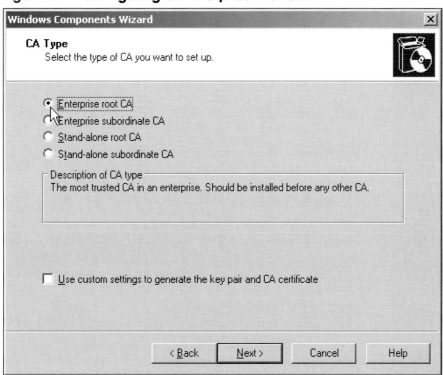

Figure 6-13 Confirming Certificate Services is running

skill 4

Selecting a Virtual Private Network Solution

exam objective

Implement secure access between private networks.

overview

A **virtual private network (VPN)** allows remote access users to connect to their corporate network over a public network infrastructure, such as the Internet. Typically, a remote user will create a connection to the Internet via common methods such as dial-up, cable, or DSL access. Once connected, they can activate the VPN, which creates a secure tunnel between the remote user and their destination network across the Internet. Access is secured by restricting communications to clients who can be authenticated via account credentials, IP address information, and encryption.

VPNs can also be used to connect two remote offices securely over the Internet. Previously it was more common to use dedicated WAN links between remote offices, but with the growth of the Internet, it is more cost effective to simply secure a transmission over the existing public network rather than install dedicated lines.

Tunneling and encryption protocols are used to establish the VPN's secure channel through the Internet to the destination LAN (**Figure 6-14**). The VPN connection is secure because the remote access server enforces authentication and encryption protocols. Any network packets that are intercepted on the public network are indecipherable without the corresponding encryption keys.

A VPN encapsulates, authorizes, and routes data by creating tunnels. A tunnel is a secure, logical link that is established between a remote user and a private network. Data is encapsulated by surrounding it with a new header. The additional header provides routing information so that the data packets can reach the destination. The encapsulated packets are communicated across the tunnel to the VPN endpoint, and then de-encapsulated.

The protocols used to secure VPN communications are usually either Point-to-Point Tunneling Protocol (PPTP) or Layer Two Tunneling Protocol (L2TP) with IPSec (**Table 6-3**).

Point-to-Point Tunneling Protocol (PPTP): PPTP is an extension of the Point-to-Point Protocol (PPP) and is installed by default during the installation of RRAS. PPTP uses MPPE for encryption purposes.

Layer Two Tunneling Protocol (L2TP): With L2TP alone, a secure tunnel is created, but the data is not encrypted. L2TP must be used in conjunction with IPSec which will provide data encryption. L2TP derives from two earlier protocols: Microsoft's PPTP and Cisco's L2F. Unlike PPTP, which works only over IP-based networks, L2TP can be deployed over a variety of different networks. L2TP uses IPSec to negotiate a security association between two computers and perform encryption services. L2TP and IPSec have several advantages over PPTP. For example, the actual encryption process starts prior to the PPP connection, and IPSec uses DES, a much stronger method of encryption.

tip

IPSec tunnel mode encrypts only that data between the two end points. Data behind the tunnel endpoint is not encrypted.

Figure 6-14 Creating a VPN

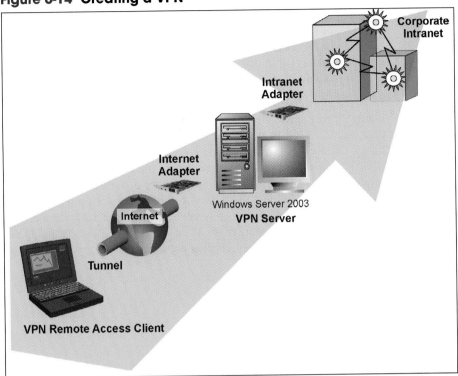

Table 6-3 Choosing a VPN Protocol

Protocol	When to Use It
PPTP	• The VPN tunnel must pass through a NAT device or firewall. • You are using older Windows clients. • Your design calls for authentication of both users and computers. • Your design calls for client-to-server or network-to-network security.
L2PT	• You want to use IPSec tunnels. • The VPN tunnel does not pass through a NAT device or firewall. • Your design calls for authentication of both users and computers. • Your design calls for client-to-server or network-to-network security.

skill 4

Selecting a Virtual Private Network Solution (cont'd)

exam objective

Implement secure access between private networks.

overview

L2TP cannot be used with NAT because IPSec protects the IP address and port number information in an IP packet.

Creating the VPN Server: To configure a VPN server, you must use RRAS. RRAS can be used to configure a computer to be a VPN server that can accept both remote access and demand-dial VPN connections from remote access clients. The VPN server must have two network interfaces installed, one for a permanent connection to the Internet, and one for the connection to the LAN.

To begin, start the **Remote Access Server Setup Wizard**. On the **Remote Access** screen, select **VPN (Figure 6-15)**, and then on the **VPN Connection** screen, select the network interface that connects the server to the Internet **(Figure 6-16)**. By default, if configured to support VPN connections, Windows Server 2003 automatically creates 128 PPTP and 128 L2TP ports for incoming VPN connections. You can change the number of ports if your VPN server needs to support more clients for either protocol. If you are not going to allow PPTP clients, you can deselect the **Allow Remote Access Connections** check box in the **Port Properties** dialog box, or if you are not going to accept L2TP connections, deselect the same box in the **L2TP** port properties. After you have configured the properties for your VPN server, you can create remote access policies and a remote access profile as per the RAS server configuration.

Figure 6-15 Creating a VPN server

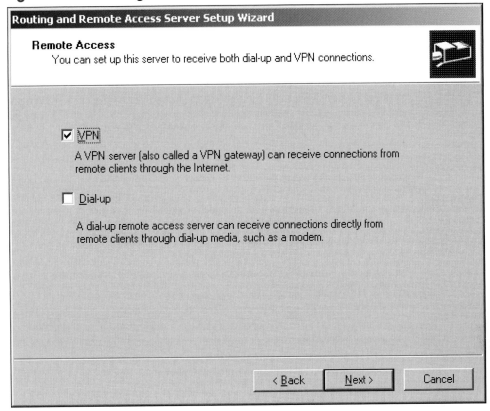

Figure 6-16 Selecting the network interface that connects to the Internet

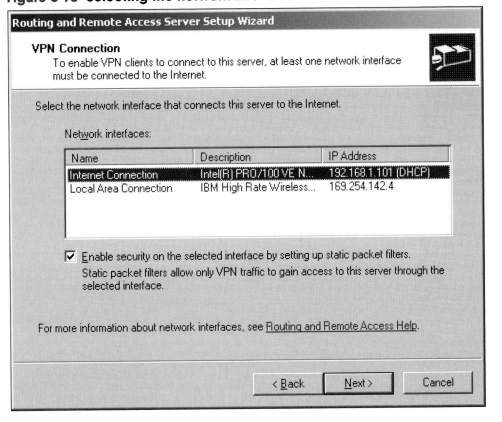

skill 5   *Implementing IPSec Policy*

exam objective

Implement secure access between private networks. Create and implement an IPSec policy. Configure network protocol security. Configure protocol security by using IPSec policies. Configure security for data transmission. Configure IPSec policy settings. Plan for network protocol security. Plan an IPSec policy for secure network communications. Plan security for data transmission. Secure data transmission by using IPSec. Configure protocol security in a heterogeneous client computer environment. Secure data transmission between client computers to meet security requirements.

overview

IPSec (Internet Protocol Security) protects Internet Protocol (IP) and higher layer protocols by using security policies to secure user communications within a local area network and/or between sites. These protocols provide a method for ensuring authentication, confidentiality, and integrity of data in IP-based communications (**Figure 6-17**). Policies are created by using the **IPSec Management** snap-in. Each policy includes a set of rules that specify the actual security requirements for different types of communications. The most common implementation of IPSec is in VPNs, but it can also be used to protect against unauthorized access to data by internal users as well.

When deploying IPSec there are two protocols that you can use: Authentication Header (AH) and Encapsulating Security Payload (ESP). These protocols can be implemented together or separately depending upon the goals of your security design. The **Authentication Header (AH)** protocol ensures authentication, integrity, and anti-replay protection for transmitted packets (**Figure 6-18**). It can identify the sender and ensure the data in the packet is accurate and complete. AH cannot protect the data from being seen, but it will ensure that it cannot be modified during transmission. The **Encapsulating Security Payload (ESP)** protocol can encrypt the actual data in the packet. ESP provides authentication, integrity, and anti-replay services as well (**Figure 6-19**). ESP protects only the TCP/UDP header (not the IP header) and the data payload from being inspected, while AH protects the IP packet and IP header from being modified.

IPSec can be used in two different modes (**Figure 6-20**):

◆ **Transport mode:** If your security design dictates that traffic must be secure over the entire path between the source and destination computers, use transport mode (the default mode for IPSec). When transport mode is used, IPSec encrypts only the IP payload by using an AH or ESP header. Only the computers that need to communicate with each other using IPSec should have their policy configured.

◆ **Tunnel mode:** You have a corporate office that connects to a branch office through the Internet and need to protect sensitive information traveling between the two locations. This type of end-to-end communication uses routers as the endpoints in the communication. Unlike transport mode, which encrypts communication between two computers as it is sent on the local network, in tunnel mode, data is sent unencrypted to the router closest to the computer. Once the data reaches that router, it is encrypted as it is passed across the public Internet. At the corporate router, it is decrypted before being sent to the destination computer.

Windows Server 2003 implements IPSec by utilizing IPSec policies. You need to create a set of IPSec policies that match the needs of your environment. Organizations that have consistent security needs and a simple network structure can create fewer and less complex policies to meet their goals. Other organizations with more stringent security needs and more complex environments require a greater number of policies and potentially more rules in their policies.

The policies contain rules that can be used to define the level of security you want to enforce on the network. When each packet is received, the IPSec driver will match them against the security settings defined in the IPSec policy. You can use a predefined IPSec policy or create your own custom policies. IPSec policies are defined by using the **IPSec Security Policy Management** snap-in.

tip

Using IPSec in tunnel mode is not recommended for remote access VPNs. Use L2TP/IPSec or PPTP for remote access connections.

Figure 6-17 Advantages of IPSec

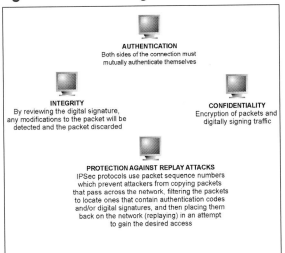

AUTHENTICATION
Both sides of the connection must mutually authenticate themselves

INTEGRITY
By reviewing the digital signature, any modifications to the packet will be detected and the packet discarded

CONFIDENTIALITY
Encryption of packets and digitally signing traffic

PROTECTION AGAINST REPLAY ATTACKS
IPSec protocols use packet sequence numbers which prevent attackers from copying packets that pass across the network, filtering the packets to locate ones that contain authentication codes and/or digital signatures, and then placing them back on the network (replaying) in an attempt to gain the desired access

Figure 6-18 Authentication Header

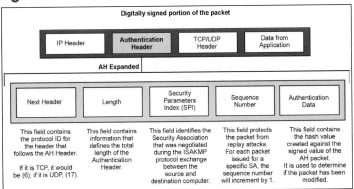

Figure 6-19 ESP Header

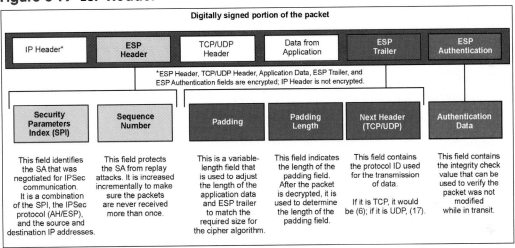

Figure 6-20 Tunnel Mode and Transport Mode

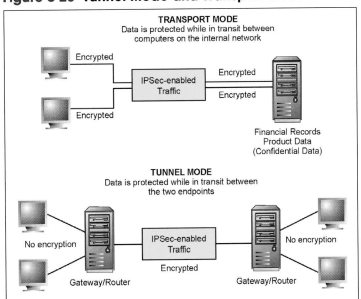

skill 5

Implementing IPSec Policy (cont'd)

exam objective

Implement secure access between private networks. Create and implement an IPSec policy. Configure network protocol security. Configure protocol security by using IPSec policies. Configure security for data transmission. Configure IPSec policy settings. Plan for network protocol security. Plan an IPSec policy for secure network communications. Plan security for data transmission. Secure data transmission by using IPSec. Configure protocol security in a heterogeneous client computer environment. Secure data transmission between client computers to meet security requirements.

overview

IPSec policies can deploy onto a local computer or if the computers are in an Active Directory-based environment, they can be assigned by using Group Policy.

Each IPSec policy consists of one or more rules. Each rule is composed of a filter, a filter action, and an authentication method.

◆ **Filter:** Identifies the type of traffic that the filter action will be applied to. Filters include protocols, ports, IP addresses, and DNS names.

◆ **Filter action:** Identifies what to do if the filter matches. Actions might be to encrypt the traffic or, in some cases, block it entirely.

◆ **Authentication method:** Determines the method used to authenticate the entities involved. Examples are Kerberos, certificates, or pre-shared keys.

Although you can design custom IPSec policies, Windows Server 2003 provides three pre-defined policies that you should consider when implementing IPSec on your network **(Figure 6-21)**.

◆ **Client (Respond Only):** Computers using this policy will never initiate a request to use IPSec for data transmissions but will enter a negotiation with Internet Key Exchange when requested to do so by another computer.

◆ **Secure Server (Require Security):** When using this policy, the computer will accept communications only if they are IPSec-enabled.

◆ **Server (Request Security):** This policy is assigned to servers or clients that will be involved in communications with both Windows Server 2003 and computers running down-level operating systems. The client will attempt to use IPSec; if it cannot initiate IPSec communication, then communication will continue unencrypted.

Figure 6-21 IPSec predefined policies

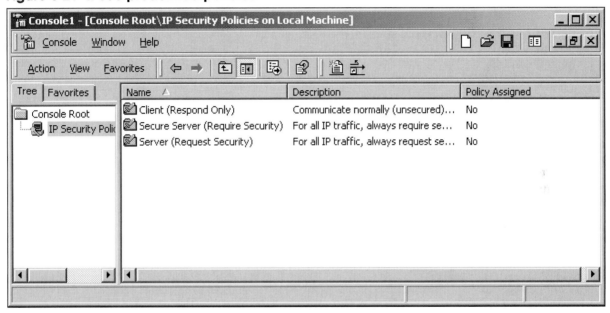

skill 6

Planning Security for Wireless Networks

exam objective

Plan secure network administration methods. Plan security for wireless networks.

overview

With the growing popularity of wireless networks, there is the challenge of ensuring that only authenticated users can access the wireless network, and that data transmitted across the wireless network cannot be intercepted. Windows Server 2003 WLANs, when used in conjunction with a Windows Server 2003 PKI, can support both of these goals by providing centralized user identification, authentication, dynamic key management, and accounting to provide authenticated network access to wireless networks and to wired Ethernet networks.

Wireless LANs (WLANs) supported by Windows Server 2003 **(Figure 6-22)** are based on IEEE standards 802.11 and 802.1X.

IEEE 802.11: This standard, developed by the Institute of Electrical and Electronic Engineers (IEEE), sets forth specifications for wireless access points, defined as a device that functions as interface between wireless clients and an existing wired network. The original 802.11 standard provides for a maximum bit rate of 2 megabits per second (Mbps). 802.11b, an extension of the 802.11 standard, supports two additional speeds, 5.5 Mbps and 11 Mbps, while 802.11g supports up to 20+ Mbps. IEEE 802.11a, the most recent member of the 802.11 family, provides for a maximum bit rate of 54 Mbps.

IEEE 802.1X: This IEEE standard is designed to enhance the security of WLANs that use the 802.11 standard. 802.1X provides an authentication framework for WLANs, allowing a user to be authenticated by a central authority. 802.1X uses Extensible Authentication Protocol (EAP) for message exchange during the authentication process.

All of the components required for a secure WLAN solution are included with Windows Server 2003, including Active Directory, DHCP, DNS, RADIUS, and PKI support. To plan the implementation of a secure WLAN, you must review your network infrastructure to make sure all of these required components are in place and then configure them to support a WLAN. For instance, to configure Active Directory for wireless clients, create a group to manage wireless accounts and then add the user and computer accounts to be used by wireless users to the group. You must also create remote access polices covering the accounts. Active Directory can also be used to create Group Policies that cover wireless connections, such as Wired Equivalent Privacy (WEP) security settings.

To configure DNS, make sure that any DNS zones where wireless clients will register DNS address records are configured to use dynamic updates or alternatively, are Active Directory-integrated zones. Configure a separate scope for wireless clients on your DHCP server, and set a shorter lease duration for those clients than the default of 8 day. Check that your RADIUS server supports EAP-TLS (an authentication protocol that provides for mutual authentication and key exchange between two endpoints via public key cryptography) or PEAP MS-CHAP v2 authentication (which provides for secure wireless authentication without the need for PKI and the installation of a user or computer certificate on each wireless client) and that your PKI supports issuing user and computer certificates to wireless clients, and computer certificates to your RADIUS server.

Wireless networking technology and wireless access points present many security risks. In wireless networks, the signals can be intercepted because the data is broadcast using an antenna. If the signals are not encrypted, a user with a compatible wireless adapter can communicate with a wireless access point and access your network.

tip

To test your wireless security, use a laptop and a wireless network scanner and patrol your network perimeter. You will be able to see if there are any existing unauthenticated or unencrypted wireless LANs on your premises.

Figure 6-22 Plan for securing a wireless LAN

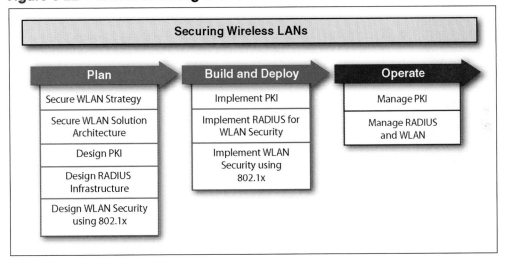

skill 6

Planning Security for Wireless Networks (cont'd)

exam objective

Plan secure network administration methods. Plan security for wireless networks.

overview

The following should be included in your design plan for wireless security:

◆ Require authorization and authentication of wireless clients before they exchange data with your WLAN. The best method is to use a RADIUS-compatible wireless access point in conjunction with a Windows Server 2003 computer running RADIUS services. Wireless access points can send connection requests and login credentials to a central RADIUS server (**Figure 6-23**). The RADIUS server can access Active Directory and authenticate the wireless access point connection request.

◆ Encrypt the data sent between wireless clients and access points. **Wired Equivalent Privacy (WEP)** is the method of encryption specified by the IEEE 802.11b standard. To further enhance the security provided by WEP encryption, use EAP-TLS, PEAP-TLS, or PEAP-MS-CHAP v2 as the authentication method.

how to

Configure a wireless network policy.

1. Click **Start**, point to **Administrative Tools**, and then click **Domain Security Policy**.
2. The **Domain Security Settings** console opens. Right-click **Wireless Network Policies** and select **Create Wireless Network Policy**.
3. The **Wireless Network Policy Wizard** appears. Click **Next >**.
4. The **Wireless Network Policy Name** screen appears (**Figure 6-24**). Enter a name in the **Name** text box and a description in the **Description** text box for the wireless network policy, and click **Next >**.
5. Click **Edit Properties...**. The **My Wireless Properties** dialog box appears (**Figure 6-25**).
6. Click the **Preferred Networks** tab, and click **Add**. The **New Preferred Settings Properties** dialog box appears (**Figure 6-26**).
7. Enter a name, such as **Wireless1**, in the **Network Name SSID** text box, and a corresponding description.
8. In the **Wireless network key (WEP)** section, make sure that the **Data encryption (WEP enabled)** and **The key is provided automatically** check boxes are selected.

Figure 6-23 Wireless RADIUS Authentication

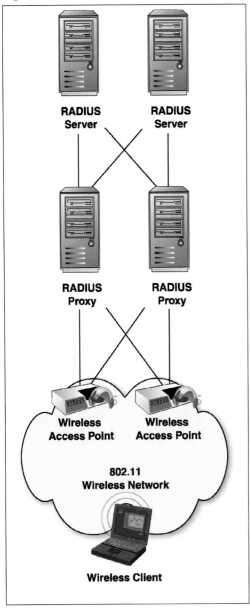

Figure 6-25 My Wireless Properties dialog box

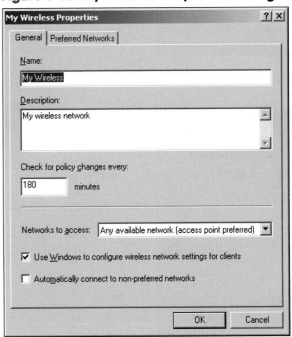

Figure 6-26 New Preferred Settings Properties dialog box

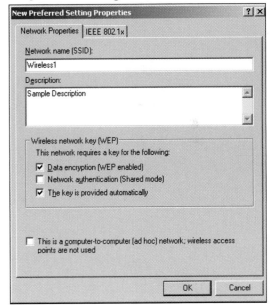

Figure 6-24 Wireless Network Policy Name screen

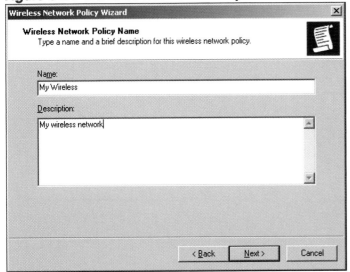

skill 6

Planning Security for Wireless Networks (cont'd)

exam objective

Plan secure network administration methods. Plan security for wireless networks.

how to

tip

You can click the Settings button in the EAP type section of the IEEE 802.1x tab to configure smart cards and certificates.

9. Click the **IEEE 802.1x** tab (**Figure 6-27**).
10. Make sure that the **Enable network access control using IEEE 802.1x** and **Authenticate as computer when computer information is available** check boxes are both selected.
11. Click **OK** to return to **My Wireless Properties** dialog box (**Figure 6-28**).
12. Click **OK** to return to the **Domain Security Settings** console and then close the console window.

Figure 6-27 IEEE 802.1x tab

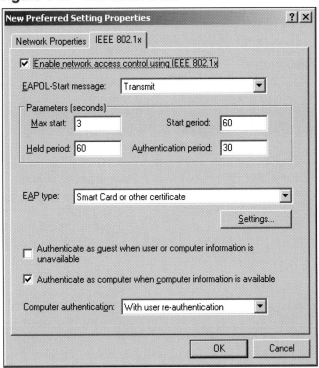

Figure 6-28 Wireless1 network with data encryption enabled

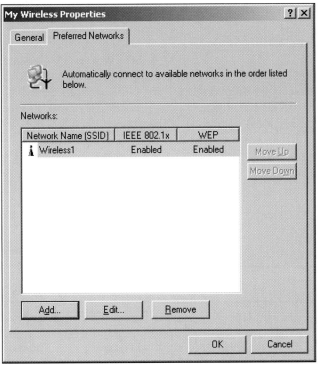

Summary

- Remote access security must include authentication, authorization, and protection of data.
- Remote access policies consist of a set of rules and conditions that must be met by a remote connection before a user can gain access.
- Remote access policies can be stored locally on a RRAS or RADIUS server.
- Access can be restricted by type of dial-in connection, IP address, and types of authentication and encryption protocols.
- Authentication protocols include PAP, SPAP, CHAP, MS-CHAP, and EAP.
- EAP is the strongest authentication protocol available, but in Windows Server 2003 it is used only when using smart cards.
- Windows Server 2003 supports the use of PKI (Public Key Infrastructure) for authentication and encryption of remote services.
- PKI methods include public/private keys, digital certificates, and the use of Certification Authorities.
- An Enterprise CA requires that Active Directory be implemented on the network. Enterprise CAs with Active Directory allow the use of smart cards and certificate templates.
- Install Certificate Services in Windows Server 2003 to configure your own Certification Authority.
- Certificates are obtained by using Web Enrollment Support pages or by using the Certification Request Wizard.
- A VPN encapsulates, authorizes, and routes data by creating tunnels.
- The protocols used to secure VPN communications are usually either Point-to-Point Tunneling Protocol (PPTP) or Layer Two Tunneling Protocol (L2TP) with IPSec.
- With L2TP alone, a secure tunnel is created, but the data is not encrypted. L2TP must be used in conjunction with IPSec, which will provide data encryption.
- To configure a VPN server, you must use the Routing and Remote Access Service (RRAS).

- By default, if configured to support VPN connections, Windows Server 2003 automatically creates 128 PPTP and 128 L2TP ports for incoming VPN connections.
- IPSec protects Internet Protocol (IP) and higher layer protocols by using security policies to secure user communications within a local area network and/or between sites.
- The Authentication Header (AH) protocol ensures authentication, integrity, and anti-replay protection for transmitted packets.
- The Encapsulating Security Payload (ESP) protocol can encrypt the actual data in the packet.
- If your security design dictates that traffic must be secure over the entire path between the source and destination computers, use transport mode (the default mode for IPSec).
- In IPSec tunnel mode, the data is sent unencrypted to the router closest to the computer. Once the data reaches that router, it is encrypted as it is passed across the public Internet. At the corporate router, it is decrypted before being sent to the destination computer.
- Windows Server 2003 implements IPSec by utilizing IPSec policies.
- IPSec policies are defined by using the IPSec Security Policy Management snap-in.
- You can use predefined IPSec policies, or create custom ones.
- Each IPSec policy consists of one or more rules. Each rule is composed of a filter, a filter action, and an authentication method.
- The Wireless LAN solution provided by Windows Server 2003 is based on IEEE standards 802.11 and 802.1X.
- Wireless users can be authenticated and authorized for access via Active Directory.
- Use a RADIUS server to authenticate wireless users to Active Directory.
- Wireless communications must be encrypted.
- IEEE 802.11b standard encryption is WEP (Wired Equivalent Privacy).

Key Terms

802.11
802.1X
Authentication Header (AH)
Certification Authority (CA)
Challenge Handshake Authentication
    Protocol (CHAP)
Condition
Digital certificate

Encapsulating Security Payload (ESP)
Enterprise CA
Extensible Authentication Protocol
    (EAP)
Internet Protocol Security (IPSec)
Layer Two Tunneling Protocol (L2TP)
Microsoft CHAP (MS-CHAP)

Microsoft Point-to-Point Encryption
    (MPPE)
Password Authentication Protocol
    (PAP)
Public key cryptography
Public Key Infrastructure (PKI)
Point-to-Point Tunneling Protocol
    (PPTP)

Remote access permission
Remote access policy
Remote access profile
Root CA

Routing and Remote Access Services
  (RRAS)
Shiva Password Authentication
  Protocol (SPAP)
Standalone CA

Subordinate CA
Transport mode
Tunnel mode
Virtual Private Network (VPN)
Wired Equivalent Privacy (WEP)

Test Yourself

1. Which of the following can be used to authenticate remote access users?
   a. MD5
   b. RADIUS
   c. TCP/IP
   d. VPN

2. Which type of remote access method encapsulates, authorizes, and routes data by creating tunnels?
   a. VPN
   b. Dial-in
   c. PAP
   d. PPP

3. Which of the following authentication protocols is the least secure?
   a. MS-CHAP v2
   b. CHAP
   c. PAP
   d. EAP

4. Which of the following components of PKI is used to authenticate digital certificates?
   a. Digital signature
   b. Active Directory
   c. Public key
   d. Certification Authority

5. Which type of CA must be used to support Active Directory features?
   a. Standalone
   b. Third-party
   c. Root
   d. Enterprise

6. What must be used in conjunction with L2TP to encrypt data during a transmission?
   a. Private keys
   b. IPSec
   c. PPTP
   d. RRAS

7. What type of remote access method typically uses IPSec?
   a. SPAP
   b. Dial-in
   c. VPN
   d. Wireless

8. What must be enabled on a wireless network to prevent eavesdropping?
   a. Authorization
   b. Authentication
   c. Encryption
   d. Access points

Projects: On Your Own

1. Examine your network and all of its remote access points and methods. Analyze the security requirements of each method, such as dial-up, VPN, or wireless, for security risks and measures that should be implemented to minimize them. Consider your security with respect to authentication, authorization, and the protection of data communications. If your network contains a variety of methods such as dial-up, VPN, and wireless access that are accessed by many users, what types of centralized authentication methods can be used to lessen the management load?

2. Design a wireless-based access solution that includes security to authenticate and encrypt all communications between the clients and the destination wired LAN.

Problem Solving Scenarios

You are the network administrator for a company that has added a large, remote sales force who are geographically spread around the world. You have been tasked to design a remote access solution that will be cost-effective, efficient, and secure. Many of the Sales teams will be based at home using a local Internet Service Provider to access the Internet, while others will be constantly traveling, and require remote access via dial-up from wherever they are located. In your solution, you must be able to balance the remote access requirements with a cost-effective solution, while maintaining strict authentication and data protection standards.

LESSON

7

Planning Remote Administration

In previous lessons, you learned about planning the major components of your network infrastructure, including server roles, the network communications that allow them to cooperate, and security policies. Your network infrastructure plan also needs to take into account the demands that will be placed on IT resources for maintenance and troubleshooting. In many cases, an IT organization will opt for centrally located staff to monitor a network that is dispersed across a very large geographical area. As the geographical distance between support personnel and physical infrastructure grows, so do the challenges in providing timely and effective support and management.

One of the greatest challenges facing organizations with large networks is administering remote computers without the delays of travel or the financial costs of providing on-site support. Previous versions of Windows provided tools that allowed for only a limited range of support tasks. However, Windows Server 2003 includes two important tools based on Terminal Services (Windows Server 2003's implementation of a centralized computing architecture that lets users execute Windows-based applications on a remote server) technology: Remote Desktop for Administration and Remote Assistance. Remote Desktop for Administration is used to manage a computer from nearly any computer on your network and Remote Assistance is used to allow a trusted party to remotely access your system. This expert can be allowed to just view your system or to both view and interact with your system. These two tools provide administrators with powerful interfaces that make remote system management effective and efficient.

Goals

In this lesson, you will review the key features and abilities of Windows Server 2003 Terminal Services and learn about Windows Server 2003's Remote Desktop for Administration and Remote Assistance remote administration tools. You will also consider some of the issues surrounding the installation, maintenance, and proper use of these tools, and become aware of some of the potential security issues involved.

Lesson 7   Planning Remote Administration

Skill	Exam 70-293 Objective
1. Planning for Remote Administration Using Terminal Services	Plan secure network administration methods. Plan for remote administration by using Terminal Services.
2. Planning for Remote Administration with Remote Desktop for Administration	Plan secure network administration methods. Plan for remote administration by using Terminal Services.
3. Planning to Use Remote Assistance	Plan secure network administration methods. Plan for remote administration by using Terminal Services. Create a plan to offer Remote Assistance to client computers.

Requirements

To complete this lesson, you will need administrative rights on a Microsoft Windows Server 2003 member server and a Windows XP Professional client computer. If you do not have access to two computers, simply perform the steps listed on your Windows Server 2003 computer; however you will not be able to create the Remote Desktop or Remote Assistance connections.

skill 1

Planning for Remote Administration Using Terminal Services

exam objective

Plan secure network administration methods. Plan for remote administration by using Terminal Services.

overview

Remote Desktop for Administration and Remote Assistance are both based on Terminal Services technologies. **Terminal Services** is the Windows Server 2003 implementation of a centralized computing architecture that lets users execute Windows-based applications on a remote server **(Figure 7-1)**. With Terminal Services, clients need not fit the typical Windows Server 2003 client/server model in which each user works from an independent client that is responsible for its own application processing, local storage, and operating system management. Terminal Services supports a full range of clients including so-called "thin clients," as well as Windows 98, NT, CE, 2000, and XP Professional computers. With the help of third-party software, it will also support Unix, Unix-based X-terminals, and Macintosh computers **(Figure 7-2)**. All processing is remotely performed on the server. The Terminal Server client software is installed on the client, the client receives the Windows Server 2003 GUI from the Terminal Server, users enter keystrokes and mouse clicks, the commands are sent to the Terminal Server for execution, and the server then refreshes the local terminal screen. An Application layer protocol called **Remote Desktop Protocol (RDP)** handles communication between the Terminal Server client and the Terminal Server. RDP, which is designed to handle the transmission of graphical data, supports automatic disconnection, remote configuration, and three levels of session encryption.

Terminal Services is a very powerful application service, designed to allow hundreds of remote users to access the Terminal Server from any location, and from nearly any device. As such, you should plan your Terminal Services implementation carefully. Your first priority should simply be to ensure that the feasibility and operational requirements are met. In this regard, financial issues need to be taken into account. While thin client solutions, such as Terminal Services, *can* save you money, they can also end up costing you much more than you expected. Thin client solutions typically reduce costs by reducing the current and recurring costs of expensive PCs on all desktops. When using a thin client solution, you can use much cheaper hardware for your desktop computers, as most of the processing requirements (and sometimes, storage as well) are handled by the Terminal Servers. However, you should not neglect to take into account the cost of the Terminal Servers themselves, which necessarily must be much more powerful computers than a simple file server. Secondarily, you may need to purchase Terminal Services licenses (unless all of your computers run an operating system with built-in licensing, such as Windows 2000), which will increase the cost of deployment. Finally, you need to take into account bandwidth requirements and network hardware throughput, and upgrade your infrastructure if necessary. Often, organizations will find that they have a "critical mass" number. If they have less thin clients than this number, Terminal Services is not financially viable.

To determine what your organization's critical mass is, you will need to examine each of your requirements in detail. First, determine how many Terminal Servers will be required to support your needs. The best option in this regard would be to simply set up a test environment. However, in many cases, this will not be an option, mostly due to financial or time constraints. You can still use approximations to get an idea of how many servers are required, using published test results as your base. You can find one good source for this information, though it is a bit dated, at the following Web site: **http://www.microsoft.com/windows2000/docs/tscaling.doc**.

Figure 7-1 Terminal Services

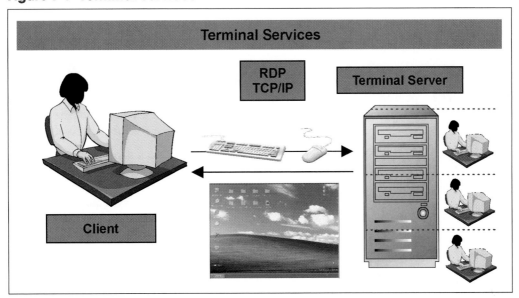

Figure 7-2 Terminal Services architecture

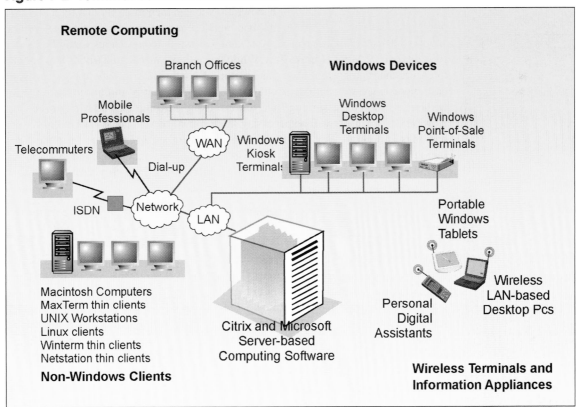

skill 1

Planning for Remote Administration Using Terminal Services (cont'd)

exam objective

Plan secure network administration methods. Plan for remote administration by using Terminal Services.

overview

tip

For more information about licensing requirements, see **www.microsoft.com /windowsserver2003 /howtobuy/licensing**.

In general, the estimated number of users a Terminal Server using modern hardware (2+ Ghz dual processor computers with 4 GB of RAM) can support is around 100-200 users. However, this number depends upon many factors, including the type of user, the applications to be supported, the server's specific configuration, and the server load imposed from other services.

Once you have determined your Terminal Services hardware requirements, you need to thoroughly examine licensing costs. At a minimum, you will require a Windows Server 2003 license, a client access license (CAL) for each session, and a Terminal Services license (a TS-CAL) for each user or device. Additionally, you may require special licensing for your client applications, so ensure that you take this into account.

Once licensing has been accounted for, you will need to examine the functionality of your client applications under a Terminal Services session. If you built a test environment when sizing your Terminal Servers, you will already have this information, but if not, you need to ensure that the applications perform properly in a Terminal Services session. Since not all applications will work properly in the Terminal Services environment, it is imperative that you do testing and research to ensure that your applications are compatible.

Next, you should plot the bandwidth requirements of your proposed environment. A good general rule is to allocate around 2,000 bytes (16,000 bits) of bandwidth for each user, each second. In most cases, users will require only 500 or so bytes per second, but allocating 16 Kbps will enable you to handle occasional spikes in bandwidth usage. If you estimate that each user will utilize 16 Kbps of bandwidth, you can then multiply that figure by the number of concurrent users to estimate total bandwidth requirements. For instance, if you needed to support 200 users simultaneously, your total bandwidth requirements would be 16 Kbps x 200 for a total of 3.2 Mbps (**Figure 7-3**). While this number may sound trivial, it is very important to ensure that you have at least this amount of bandwidth available for use by RDP. In this case, your LAN connections should be able to handle this amount in most environments without a problem, assuming that you are using full-duplex 100 Mbps or 1 Gbps links. However, if any users will be accessing the terminal servers across WAN links, this number becomes quite high. For instance, if all users were accessing your Terminal Server from remote locations, and were entering your Terminal Services hub through a single T-1 link (1.544 Mbps total bandwidth, with around 1.1 Mbps typically usable), you now have significant bandwidth shortage that needs to be addressed.

In addition to ensuring link bandwidth is adequate, you should also ensure that your network hardware can handle the additional traffic. While there is no easy way to do this, one of the simpler methods involves taking a simple statistical analysis (using SNMP, typically) of the total traffic entering and exiting critical components, such as routers. Match these statistics up with statistics on the given component's processing requirements, and you should be able to make a simple correlation between throughput and processor utilization. For instance, if you currently have a total average throughput on your router of 900 Kbps, and an average processor utilization of 28%, then the correlation between throughput and processor utilization is around 32 Kbps for every 1% of utilization. Adding an additional 3.2 Mbps of throughput to this router would theoretically put it considerably over 100% utilization. While this method is not extremely accurate, it is a quick and easy way to get an estimate of how your network components will handle the additional requirements imposed.

Figure 7-3 Bandwidth requirements

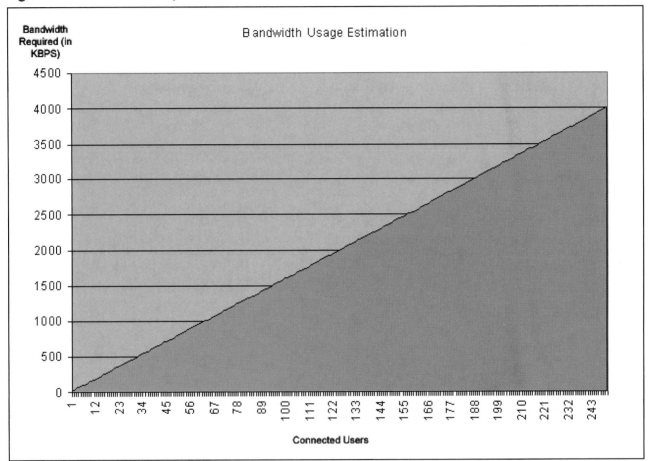

skill 1

Planning for Remote Administration Using Terminal Services *(cont'd)*

exam objective

Plan secure network administration methods. Plan for remote administration by using Terminal Services.

overview

The best approach is always to create a test environment and test the proposed solution first. However, you can make a bit more accurate base calculation by using the delta between minimum and peak usage. For instance, if your minimum processor and bandwidth usage was 10 Kbps and 15%, while your peaks were 1.5 Mbps and 32%, you would first find the delta between minimum and peak numbers. In this case, the bandwidth delta is 1.49 Mbps and the utilization delta is 17%. By dividing 1.49 Mbps by 17, you find that the more accurate assumption is that each 87 Kbps accounts for 1% processor utilization. In this case, at peak hours, an additional 3.2 Mbps will increase processor utilization to around only 68%.

Finally, once you have planned for basic functionality, you should consider redundancy and fault tolerance. Standard server fault tolerance measures should be considered almost mandatory. Remember, in a thin client environment, each user is dependent on the Terminal Server, more so than any other server. Measures such as RAID arrays, redundant power supplies, and UPS systems should not be skimped on for such a critical system.

For redundancy, your options will vary depending upon the specific applications you will be using. For simple applications using static files, or front-end applications in a tiered database design, Network Load Balancing may be a viable solution. However, if you are running a complex database application on the Terminal Server itself, clustering will most likely be your only option. In either case, you should evaluate the need for redundancy and implement a solution if uninterrupted access is an absolute necessity.

Table 7-1 summarizes the process you should follow when planning for Terminal Services.

Table 7-1 Planning for Terminal Services

1. Set up a test environment, if possible, or use estimates to determine how many Terminal Servers are required.

2. Examine licensing costs.

3. Examine functionality of client applications under Terminal Services.

4. Plot bandwidth requirements.

5. Ensure network hardware can handle additional traffic.

6. Consider redundancy and fault tolerance.

skill 2

Planning for Remote Administration with Remote Desktop for Administration

exam objective

Plan secure network administration methods. Plan for remote administration by using Terminal Services.

overview

Remote Desktop for Administration provides remote access to desktops running any of the Windows Server 2003 family, facilitating server administration from almost any computer on your network. A typical environment is illustrated in **Figure 7-4**.

Remote Desktop for Administration offers an administrator a powerful tool to access servers from remote locations, without needing assistance from local support staff. As such, Remote Desktop for Administration offers an organization the opportunity for enormous savings in travel, time, and network costs by allowing comprehensive server administration from virtually anywhere in the world, affording the IT team a great deal of flexibility in logistics. When you connect to a remote computer using Remote Desktop for Administration, you control it as if you were sitting at the console, and no physical interaction at the remote location is necessary. First, you must log on to the remote computer just as you would log on to any other computer. Note that unless you log off the remote computer, your logon session will remain active even if you terminate Remote Desktop.

Remote Desktop for Administration is designed specifically for efficient remote server administration. During the installation of any Windows Server 2003 family operating system, a connection is configured for the Remote Desktop Protocol (RDP) without having to assign the Terminal Server role. Process scheduling, multi-user and application sharing components do not install for Remote Desktop, leaving the resources of the server relatively free to perform its designated role. Moreover, unlike Terminal Server, no additional licenses are required for Remote Desktop for Administration.

Remote Desktop for Administration operates on TCP/IP over an existing network, or by remote access, using TCP port 3389 with RDP. Remote Desktop for Administration transmits not only the graphical user interface, but also keyboard input and mouse clicks from the client to the server. Because it relies on TCP/IP, the client may connect via network or dial-up connections (**Figure 7-5**) as well as through a virtual private network (VPN).

The Remote Desktop User group is provided in order to bypass the need to log on as Administrator. This group is not populated by default. Any users requiring Remote Desktop access should be granted permission through membership in the Remote Desktop Users group.

Remote Desktop Connection is the client software that is used to connect to a Terminal Server. The Remote Desktop Connection client is included in the default installations of both Windows Server 2003 and Windows XP Professional. For all other operating systems, you must install the client. The Remote Desktop Connection client is stored in *%systemroot%* **\system32\clients\tsclient\win32 (Figure 7-6)**. The 16-bit Terminal Services client can be found in the *%systemroot%***\system32\clients\tsclient\win16** folder on the Terminal Server. If you have already installed an earlier version of the Terminal Services client on a client computer with a down-level version of the Windows operating system, you should update the software so that you can take advantage of the newest features such as alternate port selection (the default Terminal Services port is TCP port 3389), the ability to save connection settings, and the ability to access network printers.

tip

You can improve performance during a Remote Desktop session by reducing the number of colors on the user's computer. Use the Color quality setting on the Settings tab in Display (in Control Panel) to reduce the number of screen colors.

tip

Sharing the folder \%*systemroot*\ system3clients\tsclient for Remote Desktop Group Users makes remote management software readily available.

Figure 7-4 A typical Remote Desktop for Administration environment

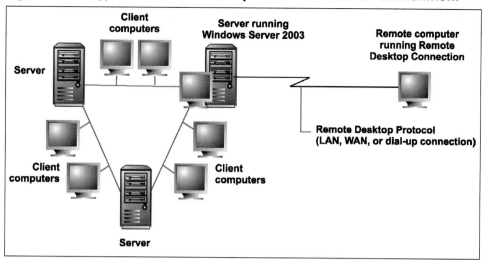

Figure 7-5 Remote Desktop for Administration accessed from dial-up or VPN

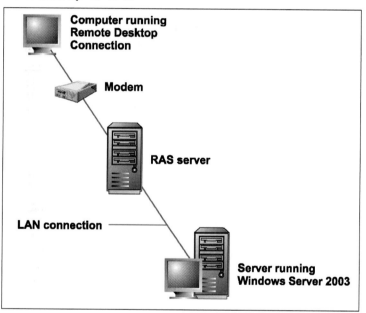

Figure 7-6 Locating the Remote Desktop Connection client

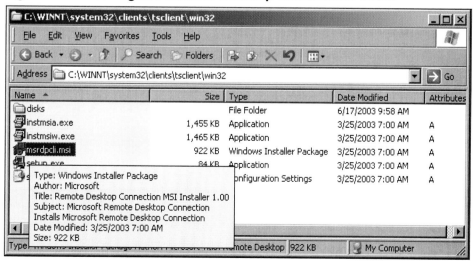

skill 2

Planning for Remote Administration with Remote Desktop for Administration (cont'd)

exam objective

Plan secure network administration methods. Plan for remote administration by using Terminal Services.

how to

Configure Remote Desktop for Administration on a server.

1. Log on to the server as an Administrator (you must be logged on as a member of the Administrators group in order to enable or disable Remote Desktop for Administration).
2. Click [Start], click **Control Panel** and then click **System**. The **System Properties** dialog box appears.
3. Click the **Remote** tab and select the **Allow users to connect remotely to this computer** check box in the **Remote Desktop** section (**Figure 7-7**).
4. The **Remote Sessions** message box opens to warn you that all accounts used for remote connections must have passwords and that the correct port must be open if you are using Internet Connection Sharing or a personal firewall. Click [OK].
5. Click [OK] to close the System Properties dialog box.

Start a Remote Desktop session.

1. Log on to your client computer. Click [start], and click **Run** to open the **Run** dialog box.
2. Enter **mstsc.exe** in the **Open** text box and click [OK].
3. The **Remote Desktop Connection** dialog box will appear. If necessary, click [Options >>] to expand the dialog box.
4. In the **Computer** list box, enter the name of the server you wish to connect to. Enter your user name, password, and the domain in the appropriate text boxes (**Figure 7-8**) and click [Connect].
5. You can now remotely administer your member server from your client computer. The member server's monitor does not display your login session, as you are logged in remotely through your client computer; however, on the client computer you are logged on to the member server.
6. Click [start], point to **Programs** (or **All Programs**), point to **Administrative Tools** and click **Services**. You can start, stop, and configure any services on your member server.
7. Close the Services window. Click [Close] on the Remote Desktop console toolbar.
8. The **Disconnect Windows session** dialog box opens. Click [OK] to end the session.

tip

When Remote Desktop Connection is installed on a client computer, a shortcut to the application is placed in the Start > Programs menu.

more

Because of the power of Remote Desktop for Administration—that is, allowing remote server control—you must pay particular attention to security. Make sure that the Terminal Server running Remote Desktop is located behind a firewall and that all users who make remote desktop connections are required to use strong passwords.

Figure 7-7 Configuring Remote Desktop on the server

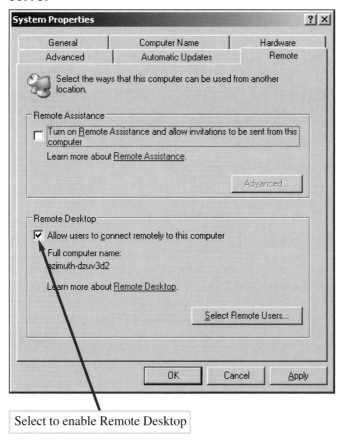

Select to enable Remote Desktop

Figure 7-8 The Remote Desktop Connection dialog box

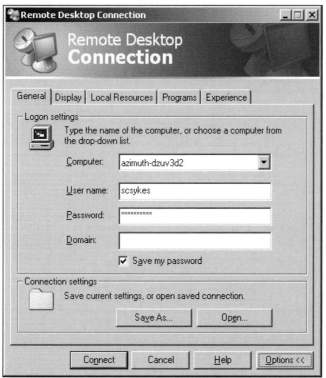

skill 3

Planning to Use Remote Assistance

exam objective

Plan secure network administration methods. Plan for remote administration by using Terminal Services. Create a plan to offer Remote Assistance to client computers.

overview

The Remote Assistance tool, introduced in Windows XP and included in the Windows Server 2003 family, allows support personnel to remotely access a user's Windows XP computer, view its desktop, and control its operation.

Though chiefly designed to offer remote assistance to users having technical trouble (such as adding a network printer), Remote Assistance provides an IT team with a very simple and reliable tool that allows an inexperienced support person or administrator to solicit the help of a more experienced colleague.

The user needing help typically initiates a Remote Assistance session through e-mail or Windows Messenger. The user, or Novice, sets a password for the support person, or Expert, to use, determines the length of time the session should last, and sends the invitation. When both parties confirm the invitation, the Remote Assistance Novice chat dialog box opens on the user's computer screen and the Remote Assistance Expert console opens on the support person's screen. The console allows the Expert to chat with the Novice in real time, view his or her desktop, and if the Novice permits, control the desktop. If full control is granted, the Expert does indeed have full control—including access to the network—as though he or she were sitting in front of the user's computer. We will address the security issues involved with granting full control later in this lesson.

In addition to allowing requests for help, Remote Assistance allows a support person to offer assistance to a user without requiring the user to initiate the Remote Assistance session. This feature must be enabled in the Group Policy Editor by using the Offer Remote Assistance policy.

The Remote Assistance utility is a powerful way of resolving problems remotely. Rather than guiding a user through changing local settings via an e-mail exchange or on the telephone, help can be given virtually "in-person," and is available to the user in a truly efficient manner. As well as saving support costs, Remote Assistance also offers an expert user the ability to train a less experienced person with live demonstrations.

Remote Assistance requires that participants in a session have either Windows XP or a version of the Windows Server 2003 family. They may be anywhere on a TCP/IP network; however, any firewalls must have TCP port 3389 open.

how to

Configure System Properties to turn on Remote Assistance and allow a local user to request assistance.

1. Click **Start**, open the **Control Panel** and select **System**.
2. On the **Remote** tab, in the **Remote Assistance** section, select the **Turn on Remote Assistance and allow invitations to be sent from this computer** check box (**Figure 7-9**).
3. Click **Advanced...** and make sure that the **Allow this computer to be controlled remotely** check box is selected (**Figure 7-10**).
4. Set the maximum amount of time invitations can remain open to **1 hour**.
5. Click **OK**.

Figure 7-9 Control Panel settings

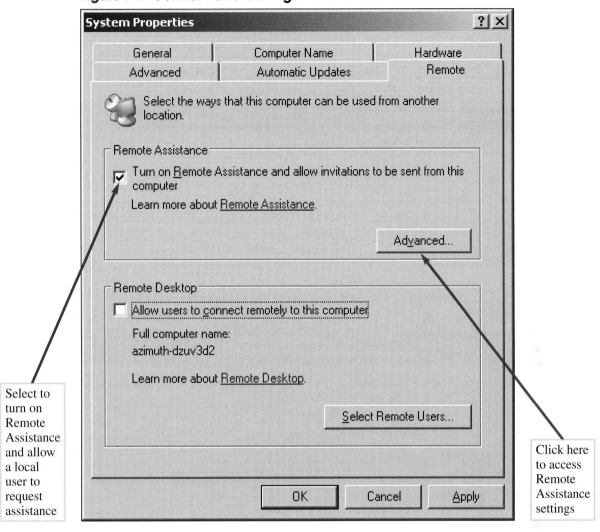

Select to turn on Remote Assistance and allow a local user to request assistance

Click here to access Remote Assistance settings

Figure 7-10 Control Panel Remote Assistance settings

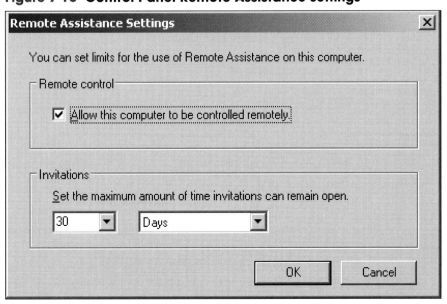

skill 3

Planning to Use Remote Assistance
(cont'd)

exam objective

Plan secure network administration methods. Plan for remote administration by using Terminal Services. Create a plan to offer Remote Assistance to client computers.

how to

Configure Group Policy to allow the use of Remote Assistance.

1. Click [Start], and then click **Run**.
2. In the **Open** text box in the **Run** dialog box, type **gpedit.msc** and click [OK].
3. Under **Computer Configuration**, double-click **Administrative Templates**, double-click **System**, and then click **Remote Assistance (Figure 7-11)**.
4. Double-click **Solicited Remote Assistance** to open the **Solicit Remote Assistance Properties** dialog box and enable or disable the setting **(Figure 7-12)**. You may also set the level of remote control desired. The Maximum Ticket Time (how long an offer of assistance is valid) and the method for sending e-mail invitations is also configured here. Click [OK].
5. Double-click **Offer Remote Assistance** to open the **Offer Remote Assistance Properties** dialog box and enable or disable the setting **(Figure 7-13)**. You may also set the level of control a helper can utilize, using the **Permit Remote Control** combo box, and set the list of allowed helpers by using the **Show** button. Only those included in the list or part of the **Administrators** group will be able to offer assistance to this computer. Click [OK].

more

There are several restrictions you can set in the configuration of Remote Assistance to enhance security.

◆ You can restrict the reach of Remote Assistance by closing TCP port 3389 on a firewall.
◆ Group Policy allows you to restrict which users may request Remote Assistance and the degree of access—either full remote control of the computer or view access only. Similarly, Group Policy can prohibit an assistant from offering unsolicited Remote Assistance to a given computer.
◆ Settings may also be restricted on the local computer to prevent the sending of any invitations.

Among your implementation plans, you should take advantage of the resource flexibility that Remote Assistance affords a team. Any IT group will have members of varying experience and expertise. By using Remote Assistance, the more experienced people on the team can provide mentoring, training, and support to junior members of the team, as well as support from remote locations.

caution

Be aware that, in order for Remote Assistance to function over the Internet, port 3389 must be opened on your firewall. By opening this port, you are also increasing the chance that an unauthorized user can gain access to RDP, and may cause harm to your system or network.

Figure 7-11 Group Policy Object Editor displaying Remote Assistance parameters

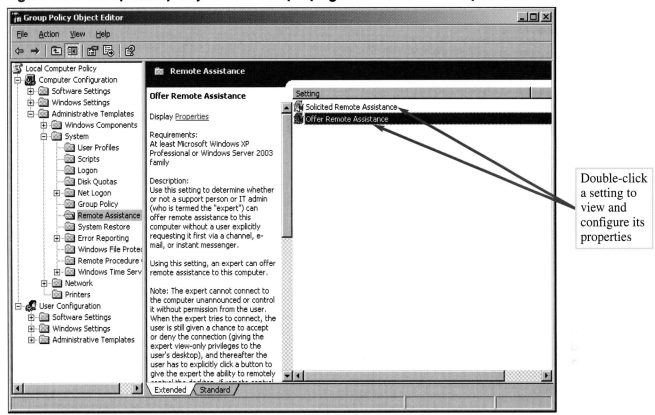

Figure 7-12 Setting Solicited Remote Assistance properties

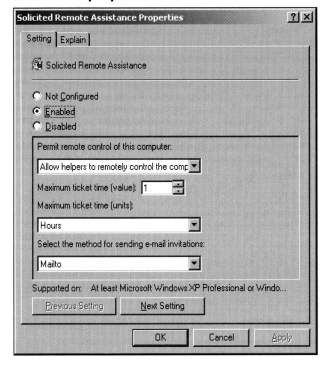

Figure 7-13 Setting Offer Remote Assistance properties

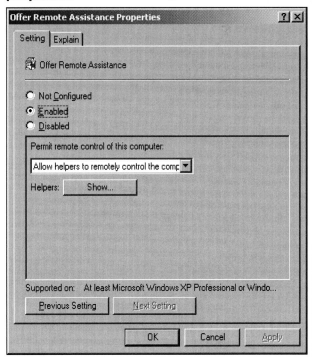

Summary

◆ Terminal Services is the Windows Server 2003 implementation of a centralized computing architecture that lets users execute Windows-based applications on a remote server.

◆ Remote Desktop for Administration provides administrators with a powerful and flexible tool for managing and maintaining large networks.

◆ Remote Assistance allows users to initiate requests for live, interactive help across a local network or over the Internet.

◆ Because Remote Assistance requires agreement between two users for access, with limited ability for administrators to verify the helper, it is most secure when protected from outside networks by a firewall.

Key Terms

Remote Assistance

Remote Desktop for Administration

Remote Desktop Protocol (RDP)

Terminal Services

Test Yourself

1. How can an administrator prevent a user from offering assistance?
   a. E-mail
   b. Windows Messenger
   c. Group Policy Editor
   d. Remote Desktop

2. A user may request Remote Assistance by: (Choose all that apply.)
   a. Using E-mail.
   b. Using Windows Messenger.
   c. Accessing the Remote Assistance Web page.
   d. Using the My Computer icon on the desktop.

3. An active Remote Desktop session provides full access to a remote computer only if:
   a. The user is in the Remote Desktop User group.
   b. TCP port 3389 is open on any firewalls between networks.
   c. A remote user grants it.
   d. None of the above

4. True or false: The terminal services client can only run on Windows XP clients?
   a. True
   b. False

5. You are the network administrator for Tiny Tots Toys, a multi-national entertainment company. Your network consists of over 70 locations worldwide, and operates on a mix of client operating systems. To reduce costs, your CIO wants to use a single user interface for all platforms company wide. However, the company does not currently have the funding to convert all PCs to a standardized Windows UI. The CIO has suggested using terminal services to provide a standard user environment for all clients. Which of the following options is not a major consideration for this solution?
   a. The number of simultaneous connections
   b. The available WAN bandwidth
   c. The supporting server hardware
   d. The client machine specifications
   e. The supporting infrastructure requirements

6. What is one major difference between Terminal Services and the Remote Desktop service?
   a. Terminal Services uses RDP, while remote desktop uses the telnet protocol.
   b. Terminal Services is used only to provide remote support, while remote desktop can be used to provide Windows Terminal Services.
   c. Terminal Services does not require additional licensing.
   d. Terminal Services uses the telnet protocol, while remote desktop uses RDP.
   e. Remote Desktop does not require additional licensing.

7. A well configured 2GHz multi-processor terminal server with 4 GB of system RAM should support approximately how many users?
   a. 50-100
   b. 200-300
   c. 150-250
   d. 100-200
   e. 350-500

8. You want to configure your Windows XP machine to allow incoming remote desktop sessions. Which of the following actions must you take to enable this (select all that apply)?
   a. Check the box labeled "Allow users to connect remotely to this computer".
   b. Run the command "regsrv32 rdpenabl.dll"
   c. Configure the maximum invitation time to be 30 or more days.
   d. Ensure that the telnet service is enabled and started.

Projects: On Your Own

1. Install Remote Desktop Connection on a previous version of Windows: Windows 95, 98, or NT 4.0.
   a. On a computer running Windows Server 2003, share the folder *%systemroot%*\system32\clients\tsclient as **tsclient$**. The **$** sign at the end of the share will hide the share from normal network browsing.
   b. On a client running a previous version of Windows, connect to the shared folder by clicking **Start**, then **Run**, and then entering *Servername*\tsclient$.
   c. Double-click the **Win32** folder.
   d. Find the file **Setup.exe** and double-click.
   e. Follow the on-screen setup instructions.
   f. Verify the installation by looking for **Remote Desktop Connection** under **Start > Programs**.

2. Configure Remote Desktop.
   a. Open the **System Properties** dialog box.
   b. Click the **Remote** tab.
   c. Select the **Allow Users To Connect Remotely To This Computer** check box and click **OK**.

3. Start a Remote Desktop Session.
   a. On the client, click **Start**, point to **Programs** and select **Remote Desktop Connection**.
   b. Enter the name of the server to which you wish to connect.
   c. Enter the domain name, user name, and password.
   d. Click **Connect**.

4. Try accessing the client you are using via the **Remote Desktop Connection** on the server you are using.

Problem Solving Scenarios

You are a server administrator located in the California-based headquarters of ABC Furniture Corporation, with a manufacturing plant in the Midwest. With an increasing need at the plant for faster access to network files, you decide to deploy a server at the plant site in order to save on network costs. Make a checklist of the user, group, and permission settings you must enable so you can remotely administer the plant's server.

LESSON 8

Planning Network Monitoring

Acquiring the knowledge necessary to effectively implement network monitoring tools allows you to be proactive in the event of a network problem. Regular monitoring increases your ability to identify potential problem areas, such as defective network interface cards and loose cables, security breaches, unauthorized access of servers and workstations, or the introduction of malicious programs to the network. If detected in time, you can prevent security breaches from causing major damage to systems connected to the network.

There are many utilities available to a network administrator for diagnosing problems in a Windows Server 2003 network. These utilities include Network Monitor, Ipconfig, and Tracert, among others. Network Monitor provides administrators with a diagnostic tool that allows for the capture and analysis of network packets. For example, Network Monitor can help administrators diagnose communication problems through the capture and analysis of network data in statistical frames, using the Capture Filter and Display Filter features. These features provide network traffic information specific to computers, protocols, and patterns.

Network Monitor is available in different versions in Windows Server 2003 and Microsoft Systems Management Server (SMS). The version of Network Monitor included in Windows Server 2003 is a limited version that only captures and displays information being sent directly to or from the Windows Server 2003 computer, as well as broadcast packets. The version of Network Monitor that is available with SMS 2003 allows the capture of all data packets sent to any MAC address which are received on the network interface. In addition, the SMS version allows data capture of any traffic sent to and from any remote computers on the network that are running the Network Monitor Driver. The Network Monitor Driver is a protocol that enables the Network Monitor utility to capture network information.

Goals

In this lesson, you will learn how to install the Network Monitor utility and Network Monitor Driver to capture and analyze network traffic data and how to use the Capture Filter and Display Filter features to specify the criteria for capturing and displaying frames. You will also learn the skills required to capture and analyze information using System Monitor and Performance logs.

Lesson 8 Planning Network Monitoring

Skill	Exam 70-293 Objective
1. Installing Network Monitor and Driver	Basic knowledge
2. Using Network Monitor to Capture Network Data	Plan network traffic monitoring. Tools might include Network Monitor and System Monitor.
3. Using Network Monitor to View Captured Data	Plan network traffic monitoring. Tools might include Network Monitor and System Monitor.
4. Using Capture Filters to Capture Data	Plan network traffic monitoring. Tools might include Network Monitor and System Monitor.
5. Analyzing Captured Data	Plan network traffic monitoring. Tools might include Network Monitor and System Monitor.

Requirements

To complete this lesson, you will need administrative rights on a Windows Server 2003 computer connected to a network.

skill 1

Installing Network Monitor and Driver

exam objective

Basic knowledge

overview

In a Windows Server 2003 network, there may be situations when two or more computers are not able to exchange data due to hardware or software problems. You can detect these problems by using the **Network Monitor** utility provided by Windows Server 2003. Network Monitor is a diagnostic utility that captures and displays network data from a local area network, in the form of frames. **Frames** are data packets that contain information about the protocol being used, the source and destination computer address, and the length of the frame.

Network Monitor includes a **Network Monitor Driver** that enables Network Monitor to receive network data in the form of frames and an administrative utility that captures and displays the data. Installing Network Monitor installs both the Network Monitor and the Network Monitor Driver by default. Network Monitor can capture and filter network data from protocols such as Hypertext Transfer Protocol (HTTP) and File Transfer Protocol (FTP). This data can help troubleshoot communication problems between a browser and a Web server.

Network Monitor is available in different versions in Windows Server 2003 and Microsoft Systems Management Server (SMS). The version of Network Monitor included in Windows Server 2003 is a limited version that only captures and displays information being sent directly to or from the Windows Server 2003 computer, as well as broadcast packets. The version of Network Monitor that is available with SMS 2003 allows the capture of all data packets sent to any MAC address that are received on the network interface.

The Windows Server 2003 version of Network Monitor allows data to be captured on a local area network (LAN). If you need to centrally capture data between two clients (not including the Windows Server 2003 computer on which Network Monitor is installed) on a LAN or on a remote network, you need to upgrade to the Microsoft Systems Management Server (SMS) 2003 version of Network Monitor. In order to capture and display network frames from remote computers using the SMS 2003 version of Network Monitor, the Network Monitor Driver needs to be installed separately on all client and Windows Server 2003 computers on the different network segments from which frames will be captured.

tip

In order to capture packets from remote segments, your routers need to be configured to support multicasts.

how to

Install Network Monitor on a Windows Server 2003 computer.

1. Log on to the computer as an **Administrator**.
2. Click ⊞**Start**, point to **Settings**, and then click the **Control Panel** command. The **Control Panel** window is displayed.
3. Double-click the **Add/Remove Programs** icon. The **Add/Remove Programs** dialog box is displayed.
4. Click the **Add/Remove Windows Components** option in the Add/Remove Programs dialog box. The **Windows Components Wizard** is displayed.
5. Select the **Management and Monitoring Tools** check box in the **Components** list box (**Figure 8-1**).
6. Click Details... . The **Management and Monitoring Tools** dialog box is displayed.

Figure 8-1 Selecting Management and Monitoring Tools

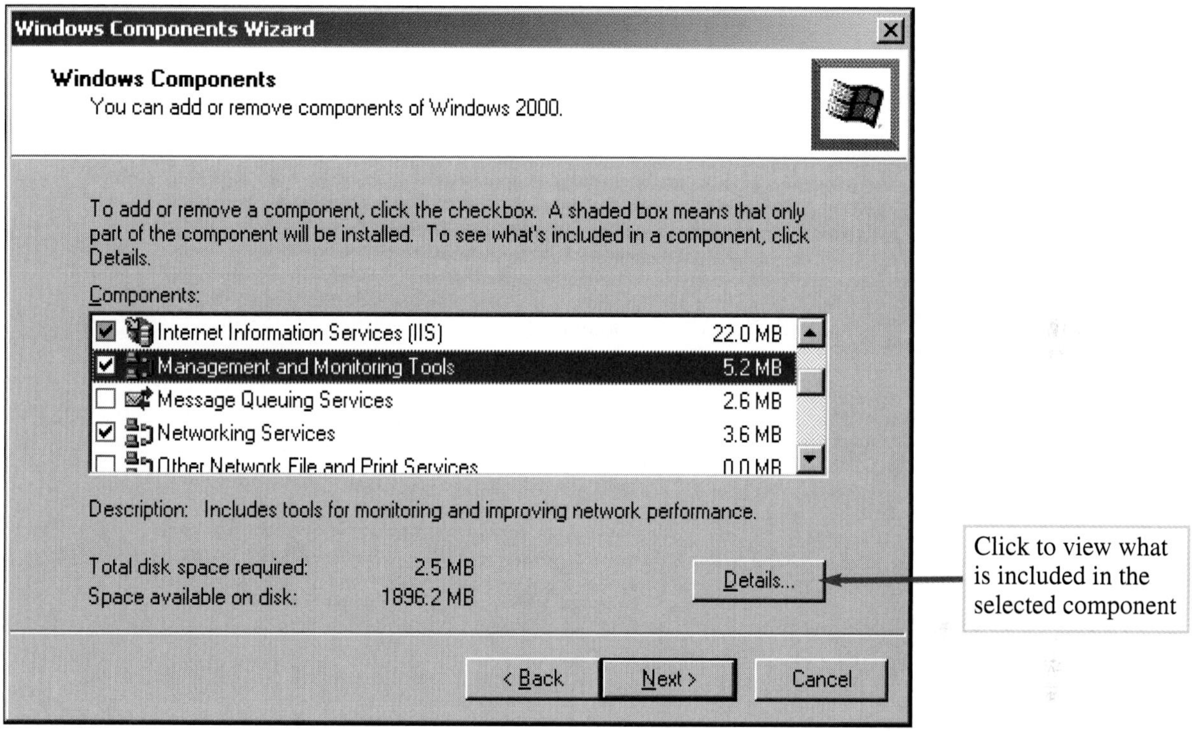

Click to view what
is included in the
selected component

skill 1

Installing Network Monitor and Driver (cont'd)

exam objective

Basic knowledge

how to

7. Select the **Network Monitor Tools** check box in the **Subcomponents of Management and Monitoring Tools** list box (**Figure 8-2**).
8. Click [OK] to close the **Management and Monitoring Tools** dialog box and display the **Windows Components Wizard**.
9. Click [Next >] to continue. You may be asked to provide the path for the Windows Server 2003 files necessary to install the Network Monitor.
10. The final screen of the Wizard informs you that the installation has completed successfully. Click [Finish] to close the **Windows Components Wizard**.

Install the Network Monitor Driver on the computer.

1. Open the **Control Panel** window, click **Network Connections**, right-click **Local Area Connection**, and then click **Properties**. The **Local Area Connection Properties** dialog box is displayed.
2. Check the **Network Monitor Driver** option in the item list (**Figure 8-3**).

more

Network Monitor is a diagnostic tool that allows for the capture and analysis of network packets. However, you can also use some other utilities provided by Windows Server 2003 to identify network problems in a Windows Server 2003 network:

◆ **Ipconfig** enables you to verify the TCP/IP configurations for the network interface cards on your system. An incorrect configuration (such as duplicate IP addresses, duplicate host names, an incorrect gateway/router address, an incorrect DNS server address, or different network masks on the same subnet, etc.) can cause network communication problem between clients.

◆ **Tracert** enables you to verify connectivity between networks.

Figure 8-2 Adding Network Monitoring Tools

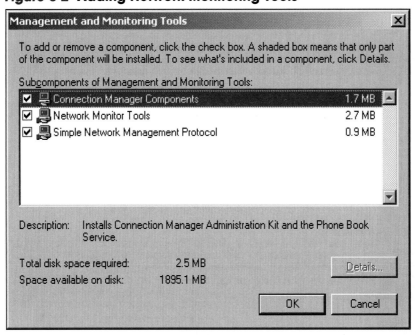

Figure 8-3 Specifying Local Area Connection Properties

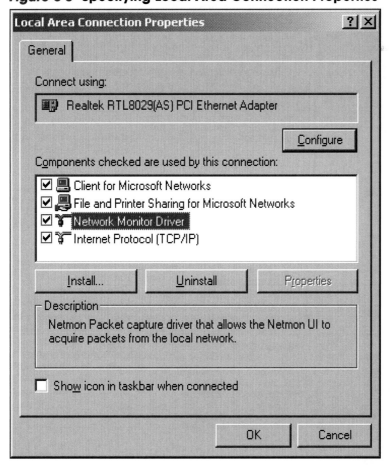

skill 2

Using Network Monitor to Capture Network Data

exam objective

Plan network traffic monitoring. Tools might include Network Monitor and System Monitor.

overview

Network Monitor uses a process called "capturing" to collect and display network traffic flow information in the form of frames. These frames are of a particular length and contain information including the protocol used on the network, the IP address of the source computer, and the IP address of the destination computer.

If the Windows Server 2003 computer running Network Monitor is multi-homed (more than one network card) and you want to simultaneously capture and display frames from all of the adapters, a separate instance of Network Monitor is needed for each adapter. One instance of Network Monitor can be used to collect data from all network cards in the server; however, data from only one network card can be displayed at a time.

how to

Capture network frames.

1. Click [Start], point to **Programs**, point to **Administrative Tools**, and then click the **Network Monitor** command. The **Network Monitor Capture** window is displayed.
2. Click **Capture** on the menu bar, and then click the **Networks** command. The **Select a network** dialog box is displayed.
3. Click **Local Computer** to display the available network adapters that are in the computer (**Figure 8-4**). Click the network adapter of the network whose data needs to be captured.
4. Click [OK] to close the Select a network dialog box. The **Network Monitor Capture** window is displayed.
5. Click **Capture** on the menu bar and then click the **Start** command to start capturing frames over the network (**Figure 8-5**). You can capture frames for a specified amount of time, for a specific instance, or for a time interval during which you want to examine your network's activity. Be aware that, by default, Network Monitor will capture only a small amount of data. You can increase the amount of data network monitor will capture by changing the Network Monitor buffer size.
6. Click **Capture** on the menu bar and click the **Stop** command. The statistics of the captured frames are viewable in the **Network Monitor Capture** window.

tip

If you have more than one network adapter, you can determine which network adapter is which by running Ipconfig /all from the command prompt. This will show you the MAC address of the adapter that you can then use to identify the adapter in Network Monitor.

more

You can also save the captured frames displayed in the **Network Monitor Capture** window for future reference or to forward to a network expert for diagnosis. To save the captured frames, click **File** on the menu bar. Then click the **Save As** command on the **File** menu. The **Save As** dialog box is displayed. Specify a name for the file in the filename text box and click [Save]. The captured frames save as **.cap** files.

Figure 8-4 Selecting a network to monitor

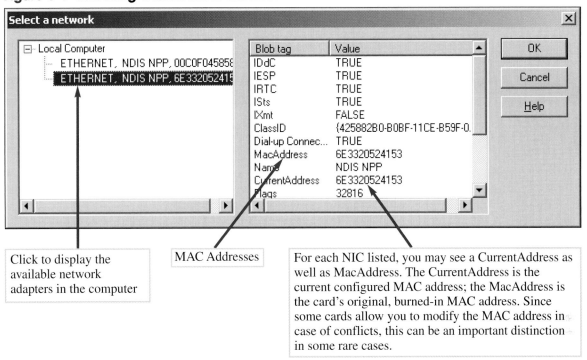

Click to display the available network adapters in the computer

MAC Addresses

For each NIC listed, you may see a CurrentAddress as well as MacAddress. The CurrentAddress is the current configured MAC address; the MacAddress is the card's original, burned-in MAC address. Since some cards allow you to modify the MAC address in case of conflicts, this can be an important distinction in some rare cases.

Figure 8-5 Starting a Network Monitor Capture

Click Capture, then Start to start capturing frames over the network

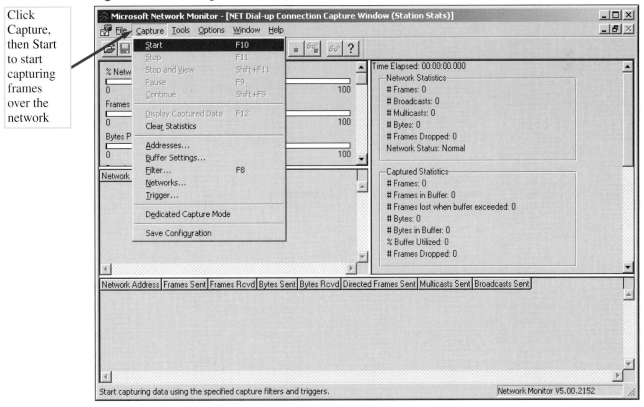

skill 3 — *Using Network Monitor to View Captured Data*

exam objective

Plan network traffic monitoring. Tools might include Network Monitor and System Monitor.

overview

After Network Monitor captures the data frames of a network, it presents the data in logical frames. The data frames are displayed in four different panes, along with several statistics relevant to the speed and nature of the network traffic, such as broadcast frames, multicast frames, network utilization, total bytes received per second and total frames received per second.

Network administrators use the saved statistics of captured data to diagnose faults or to detect potential problems in the network. Network Monitor displays the session statistics of captured data in the following panes of the **Network Monitor Capture** window (**Figure 8-6**):

◆ **Graph:** Displays a graphical representation of current network activity.
◆ **Station Stats:** Displays statistics about sessions established with the computer running Network Monitor.
◆ **Total Stats:** Displays summary statistics of network activity since the capture process started.
◆ **Session Stats:** Displays statistics about the current sessions of the network.

The statistics displayed in the Network Monitor Capture window are difficult to analyze in their numerical form. Network Monitor simplifies data analysis by interpreting raw data collected during the capture and displaying it in the **Capture Summary** window. To display the Capture Summary window, click the **Display Capture Data** command (or press the **[F12]** key) on the **Capture** menu of the Network Monitor Capture window main menu. The Capture Summary window then displays a summary of the captured data. (**Figure 8-7**).

The Capture Summary window can display the captured data in the following panes:

◆ **Detail:** Displays the contents of the frames, including the protocols used to send them.
◆ **Hex:** Displays captured data in hexadecimal and ASCII format.

You can view these panes by selecting the **Show Details Pane** and **Show Hex Pane** commands on the Window menu of the Capture Summary window (**Figure 8-8**).

more

At any point in time, Network Monitor displays statistics for only the first 100 frames it has captured. You need to use the **Clear Statistics** command on the Capture menu to display the statistics for an additional 100 frames.

Figure 8-6 Network Monitor Capture window

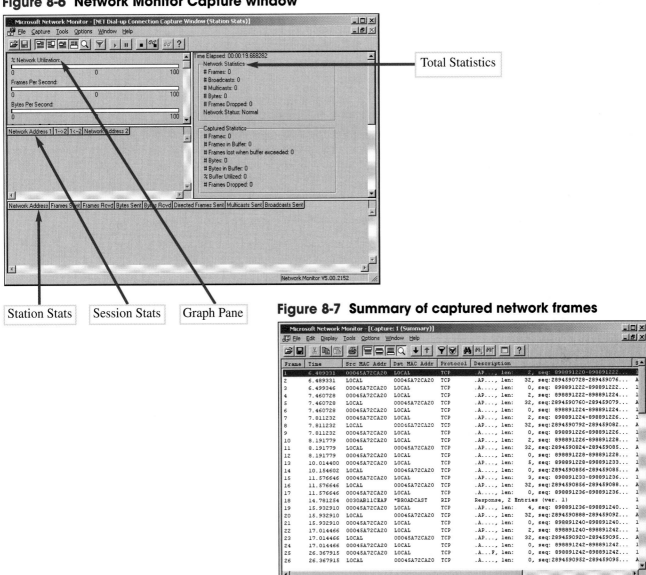

Station Stats   Session Stats   Graph Pane

Figure 8-7 Summary of captured network frames

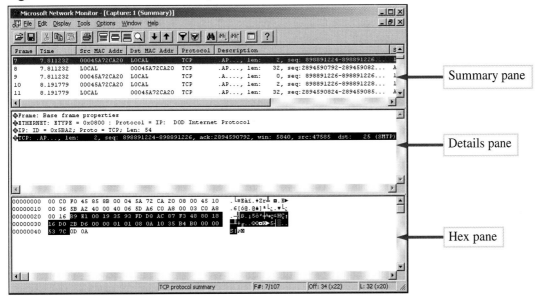

Figure 8-8 Detailed view of captured frames

Summary pane

Details pane

Hex pane

skill 4

Using Capture Filters to Capture Data

exam objective

Plan network traffic monitoring. Tools might include Network Monitor and System Monitor.

overview

When you capture data using the fully functional Network Monitor Capture window, you receive data about all protocols and computers on a network in a single window. Therefore, it becomes very difficult to trace and segregate specific data. You can use the **Capture Filter** feature of Network Monitor to capture information about specific protocols in use on your network.

In general, network frames can be filtered on the basis of the following:

◆ Protocol used to transmit the frame.
◆ Source or destination address of the frame.
◆ Content of the frame.

In the **Capture Filter** dialog box, you can specify the criteria for capturing specific data. The Capture Filter feature is similar to the query feature of a database application, and allows you to specify the criteria for capturing or viewing frames. You can define criteria for capturing frames specific to a computer, protocol, or pattern using the branches of the Capture Filter dialog box. **Table 8-1** provides the description of the branches of the Capture Filter dialog box.

To capture data from specific computers in a network, you need to know the IP addresses of those computers. The IP addresses of the computers are then associated with their host names by the network administrators using the Capture Filter dialog box. The host names of the computers are saved to a database file with the extension **.adr**. This database file is used to select addresses of the computers while specifying the filtering criteria.

The process of capturing data using Network Monitor can be automated using **Capture Triggers**. Triggers require criteria and a condition to function properly. Two primary types of triggers can be used to specify capturing criteria: **Pattern Match** and **Buffer Space**. You use the Pattern Match trigger type to initiate a trigger based on the occurrence of a specified pattern in the captured frame. You use the Buffer Space trigger type to initiate a trigger when a specified portion of the capture buffer is used. You can combine the functionality of both of these trigger types by using the **Pattern Match Then Buffer Space** trigger type or the **Buffer Space Then Pattern Match** trigger type. If you want to take no action when a specific trigger condition is met, you use the **No Action** trigger. Other trigger types included with the Network Monitor are: **Stop Capture**, **Execute Command Line**, and **Nothing**; by default, the **Nothing** trigger type (which does not initiate any trigger) is used. A trigger also needs to be configured with a set of actions to be performed. For example, when the capture buffer fills to a specified limit, a predetermined action takes place.

caution

Using Capture Filters increases the workload on the processor, as each frame is compared with the criteria specified in the Capture Filter. If the frame data match the filter criteria, the frame is captured. Otherwise, the frame is discarded.

how to

Use a Capture Filter to capture data.

1. Click **Capture** on the menu bar of the main **Network Monitor Capture** window and then click **Filter**. (If the Windows Server 2003 version of Network Monitor is installed, a message box displays stating that the Network Monitor will only be able to capture data to and from the local computer.)

2. Click <u>OK</u> to continue. The **Capture Filter** dialog box is displayed. Click the **SAP/ETYPE** branch in the **Capture Filter** dialog box. The SAP/ETYPE defaults to **Any SAP** or **Any ETYPE**.

3. To change the default settings, click <u>Edit...</u>. This displays the **Capture Filter SAPs and ETYPEs** dialog box. The Capture Filter SAPs and ETYPEs dialog box displays two list boxes, **Enabled Protocols** and **Disabled Protocols (Figure 8-9)**.

tip

You should review your Capture Filter criteria before applying them, as it is possible to specify criteria that are mutually exclusive or cannot be met in a given environment.

Table 8-1   Branches of the Capture Filter dialog box

Branch	Description
SAP/ETYPE	SAP is an acronym for Server Access Point. ETYPE is an acronym for Ethertype or Ethernet type. Used to specify protocols such as Transmission Control Protocol (TCP) and Address Resolution Protocol (ARP). By default, this is set to Any SAP or Any ETYPE.
Address Pair	Used for specifying computer addresses for capturing frames.
Pattern Matches	Used for specifying the capture pattern of ASCII or hexadecimal data.

Figure 8-9 Capture Filter SAPs and ETYPEs dialog box

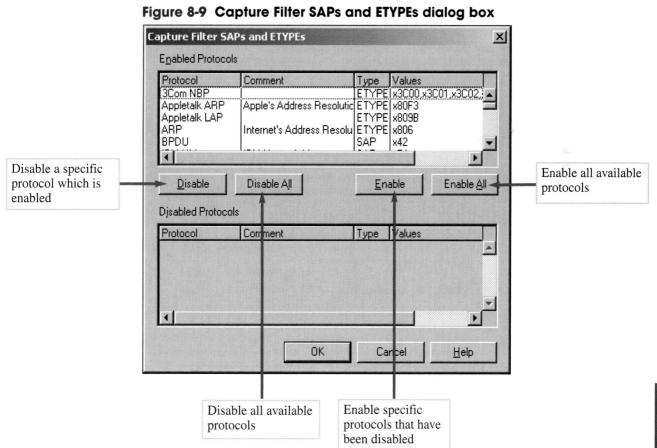

skill 4

Using Capture Filters to Capture Data (cont'd)

exam objective

Plan network traffic monitoring. Tools might include Network Monitor and System Monitor.

how to

4. To enable capturing only TCP protocol frames, click [Disable All]. All the protocols are disabled and displayed in the **Disabled Protocols** list.
5. Click the **TCP** option from the **Disabled Protocols** list and then click [Enable]. Now the TCP protocol displays in the **Enabled Protocols** list.
6. After specifying the enabled and disabled protocols, click [OK] to close the **Capture Filter SAPs and ETYPEs** dialog box.
7. Click [OK] once you have specified the Capture Filter criteria. All subsequent frames captured by the Network Monitor in this session will use this Capture Filter.

more

Similar to the filters specified to capture specific data, the **Filter** command on the Display menu (in the **Network Monitor Capture** window) can be used to specify conditions for displaying previously captured data; this filter does not affect the Capture Filters that are applied to newly captured data. To display specific information, add the conditions in the **Display Filter** dialog box. To specify a Display Filter, click **Display** on the menu bar and then click **Filter**. The **Display Filter** dialog box opens **(Figure 8-10)**. Conditions in the Display Filter dialog box can be specified using logical operators such as AND, OR, and NOT. Similar to the **Capture Filter** dialog box, the **Display Filter** dialog box has options for applying filters on basis of the **Address Pair**, **Protocol**, and **Properties** of the captured frames. These three option types for the Display Filter are defined as follows, and are shown in **Figure 8-11(a)** and **Figure 8-11(b)**:

◆ **Address Pair:** Specifies the logical or physical addresses from which you want to display a data frame.
◆ **Protocol:** Specifies the protocols you want to find in the Frame Viewer window.
◆ **Property:** Specifies which protocol properties you want to find or add to the filter decision tree.

The **Save** command allows you to save a display filter for later use. Upon saving, the display filter frames are written to a **.df** file. To load a previously saved filter, use the **Load** command. By saving the filter, you can reuse it on other captured data without recreating it. Saving a filter does not save the captured frames; you must save the capture itself to save the captured frames.

Figure 8-10 Display Filter dialog box

Specifies protocol for display

Specifies computer addresses for display

Opens Expression dialog box, which is used to specify computer address pair and protocols that you want to display

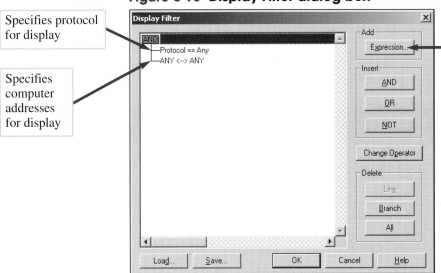

Figure 8-11(a) IP address of source computer and destination computer and protocol of the captured frames

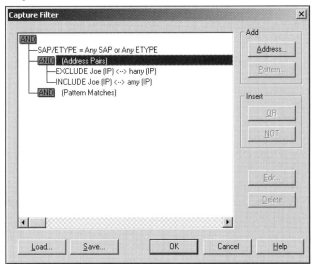

Figure 8-11(b) IP address of source computer and destination computer and protocol of the captured frames

* **SAP\ETYPE = LINE OF CAPTURE FILTER**

  For example, to capture only IP frames, disable all protocols and then enable IP ETYPE 0x800 and IP SAP 0x6.

* **<INCLUDE JOE ←→ ANN EXCLUDE JOE ←→ AMY**

  To capture frames from specific computers on your network, specify one or more address pairs in a capture filter (as above). You can monitor up to four specific address pairs simultaneously.

* **An address pair consists of:**

  * The addresses of the two computers you want to monitor traffic between. IP addresses are configured and shown as host names.

  * Arrows that specify the traffic direction you want to monitor.
  * The INCLUDE or EXCLUDE keyword, indicating how Network Monitor should respond to a frame that meets a filter's specifications.

* **By specifying a pattern match in a capture filter, you can:**

  * Limit a capture to only those frames containing a specific pattern of ASCII or hexadecimal data.
  * Specify how many bytes (offsets) into the frame the pattern must occur.

skill 5

Analyzing Captured Data

exam objective

Plan network traffic monitoring. Tools might include Network Monitor and System Monitor.

overview

In order to diagnose potential problems in a network after capturing data, you need to analyze the data. Analyzing captured data frames helps network administrators to:

◆ Understand the effect of network traffic load on the system's resources.

◆ Test the impacts of configuration changes on the system. For instance, you can change the current protocol suite (for instance, going from IPX/SPX to TCP/IP) of your network and compare the performance against the previous protocol.

◆ View trends and changes in the captured data frames. This may indicate a trend in resource usage on the network and help you plan your future upgrades.

Use the following guidelines when analyzing the statistics displayed in the Network Monitor Capture window:

◆ If you come across a **reset** (which occurs when a frame fails to reach its destination), you need to consider the sequence numbers and pre-acknowledgements associated with the data frames. Every data frame has a particular time of existence. If, within a designated period, a frame is not able to reach its destination, a reset occurs to resend the data packets. Resets originating in Transmission Control Protocol (TCP)-based network traffic are easier to trace than in higher layer protocols, such as Server Message Block (SMB).

◆ View the time interval between the captured data frames and the number of retries made by the network protocol to resend the data packet. By default, the number of retries for TCP is five.

◆ Analyze the time interval, source IP address and TCP port, and destination IP address and TCP port of the captured data frames to determine the acknowledgement associated with them.

◆ Observe the trend in the captured data frames to find out whether the sender is performing a retry, a backup, or a reset for the data frames, or if the receiver is asking for a missed frame by acknowledging a previous sequence.

Table 8-2 describes the nine types of data that appear in the Network Monitor Capture summary pane.

Table 8-2   *Types of Data in the Network Monitor Capture summary pane*

Column Heading	Description
Frame	Lists a frame number for each frame captured in the capture session. Frames are listed in the order in which they are captured.
Time	Displays a frame's capture time, in terms of either time of day or elapsed time since previous frame captured.
Src MAC Addr	Displays the source MAC address (the hardware address of the computer sending the frame or the router forwarding it).
Dst MAC Addr	Displays the destination MAC address (the hardware address of the destination computer).
Protocol	Displays the protocol type used by the frame.
Description	Displays a brief description of the contents of the frame, such as first protocol used in the frame, last protocol used, etc.
Src Other Addr	Displays the IP/IPX address of the frame source, rather than the MAC address.
Dst Other Addr	Displays the IP/IPX address of the frame destination.
Type Other Addr	Displays the type of address displayed in the previous two columns.

Summary

◆ Monitoring a network can help an administrator to prevent network problems.

◆ Windows 2003 provides a utility known as Network Monitor that captures and displays data transmitted across a Windows Server 2003 network.

◆ Windows Server 2003 includes a limited version of Network Monitor that enables you to capture and display frames transmitted between the Windows Server 2003 computer running Network Monitor and a client located on the same local area network. The Windows SMS 2003 version of Network Monitor enables a Windows Server 2003 computer to monitor network traffic between two or more computers on the LAN or remote network segments.

◆ The installation of the Network Monitor Driver enables Network Monitor to capture frames from client network adapters and forwards the information to Network Monitor for analysis and display.

◆ During the installation of Network Monitor in a Windows Server 2003 system, the Network Monitor Driver installs by default.

◆ Network Monitor captures the data sent to and from computers. Additionally, Network Monitor can interpret application layer protocols such as HyperText Transfer Protocol (HTTP) and File Transfer Protocol (FTP).

◆ The conditions for capturing and displaying specific information can be defined by using the Capture Filter and the Display Filter.

◆ The statistical summary of captured data displays in different panes of the Network Monitor Capture window and can be saved into a file for later use.

◆ Network Monitor simplifies data interpretation by displaying captured data in three different panes in the Frame Viewer window.

Key Terms

Capture Filter	Frame	Network Monitor Driver
Capture Trigger	Ipconfig	Reset
Display Filter	Network Monitor	Tracert

Test Yourself

1. The four panes of the Network Monitor Capture window are: Station, Total, Session, and _____.
   a. Summary
   b. Detail
   c. Graph
   d. Hex

2. Which of the following options captures frames containing a specific pattern of ASCII or hexadecimal data?
   a. Buffer Space
   b. SAP/ETYPE
   c. Buffer Space THEN Pattern Match
   d. Pattern Match

3. Which of the following options can you specify in the Display Filter dialog box?
   a. Length of the frame
   b. Content of the frame
   c. Time
   d. Protocol

4. Which of the following panes in the Network Monitor Capture window displays statistics about sessions started from or to the computer running Network Monitor?
   a. Graph
   b. Total
   c. Station
   d. Session

5. A _____ copies frames to the Capture buffer, which is a resizable storage area in the memory of the computer.
  a. Network Monitor
  b. Network Driver Interface Specification (NDIS) feature
  c. Network Monitor Driver
  d. Network Capture window

6. When you save a captured frame, it has a file extension of _____.
  a. .cap
  b. .adr
  c. .frm
  d. .df

7. Which of the following TCP/IP packets can you monitor on a switched network using Network Monitor?
  a. Only the packets sent from the server.
  b. Only the packets addressed to the server.
  c. All the packets addressed to and sent from the server.

8. The Network Monitor utility installs by default when installing Windows Server 2003.
  a. True
  b. False

9. To capture and display frames sent to and from remote computers, you need to install the _____ on your system.
  a. Windows Server 2003 version of Network Monitor
  b. Network Monitor Driver protocol
  c. SMS 2003 version of Network Monitor
  d. Gathering agent

Projects: On Your Own

1. Install the Network Monitor on your system.
  a. Open the **Control Panel** window.
  b. Open the **Add/Remove Windows Components** window.
  c. Open the **Network Component Wizard**.
  d. Select the **Management and Monitoring Tools** option and open the **Management and Monitoring Tools** dialog box.
  e. Select the **Network Monitor Tools** option.
  f. Complete the process of installing Network Monitor.
  g. Close the **Windows Components** Wizard.

2. Capture network frames and display a summary of the captured information.
  a. Open the **Network Monitor Capture** window.
  b. Select the network that you want to monitor.
  c. Start the capture process.
  d. Stop the capture process.
  e. Display the captured data.

3. Use **Capture Filter** to capture network frames.
  a. Open the **Network Monitor Capture** window.
  b. Click **Filter** on the **Capture** menu.
  c. Select the **SAP/ETYPE** branch in the **Capture Filter** dialog box.
  d. Display the **Capture Filter SAPs and ETYPEs** dialog box.
  e. Disable all protocols.
  f. Enable the **TCP** protocol.
  g. Close the Capture Filter dialog box.

Problem Solving Scenarios

You are a network security officer at a company. Intrusions into your corporate Web server occur frequently. The primary suspects are computer users within your own company. It is your job to identify the intruders. Through initial monitoring of the network, you suspect that the intrusions are HTTP (TCP)-based. Since the network is heavily loaded, you want to reduce the amount of captured data. Prepare a document describing the plan you will follow in order to efficiently monitor the traffic and identify the intruders.

Planning Data Protection and Recovery

Before making backups, you should create a backup plan so that you can retrieve lost data quickly and efficiently. First, you must identify the data that needs to be backed up and the medium you are going to use. Then, you must decide upon a backup schedule and a backup type. Backup types differ depending on how the archive attribute or backup marker (also referred to as the archive bit) is treated. The archive attribute is set on a file when it has changed. Some backup types will remove the archive bit when the file has been backed up, while others will leave it at its present state.

There are several tools and utilities that are used to protect your data and system in the event of a catastrophe such as a disk drive crash, a virus, or a power outage. The Windows Server 2003 Backup utility includes the Backup Wizard, the Restore Wizard, and the Automated System Recovery Wizard. You use the Backup Wizard to create copies of vital enterprise data that are either stored in a backup file on a different hard disk, or to a dedicated backup device such as a magnetic tape drive. If data is lost or damaged, you can use the Restore Wizard to recover it from the backup copies. You must also back up all system files, the startup environment files, the partition boot sector, and the Registry, because they can also be accidentally deleted or become corrupted. The Automated System Recovery Wizard will be used to back up the operating system files, configuration settings, and System State data so that you can rebuild your system if the system files become corrupt or the operating system will not start.

Goals

In this lesson, you will learn how to use the Windows Backup utility, how to plan a backup strategy, and how to schedule backups. You will also learn how to restore files from your backups.

Requirements

To complete this lesson, you will need administrative rights on a Windows Server 2003 computer. You will also need a folder named Reports (with miscellaneous files contained therein to suit your backup media storage limits) stored on the C: drive on your computer, and between 300 and 400 MB of space on your storage medium for the System State data.

skill 1

Understanding the Windows Backup Utility

exam objective

Plan a backup and recovery strategy.

overview

The data stored on any computer can be categorized as either user data or System State data. **System State data** consists of several key components related to the operating system or applications. Loss of System State data can render a computer non-operational.

While System State data is critical to the operation of the computer, user data can be even more vital to the operation of the organization. You must make sure that user data is protected from losses due to viruses, disk drive failures, or user deletion. You can safeguard data by creating backups of the files and folders saved on network file servers or on a local computer. Lost or damaged data can be retrieved if you have properly designed and implemented a comprehensive backup plan. You can use the Windows Backup utility to perform backups and to schedule backups to be performed at a specified date and time.

Before you perform a backup, you must decide whether you want to back up user data or System State data, or both. If you are backing up user data, you can either back up all the files and folders on a computer or only specific files and folders. You back up the System State data so that you can restore the operating system to its original state in the event of a system failure. A System State restore is performed on a clean installation of the operating system to recover all of the configuration changes. System State backups should frequently be part of the backup process because the System State will change when system components, such as the Registry, change.

In order to back up data, you must have the necessary user rights to access the data being backed up. Any user can back up files and folders that they have created (files they own) and files for which they have the Read, Read and Execute, Modify, or Full Control permission. Local Administrators and Backup Operators can back up any file or folder on the local computer, regardless of permissions settings. Domain Administrators and members of the built-in **Backup Operators** group on a domain controller can back up any file or folder in the domain or in other trusted domains because they are granted the **Back up files and directories** user right by default.

Similarly, to restore a backed up file or folder, you must have the appropriate user rights and permissions. File or folder owners can restore the backup copy. Other users can restore files or folders if they have the Write, Modify, or Full Control permission. Members of the local Administrators and Backup Operators groups can restore any file or folder on the local computer. Domain Administrators and Backup Operators on the domain controller have the **Restore files and directories** user right by default and can restore any backup file or folder on the domain.

Next, you must decide on the media you will use. Typically, a server will have a large amount of data to back up, requiring the speed and storage capacities magnetic tape provides. Magnetic tape has been the most widely used backup medium because it is inexpensive and you can store large amounts of data on it; however, tape can deteriorate over time. **Table 9-1** lists types of backup media and their comparative advantages and disadvantages.

There are five different backup types from which you can choose either in the Backup Wizard or on the Backup Type tab in the Options dialog box. The different types of backup and their characteristics are explained in **Table 9-2**. In order to choose one of these types, you must first understand what the archive attribute or archive bit is and how each backup type handles it. The **archive attribute** is a property for files and folders that is used to identify them when they have changed. When a file has changed, the archive attribute, which is actually an attribute of the file header, is automatically set. This can be viewed on an NTFS partition in the **Advanced Attributes** dialog box. To access the Advanced Attributes dialog box, click the **Advanced** button on the **General** tab in the Properties dialog box for a file or folder.

tip

Some organizations use third-party backup and restore systems, such as Tivoli Storage Manager (TSM), to back up and recover data on all platforms. While TSM takes care of backup and restoration of user data, it is still vital and essential to use the platform's operating system utilities to back up (and restore, if necessary) System State data.

Table 9-1 Storage media

Media	Description
Online	Used to back up data onto a local or remote server. Online backups to a remote server are typically beneficial only if the WAN connection is fast and you have few files to store. If the WAN connection is slow or you have a large amount of data to back up, this can take a long time. Online backups allow you to avoid the management of storage media because you can have the server back up data on a regular basis. When you back up data to a remote server, your backed up data is safe if a natural calamity occurs at your location, because it is stored at another location.
Magnetic tape drives	Used to store backup data sequentially. This traditional backup media is often still the best choice because of its high capacity and low cost. Since hard disk size on new computers now averages several gigabytes, tape is generally the only media you can use to completely back up a hard disk without having to change media. Technological obsolescence can also present a problem. However, you must carefully mark and store the tapes, and tapes can deteriorate over time. DLT (Digital Linear Tape) drives are the most common backup devices. They are single-spindled and use magnetic tapes that can hold 20 GB to 40 GB of data and they transfer data at approximately 5 megabytes/sec. Super DLT drives have an average transfer rate of 11 megabytes/sec and can store up to 110 GB per tape, uncompressed. DLT and SDLT units are often not compatible. Mid-range and low-end systems generally use 8mm helical scan technology because of their high capacity. A disadvantage is that a complex tape path puts a lot of pressure on the tape. Low-end systems that have less demanding backup requirements can use 4mm helical scan digital audio tape (DAT) or quarter-inch cartridge (QIC) linear tape.
Optical	This category of media includes CD-R, CD-RW, DVD-R, and DVD-RAM. CD-R and CD-RW media can store up to 700 MB of data per CD, and DVD-R and DVD-RAM media can store up to 9.4 GB per DVD (4.7 GB per side). While this is a cheap and easy method for many to use, it requires the purchase of additional software, as the Windows Server 2003 Backup utility does not support the use of this media type.
DAT	Originally a format for storing music on magnetic tape, DAT was adopted for general data storage through an ISO (International Organization for Standardization) standard. You can sequentially store between 4 and 40 GB of backup data on a 120 meter tape depending on the standard and compression. Compression is designated from DDS-1 through DDS-4 (Digital Data Storage). DAT is a cost efficient choice for tape backups because the tapes and the drive are generally far less expensive than DLT, but because the sustained transfer rate is still considerably slower than DLT, DAT is generally only used in small network or workgroup environments.

Table 9-2 Types of backups

Backup Type	Criteria for Backing Up Files	Archive Attribute
Normal	All selected files/folders are backed up whether or not they have the archive attribute set.	Archive attribute is cleared.
Differential	Only the selected files/folders with the archive attribute set are backed up.	Archive attribute is not changed.
Incremental	Only the selected files/folders with the archive attribute set are backed up.	Archive attribute is cleared.
Copy	All selected files/folders are backed up whether or not they have the archive attribute set.	Archive attribute is not changed.
Daily	All selected files/folders that have been modified that day are backed up.	Archive attribute is not changed.

skill 1

Understanding the Windows Backup Utility (cont'd)

exam objective

Plan a backup and recovery strategy.

overview

tip

Always store at least one verified copy of your backups off site, in case a natural disaster (e.g., fire or flood) destroys the facility where the servers are hosted. Also, regularly verify that these backups actually work by performing a test restore on an offline computer.

Some backup types remove the archive attribute to mark files as having been backed up, while others do not. For example, in a **Normal backup**, the archive attribute is removed to denote that the file has been backed up, but in a **Copy backup**, the archive attribute is not removed. Copy backups are used between Normal and Incremental or Normal and Differential backups so that when they take place the backup process will not be affected by the removal of the archive bit. The Copy backup type essentially "ignores" the archive attribute, creating a representation of your data at a particular point in time. An **Incremental backup** backs up only selected files and folders that have the archive attribute and the archive attribute is then removed. Thus, if a file has not changed since the previous backup, it will be skipped during the next Incremental backup. A **Differential backup**, on the other hand, backs up only selected files and folders with the archive attribute, and it is not removed. Therefore, even if a file has not changed since the previous Differential backup, it will be backed up again because it still has the archive attribute. A **Daily backup** is used to back up all selected files and folders that have changed on that day, but the archive bit is not removed.

how to

Back up and restore the Reports folder.

1. Click **Start**, point to **All Programs**, point to **Accessories**, point to **System Tools**, and click **Backup** to open the **Backup or Restore Wizard (Figure 9-1)**.
2. Click the **Advanced Mode** link to open the **Backup Utility Advanced Mode window (Figure 9-2)**.
3. Click the **Backup** tab.
4. Expand the local disk (C:).
5. Scroll down the list of folders to locate the **Reports** folder. Click in the check box to the left of the Reports folder to select it.
6. In the **Backup media or file name** text box, type: *x*:\Backup-Reports.bkf (where *x* represents the drive letter you are using) **(Figure 9-3)**.
7. Click **Start Backup**.
8. The **Backup Job Information** dialog box opens. Check the information entered in the dialog box, and click **Start Backup** **(Figure 9-4)**.

Figure 9-1 The Backup or Restore Wizard

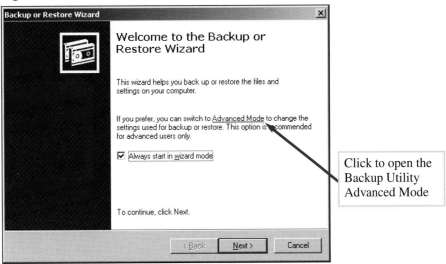

Figure 9-2 The Backup Utility Advanced Mode

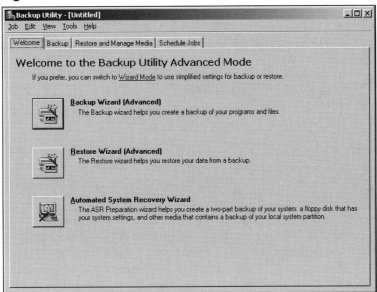

Figure 9-3 Selecting the folders and files to backup

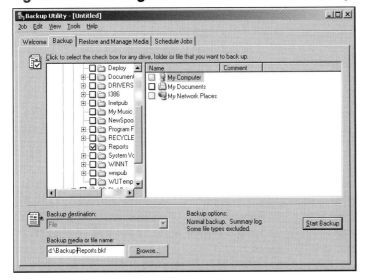

Figure 9-4 The Backup Job Information dialog box

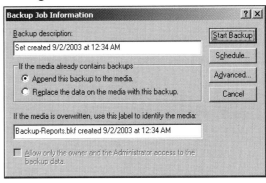

skill 1

Understanding the Windows Backup Utility *(cont'd)*

exam objective

Plan a backup and recovery strategy.

how to

9. The **Backup Progress** dialog box opens and displays the status of the backup process including the backed up files, the time taken by the backup process, and the backup media used. After the backup is complete, the **Status** text box will show **Completed**, as shown in **Figure 9-5**.
10. Click [Report...] to open the text file, which contains the details of the backup process **(Figure 9-6)**.
11. Close the report. Close the Backup Progress dialog box.
12. Click the **Restore and Manage Media** tab.
13. Expand the **File** icon.
14. Expand the local disk (**C:**).
15. Click the check box next to the Reports folder. Select the Reports folder to view the contents of the folder.
16. In the **Restore files to** list box, select **Alternate location**. Type: *x:* **\Reports-Backup** in the **Alternate location** text box **(Figure 9-7)**.
17. Click [Start Restore]. In the **Confirm Restore** dialog box, click [OK].
18. The **Restore Progress** dialog box opens. When the job is complete, close the Restore Progress dialog box and the Backup Utility window.
19. Click [Start]. Click **My Computer**. Locate the drive on which you backed up and restored the Reports folder.
20. Verify that both Backup-Reports.bkf and Reports-Backup have been saved on the backup media.

more

Organizations use a blend of the different backup types in order to optimize the time spent on both the backup and the restore processes. For example, a Normal backup will take longer than an Incremental backup because with a Normal backup, all selected files are backed up whether or not they have the archive attribute; however, you can quickly restore all of your files using the most recent copy of the backup file. On the other hand, if you used only Incremental backups you would likely need to restore numerous backup files in order to recover all of your data. Since an Incremental backup only backs up files and folders with the archive attribute, you would not be starting with a full set of files, as each backup would include only files that changed on that day. Therefore, although the backup process would be quick, the restore process would be unwieldy, if not impossible. For these reasons, you should use a combination of Normal and other backup types to effectively manage your backup and restore times and ensure that all lost data can be recovered. For example, if you create a backup schedule that uses a combination of the Normal and Differential backup types, you will only have to restore the last Normal backup and the last Differential backup. On the other hand, if you use a combination of Normal and Incremental backups, you will have to restore the last Normal backup and all Incremental backups since that date. A Normal/Incremental strategy will take less time to back up files because each Incremental backup will only capture changed files, whereas each Differential backup will capture all files that have changed since the last Normal backup. However, a Normal/Incremental strategy will take more time to restore files.

In most modern networks, however, the strategy is much simpler. Since tape drive speeds and capacities have increased so rapidly in the past few years, most large companies simply perform a full normal backup of the servers nightly.

Figure 9-5 The Backup Progress dialog box

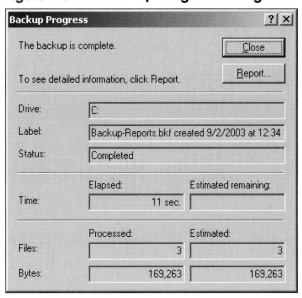

Figure 9-6 The backup log file

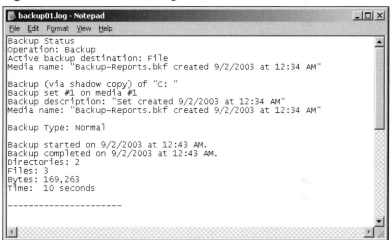

Figure 9-7 The Restore and Manage Media tab

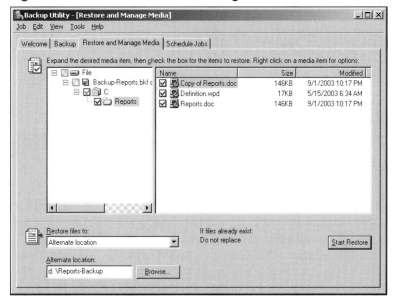

skill 2

Scheduling a Backup

exam objective

Plan a backup and recovery strategy.

overview

The System State changes when any system component, such as the Registry, changes. For example, when you install new software or hardware on your Windows Server 2003 computer, if the application makes Registry entries, the System State data will change. To keep up-to-date with these changes, you should perform a backup of the System State data regularly—typically, every night and before installing new hardware or software on your server. It is critical to back up this data because it will allow you to restore the Registry data, the system startup files, all files under Windows File Protection, the Component Service Class Registration (COM +) database, and the Certificate Services database, if it is installed, to its most recent state using the latest backup.

You can use the Backup utility (Ntbackup) to schedule backups to run at specified dates and times. Ntbackup uses the **Task Scheduler** to schedule the backup. For example, if you want to back up the System State data on your member server twice a week at 7:00 PM, you can specify the two days along with the start time in the **Schedule Job** dialog box, which you can access from the Backup Wizard. The Task Scheduler will then automatically initiate the backup operation at the scheduled date and time. You can also set the number of weeks, months, or years that you want this schedule to continue. The backup job will be put on the calendar on the Schedule Jobs tab in the Backup window. If the server you are backing up is running Certificate Services, you must also schedule Certificate Services to stop before the backup is run. The backup will not succeed if Certificate Services is running. You can also use the Task Scheduler to restart Certificate Services when the backup job is complete.

how to

Schedule an Incremental backup of the System State data from your member server to a backup device to occur three times a week for three weeks at 11:00 PM on a backup device. (You may use a Zip or Jaz drive, or the local hard disk, to complete this exercise. You will generally need between 300 and 400 MB of space on your storage medium for the System State data.)

1. Click **Start**, point to **All Programs**, point to **Accessories**, point to **System Tools**, and click **Backup** to open the **Backup or Restore Wizard**.
2. Click the **Advanced Mode** link to open the **Backup Utility Advanced Mode** window.
3. Click the **Schedule Jobs** tab. Click **Add Job** to start the Backup Wizard.
4. Click **Next** to open the **What to Back Up** screen. Select the **Only back up the System State data** option button (**Figure 9-8**).
5. Click **Next** to open the **Backup Type, Destination, and Name** screen. Select the drive you are using for your backup media in the **Choose a place to save your backup** list box, or use the **Browse** button to locate the drive. In the **Type a name for this backup** text box, type **BackupSSD.bkf** (**Figure 9-9**).
6. Click **Next** to open the **How to Back Up** screen. Select the **Verify data after backup** check box.
7. Click **Next** to open the **Backup Options** screen. Select the **Replace the existing backups** option button. Select the **Allow only the owner and the Administrator access to the backup data and to any backups appended to this medium** check box.
8. Click **Next** to open the **When to Back Up** screen. In the **Job name** text box, type **SSD Backup**.
9. Click **Set Schedule** to open the **Schedule Job** dialog box.
10. Select **Weekly** in the **Schedule Task** list box.
11. Select the current day of the week.
12. Enter a time 5 minutes ahead of the current time as displayed on the computer's clock in the **Start time** box. (**Figure 9-10**).

Figure 9-8 Backing up the System State data

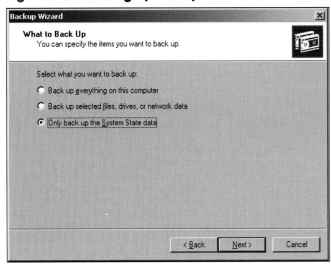

Figure 9-9 The Backup Type, Destination, and Name screen

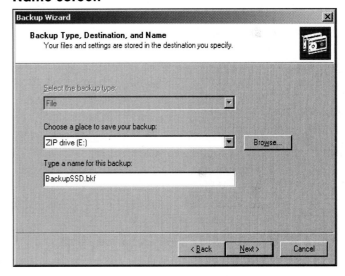

Figure 9-10 The Schedule Job dialog box

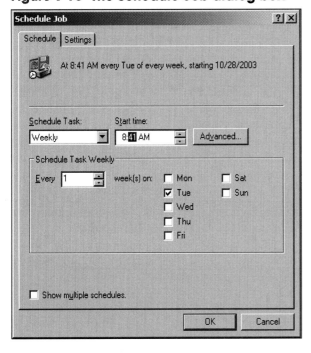

skill 2

Scheduling a Backup (cont'd)

Plan a backup and recovery strategy.

how to

13. Click [Advanced...] to open the **Advanced Schedule Options** dialog box. You use this dialog box to specify the start and end dates for the job. By default, the current date appears as the start date.
14. Select the **End Date** check box. Click the list arrow on the **End Date** list box. A calendar for the current month appears (**Figure 9-11**).
15. To schedule the backup operation to continue for three weeks, select a date that is 21 days from the start date. Click [OK] to apply the settings and return to the Schedule Job dialog box.
16. Click [OK] to apply the settings and return to the **When to Backup** screen. The **Set Account Information** dialog box opens. In this dialog box, you must enter a valid account name and password for a user who is a member of either the Administrators or Backup Operators group. By default, *<computername>***\administrator** is entered in the **Run as** text box if you are logged on using the Administrator account. Otherwise, the account that you are logged in as is displayed.
17. Type the administrator password in the **Password** and **Confirm Password** text boxes, and click [OK] (**Figure 9-12**).
18. Click [Next >] to open the **Completing the Backup Wizard** screen.
19. Click [Finish] to complete the Backup Wizard and return to the Schedule Jobs tab in the Backup window. The System State backup you configured displays on the calendar for the next three weeks (**Figure 9-13**).
20. Close the Backup window.
21. Click [Start], point to **All Programs**, point to **Accessories**, point to **System Tools**, and then click **Scheduled Tasks** to open the **Scheduled Tasks** window. The presence of the SSDBackup task in the Scheduled Tasks folder verifies the successful creation of the backup operation (**Figure 9-14**).
22. Double-click the **SSD Backup** icon to open the **SSD Backup** dialog box. Click the **Schedule** tab to verify the schedule details.
23. Click [OK] to close the SSDBackup dialog box.
24. Close the Scheduled Tasks folder. The Task Scheduler will initiate the backup operation shortly.

more

On the Schedule Jobs tab in the Backup window, you can click the icon for a scheduled job to open the **Scheduled Job Options** dialog box. Here you can change the job name on the **Schedule data** tab and view the job details on the **Backup details** tab. The **Job summary** section displays the backup type and the properties that were set for the backup job such as whether **Verify data** has been set, whether hardware compression is to be used, and if access is restricted to the owner or administrator. Here, you can also find out the media name that will be used for the job and the Backup Set description.

When you restore files, you have three choices as to where you want them to be restored. You can restore them to the original location, restore them to an alternate location, or restore them to a single folder. If you restore to the original or an alternate location, you retain the original folder structure. However, if you restore the backup file to a single folder, the original folder structure is no longer kept and the single folder will contain all of the files that were in all of the folders that were backed up.

Figure 9-11 The Advanced Schedule Options dialog box

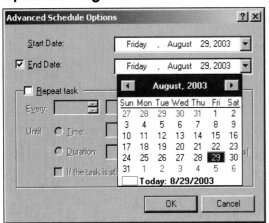

Figure 9-12 The Set Account Information dialog box

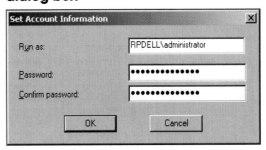

Figure 9-13 Scheduled jobs on the calendar on the Schedule Jobs tab

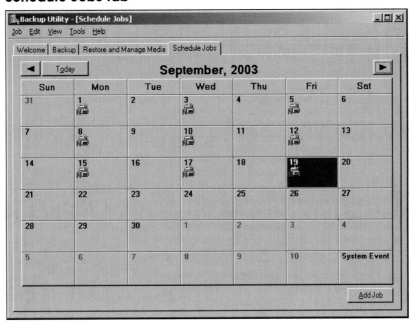

Figure 9-14 The Scheduled Tasks window

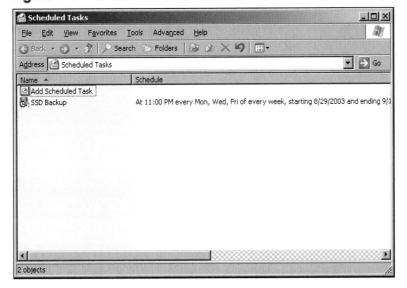

skill 3

Restoring System Data

exam objective

Plan a backup and recovery strategy. Plan a backup strategy that uses volume shadow copy. Plan system recovery that uses Automated System Recovery (ASR).

overview

The purpose of backing up data is to enable you to retrieve it in the event of a virus attack, a system or disk failure, or for any other reason. To retrieve data from an existing backup, you can either use the **Restore Wizard** in Ntbackup, or you can use the **Restore** tab in the Backup Utility window to manually run the restoration process. You should test the restoration process regularly to ensure that you will be able to restore your data to its original state in the event of a catastrophe. To test the restoration process, you should restore data to an alternate location and compare the restored data with the original data on the hard disk. Your restore strategy is often based on the backup strategy you chose. For example, if you used a combination of Normal and Incremental backups, you will have to restore the last Normal backup you made along with all Incremental backups since that date. If you used a Normal/Differential strategy, you will have to restore the last Normal backup and the last Differential backup. It is also important to keep records of each backup job that is performed. Good recordkeeping may allow you to restore tapes from only a specific date, depending on what you need to restore. You should create and print a backup log for each job that will detail all backed up files and folders and which tape, disk, or other storage media the job is stored on.

By default, the Restore Wizard restores data to its original location. For example, if you back up the My Documents folder, which is stored in the C:\Documents and Settings\user_account_name\My Documents folder, when you restore the My Documents folder, the wizard will automatically restore the folder to the correct folder for the user account in C:\Documents and Settings. If you restore files that are already on your system, you must decide whether you want to replace the existing files with the files from the backup set. When you back up a file, the security settings, such as the user permissions, are preserved with the file. If you must restore the file, you have the option to restore the original security settings.

Thus, if you restore a file from an NTFS partition to an NTFS partition, the security settings for the file can optionally be retained. Even when you restore files to a different directory, they can retain the full NTFS permissions set when the file was backed up because they are set not to inherit permissions from the parent folder. However, if you restore an NTFS file or folder to a FAT partition, you will lose the security settings because a FAT partition does not support NTFS security settings.

If you are restoring System State data, including Active Directory objects on a domain controller, you can perform one of the following types of restores.

◆ **Non-Authoritative restore (Normal):** You use this method when you need to recover a domain controller from hardware failure or replacement and you are sure that the data on the other domain controllers in the forest is correct. Under these circumstances, all you must do is restore the most recent backup of the domain controller. Restored data, including Active Directory objects, will have their original update sequence number. The update sequence number is used to detect and propagate Active Directory changes among the servers on the network. The Active Directory replication system will view data that is restored non-authoritatively as old data, and so it will thus not be replicated to the other servers. If more recent data is available on other servers, the Active Directory replication system will use this to update the restored data.

◆ **Authoritative restore (Figure 9-15):** You use an authoritative restore in order to replicate restored data to other servers. Authoritative restores are typically used when accounts or other Active Directory objects have been deleted in error. You perform an authoritative restore by restoring the backup non-authoritatively, then running the Ntdsutil utility. In Ntdsutil, you choose authoritative restore and enter the distinguished

Figure 9-15 Authoritative restore

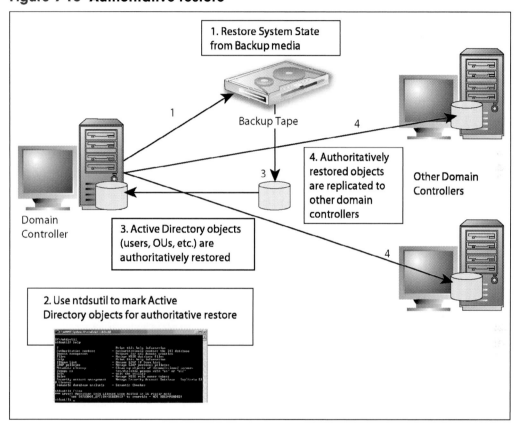

skill 3

Restoring System Data (cont'd)

exam objective

Plan a backup and recovery strategy. Plan a backup strategy that uses volume shadow copy. Plan system recovery that uses Automated System Recovery (ASR).

overview

names for the object or objects you wish to restore. This increases the update sequence number (USN) on the specified objects, making them the "most current" copies of the objects. This, in turn, causes the restored objects to be replicated to the other domain controllers.

◆ **Primary restore:** You do a primary restore when you must rebuild the domain from backup because all domain controllers in the domain have been lost. You perform a primary restore on the first domain controller and non-authoritative restores on all the other domain controllers.

how to

Restore the System State data on your member server. (If the task you created in the previous skill has not yet run, open the Scheduled Tasks window, right-click SSD Backup, and click Run. You will have to wait until the System State data has been backed up before you can perform this exercise.)

1. Click **Start** and click the **Run** command to open the **Run** dialog box.
2. In the **Open** text box, type **ntbackup**, and click **OK** to open the **Backup or Restore Wizard**.
3. Click **Next >** to open the **Backup or Restore** screen. Select the **Restore files and settings** option button.
4. Click **Next >** to open the **What to Restore** screen. Insert the disk with your System State backup into the appropriate drive.
5. In the **Items to restore** box, expand the **File** folder.
6. In the File node, expand **BackupSSD.bkf created on mm/dd/yyyy** node.
7. Click in the check box next to **System State (Figure 9-16)**.
8. Click **Next >** to open the **Completing the Backup or Restore Wizard** screen.
9. Click **Advanced...** to open the **Where to Restore** screen. Keep the default **Original location** in the **Restore files to** list box.
10. Click **Next >** . In the warning dialog box, click **OK** to overwrite the current System State. The **How to Restore** screen opens. Select the **Replace existing files** option button.
11. Click **Next >** to open the **Advanced Restore Options** screen. Choose any that apply.
12. Click **Next >** to open to the **Completing the Backup or Restore Wizard** screen. Click **Finish** .
13. The **Restore Progress** dialog box opens showing the status of the operation, the estimated and actual amount of data being restored, the time that has passed, and the time left until the operation is complete (**Figure 9-17**).

Figure 9-16 Restoring the System State data

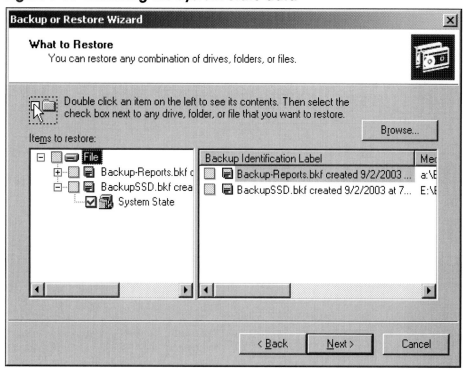

Figure 9-17 The Restore Progress dialog box

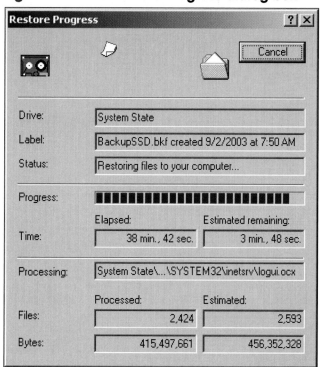

skill 3

Restoring System Data (cont'd)

exam objective

Plan a backup and recovery strategy. Plan a backup strategy that uses volume shadow copy. Plan system recovery that uses Automated System Recovery (ASR).

how to

14. When, the operation is complete, click [Report...] in the Restore Progress dialog box to view information on the restore process. The restore log, which will open in Notepad, shows the number of files that have been restored, the duration of the restore process, the total size of the files restored, the start and end time for the restore operation, the restore destination, and the media type and label. This information will be appended to the backup log (**Figure 9-18**). The report log can prove useful at a later date to confirm what files were restored.

15. Close the log file. Close the Restore Progress dialog box. You will be prompted to restart the computer.

more

The Restore utility is used to retrieve lost data from the backup copies. An Automated System Recovery (ASR) is a backup of your system configuration including critical system files and the Registry. The ASR backup set includes a backup of all system files needed to start your system and a floppy disk that lists the Windows system files installed on your computer. It is used to repair your system partition in the event of a complete malfunction due to a hard drive failure or corrupt system files.

When creating an ASR set, all System State data, services, and disks associated with operating system files are completely backed up. However, no user data is backed up, so a separate backup is required to ensure the validity of user data. To restore the ASR backup set, you must have the original ASR backup, the ASR floppy disk, and your Windows Server 2003 installation CD. Since each ASR floppy disk is unique, an ASR floppy disk from a different ASR set cannot be used to restore the ASR backup. For this reason, you should create multiple copies of the ASR floppy disk.

The **Volume Shadow Copy Service (VSS)** provides two new services in Windows Server 2003. You can configure VSS so that previous versions of saved files stored in a shared directory can be recovered if they are accidentally deleted or overwritten. VSS can also be used by applications to access locked files or files that are in use by other services or applications. The Backup Utility in Windows Server 2003 uses the API for VSS so that all files, including those that are open or locked, can be backed up.

When configured, VSS keeps a history of your files on a volume. This allows you or your users to go back to previous versions of files stored on the volume. By default, VSS creates two copies of changed files per day, at 7:00 AM and 12:00 PM, local server time. While this schedule is appropriate for most organizations, if your organization has users who work non-standard hours (such as 3:00 PM to 11:00 PM), or users who access the server from different time zones, you may need to modify the schedule to fit your needs. However, keep in mind that VSS has a maximum limit of 64 copies of any given file. For this reason, extremely rapid copy schedules are not recommended. Microsoft recommends that you configure VSS to create shadow copies no more than once per hour.

Figure 9-18 The restore log

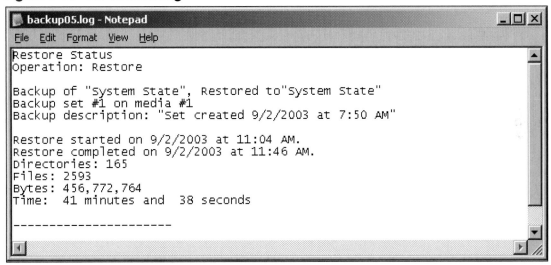

Summary

- You can categorize the data stored on any computer as either user data or System State data.
- System State data consists of files related to the operating system. Loss of System State data can render a machine non-operational.
- The archive attribute is a property for files and folders that is used to identify them when they have changed.
- There are five different backup types, which are identified according to how they handle the archive attribute.
- In a Normal backup, all selected files and folders are backed up whether or not they have the archive attribute and the archive attribute is removed.
- In a Differential backup, only the selected files and folders with the archive attribute are backed up and the archive attribute is not removed.
- In an Incremental backup, only the selected files and folders with the archive attribute are backed up and the archive attribute is removed.
- In a Copy backup, all selected files and folders are backed up whether or not they have the archive attribute and the archive attribute is removed.
- In a Daily backup, all selected files and folders that have been modified that day are backed up and the archive attribute is not removed.

- To retrieve data from an existing backup, you can either use the Restore Wizard or you can use the Restore tab in the Backup Utility window to manually run the restoration process.
- Your restore strategy is often based on the backup strategy you chose. If you used a combination of Normal and Incremental backups, you will have to restore the last Normal backup you made along with all Incremental backups since that date.
- If you used a Normal/Differential strategy, you will have to restore the last Normal backup and the last Differential backup.
- When you back up a file, the security settings, such as the user permissions, are preserved with the file. If you must restore the file, you have the option to restore the original security settings.
- If you restore a file from an NTFS partition to an NTFS partition, you have the option to retain the full NTFS security settings for the file. This is true even when you restore files to a different directory, because they are set not to inherit permissions from the parent folder.
- If you restore an NTFS file or folder to a FAT partition, you will lose the security settings because a FAT partition does not support NTFS security settings.

Key Terms

Archive attribute
Authoritative restore
Backup
Copy backup

Daily backup
Differential backup
Incremental backup
Non-authoritative (normal) restore

Normal backup
Parity bit
System State data
Volume Shadow Copy Service (VSS)

Test Yourself

1. You are working as an administrator at DataNet, Inc. One of your duties is to back up large data files three times per week on magnetic tape drives. The time taken to perform the Normal backup is about 6 hours. Which of the following backup options will you use on Wednesdays and Fridays if reducing the amount of time it takes to perform the backup on those days is your top priority?
   a. Incremental backup
   b. Normal backup
   c. Copy backup
   d. Differential backup

2. Users who have the _____ permission for a file or folder, or who have backup operator rights, will be able to back up and restore other user's files.
   a. Read
   b. Write
   c. Read and Execute
   d. Modify

3. Which of the following statements is true about the archive attribute? (Choose all that apply.)
   a. The archive attribute is also called the backup marker or the archive bit.
   b. In a Normal backup, all selected files and folders are backed up whether they have the archive attribute or not, and the attribute is removed to denote that a file has been backed up.
   c. The archive attribute is used to mark files that have been modified since the last backup.
   d. In a Copy backup, all selected files and folders with or without the archive attribute are backed up and the archive attribute is removed.
   e. A Differential backup backs up all selected files and folders and the attribute is not removed.

4. Which of the following should be done to ensure the integrity of backups? (Choose all that apply.)
   a. Back up all files to the system partition.
   b. Use only one set of backup media.
   c. Store backups off site.
   d. Perform regular test restorations.
   e. Use a RAID array instead of backups.

5. You are the junior administrator at Gecko Corp. Your boss, the senior administrator, has configured a rather complex backup consisting of the following:

   · Monday: Incremental Backup at 3 AM
   · Tuesday: Copy Backup at 3 AM
   · Wednesday: Differential Backup at 3 AM
   · Thursday: Incremental Backup at 3 AM
   · Friday: Normal Backup at 12 AM
   · Saturday: Copy Backup at 6 AM
   · Sunday: Differential Backup at 9AM

   The server fails around 4 PM on Thursday. Assuming that all tapes are valid, which order will be fastest in restoring as close to the point of failure as possible?
   a. Restore the backups in the following order: Friday, Saturday, Monday, Wednesday.
   b. Restore the backups in the following order: Tuesday, Thursday.
   c. Restore the backups in the following order: Tuesday, Wednesday, Thursday.
   d. Restore the backups in the following order: Friday, Sunday, Wednesday.
   e. Restore the backups in the following order: Friday, Monday, Thursday.

6. Which of the following users and/or groups can back up files? (Choose all that apply.)
   a. Members of the Domain Administrators group
   b. Members of the Administrators group
   c. Members of the Account Operators group
   d. Users that have Read permissions to the files
   e. Users that have been denied read permission but have the backup files and directories right

7. Which of the following backup types clear the archive bit? (Choose all that apply.)
   a. Normal
   b. Daily
   c. Differential
   d. Incremental
   e. Copy

8. Which of the following must be done to restore the SYSVOL directory?
   a. Press F8 during boot and choose "Safe Mode."
   b. Press F8 during boot and choose "Safe Mode with Command Prompt."
   c. Perform a normal system state restore.
   d. Press F8 during boot and choose "Recovery Console."
   e. Press F8 during boot and choose "Directory Services Restore Mode."

9. You are the network administrator for Kingdom Beds, Inc. You return from lunch one day to find that your junior administrator has deleted an OU containing over 200 user accounts. The deletion has been replicated. To properly restore the user accounts, which of the following actions should you take? (Choose all that apply.)
   a. Restore the last System State backup.
   b. Reboot the Server.
   c. Press F8 and choose "Directory Services Restore Mode."
   d. Run the Ntbackup utility.
   e. Run Adrestor.exe at the command prompt.
   f. Copy the SYSVOL folder from a functioning domain controller.
   g. Run ntdsutil.exe.

Projects: On Your Own

1. Schedule a normal backup of the My Documents folder to occur three times a week.
   a. Click **Start**, point to **All Programs**, point to **Accessories**, point to **System Tools**, and click **Backup**.
   b. Click the **Advanced Mode** link.
   c. Open the **Backup** tab.
   d. Select the **My Documents** folder for backup.
   e. Click **Start Backup**.
   f. Enter the backup description, select how to write on the media if it already contains backups, and enter a label for the backup.
   g. Click the **Schedule** button.
   h. Click **Yes** to save the backup selections.
   i. Enter a filename for saving the selection parameters for the backup job and click **Save**.
   j. Enter and confirm the password for the account from which the job will be run and click **OK**.
   k. In the **Scheduled Job Options** dialog box, enter the job name in the **Job name** text box.
   l. Click **Properties**.
   m. Select **Weekly** in the Scheduled Task list box.
   n. Select the **Mon**, **Wed**, and **Fri** check boxes.
   o. Enter the **Start time** of your choice.
   p. Click **OK** to close the **Schedule Job** dialog box.
   q. Click **OK** to close the **Scheduled Job Options** dialog box.
   r. Close the Backup Utility window.

2. Back up the System State data and system protected files.
   a. Click **Start**, point to **All Programs**, point to **Accessories**, point to **System Tools**, and click **Backup**.
   b. Click the **Advanced Mode** link
   c. Open the **Backup** tab.
   d. Click the **System State** check box in the left pane.
   e. Click **Start Backup**.
   f. In the **Backup Job Information** dialog box, click **Advanced**.
   g. Make sure the **Automatically backup System Protected Files with the System State** check box is selected.
   h. Close the **Advanced Backup Options** dialog box.
   i. Click **Start Backup**.
   j. When the backup is complete, click **Report** to view the backup log file.
   k. Close the log file, the **Backup Progress** dialog box, and the Backup Utility window.

Problem Solving Scenarios

You are the system administrator for a garden tools and supplies company. The CEO has asked you to confirm for her that a comprehensive backup plan has been designed and implemented for the network. Prepare a report for her explaining how you have provided for backing up the file server on which users save their daily reports, backing up the domain controller, and backing up four shared folders that contain sales data that will be imported into a database for analysis and archival.

10 Troubleshooting Network Infrastructure Problems

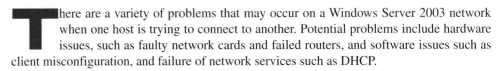

There are a variety of problems that may occur on a Windows Server 2003 network when one host is trying to connect to another. Potential problems include hardware issues, such as faulty network cards and failed routers, and software issues such as client misconfiguration, and failure of network services such as DHCP.

When troubleshooting network connectivity issues, there are many network services that must be checked to ensure they are working properly. These network services include:

◆ **DHCP:** This service automatically assigns IP address information, including addresses for DNS and WINS servers, to a client when they connect to the network.

◆ **TCP/IP routing:** Hosts must communicate with each other over a TCP/IP network. If there is a disruption anywhere on the network between the hosts, the communication will not be received. Utilities such as Ping and Tracert can be used to diagnose TCP/IP connectivity and routing issues.

◆ **DNS:** This service maps host names to IP addresses. To allow a host to communicate with another host by its host name, the DNS service needs to be available to translate the host name to an IP address. DNS is a vital service in a Windows Server 2003 domain.

◆ **WINS:** Similar to DNS, WINS translates NetBIOS names to IP addresses. If this service is not working, you will not be able to connect to remote systems using NetBIOS names if your client relies on WINS for name resolution.

◆ **NAT:** Network Address Translation translates internal IP addresses into external addresses for communication on the Internet. If this service is not working or is misconfigured, hosts will not be able to access the Internet, or vice versa.

◆ **IPSec:** When using IPSec for encryption services, the hosts involved must all be configured correctly with compatible IPSec encryption settings for communications to occur.

◆ **Remote access and authentication:** When accessing a network remotely, you must be authenticated to the network before being allowed to continue. There are many things that can go wrong with the remote access and authentication process which will prevent a client from accessing the network.

Goals

In this lesson, you will learn how to troubleshoot network infrastructure problems with respect to DHCP, TCP/IP routing, name resolution, NAT, IPSec, remote access and authentication, and client configuration.

Lesson 10   Troubleshooting Network Infrastructure Problems

Skill	Exam 70-293 Objective
1. Troubleshooting DHCP	Diagnose and resolve issues related to DHCP server address assignment. Troubleshoot TCP/IP addressing.
2. Diagnosing Name Resolution Problems	Diagnose and resolve issues related to name resolution cache information. Diagnose and resolve issues related to DNS services. Troubleshoot connectivity to the Internet.
3. Troubleshooting TCP/IP Routing	Troubleshoot TCP/IP routing. Tools might include the route, tracert, ping, pathping, and netsh commands and Network Monitor.
4. Resolving NAT Problems	Diagnose and resolve issues related to Network Address Translation (NAT). Troubleshoot connectivity to the Internet.
5. Analyzing IPSec Issues	Troubleshoot security for data transmission. Tools might include the IP Security Monitor MMC snap-in and the Resultant Set of Policy (RSoP) MMC snap-in.
6. Troubleshooting Remote Access and Authentication	Basic knowledge
7. Correcting Client Configurations	Diagnose and resolve issues related to client computer configuration.

Requirements

To complete this lesson, you will need administrative rights on a Windows Server 2003 computer with DHCP, DNS, and RRAS installed and access to a client running Windows 2000 or XP.

skill 1

Troubleshooting DHCP

exam objective

Diagnose and resolve issues related to DHCP server address assignment. Troubleshoot TCP/IP addressing.

overview

DHCP services, when enabled, are critical to the operation of a network. When clients connect to a network, DHCP automatically configures them with the information they need to communicate on that network, such as an IP address, subnet mask, and addresses of DNS and WINS servers. Without proper configuration from a DHCP server, a client will be unable to communicate with the network. DHCP services must be working at all times to ensure that network devices can communicate with each other.

Major areas of DHCP troubleshooting include client configuration, server configuration, and database corruption. You should begin your troubleshooting process at the client, and then work your way to the DHCP server.

Client configuration: If a client cannot connect to resources on a network, you should begin troubleshooting by examining the client configuration to make sure that it is set up correctly to receive information from the DHCP server.

tip

Ensure that the IP address information you are receiving from the DHCP server is for your subnet. Wrong information could mean you are getting information from the wrong DHCP server or a rogue DHCP server.

◆ First, make sure that all network connections and cabling are present and connected properly.

◆ From the command line, enter the **ipconfig /all** command to help you determine the source of the connectivity problem. This command displays your network configuration information, including whether you have received an IP address from a DHCP server. You can also check the origin of the client's address by opening the **Local Area Connection Status** dialog box and selecting the **Support** tab, which indicates whether the IP address was assigned by DHCP **(Figure 10-1)**.

◆ If you have not received an address from the DHCP server, try assigning the client a static address temporarily and performing connectivity tests such as pinging another device. This ensures that you have network connectivity.

◆ If the client's IP address has been properly obtained from the DHCP server, try to determine if this address is in use by another system on the network. Evidence of address conflicts can appear both in the System log and in warnings that pop up from the client's system tray (notification area in Windows XP). Address conflicts can result from having multiple DHCP servers that are configured to assign addresses from the same pool, or from scopes being redeployed. There is the possibility that clients are receiving IP addresses from the wrong scope. This situation can occur when a rogue server is present, or when a relay agent or router has been addressed incorrectly. You can search for rogue DHCP servers by running the **Dhcploc.exe** program from the **Windows Support Tools** folder on the server. If the conflict was the result of scope redeployment, renew the client's DHCP lease by using the **ipconfig /renew** command, or by clicking the **Repair** button on the **Support** tab of the **Local Area Connection Status** dialog box. **Table 10-1** describes the steps taken when the Repair option is used.

◆ If a client cannot obtain a DHCP address, try the **ipconfig /renew** command or use the **Repair** button from the client. If this does not work, you should verify that there is a working DHCP server deployed on the network, or, if the DHCP server resides on another subnet, that a relay agent is present and functioning.

◆ If there is still a problem, move on to troubleshooting the DHCP server itself.

Figure 10-1 The Support tab in the Local Area Connection Status dialog box

Table 10-1   Steps completed by clicking the Repair button

Command description	Equivalent at command prompt
1. Broadcasts a DHCPRequest message to renew lease	
2. Flushes the ARP cache	arp -d *
3. Flushes the NetBIOS cache	nbtstat -R
4. Flushes the DNS cache	ipconfig /flushdns
5. Reregisters the client's IP address and NetBIOS name with WINS server	nbtstat -RR
6. Reregisters the client's name and IP address with DNS	ipconfig /registerdns

skill 1

Troubleshooting DHCP (cont'd)

exam objective

Diagnose and resolve issues related to DHCP server address assignment. Troubleshoot TCP/IP addressing.

overview

Server configuration: If the DHCP problems do not seem to be coming from the client, you must examine the DHCP server and its configuration.

◆ Verify that the DHCP Server role is installed and configured on your specified DHCP server, and that the server is authorized.

◆ Verify that the scope is active and that it has not run out of IP addresses in its range. If address availability is a problem, you can decrease the lease duration setting so that clients do not unnecessarily occupy address space when they do not require a lease. Also, ensure the address exclusions and reservations are configured properly, and that there are no conflicts between them.

◆ The DHCP server itself must be addressed correctly, and its network ID must be the same as that of the subnet that it services. If a DHCP server is not on the same subnet as the client, there must be a DHCP relay agent on the client's subnet so that requests can be relayed to the DHCP server.

◆ In addition, the DHCP server must be bound to the connection that it uses for the subnet. You can view the network bindings of a DHCP server by opening its **Properties** dialog box, selecting the **Advanced** tab, and clicking the **Bindings** button. Finally, ensure the server is authorized in Active Directory. Verify this via the DHCP console. A green arrow pointing upward inside a white circle on the server icon indicates that the server is authorized.

Database corruption: The DHCP database stores information about scope IP address leases. If information in the DHCP console is not displaying correctly, there could be DHCP addresses or leases in conflict. To fix these inconsistencies, you must reconcile the DHCP database or an individual scope.

how to

Reconcile a DHCP database.

1. Click ⟨Start⟩, point to **Programs**, point to **Administrative Tools**, and then click **DHCP** to open the DHCP console.
2. Click the name of your DHCP server in the console tree to select the server.
3. Click **Action** on the Menu bar, and then select **Reconcile All Scopes (Figure 10-2)**.
4. The **Reconcile All Scopes** dialog box opens **(Figure 10-3)**. Click ⟨Verify⟩.
5. If no data needs to be reconciled, click ⟨OK⟩ to close the dialog box.
6. If you do need to reconcile a scope, it will appear in the dialog box. Select the scope you want to reconcile **(Figure 10-4)** and click ⟨Reconcile⟩ to fix the discrepancies in the database.
7. Click ⟨OK⟩ to close the **Reconcile All Scopes** dialog box.
8. Close the DHCP console.

Figure 10-2 Reconciling the DHCP database

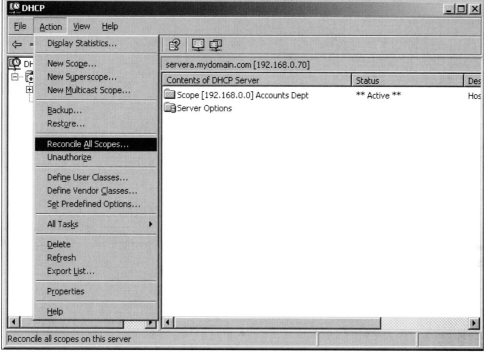

Figure 10-3 The Reconcile All Scopes dialog box

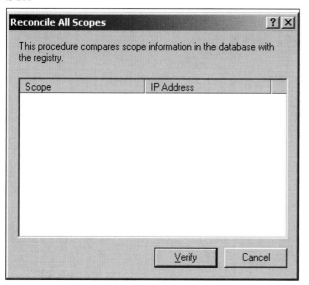

Figure 10-4 Reconciling a scope that has inconsistencies

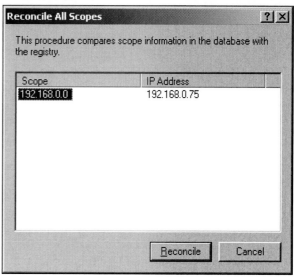

skill 2

Diagnosing Name Resolution Problems

exam objective

Diagnose and resolve issues related to name resolution cache information. Diagnose and resolve issues related to DNS services. Troubleshoot connectivity to the Internet.

overview

tip

It is recommended that you do not configure a large number of secondary WINS servers because all servers will be checked before a failed query response is returned.

While implementing WINS for name resolution on a network, you might encounter problems such as failed name resolution queries. To troubleshoot name resolution problems effectively, you need to identify the cause of the problem. In most cases, the issue is either with the client or server configuration.

Client configuration: There are a number of items that can be checked on the client to troubleshoot name resolution.

◆ There may be network problems preventing the client from contacting the WINS server. Try using the **ping** command to test the connection between the WINS server and the client.

◆ If you are using the local NetBIOS cache and cannot resolve a certain host, try clearing and reloading the cache using the **nbtstat –r** command from the command prompt. This will clear and reload the name cache and may help resolve host names that are new to the network.

◆ Examine the client's WINS settings by examining the TCP/IP network settings, and then clicking the **WINS** tab of the **Advanced TCP/IP Settings** dialog box (**Figure 10-5**). Ensure that the WINS server addresses are correct, and that these servers are running the WINS service. This information can also be found by running **ipconfig /all** from the command prompt.

◆ Also, check if the **NetBIOS over TCP/IP** setting is disabled. If this is disabled, the client will not be able to resolve names via NetBIOS.

If the client configuration is correct, you must now check your WINS server status and configuration.

Server configuration: Check the following items on your WINS server:

◆ Ensure that the WINS service is started by checking the WINS console or the Services list.

◆ Corruption of the WINS database can be caused by improper shutdown of your computer. Check the Event Log to identify these problems. If necessary, you can restore the WINS database from a backup copy.

◆ If you updated a non-WINS client to a WINS client, the static mapping for the client is not updated automatically, and this can cause name resolution problems. To fix this issue, you must set up the WINS server to update static mapping information dynamically. To update static mappings dynamically, right-click the **Replication Partners** folder for the WINS server, and then click **Properties** to open the **Replication Partners Properties** dialog box. On the **General** tab, select the **Overwrite unique static mappings at this server (migrate on)** check box to instruct the WINS server to overwrite old name mappings dynamically with new name mappings.

DNS name resolution: After you install and configure DNS, you need to test whether you have implemented DNS correctly on the network. You can use the DNS console to test DNS by sending two types of queries:

◆ **Simple query:** To test the active DNS server
◆ **Recursive query:** To test other DNS servers on the network from the active DNS server

You can access the options to run these queries from the **Monitoring** tab of the Properties for your DNS server (**Figure 10-6**). The results of the query that you run are displayed in the dialog box. If the DNS server is implemented correctly and able to answer the queries, a **Pass** status property is listed in the appropriate column of the **Test results** box on the **Monitoring** tab, otherwise, a **Failed** status appears.

Figure 10-5 WINS tab in Advanced TCP/IP Settings dialog box

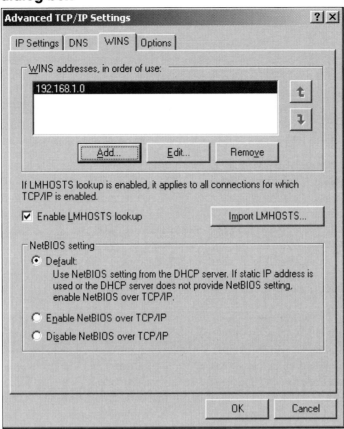

Figure 10-6 The Monitoring tab

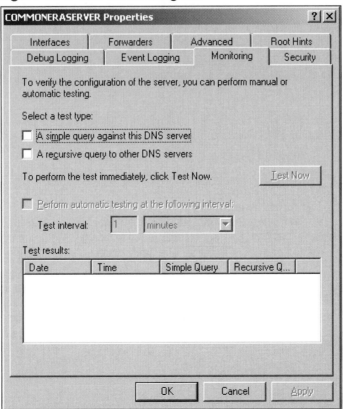

skill 2

Diagnosing Name Resolution Problems (cont'd)

exam objective

Diagnose and resolve issues related to name resolution cache information. Diagnose and resolve issues related to DNS services. Troubleshoot connectivity to the Internet.

overview

In addition to using the DNS console, you can use other diagnostic utilities such as Ping, Nslookup, and Ipconfig /flushdns to check the connectivity between two IP hosts on a TCP/IP network, or to check your DNS server for communication problems with other name servers.

Ping: Use the Packet Internet Groper (Ping) utility to check the connectivity between two IP hosts on a TCP/IP network. You can use the IP address or the host name of the destination host to check for connectivity between the source host and the destination host. If you have implemented DNS, you can also use the FQDN of the destination host. The syntax for the Ping command is: **ping <destination IP address>** or **<destination host>**. To test your DNS setup using the Ping utility, ping the destination host using its IP address to ensure that you have connectivity. Next, ping the destination host by using its FQDN. If the FQDN is resolved successfully to its associated IP address, then you know that DNS is working and resolving host names correctly.

Nslookup: The Nslookup utility can be used to diagnose problems with DNS name servers on your network by making DNS queries to these DNS servers. The Nslookup utility has a simple (non-interactive) mode and an interactive mode. In the simple mode, you enter **nslookup** at the command prompt followed by the FQDN whose IP address you wish to find **(Figure 10-7)**. To use the interactive mode, which enables you to use a number of troubleshooting and look-up functions, type **nslookup** at the command prompt and press **[Enter]**. This will return the Nslookup command prompt, from which you can run various functions (enter **?** to view the available functions). You can verify a DNS server's ability to resolve host names by typing the host name of any network host at the Nslookup command prompt. If the IP address of the desired host is returned, DNS is working properly. By default, Nslookup uses the DNS server assigned to the local computer, but you can use Nslookup to check other DNS servers by typing **server <host name of the desired DNS server>** at the Nslookup prompt.

Ipconfig /flushdns: This command allows you to flush and reset the DNS client resolver cache. If you are having problem with name resolution, use this utility to discard any unresolvable entries, including dynamically-added entries, from the cache.

tip

Use ping to look for packets lost and varying round trip times for an indication of intermittent responses. There may be network problems that are preventing DNS queries from reaching the DNS server.

how to

Test the DNS server configuration.

1. Open the **DNS** console.
2. Right-click the name of the DNS server in the console tree, and then click **Properties** to open the **Properties** dialog box for the DNS server.
3. Click the **Monitoring** tab.
4. Select the **A simple query against this DNS server** check box **(Figure 10-8)**. In this test, the resolver on the DNS server computer will send a simple query, also known as an iterative query, to the name server on the computer selected in Step 2.
5. Click [Test Now] to send the simple query to the DNS server. The result of the query appears in the **Test results** box **(Figure 10-9)**. If **Pass** appears in the **Simple Query** column of the **Test results** box, DNS is working properly; if **Failed** appears, DNS is not working properly.
6. Click [OK] to close the Properties dialog box of the DNS server and return to the DNS console.
7. Close the DNS console.

Figure 10-7 Using Nslookup

Figure 10-8 Testing DNS with a simple query

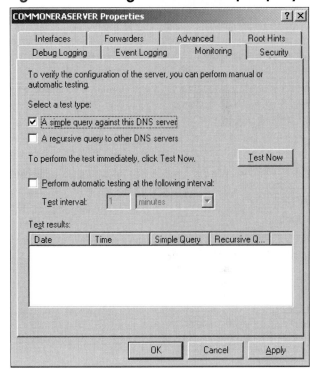

Figure 10-9 DNS query test results

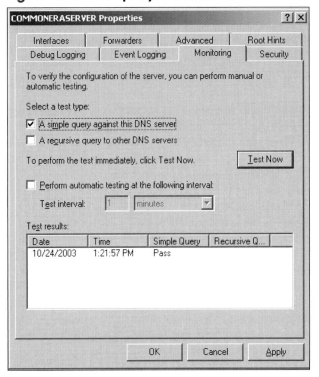

skill 3

Troubleshooting TCP/IP Routing

exam objective

Troubleshoot TCP/IP routing. Tools might include the route, tracert, ping, pathping, and netsh commands and Network Monitor.

overview

Networking problems can easily disrupt network communications between hosts on a network. From misconfiguration, network equipment failure, to cabling and routing problems, there are a wide variety of issues that can affect network traffic.

Windows Server 2003 includes a number of command-line utilities that can help you troubleshoot problems with TCP/IP routing, communication, and configuration.

tip

Some network hosts behind a firewall will not receive ping requests because they are being blocked by the firewall. This prevents Denial of Service type of attacks which send multiple ping requests to a host to prevent it from responding to legitimate requests.

◆ **Ping:** Using the Ping command sends an Internet Control Message Protocol (ICMP) ECHO request to the destination host. ICMP is used to check and report the status of the information that is transmitted over a TCP/IP network. If routing from the source to the destination is available and configured correctly, the destination host receives the ICMP packets sent by the source host. The destination host then returns the ICMP ECHO reply message to the original source host, if the routing back to the original host is available and configured correctly. If the number of ICMP packets returned is the same as the number of packets sent, then the network is properly routed from source to destination and back again. The time values generated by Ping indicate levels of network congestion. A mixed result of successful and dropped packets can also indicate congestion. If all packets are dropped, then you have evidence of a malfunction in the network, such as the destination host or router being down, or a firewall blocking Ping packets.

Table 10-2 describes the various Ping commands that you can use to test TCP/IP connectivity. There are also a number of other switches that you can use with the Ping command. For example, you can control how many ICMP echo messages will be sent. Use **ping -t *IP_address*** to send a continuous ping to a host. To see the other switches that can be used with the Ping command, enter **ping/?**

◆ **Ipconfig:** This utility provides information about the host computer configuration, IP address, subnet mask, and default gateway. You can display a summary of the TCP/IP configuration of your computer by typing **ipconfig** at the command prompt **(Figure 10-10)**. You can also display a detailed description of the TCP/IP configuration by typing **ipconfig /all**. The Ipconfig utility enables you to determine whether an IP address has been assigned to your computer and confirms that the TCP/IP protocol is running. You can also use this utility to renew the IP address for your computer using the command **ipconfig /renew**, or you can release an IP address manually by entering **ipconfig /release**.

◆ **Tracert:** This utility is used to search for the route used by data when it is transferred between communicating devices. It can also provide information about where a communication link has failed. Tracert displays the Fully Qualified Domain Name, if possible, and IP address of each gateway along the route to a remote host. Enter **tracert** [*destination hostname* or *IP address*] at the command prompt to see the route between your own system and a destination host.

◆ **Route:** This command is used to display and modify the local routing table. You can use it to set the route you want packets to take to a particular network, including the default gateway. To display the routing table on your computer, type **route print** at the command prompt **(Figure 10-11)**. The **route delete** command can be used to remove routes from your routing table, while **route add** is used to add routes.

◆ **Pathping:** This utility is a combination of Ping and Tracert. It provides a statistical analysis of results over a period of time. The time period can vary depending upon how many jumps must be analyzed. **Pathping** displays the computer name and IP address for each jump and also calculates the percentage of lost/sent packets to each router or link, making it easier for you to determine where the network problem is located.

Table 10-2   Using the Ping command to test TCP/IP connectivity

Ping command	Description
ping 127.0.0.1	This command is also known as the loopback address. It is used to see if TCP/IP is correctly installed and configured on your computer. If there is no reply, it means that TCP/IP is not installed correctly and you must reinstall it.
ping *IP_address_of_hostcomputer* and ping *localhost*	This command is used to verify that the local computer is correctly added to the network. If the routing table is correct, this forwards the packet to the loopback address 127.0.0.1. Failure implies that the IP address is not bound properly, the routing table has errors, or that you have typed an incorrect IP address.
ping *IP_address_of_default_gateway*	This command enables you to determine whether you can reach the default gateway (router). If you fail to get a reply, either the network connection is not available, or there is a hardware or software problem preventing you from reaching the gateway
ping *IP_address_of_remote_host*	This command is used to confirm that you can communicate through a router. Failure to receive a reply means that you have entered an incorrect default gateway address, that the remote system is offline, that one of the routers along the path is down, or that the routing table on one of the routers along the path is defective.
ping *name_of_remote_host*	This command is used to confirm that DNS name resolution is functioning.

Figure 10-10 Using Ipconfig to display a summary of the TCP/IP configuration

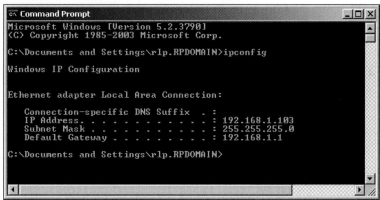

Figure 10-11 Using Route print to display the routing table on your computer

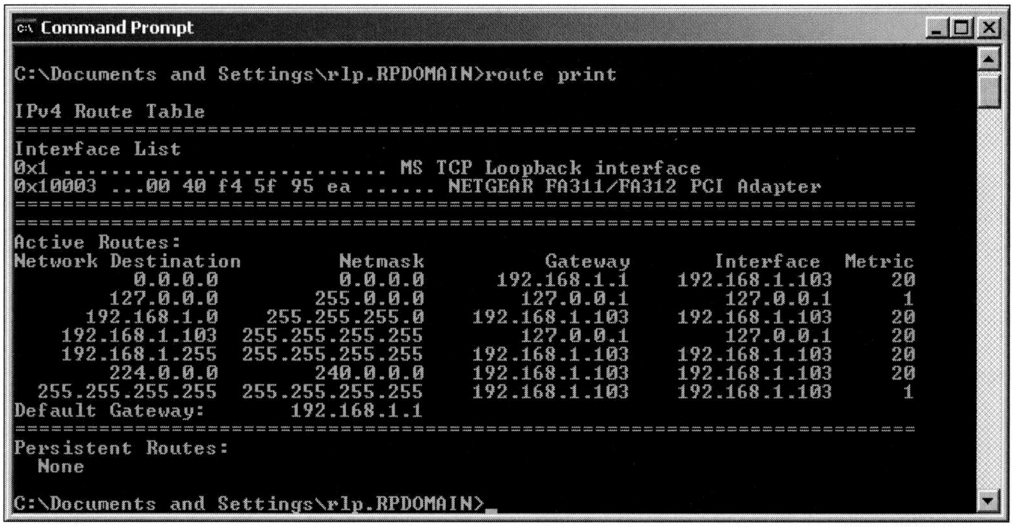

skill 3

Troubleshooting TCP/IP Routing
(cont'd)

exam objective

Troubleshoot TCP/IP routing. Tools might include the route, tracert, ping, pathping, and netsh commands and Network Monitor.

overview

◆ **Netsh:** This is a command-line and scripting utility for networking components for local or remote computers. The **Netsh** utility can also save a configuration script in a text file for archival purposes or for configuring other servers. There are a variety of networking functions that can be performed with this utility. Type **netsh** to start the utility and then type **?** to see a list of commands. The main IP routing commands are described in **Table 10-3**.

◆ **Network Monitor:** Use the Network Monitor utility **(Figure 10-12)** to log and examine network frame information. Network Monitor is a useful utility for troubleshooting networking problems, and can monitor for specific network events. Network Monitor is installed by using **Add/Remove programs** and selecting **Network Monitor Tools** under the **Management And Monitoring Tools** option. If you install the Network Monitor tool, the **Network Monitor agent** is installed automatically on the same computer. You have to install the agent itself on any Windows XP, Windows 2000, or Windows Server 2003 computer you want to monitor.

how to

Use **Ipconfig** to check network settings.

1. Open a command prompt window. At the command prompt, type **ipconfig** and press **[Enter]**. Examine the IP address, netmask, DNS information, and gateway to ensure that all settings are correct.
2. At the command prompt, type **ipconfig /all** and press **[Enter]** to see all network settings, including WINS, DNS, and DHCP lease information.
3. Test DHCP by releasing and renewing your IP address. At the command prompt, type **ipconfig /release** and press **[Enter]**. This command will release your IP address.
4. At the command prompt, type **ipconfig** and press **[Enter]** to check the current value of your IP address, which should be unassigned. The output should be **0.0.0.0**.
5. At the command prompt, type **ipconfig /renew** and press **[Enter]** to renew your IP address from the DHCP server.
6. At the command prompt, type **ipconfig** and press **[Enter]** to ensure that you have an assigned IP address.

Table 10-3   Netsh commands

Command	Description
routing ip add/delete/set/show interface	Adds, deletes, configures, or displays general IP routing settings on a specified interface.
routing ip add/delete/set/show filter	Adds, deletes, configures, or displays IP packet filters on a specified interface.
routing ip add/delete/show boundary	Adds, deletes, or displays multicast boundary settings on a specified interface.
routing ip add/delete/set/show rtmroute	Adds, deletes, configures, or displays a non-persistent Route Table Manager route.
routing ip add/delete/set/show persistentroute	Adds, deletes, configures, or displays persistent routes.
routing ip add/delete/set/show preferenceforprotocol	Adds, deletes, configures, or displays the preference level for a routing protocol.
routing ip add/delete/set/show scope	Adds, deletes, or displays a multicast scope.
routing ip set/show loglevel	Configures or displays the global IP logging level.
routing ip show helper	Displays all Netsh utility subcontexts of IP.
routing ip show protocol	Displays all running IP routing protocols.
routing ip show mfe	Displays multicast forwarding entries.
routing ip show mfestats	Displays multicast forwarding entry statistics.
routing ip show boundarystats	Displays IP multicast boundaries.
routing ip show rtmdestinations	Displays destinations in the Route Table Manager routing table.
routing ip show rtmroutes	Displays routes in the Route Table Manager routing table.

Figure 10-12   Network Monitor

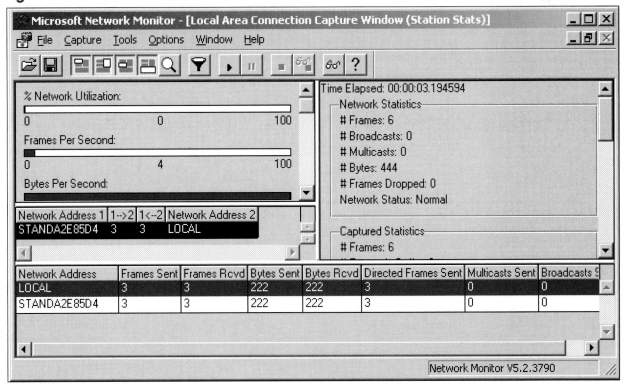

skill 4

Resolving NAT Problems

exam objective

Diagnose and resolve issues related to Network Address Translation (NAT). Troubleshoot connectivity to the Internet.

overview

Network Address Translation (NAT) is a service that can translate private IP addresses to public IP addresses and vice versa as they are being forwarded from client computers to a server or from the server to client computers **(Figure 10-13)**. With NAT, you can determine your own internal IP address ranges. Windows Server 2003 Network Address Translation also includes simple firewall functionality to protect your network.

When troubleshooting NAT issues, it is helpful to know the process for how NAT translates addresses:

1. The client sends a data packet to the RRAS (Routing and Remote Access Services) server configured as a NAT router.
2. The server modifies the packet header, replacing the source IP address with the IP address of the router's external interface. The source port number is also changed. A new source port number is randomly generated on the router's external interface. The data packet is then ready to be sent over the Internet to a Web server.
3. The NAT table stores the original source IP address, the original source port number, and the new source port number. This data is referred to as the translation data.
4. The Web server that received the data packet sends the reply to the RRAS server addressed to the external interface on the NAT router (destination IP address and port number). When the NAT router receives the reply, the port number is looked up in the NAT table. The IP address of the client is inserted in place of the destination IP address, and the port number for the client is inserted in place of the destination port.
5. After the RRAS server modifies the packet header and determines the destination, it sends the packet to the client.

Check the following if you are having problems with NAT:

◆ Examine your NAT configuration to ensure that all settings are correctly set up for your network.
◆ Examine your settings for NAT address assignment **(Figure 10-14)**. This setting allows you to allocate IP addresses using the DHCP allocator. Ensure that the IP address range you have set up is correct for your network.
◆ Check the DNS settings for NAT to ensure that host names are being resolved to IP addresses **(Figure 10-15)**.
◆ Check your filtering settings if you have NAT configured for firewall functionality **(Figure 10-16)**. Check both inbound and outbound filters for any filtering rules that may block your communications.

Figure 10-13 NAT Process

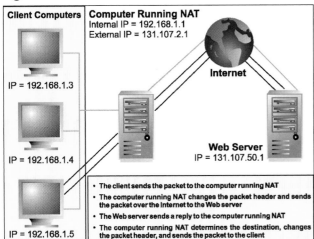

Figure 10-14 NAT Address Assignment settings

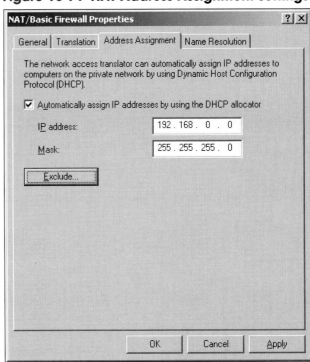

Figure 10-15 NAT Name Resolution settings

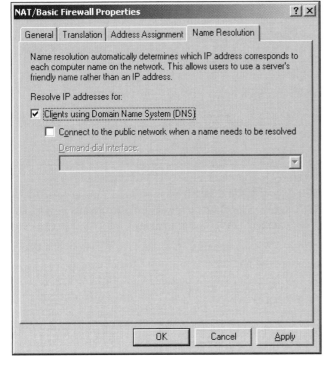

Figure 10-16 The Network Address Translation Properties dialog box

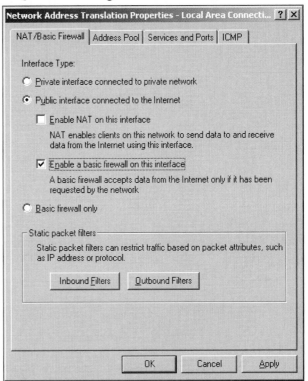

skill 5

Analyzing IPSec Issues

exam objective

Troubleshoot security for data transmission. Tools might include the IP Security Monitor MMC snap-in and the Resultant Set of Policy (RSoP) MMC snap-in.

overview

Internet Protocol Security (IPSec) protects Internet Protocol (IP) and higher layer protocols by using security policies to secure user communications within a local area network and between sites.

When troubleshooting IPSec issues, it is useful to know the communications path and procedure for an IPSec communication.

1. When Computer A sends a packet to Computer B, the **IPSec driver** on Computer A will intercept the packet and compare the destination IP address and protocol with the IPSec filters configured on Computer A.
2. If there is a matching IPSec filter, the IPSec driver on Computer A will send the packet to the **Internet Key Exchange (IKE)** module to begin the negotiation process with Computer B to establish a security association (SA). This occurs in two phases, Main Mode and Quick Mode (described below).
3. The IPSec driver on Computer A will then apply the appropriate level of encryption as well as the data integrity algorithm and send the packet to the network adapter, which sends it on to Computer B.
4. When the packet is received on Computer B, it is passed to the IPSec driver where it is decrypted, checked for data integrity, and passed to the appropriate application.

During the Main Mode phase, Computers A and B go through the process of authenticating each other using IKE. The authentication methods available include Kerberos, certificates, or pre-shared keys. Once the Main Mode phase has been completed, a Main Mode security association is created. For both computers to be able to communicate using IPSec, they must establish a security association.

In the second phase of negotiations (Quick Mode), the security protocols are established. During this phase, the computers must agree on the security protocols to use, either Authentication Header, Encapsulating Security Payload Header, or both. The protocols used depend upon the settings of the IPSec policy used. Once the security protocols are agreed, IKE sends the security association to the IPSec Driver for processing.

To troubleshoot problems with IPSec communications, the best method is to first ensure that basic communications are working properly, and then monitor the actual connections using Window Server 2003 tools such as Netsh, IP Security Monitor, Event Viewer, and Network Monitor. When experiencing a problem with IPSec, you should first determine if it is related to IPSec or if it is a basic network connectivity problem. Stop all IPSec services on both of the systems and then try using the Ping command to confirm connectivity. If you do not get a response, then you must check all the basic networking settings such as TCP/IP configuration, cabling, routing, and so on, until you have established connectivity. Start IPSec services again, and if your policies are still not working, you have to troubleshoot IPSec-related issues.

Netsh is a command line tool that can be run from a batch file or from the command prompt. Although it can be used to create a policy, it can also be used for monitoring IPSec sessions. Any information that is available in the IP Security Monitor snap-in is also available using this tool.

IP Security Monitor is a tool that is added into a Microsoft Management console as a snap-in. It provides information on which IPSec policy is active on the computer and whether a secure association has been established.

Determine which policy is actually assigned to the computers involved. This can be checked by using the **IP Security Policy Management** snap-in. **Netsh** can also provide information by using the **netsh ipsec static show gpoassignedpolicy** command **(Figure 10-17)**.

Figure 10-17 Using the Netsh command

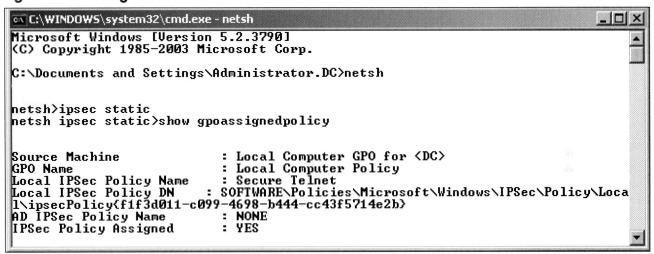

skill 5

Analyzing IPSec Issues (cont'd)

exam objective

Troubleshoot security for data transmission. Tools might include the IP Security Monitor MMC snap-in and the Resultant Set of Policy (RSoP) MMC snap-in.

overview

If your IPSec policies are being distributed by using Group Policy and the computer is not assigning the correct policy, you can use the **Resultant Set of Policy** snap-in in the Microsoft Management console to see which Group Policy object is responsible. When policies are assigned at different levels (site, domain, organizational unit), some settings may conflict and produce unexpected results. The Resultant Set of Policy (RSoP) snap-in can help you determine the policies that have been applied to the computer as well as their precedence.

The **Event Viewer** can also provide information to assist you in troubleshooting IPSec communication problems. In general, look for events in the System log that are generated by the IPSec Policy Agent or IPSec Driver. Security association details can be seen in the Security log. In order to review these types of events in the Security log, you will need to ensure that auditing is enabled.

Figure 10-18 shows a successful IKE Quick Mode security association. This indicates the two computers have already completed the security association and agreed upon the authentication method to use. With a basic understanding of the Main Mode and Quick Mode phases you can begin to identify the area of your configuration that may need to be reviewed if communication is failing. The details of the existing policies, such as authentication modes and encryption settings, can be obtained by using **netsh ipsec static show all (Figure 10-19)** or by using the IP Security Policy Management snap-in.

Network Monitor can also be used to capture IPSec packets. You will be able to see if the packets are actually reaching the server and that they are protected by IPSec **(Figure 10-20)**.

Figure 10-18 Viewing the Security log

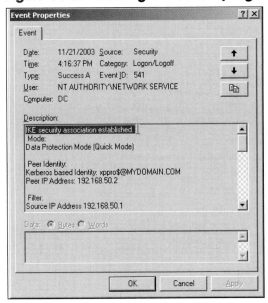

Figure 10-19 Reviewing policy details using Netsh

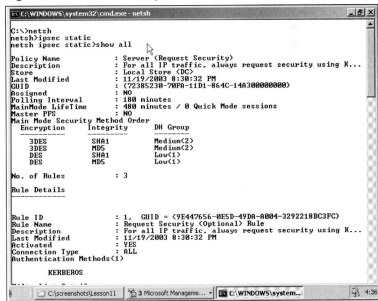

Figure 10-20 Using Network Monitor to capture IPSec traffic

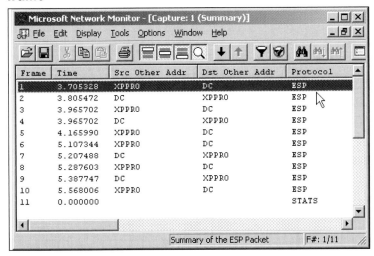

skill 6	**Troubleshooting Remote Access and Authentication**

exam objective	Basic knowledge

overview

Troubleshooting remote connections can be a difficult procedure, as there are many different parts of the remote access process that need to be checked, including initial communication and handshaking, authentication, and remote access and policy configurations. When troubleshooting remote access problems, you should start with the client and work towards the remote destination.

Initial examination should include the type of connection. If using a modem, for example, make sure that it is configured properly, that the client is dialing out successfully, and that a connection can be made. Anything from bad cabling, line noise, or connection settings can stop the remote access process.

If the connection is established properly, but you cannot access remote resources, the problem is most likely with the RRAS server configuration or remote access policies.

Remote access policies are used to control what connection attempts will be rejected or accepted by the RRAS server. These include items such as time conditions, where a client can only access the remote network within a certain time range. If the user does not match all of the conditions in a given policy, then a match is attempted against the next policy. If the user does not match any policies, he or she is disconnected.

You need to examine authentication methods to ensure the client and server are using compatible methods, such as PAP, SPAP, CHAP, and so on. If there is no match, the caller will be disconnected. The same process needs to be used to check encryption settings. If the client and server are not using compatible methods or types of encryption, that caller will be disconnected.

The authentication protocols used by Routing and Remote Access Services, and which must be configured on both the remote client and the remote access server, are listed in **Table 10-4**.

Windows Server 2003 provides several tools and logs that can provide information to an administrator about login authentication attempts.

Event Viewer provides information about events that have occurred on the remote access server. This information is stored in Application, Security, and System event logs. When event logging is configured on the remote access server (as discussed in the next paragraph), the RRAS server will enter RAS system events in the System log. To view information in the Security log **(Figure 10-21)**, you may need to enable auditing and logging of specific security events. This can be enabled via the Local Security Settings if you are configuring auditing on a local computer. If you are configuring auditing on domain controllers, you can enable it by accessing the Domain Controller Security Policy.

RRAS servers support event logging, local authentication and accounting logging, and RADIUS-based authentication and accounting logging. Event logging records remote access server warnings, errors, and other information in the system event log. To enable event logging, select the server name in the **Routing and Remote Access** console, right-click and select **Properties**. On the **Logging** tab in the server's Properties dialog box, select the event types you want to log **(Figure 10-22)**. Information recorded in the System event log can be reviewed by using the Event Viewer tool.

To track remote access usage and authentication attempts on a server running Routing and Remote Access Services, you should review the information stored in the *%systemroot%* **\System32\Logfiles** folder. Each time an authentication attempt is made, the information is stored in this log indicating the remote access policy that accepted or rejected the connection. In order to use this type of logging, you will need to enable Windows Authentication as the

Table 10-4   Authentication protocols

Protocol	Description
Password Authentication Protocol (PAP)	When using this protocol, the user name and password are requested by the remote access server and are sent by the remote client in plain text.
Shiva Password Authentication Protocol (SPAP)	Used with SHIVA remote access products. SPAP does not support encryption of the connection.
Challenge Handshake Authentication Protocol (CHAP)	An industry standard authentication protocol that supports non-Microsoft remote access clients that cannot use more secure methods such as MS-CHAP or EAP. CHAP is more secure than PAP, and utilizes a challenge from the authenticating server, which the client responds to using a one-way hash encryption.
Microsoft Challenge Handshake Authentication Protocol (MS-CHAP) v1	Encrypts password information before it is sent over communication link.
Microsoft Challenge Handshake Authentication Protocol (MS-CHAP) v2	Enhanced version of MS-CHAP v1 that utilizes mutual authentication.
Extensible Authentication Protocol-Transport Layer Security (EAP-TLS)	EAP-TLS is a certificate-based authentication scheme that uses mutual authentication. It is commonly used with smart card implementations.

Figure 10-21 Security log contents

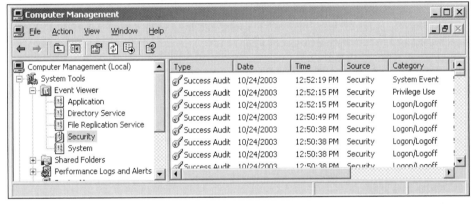

Figure 10-22 Selecting event types to log

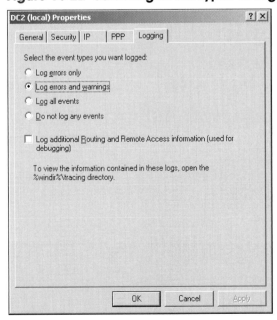

skill 6

Troubleshooting Remote Access and Authentication (cont'd)

exam objective

Basic knowledge

overview

Authentication provider or Windows Accounting as the Accounting provider in the server's Properties dialog box. Once these have been enabled, you can configure what you want to log by selecting the **Remote Access Logging** folder and then right-click the log file in the right pane to configure its properties. On the **Settings** tab, select the information you want to log.

Netsh will allow you to display or modify the network configuration of a computer that is currently running. When used on a remote access server, the **netsh ras diagnostics show logs** command can be used to dump information regarding the server's configuration into a diagnostic report. This includes tracing logs (modem logs, connection manager logs, IP Security logs), remote access event logs, as well as Security event logs (**Figure 10-23**).

If you are experiencing problems with remote connectivity or want to monitor a specific connection to the server, you can use **Network Monitor** to capture packets that are sent between the remote access client and the server (**Figure 10-24**).

how to

Activate security auditing for successful and failed log on events on your RRAS server.

1. Click ⊞Start, point to **Administrative Tools**, and then click **Local Security Policy** to open the **Local Security Settings** console.
2. Double-click **Local Policies** to expand the console tree.
3. Click **Audit Policy** to display the policies in the right pane (**Figure 10-25**).
4. Double-click the **Audit logon events** attribute in the right pane to activate security auditing.
5. In the **Audit logon events Properties** dialog box, select the **Success** and **Failure** check boxes under the **Audit these attempts** section (**Figure 10-26**).
6. Click ☐ OK ☐ to activate the audit entry for the **Audit logon events** attribute and close the dialog box. Using this same MMC, you can activate audit entries for the other attributes you need.
7. Close the Local Security Settings console window.

Figure 10-23 Diagnostic report using Netsh command

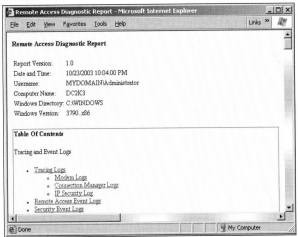

Figure 10-24 Diagnostic report using Network Monitor

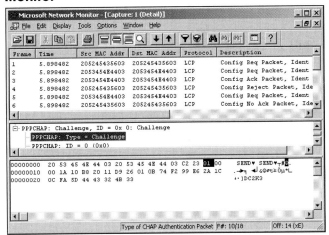

Figure 10-25 List of audit policies

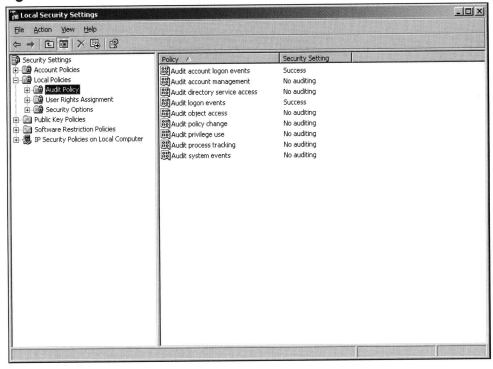

Figure 10-26 Configuring audit policy

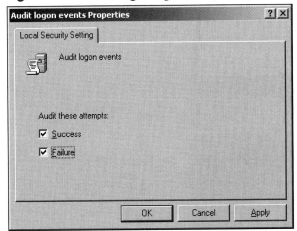

skill 7

Correcting Client Configurations

exam objective

Diagnose and resolve issues related to client computer configuration.

overview

Many problems occur simply because of a client misconfiguration issue. If the client's TCP/IP settings are configured manually, you must ensure that the IP address, subnet mask, and gateway settings are correct for your network. Using the wrong subnet mask or wrong gateway setting will prevent the client from properly connecting to the network. You must also ensure that a particular IP address has not been assigned to more than one host. Two hosts with the same IP address or host name connected to the same network will result in communication problems for both systems.

TCP/IP Settings: Open the client's TCP/IP Properties dialog box (**Figure 10-27**). If you are using DHCP, make sure that **Obtain an IP address automatically** is selected. Select **Obtain DNS server address automatically** if you want to receive DNS server settings from the DHCP server. If you are configuring your TCP/IP properties manually, make sure that **Use the following IP address** is selected, and that the **IP address**, **Subnet mask**, and **Default gateway** are set appropriately for your network.

For most network services such as DNS, WINS, and DHCP to work properly, the client must be set up with the proper settings to connect to these services.

DHCP Configuration: In the client's TCP/IP Properties dialog box, make sure that **Obtain an IP address automatically** is selected. To check your current IP address settings, enter the **ipconfig** command at the command prompt. Make sure that you have been assigned an address by the DHCP server, and that the subnet mask, DNS, and WINS settings are appropriate for your network.

DNS Configuration: In the client's TCP/IP Properties dialog box, make sure that **Obtain DNS server address automatically** is enabled if you are using DHCP. If not, the preferred DNS server should be defined, and it is recommended to enter an address for an alternate DNS server. Click **Advanced** to open the **Advanced TCP/IP Settings** dialog box, and select the **DNS** tab to see the advanced DNS settings (**Figure 10-28**). Ensure that your DNS servers will be searched in the proper order. Also, check your settings for adding DNS suffixes.

WINS Configuration: In the Advanced TCP/IP Settings dialog box, select the **WINS** tab (**Figure 10-29**). Make sure that your WINS server addresses are correctly listed in the required order. **Enable NetBIOS over TCP/IP** should be enabled if you need to communicate with other NetBIOS systems on a TCP/IP network, otherwise disable it, or select to receive this setting from the DHCP server. Select **Enable LMHOSTS lookup** if you want to search a local LMHOSTS file for NetBIOS address mappings.

Advanced TCP/IP settings: Click the **Option** tab in the Advanced TCP/IP settings dialog box and check your settings for **IPSec** and **IP filtering**. Make sure that you are not inadvertently blocking any protocols and ports in the IP filtering.

how to

Use **ipconfig** to check network settings.

1. At the command prompt, type **ipconfig** and press **[Enter]**. This will show you your basic TCP/IP settings (**Figure 10-30**).
2. Type **ipconfig /all** and press **[Enter]**. This will show you additional information such as DHCP, DNS, WINS server addresses, NetBIOS status, and DHCP address lease information (**Figure 10-31**).

Figure 10-27 Client Internet Protocol (TCP/IP) Properties dialog box

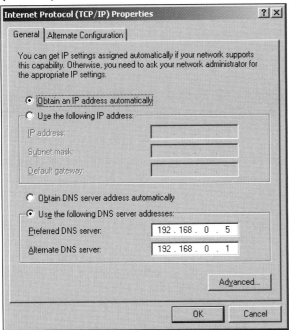

Figure 10-28 Advanced TCP/IP Settings dialog box

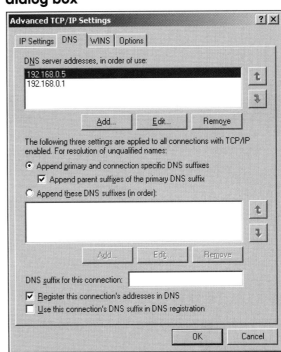

Figure 10-29 Advanced WINS settings

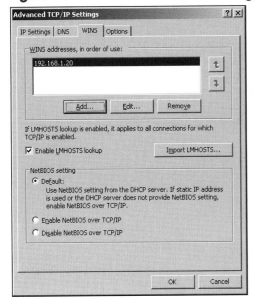

Figure 10-30 Ipconfig command

```
C:\>ipconfig

Windows 2000 IP Configuration

Ethernet adapter Local Area Connection:

        Connection-specific DNS Suffix  . :
        IP Address. . . . . . . . . . . . : 192.168.2.35
        Subnet Mask . . . . . . . . . . . : 255.255.255.0
        Default Gateway . . . . . . . . . : 192.168.2.1

C:\>
```

Figure 10-31 Ipconfig/all command

```
C:\>ipconfig /all

Windows 2000 IP Configuration

        Host Name . . . . . . . . . . . . : cr1048382-a
        Primary DNS Suffix  . . . . . . . :
        Node Type . . . . . . . . . . . . : Broadcast
        IP Routing Enabled. . . . . . . . : No
        WINS Proxy Enabled. . . . . . . . : No

Ethernet adapter Local Area Connection:

        Connection-specific DNS Suffix  . :
        Description . . . . . . . . . . . : 3Com EtherLink XL 10/100 PCI TX NIC (3C905B-TX)
        Physical Address. . . . . . . . . : 00-50-04-1D-F3-DF
        DHCP Enabled. . . . . . . . . . . : Yes
        Autoconfiguration Enabled . . . . : Yes
        IP Address. . . . . . . . . . . . : 192.168.2.35
        Subnet Mask . . . . . . . . . . . : 255.255.255.0
        Default Gateway . . . . . . . . . : 192.168.2.1
        DHCP Server . . . . . . . . . . . : 192.168.2.1
        DNS Servers . . . . . . . . . . . : 192.168.2.1
        NetBIOS over Tcpip. . . . . . . . : Disabled
        Lease Obtained. . . . . . . . . . : Saturday, January 03, 2004 3:49:39 PM
        Lease Expires . . . . . . . . . . : Monday, January 18, 2038 10:14:07 PM

C:\>_
```

Summary

- Major areas of DHCP troubleshooting include client configuration, server configuration, and database corruption.
- You can repair inconsistencies in the DHCP database by reconciling scopes.
- While implementing the WINS service, you might encounter problems that require troubleshooting. The first step is to identify whether the problem occurred due to an error on the WINS client, on the WINS server, or on the network itself.
- Client-related problems may occur for the following reasons:
    - Incorrect WINS server IP address or configuration of the WINS DHCP scope option.
    - Interruption in connectivity between a WINS client and server.
    - Multiple secondary WINS servers are installed on the network, leading to increased network traffic and delayed failed query responses.
    - NetBIOS is disabled.
- Server-related problems may occur for the following reasons:
    - Corruption of the WINS database, possibly caused by improper shutdown.
    - Incorrect static mapping entries.
    - Improper functioning of the WINS services.
    - Over-utilization of network bandwidth.
- The DNS console provides you with a method of testing the DNS setup by sending a DNS query to the DNS server.
- Command-line utilities such as Ping and Nslookup can also be used to help you test your DNS setup.
- Network troubleshooting utilities include Ping, Tracert, Route, Pathping, Netsh, and the Network Monitor.
- When troubleshooting Network Address Translation (NAT), examine its configuration including scope of IP addresses for DHCP, DNS settings, and any inbound and outbound filtering rules.
- For IPSec communications, make sure that basic network connectivity is already established before testing IPSec. Use tools such as Netsh, IP Security Monitor, Event Viewer, and Network Monitor.
- Check the remote access communications method first, such as the modem, phone line, ISDN line, and so on, before checking the remote access process itself.
- Check the remote access policy for any rules that would cause the client to be disconnected.
- Make sure the remote access authentication methods match between the client and remote server. Check that encryption settings are correctly setup.
- Make sure that remote access security logging is enabled.
- Remote access troubleshooting tools include Event Viewer, Netsh, and Network Monitor.
- Check the client network configuration settings to make sure that they are set up properly for your network for TCP/IP settings, DHCP, DNS, andWINS.
- Make sure that there are no client-side IP filtering rules blocking required protocols and ports.

Key Terms

DHCP relay agent	Ipconfig	Pathping
Dhcploc	Nbtstat	Ping
Event Viewer	Netsh	Route
IP filtering	Network Monitor	Tracert
IP Security Monitor	Nslookup	

Test Yourself

1. When connected to the network, the client does not have an IP address to communicate. Which of the following services should you examine?
   a. WINS
   b. IPSec
   c. DHCP
   d. DNS

2. A client is able to connect to a host using its IP address, but not its NetBIOS name. Which of the following could be the problem?
   a. Network cabling
   b. WINS
   c. DNS
   d. No route to host

3. What should be done to a DHCP server whose database has been corrupted?
   a. Start a new scope.
   b. Start a new database.
   c. Release and renew the address on the client.
   d. Reconcile the database.

4. What command-line utility is typically used to send name resolution queries to a DNS server?
   a. Nslookup
   b. Ipconfig
   c. Tracert
   d. Nbtstat

5. What is the primary purpose of the Ping command?
   a. Resolve DNS queries
   b. Test connectivity to a host
   c. Leasing an IP address from a DHCP server
   d. Flush the hostname cache

6. Which of the following commands is used to examine a client's TCP/IP settings?
   a. Nslookup
   b. Netsh
   c. Nbtstat
   d. Ipconfig

7. Which of the following tools can be used to troubleshoot IPSec issues?
   a. IP Security Monitor
   b. Nslookup
   c. Performance Monitor
   d. Ipsecsh

8. When troubleshooting a dial-in remote access issue, which of the following items should you check first?
   a. Client modem
   b. Remote access server
   c. Encryption settings
   d. Authentication settings

9. Which of the following utilities can be used to capture and analyze network information?
   a. Ping
   b. Ipconfig
   c. IP Security Monitor
   d. Network monitor

10. Which of the following utilities is best suited for troubleshooting routing problems to a destination host?
    a. Nbtstat
    b. Ipconfig
    c. Tracert
    d. Network monitor

Projects: On Your Own

1. Examine your client network configuration.
   a. Click **Start**, **Run**, and enter **cmd** in the **Run** dialog box to open the command prompt.
   b. Type **ipconfig** and press **[Enter]** to examine your basic network settings.
   c. Type **ipconfig /all** and press **[Enter]** to examine the detailed network settings.

2. Test connectivity between a client and server.
   a. Click **Start**, **Run**, and enter **cmd** in the **Run** dialog box to open the command prompt.
   b. Pick a server on your network, type **ping [server name]** and press **[Enter]** to see if you have connectivity.

   c. If you are successful, type **nslookup [server name]** and press **[Enter]**. This should return the server's IP address, if your DNS services are working.
   d. Use ping to test connectivity to the server again, but this time using the IP address, such as **ping [IP address]**.
   e. Type **tracert [server name]** and press **[Enter]** to see how many routing hops there are between you and the server.
   f. Try the same command again, but on the Internet, with an address such as the following:
   tracert www.azimuth-interactive.com.

Problem Solving Scenarios

As the network administrator for the Sales department, you have just set up a new Windows XP laptop for the Vice President of Sales. Unfortunately, when you connect it to the network, it cannot connect. As this laptop will also be used for remote access, you try to dial-in to the company's remote access server with the laptop's built-in modem. Although you get a connection established, the laptop cannot log in and authenticate to the network.

As part of your troubleshooting plan, how will you first examine the problem of connecting to the LAN? Make a list of the things to check, from the simplest components to the more complex. Perform the same procedure for the remote access connection. What aspects of the system must you check differently for connecting remotely?

11 Creating the Master Network Infrastructure Plan

During the planning phase of a Windows Server 2003 infrastructure deployment, you must make sure that you have integrated all factors of your current and proposed new environment. To understand and properly plan for your new environment, you must document your current infrastructure, and use this information for your deployment plans.

This documentation includes hardware and software inventories and network diagrams that fully describe the architecture, services, and devices that comprise your current environment. Additional documentation includes the Functional Specification document, which describes the features that you plan to implement in your new deployment. This document will help you create a test plan to test the new features of the proposed infrastructure before actual deployment in a production environment. The test plan ensures that you have thoroughly tested the proposed deployment in a lab environment before actual implementation.

As part of the test phase, you need to create a proper test lab environment to accurately test the performance of the proposed infrastructure. This environment must be carefully designed to simulate your production environment, or you may find that the proposed deployment does not work well under "real" loads.

Following the test phase, you should roll out a limited pilot deployment that can test your proposed infrastructure in a production environment. The pilot deployment allows you to discover and test any cases that were not fully tested in the lab environment. Allowing the end users to test the system during the deployment may reveal further cases that were not planned for during the test phase. The information from the test lab and pilot deployment will allow you to refine your network infrastructure plan accordingly, before rolling out a full production deployment.

Goals

In this lesson, you will learn what documentation is required during the deployment planning process for a Microsoft Windows Server 2003 infrastructure deployment. You will learn how to create various infrastructure plans for describing specifications, testing, and planning pilot deployments. You will also learn how to set up a proper test environment.

Requirements

There are no special requirements for this lesson. However, access to a suite of documentation tools, such as Microsoft Word, Excel, Project, and Visio may be helpful.

skill 1

Creating Planning Documentation

exam objective

Basic knowledge

overview

As you learned in Lesson 1, deploying a Windows Server 2003 network infrastructure using the Microsoft Solutions Framework (MSF) process model has a several phases: the envisioning phase, the planning phase, the developing phase, the stabilizing phase, and the deploying phase. Before you begin the envisioning phase, you first should assess your organization's current network environment, so that you can be sure that your deployment plan accurately reflects the current state of affairs. To do so, you need to conduct a hardware and software inventory, and document your current network infrastructure.

For each computer, document the following information:

- ◆ Location – geographic and departmental
- ◆ Processors – number and speed
- ◆ RAM – type and amount
- ◆ Disk drive capacity – used and available
- ◆ BIOS settings
- ◆ Peripheral devices, such as printers, scanners, and input devices.
- ◆ Network devices, such as network adapters, etc.
- ◆ Drivers and other hardware-related software and firmware information.
- ◆ Operating system installed – including version number, and any service packs, updates or patches installed
- ◆ Applications installed – including version number, and any service packs, updates or patches installed, and whether application is custom (built "in-house") or off-the-shelf.

Document your current network infrastructure (making sure to include all local and remote sites) by identifying:

- ◆ Network topology
- ◆ Network bandwidth
- ◆ Network hardware, such as routers, switches, firewalls, etc.
- ◆ Network protocols
- ◆ Network services, such as name and address resolution methods (WINS and DNS), configuration protocols (DHCP).

After doing so, create physical and logical network diagrams **(Figure 11-1)** based on your network's physical and logical network features. A **physical network diagram** focuses on the actual hardware devices and communications links between them. A **logical network diagram** identifies the structure of upper layer network services and applications such as Active Directory, domains and trust relationships, DNS, WINS, DHCP, and so on.

The physical network diagram should include the following information:

- ◆ Physical communication links (LAN and WAN), including their speed and available bandwidth between sites.
- ◆ Server names, IP addresses, and domain membership.
- ◆ Location of printers, hubs, switches, routers, bridges, proxy servers, and other network devices.
- ◆ Number of clients supported
- ◆ Addressing infrastructure and name resolution conventions
- ◆ Security and authentication infrastructure.
- ◆ Connectivity required with other network environments such as Unix or Novell Netware
- ◆ Internet service providers

tip

Use diagram and drawing software such as Microsoft Visio to create physical and logical network diagrams.

Figure 11-1 Logical and physical network diagram

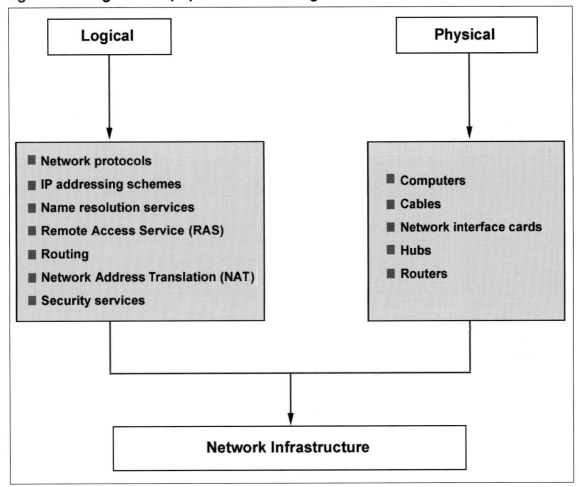

skill 1

Creating Planning Documentation
(cont'd)

exam objective

Basic knowledge

overview

The logical network diagram should include the following information:

◆ Domain architecture
◆ Server roles
◆ Trust relationships and any policy restrictions that might affect your deployment.

After you have assessed your current network environment, the next step is to create a functional specification document. The **functional specification** is a design document that describes the Windows Server 2003 features you plan to implement, and how they will be configured. The functional specification document will help you test the proposed implementation and allow you to determine the best way to use Windows Server 2003 features to meet your project objectives. Creating the functional specification document begins in the MSF planning phase and continues through the developing and stabilizing phases.

You should also create a test plan as you develop the functional specification. The **test plan** defines the objectives and scope of the test effort, and identifies the methodology that will be used to conduct tests. It describes the hardware, software, and other testing tools and equipment required. It also identifies the various features and functions of the functional specification that will be tested. The test plan typically also includes a schedule, and outlines any risk factors that may delay the testing process **(Figure 11-2)**. Once the test plan has been developed, you implement it in a test lab environment. A **test lab** is designed in a way that allows you to test as much of the proposed logical and physical network design as possible in a simulated production environment. Skill 2 examines the process of establishing a testing environment in further detail.

After you have tested the functional specifications in the test lab environment, the next step in a deployment project is the creation of the pilot plan. This step typically occurs during the stabilizing phase of the MSF process. The **pilot** tests your deployment in a controlled production environment. The **pilot plan** defines the scope and objectives of the pilot, including the participants and the pilot location. It also includes a schedule for deploying and conducting the pilot. The pilot plan helps project managers to manage the pilot project by clarifying the tasks and roles of the release management team and the pilot participants. The pilot plan includes a number of documents that provide procedures for successfully rolling out the pilot in a full production environment. The components of the pilot plan are listed in **Table 11-1**.

how to

Create a pilot plan for an infrastructure deployment:

1. Define the scope and objectives of the test pilot.
2. Identify the ideal participants and location for the pilot.
3. Create plans for training the pilot participants, and for support and communication during the pilot period.
4. What are your risk and contingency plans for the project? Describe and assess the risks involved and how they will be handled.
5. Create a backup and recovery plan to ensure that the participant's data is safe during the pilot, and that there is a plan in place to revert back to the original configuration.
6. Define a schedule for deploying and conducting the pilot, including how the results will be assessed.

Figure 11-2 Creating a test plan

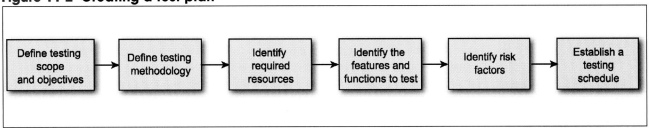

Table 11-1   Components of the pilot plan

Component	Function
Training plan for participants	Ensures that participants have the necessary skills to carry out the plan.
Support plan	Describes how problems that arise for participants during the pilot will be resolved.
Communication plan	Describes how you will keep participants informed about what is happening in the project.
Evaluation plan	Describes how you plan to obtain feedback from participants. This information can then be used to assess design changes that might be required before the pilot is rolled out to the rest of the organization.
Risk and contingency plan	Describes potential risk factors and how you plan to assess and diffuse them.
Backup and recovery plan	Allows you to revert to the infrastructure's initial state if problems arise during the pilot.
Schedule	Includes milestones for evaluating and making necessary changes to the pilot plan

skill 2 | *Establishing the Testing Environment*

exam objective | Basic knowledge

overview

As noted in Skill 1, testing your proposed functional specification in a test environment is an important part of the deployment process. A **test environment** typically consists of one or more test labs. Testing the functional specifications in a test lab before they are actually deployed (even in a pilot plan) helps to ensure that your proposed infrastructure will work properly, resulting in minimal downtime in your production environment. If you defer testing, you risk having to troubleshoot deployment errors during production, resulting in costly downtime.

Designing the Test Environment. Before you can actually test your functional specifications, you must design the testing environment. First, document the current production environment so that you can create a test environment that accurately reflects your production system requirements. Take note of server hardware and drivers, services and their configuration, domain and Active Directory structure, user and group accounts, networking topology and protocols, WAN connections, remote connectivity, fault tolerance and clustering configuration, and interoperability with other non-Windows systems. Client configuration settings should be copied as closely as possible from the production environment. Ensure that hardware and software are compatible and use the same versions of firmware, drivers, service packs, and so on.

Setting up the Test Lab. You need a test lab early in the project's planning phase to test and validate your proposed solution. Depending on the size of your company and available resources, you may have a permanent test lab, or you might create a temporary one with the resources that you have available. A test lab can be centralized in one location, or distributed across two or more physical or geographical locations. A single centralized test lab has the advantage of all resources being located at one site, allowing you to create a more complex and complete lab that is easy to manage. If you use a centralized test lab, you can create several smaller labs within the site for different testing purposes, such as network infrastructure and server testing, or client computer and application testing. A distributed test environment, especially one that includes different geographical locations, allows you to test the functionality of a network infrastructure deployment across WAN links. If testing over an actual WAN is not possible, there are tools available that can simulate using bandwidth-limited WAN links in your local LAN. While this has the advantage of being less intrusive to the current environment, it is also not quite as accurate as a WAN test using true WAN links.

After you have selected the type and location of your lab, you must assess hardware, software, and personnel requirements for the testing environment and document them in your test plan. You can build a small Windows Server 2003 LAN with DNS, DHCP, and WINS services, and then use this to perform initial baselining for further testing and development. It is important, however, to ensure that your solution is fully tested using the same amount of resource loads that the deployment would use in a production environment. For example, you would not be able to properly baseline a deployment using test resources consisting of only a few servers and clients, when in production, the actual load would require hundreds of clients and servers. It is possible to simulate the production loads by using scripts or multi-session clients. There are also capacity planning tools, such as BEST/1, which can model large-scale environments. Even with modeling tools, simulation tools, multi-session benchmark scripts, and so on, you are still making best-efforts guesses about how a new infrastructure will perform in an actual production environment.

Table 11-2 sets forth some of the other infrastructure factors to consider when planning and designing your test facilities.

Table 11-2   Infrastructure factors affecting test environment design

◆ Whether you plan to implement a domain that spans multiple sites, or require several domains dedicated for each site.

◆ Whether you plan to implement a virtual private network (VPN).

◆ Whether you are using the same standard equipment and applications, or if you need to use several different types of hardware and software in the same environment.

◆ The level of complexity in your network configuration, such as whether you have more than one type of topology. This includes the physical layout of computers, cables, switches, routers, and the underlying network architecture, such as Ethernet or Token Ring.

◆ Requirements for interconnecting with other systems, such as a mainframe or Unix system.

skill 2

Establishing the Testing Environment
(cont'd)

exam objective Basic knowledge

how to

Plan your test environment.

1. Document your current production environment, including all server/client hardware and software configurations, and networking infrastructure.
2. Plan your test lab, including the decision on the use of a central or distributed environment. Does your production environment use multiple sites? VPNs? Do you need to test communications across slow WAN links and dial-up connections?
3. Design your test lab and document all hardware, software, and networking considerations.

more

Figure 11-3 lists some of the tasks that can be performed in the test lab and indicates the MSF phases during which each of these activities might occur.

Figure 11-3 Test lab tasks and MSF phases

	Envisioning	Planning	Developing	Stabilizing	Deployment
○ Evaluate new technologies		■			
○ Examine new features		■	■		
○ Create Prototype		■	■		
○ Design test processes		■	■		
○ Check network compatibility			■		
○ Test interoperability			■		
○ Test tools			■		
○ Check Hardware/Software Compatibility			■	■	■
○ Test roll out process			■	■	■
○ Analyze and fix problems			■	■	■

○ Boxes highlighted in white indicate the phase in the MSF process during which the task is typically performed.

skill 3

Refining the Network Infrastructure Plan

exam objective

Basic knowledge

overview

Based on the results and feedback during the testing and pilot phases of the deployment, you will need to adjust and refine your network infrastructure plan as required. Your network infrastructure plan is a "living" document, and the planning process is inherently an iterative one. For example, you may find during testing that your server cannot handle the simulated production loads. During a pilot evaluation, the proposed network design may not have taken into account certain factors such as slow WAN links that affect the performance of networking services to remote sites. All of these factors must be documented during your testing and pilot phases, and then integrated into a refined infrastructure plan.

Your new, refined infrastructure plan may include additional servers, such as additional domain controllers, DNS, WINS, or DHCP servers to handle additional loads. Alternatively, the performance issues may be solved via hardware upgrades, such as additional RAM, processing power, or hard disk space. Network bandwidth is also a common issue, and the links between WAN sites may need to be upgraded, or on a local LAN, the backbone of the network may need to be upgraded to handle additional loads. Your proposed network infrastructure may have encountered hardware and software compatibility problems during the testing and pilot phase. Depending on the severity of the incompatibility, you may need to significantly revise your hardware and software requirements, including ordering additional hardware, ordering additional software licenses, or applying additional software upgrades. During testing, you may also have encountered a problem with one particular network site, where certain local conditions require that the infrastructure plan be changed for that location.

When refining the infrastructure plan, you should gather the information collected during the testing and pilot phases and analyze the data to ensure that your final plan takes into account any further expansion and scalability. You may find that although your current plan is working well, it may not handle further growth. Make any adjustments necessary to your system hardware and networking infrastructure to ensure that it can handle both current and future requirements. Similarly, although the current infrastructure works, a failure in one aspect may cause problems with the rest of the infrastructure. Make sure you have addressed any fault tolerance and high availability issues with your original plan, such as adding redundant network equipment, servers, and creating primary and secondary servers for DHCP, WINS, and DNS services. When finished revising your network infrastructure plan, it is important, if possible, to retest the new configuration to ensure that the new changes and additions to the plan will not interfere with current functionality and performance (**Table 11-3**).

how to

Refine a network infrastructure plan.

1. Analyze issues from the test lab and pilot project.
2. Determine weaknesses in the current infrastructure plan, including hardware, software, networking, availability of network services, fault tolerance, and scalability.
3. Refine your plan accordingly, and re-test to ensure that any changes have not interfered with aspects of the original plan.

Table 11-3   Refining the network infrastructure plan

Potential Problems	Possible solutions
Performance of network services in remote locations	Upgrade WAN links
Overloaded servers	Deploy additional, or upgrade existing, servers to help distribute the load
General performance issues	Upgrade hardware (processors, RAM, hard disks, etc.)
Hardware compatibility issues	Revise hardware requirements and/or order new hardware
Software compatibility issues	Revise software requirements and/or upgrade software
Future roadblocks	Plan for expansion and scalability so that future growth does not result in additional problems

skill 4

Planning an Example Network

exam objective

Basic knowledge

overview

In this skill, we will examine a sample network and show how to build a simple network design plan that increases reliability and uptime. Walking through the steps of the planning process lets you examine the decision points that shape the final design. Note that the planning process in real life may be more complex, but this example should give you a good idea of how Microsoft would prefer you to step through the planning process on the test.

The first thing that you will typically do in the planning process is to determine your objectives. This activity will require interviewing many people in order to get feedback on what the final goals of the project are. You will also be looking for detailed information on the current environment. It is during this phase that you will analyze your hardware and software inventories, as well as build your logical and physical network diagrams of the current environment. All of this information will be used to build the functional specification document.

For this example, you will interview three key members of the project, the CEO, the CIO, and the Network Administrator. **Figure 11-4** provides you with the results of those interviews.

Based on the information from these interviews, you can begin to formulate the goals for the redesign. First and foremost, reliability is a major concern, as voiced in all three interviews. Based on the Network Administrator and CIO interviews, it appears that part of the problem with network reliability is due to high bandwidth consumption. While it will take some testing to determine the specific cause, this should be a key concern. Finally, as mentioned by the CIO, money is not a huge concern, but is still important. You need to deliver the best solution possible on or under budget.

The next step would be to examine and inventory hardware and software. During this process, you may compile a list for each computer that includes all hardware and software on the computer. Using this list, you can determine which applications may be causing network problems. For instance, if you noticed several Internet file sharing applications were installed on employee computers, you may need to lock down that application using filters on the firewall, to prevent it from using Internet bandwidth. While system configuration was not mentioned as a concern, you should still look for problems with system configuration in the hardware inventory as well.

After examining the software and hardware inventory, you should examine the current network and create logical and physical diagrams of the current environment (assuming the company does not already have them). Once this is done, you may begin to see possible causes of bottlenecks in the current design, which would tell you a little better what specific problems to look for with protocol analyzers and other network monitoring tools.

For instance, in this company's physical diagram, you can see that the use of hubs throughout the network, as well as low bandwidth allocation to WAN links, is most likely the cause of the issues mentioned by the CIO and the Network Administrator **(Figure 11-5)**. This would lead you to use tools to monitor collisions and WAN bandwidth usage to precisely determine the cause of the problem.

After examining the diagrams, you should use monitoring tools to pinpoint the exact problem. In this case, you may use a protocol analyzer to determine the protocols that are using significant WAN bandwidth. You may then use SNMP counters along with an SNMP management application to determine if the routers are overloaded with WAN traffic. Finally, you will use the same SNMP tools to determine the level of traffic and collisions on the current LANs.

Figure 11-4 Interviewing the CEO, CIO, and Network Administrator

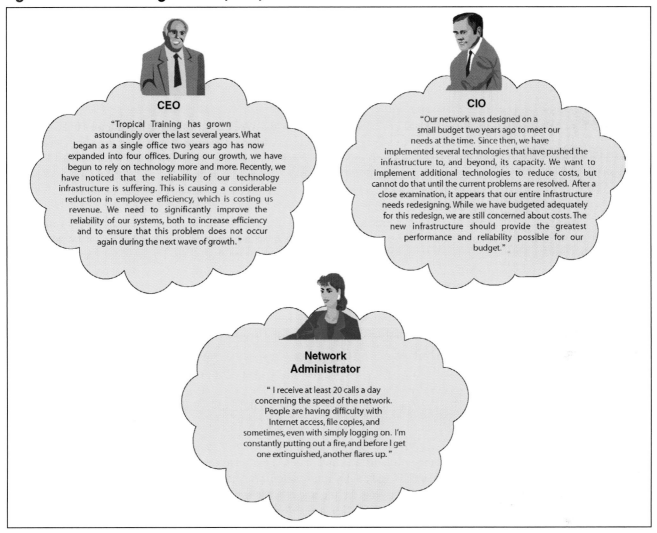

Figure 11-5 Headquarters physical diagram with problem areas

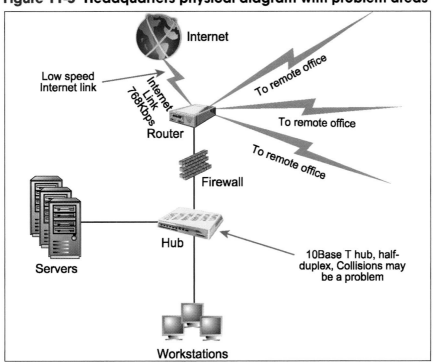

skill 4

Planning an Example Network (cont'd)

exam objective

Basic knowledge

overview

In **Figure 11-6**, you see an example of the WAN bandwidth for the Internet link, shown in chart form. In this example, the protocols are already associated to the applications that typically use those protocols, in order to make the chart easier to digest. In real life, this process is typically a bit more complex, as several applications may use the same upper-layer protocols, but the end result is the same. In this chart, you can easily see that Internet file sharing applications previously seen in the software inventory are indeed responsible for a large part of your WAN traffic usage. Since Internet file sharing is not a business application, you can significantly reduce bandwidth usage without upgrading any portions of the network by simply blocking that traffic. Another application that is not business related but is using a significant portion of the bandwidth is online games. Again, simply by creating filters, you can reduce bandwidth consumption. After removing the non-business traffic, you still see that the Internet bandwidth will need to be upgraded, as your current link is only 768 Kbps, and business traffic requires around 900 Kbps. However, by removing the non-business traffic, you can significantly reduce the cost of the upgrade by reducing the total bandwidth increase that is required.

After examining the WAN bandwidth, you should examine the LAN bandwidth on each segment. In this case, the protocol analyzer may show that there are a high number of collisions on the local LANs, which would cause a significant reduction in available bandwidth.

Once these activities are performed, you should have a pretty good idea of what the root causes of the problems are, and should be able to design a solution to reduce or eliminate those problems. Based on this information, you may then create a functional specification that states the problems and the methods that will be used to eliminate those problems. In this case, the key problems in the current design would be:

◆ Improper usage of Internet bandwidth by non-business applications.
◆ Too little Internet bandwidth available to support business applications.
◆ Large numbers of collisions on LANs are reducing available bandwidth at each facility.

To resolve these problems, the functional specification might propose the following solutions:

◆ Create new packet filters on the firewall to block all non-business traffic.
◆ Remove all non-business applications from the local computers.
◆ Increase the Internet bandwidth to 900 Kbps or higher.
◆ Replace the 10 Mbps hubs with 100 Mbps, full-duplex switches to eliminate collisions.

In a larger scenario, you might then build a detailed test plan, which would include metrics for evaluation, evaluation methods, risk assessments, and specifications for the test environment. Then, you would create a detailed pilot to fully test your implementation in a live environment. However, in a small environment, you most likely would simply create a deployment plan and begin the upgrade, as the risk of the upgrade (since it primarily involves just hardware upgrades) is fairly low.

Figure 11-6 Internet bandwidth usage analysis

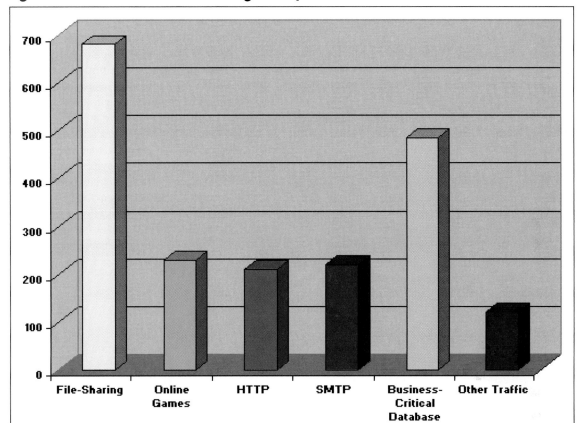

Summary

- Perform a hardware and software inventory of the current infrastructure when planning a new deployment
- When documenting current software, include the operating system, installed application (including in-house custom applications), current patch/service pack levels, and .dll versions.
- Document the network infrastructure using physical and logical network diagrams.
- A physical network represents the physical network connections and their characteristics, network attached devices, and servers along with their function and IP address.
- A logical network diagram represents the domain architecture, server roles, and trust relationships for a network infrastructure.
- A functional specification document specifies the features that you intend to implement in your deployment, and how they are configured and deployed to support the goals of the project.
- A test plan defines the objectives and scope of the testing effort and identifies the methodology that your team will use to conduct tests.
- A pilot plan defines the scope and objectives of the test pilot, including the participants and where the pilot will be conducted.

- The testing lab and process provide a controlled environment that will allow you to fully test your proposed deployment infrastructure.
- A centralized test lab has the advantage of all resources being located on one site, allowing you to create a more complex and complete lab that is easy to manage.
- A distributed test lab allows you test functionally of a network infrastructure deployment across WAN links if the sites are located at geographically remote sites.
- Make sure that your solution is fully tested using the same amount of resource loads that the deployment would use in a production environment.
- Gather information on your current environment including number of servers and clients, networking topologies, hardware and software requirements, and so on, to help create a test environment that accurately reflects your production system requirements.
- Make sure that server and client test environments resemble the production network as closely as possible.
- Analyze the results of the test lab and pilot deployment to refine your network infrastructure plan.

Key Terms

Functional specification document	Pilot plan	Test lab
Logical network diagram	Software inventory	Test plan
Physical network diagram	Test environment	

Test Yourself

1. During your initial planning for a Windows 2003 deployment, what should be the first item to document?
   a. Pilot plan
   b. Test cases
   c. Test plan
   d. Current hardware/software and networking infrastructure.

2. Which of the following network diagrams focuses on protocols, applications, and network services?
   a. Logical network diagram
   b. Protocol network diagram
   c. Physical network diagram

   d. Active Directory structure diagram

3. Which of the following documents is used to describe what features will be implemented in a deployment?
   a. Network diagrams
   b. Deployment plan
   c. Functional specification plan
   d. Test plan

4. Which of the following is NOT an aspect of a Pilot plan?
   a. Training plan
   b. Backup and recovery plan

c. Support plan

d. DNS namespace plan

5. Which type of testing lab is better suited for testing a deployment that will be installed across several remote sites?

a. Centralized test lab

b. Distributed test lab

c. Temporary test lab

d. Ethernet test lab

6. During a pilot deployment, it is discovered that when a DHCP server fails, clients are not assigned an IP address and cannot connect to the network. Which of the following should be included in a refined network infrastructure?

a. Backup domain controller

b. Backup DNS server

c. Backup DHCP server

d. Backup and recovery solution

Projects: On Your Own

1. Design a test lab that will be used to test a deployment of a small Windows Server 2003 LAN, including basic DHCP, WINS, and DNS services.

2. Create a functional specification document that fully describes how the new features of Windows Server 2003 will be implemented in a new deployment.

Problem Solving Scenarios

You are rolling out a pilot deployment of a Windows Server 2003 infrastructure to your local office. After the pilot, you want to deploy the infrastructure to all remote offices. During the pilot testing process, a number of hardware and software compatibility issues have been found. Also, you realize that you have not been able to test how the limited bandwidth WAN connectivity to remote sites will affect the deployment. In light of these considerations, summarize how you would refine your network infrastructure. In addition, develop a second pilot plan to include the remote sites in your testing of the deployment.

Glossary

802.11 The standard for wireless local area networks (WLANs).

802.1X Defines port-based network access control to provide authenticated network access for Ethernet networks.

Access Point Under the 802.11 standard, a device that functions as a transparent bridge between wireless clients and the existing wired network. It contains at least one interface to connect to the existing wired network and contains transmitting equipment to connect with wireless clients.

Address (A) Record DNS record that identifies a host.

American Standard Code for Information Interchange (ASCII) A binary code for letters, numbers, symbols, and other keyboard characters and for communications and printer control.

AppleTalk LAN architecture built into Apple Macintosh computers and laser printers used to interact with the OSI model.

Application Log Event log in which warnings, alerts, and messages that are generated by applications are recorded.

Auditing Monitoring a network for security issues by keeping and examining audit logs and using real-time monitoring applications.

Authoritative server A server that has the authority over other DNS servers in the same zone. This is the server that stores the primary zone database file.

AXFR Complete DNS zone transfer.

Bandwidth The maximum amount of data that can be delivered each second over a network. The data bits per second using the maximum possible number of network frames, or trucks, carrying the most data per frame, sent without any delay.

Baseline A record made of the known and state of a component in a solution that is used as a comparison to identify changes that have occurred within the environment.

B-Node Broadcast node WINS client.

Boarder Gateway Protocol (BGP) An exterior routing protocol used to exchange information between networks administered under different administrative authorities.

Bottleneck A factor that limits overall system performance; often found in memory, processors, disks, and networks.

Broadcast domain A group of devices that receive a broadcast frame transmitted by one of the devices.

Cache pollution protection A security enhancement that, when enabled, ensures the security of your system by telling the DNS server to disregard DNS resources records originating from DNS servers that are not authoritative for those records.

Caching-only DNS server A computer that uses caching to store information collected during name resolution; also called the caching-only name server.

Capture Filter A feature of Network Monitor used to capture information about specific protocols in use on your network.

Carrier Sense Multiple Access/Collision Detect (CSMA/CD) A protocol that specifies that multiple devices can attach to a single network segment and that each must listen before transmitting to ensure that the cable is free.

Certificate Authority An entity that issues, manages, and vouches for the authenticity of the public keys that they issue to users, computers, and services. It also can vouch for other CAs.

Challenge Handshake Authentication Protocol (CHAP) Sends a key to the client to encrypt the user name and password.

Class-based addressing Dividing up an appropriate address space into five blocks, of which the first three can be used for host addresses. Such addressing enables the subnet mask associated with an address to be implicitly determined by examining the first few bits in the address.

Classless Inter-Domain Routing (CIDR) Internet routing method that uses classless IP addressing to allow for the more efficient allocation of IP addresses. By using a configurable, rather than static, subnet mask, the problems of wasted addresses and the diminishing capacity of Internet global routing tables are alleviated. Using CIDR, a single routing table entry can replace hundreds or thousands of entries in a global routing table.

Classless routing Using any number of contiguous left-justified bits to identify a network, rather than representing the network portion of an address with a fixed number of bits defined by the address class.

Cluster.exe A command-line tool that enables creation and management of server clusters.

Clustering In Windows Server 2003, an arrangement of up to eight computers interconnected and operating as a single system.

Collision The situation on a network when two devices happen to transmit at the same exact instant; the network detects the impact of the two packets, discards both, and tries again a random length of time later.

Collision domain Any group of devices whose transmissions can collide.

Critical Path The path and time needed to complete all of the interrelated tasks that are required to reach a specified goal.

Customer The person or group who commissions or funds a project and derives business benefit from it.

Customer Focused Mindset Understanding that satisfying the customer by providing a solution that matches their requirements and solves their business problem is the team's first priority.

Cyclic Redundancy Checking (CRC) See frame check sequence (FCS).

Debug logging A tool to help investigate specific issues or to supplement existing monitoring utilities.

Demilitarized Zone (DMZ) A perimeter network between an internal and external firewall that hosts services that must be provided to both internal and external users.

Developing phase The third phase of the MSF process model during which the majority of the components of a solution are built and tested. At the completion of the developing phase, the solution is ready for extra testing and stabilization.

DHCP See Dynamic Host Control Protocol.

DHCP Relay agent A routing protocol that makes it possible for DHCP clients to request an IP address from a DHCP server that is located on a remote subnet. Without a relay agent, broadcast packets cannot travel through routers.

DHCP server Provides dynamic TCP/IP addressing configuration to any network host that requests it.

DHCP Server service Responsible for, among other things, assigning an IP address, subnet mask, and optional IP configuration settings to any host that requests them.

Dhcploc.exe A program in the Windows Support Tools folder on the server used to find rogue DHCP servers, and to reduce address conflicts.

Digital Certificate A digitally signed document that functions as a component of the Public Key Infrastructure (PKI), and which verifies the identity of a user, computer, or service.

Display Filter A database query used to specify conditions for display of previously captured frames.

DNS Forwarding Queries that cannot be resolved on a local DNS server are forwarded to another server.

DNS server Resolves host names and Fully Qualified Domain Names into IP addresses. Normally stores a zone file for a specified portion of the DNS namespace for which the server is considered authoritative.

Domain A structure of named nodes within a DNS hierarchy.

Domain controller A server that holds a copy of the Active Directory for its domain and provides services to allow authentication of users and computers and querying of the Active Directory.

Domain directory partition A storage location where data pertaining to a particular Active Directory domain is stored, such as data about objects like users and computers.

Domain Name System (DNS) The main name resolution service for Windows Server 2003, it enables IP-based computers to locate other computers and services on a network by using a host name and a domain name.

Dynamic DNS (DDNS) A feature of Windows Server 2003 DNS that permits clients to automatically update their records, rather than requiring manual updates each time a record changes.

Dynamic DNS updates The automatic updating of records, via DNS, each time that a record changes.

Dynamic Host Configuration Protocol (DHCP) A service used to allocate IP addresses dynamically to network clients that are configured to obtain an address automatically.

EAP See Extensible Authentication Protocol.

EAP-TLS See Extensible Authentication Protocol.

Efficiency The relationship between the amount of data a frame contains and the total frame size. Efficiency rises or drops according to how full network frames, or trucks, are—that is, the amount of data a frame is carrying compared to the amount that it can carry.

Empower To provide a team member with the resources necessary to fulfill their commitments to the team and give them the authority required to make decisions necessary to achieve their goal.

Envisioning phase The first phase in the MSF process model during which the majority of the design work for a project is completed.

Event Viewer Snap-in used to monitor information about server events. Events are documented in event logs as errors, warnings, or information. The default event logs are the Application, Security, and System logs.

Extensible Authentication Protocol (EAP) Extended Point-to-Point Protocol that supports multiple authentication mechanisms and settles an authentication method at the connection time instead of selecting a single authentication method. It supports authentication using either TLS (Transport Layer Security) or MD5-CHAP. TLS supports smart cards and certificates. MD5-CHAP uses a Message Digest 5 (MD5) algorithm to encrypt user names and passwords.

File Transfer Protocol (FTP) Provides network data to Network Monitor so the monitor can troubleshoot communication problems between a browser and Web server.

Forward Lookup Zone DNS zone used to resolve host names to IP addresses.

Frame A logical grouping of information created at the Data link layer of the OSI model. It uses source/destination MAC addresses in the header.

Frame Check Sequence (FCS) A cyclical redundancy check (CRC) used to verify the integrity of a frame.

Full-duplex Communication enabled when using typical Unshielded Twisted Pair (UTP) cabling because one pair of wires can be used to receive at the same time that the other pair is used to transmit.

Fully Qualified Domain Name (FQDN) The full DNS path name, containing all domains and subdomains along the path to the host. For example, www.sales.corp.com. is an example of a FQDN. www is the hostname (the name of the computer), sales is a sub-domain, corp is the second level domain, com is the top-level domain, and the "." at the end signifies the root of DNS.

Functional specification document Describes the features you plan to implement in a new network infrastructure deployment. It helps to create a test plan to test new features of a proposed infrastructure before actual deployment occurs.

Gantt chart A chart that displays project tasks and indicates their duration by the length of line used to represent the task.

Global Catalog server Stores a copy of all objects in the entire forest along with a subset of each object's attributes. The Global Catalog server always resides on a Domain Controller.

Hardware Abstraction Layer (HAL) A modular software interface that allows the Windows Server 2003 operating system to operate on different hardware platforms without changes to other core operating system files. A unique HAL must be created for each unique hardware platform.

H-Node Hybrid node WINS client querys a WINS server first, then uses broadcast if query fails. Default WINS client mode.

Hypertext Transfer Protocol (HTTP) The Internet protocol used to transfer information over the World Wide Web (WWW).

In-band management Using the network connections supplied by a network device to manage it. See also out-of-band management.

Internet Authentication Service (IAS) Microsoft's implementation of a RADIUS server. This service provides centralized authentication and logging of remote access connections.

Internet Connection Sharing (ICS) A feature that enables users to connect to the Internet through a single connection that uses a single public IP address.

Internet Group Management Protocol (IGMP) Protocol responsible for the management of IP multicasting, which is the transmission of an IP datagram to a set of hosts called the IP multicast group that is identified by a single IP multicast address.

Internet Naming Authority An Internet authority that controls the registration of domain names.

Internet Protocol version 6 (IPv6) New version of Internet Protocol that has been developed to replace IPv4.

IP Security Monitor A tool for testing whether IPSec communications are secure.

Ipconfig A command-line tool used to verify TCP/IP configuration settings.

IPSec A network encryption protocol implemented at layer 3 of the OSI model.

ITIL The IT Infrastructure Library defines industry-standard best practices for managing an IT infrastructure. The Central Computer and Telecommunications Agency, an agency of the UK government, produced them.

IXFR Incremental DNS zone transfer.

Kerberos v5 Secure authentication protocol developed by MIT and implemented by Microsoft in Windows XP, 2000, and 2003 when authenticating against the Active Directory.

Layer Two Tunneling Protocol (L2TP) A protocol that creates a secure tunnel across an untrusted communication channel.

Line speed The theoretical maximum number of bits per second (bps) that can be transmitted on an Ethernet-based network. This peak speed does not represent the amount of data sent each second. Also called media speed.

Link state protocol A protocol that sends Link State Advertisements (LSAs) when an interface on a router changes state and does not learn routes by rumor.

LMHOSTS file A text file available on the local computer that contains the static mappings of NetBIOS names to IP addresses of computers and is used to resolve NetBIOS names to IP addresses.

Logical network diagram A diagram representing the domain architecture, server roles, and trust relationships for a network infrastructure.

Master Project Plan A collection or "roll-up" of all of the individual plans created by the various roles during the planning phase of the MSF model.

Master Project Schedule A composite schedule made up of all of the individual detailed project schedules produced by each role holder.

Master server The source of zone information, and can be a primary or secondary server.

Maximum transmission unit (MTU) On an Ethernet frame, the maximum amount of Layer 3 data.

Media speed See line speed.

Memory leak When a program allocates memory and does not release it, a memory leak is created. Over time a memory leak can slowly consume all available memory on a system.

Micro-segmentation A configuration in which all devices in a network infrastructure are attached to their own switched ports. This configuration removes collisions from the environment.

Microsoft Baseline Security Analyzer (MBSA) A security assessment tool for scanning Windows systems for security issues in the operating system and supporting services such as IIS, SQL, and desktop applications, as well as for checking for missing security updates for the operating system and application software.

Microsoft Software Update Services (SUS) A service that enables administrators to deploy the latest critical updates and security updates to Windows Server 2003-based servers. These updates are available at the Windows Update Web site.

Milestone Predefined points in a project that act as progress indicators and often signal the transition from one phase of the project to another.

M-Node Mixed node WINS clients use broadcast, and then query a WINS server if broadcast fails.

MOF The Microsoft Operations Framework provides a proven set of best practices for managing the operations of an IT infrastructure.

MS-CHAP (Microsoft Challenge Handshake Authentication Protocol) A protocol that encrypts password information before it is sent over a communication link, utilizing one-way authentication. An enhanced version, MS-CHAPv2, utilizes mutual authentication.

MSF Microsoft Solutions Framework provides guidance in managing people and processes to plan, build, and deploy successful IT solutions.

Multicast A session in which you transmit a message to a select group of recipients.

Namespace A hierarchical arrangement of domains in DNS.

Nbtstat Used with different parameters to flush, or clear and reload, the NetBIOS cache or to re-register a client's IP address and NetBIOS name with a WINS server.

NetBEUI NetBIOS Extended User Interface. Non-routable protocol used to share resources in a small LAN.

NetBIOS An Application Programming Interface (API) that provides network commands used by applications to allow them to communicate over a network. One function of NetBIOS allows you to provide names to computers on a LAN.

Netsh A command-line utility used to configure and monitor IPSec and to perform DHCP and other administrative tasks from a command prompt.

Network Address Translation (NAT) A service that is a component of the Remote Access services. It allows a single external address to provide connectivity for a number of internal hosts, hiding the internal addressing structure from anyone outside of the private network.

Network Load Balancing A Windows service that distributes incoming connection requests across multiple servers to balance network load.

Network Monitor A set of tools for capturing and monitoring packets. You use it primarily to examine protocols and data used on a network.

Network Monitor Driver A protocol that enables Network Monitor to capture information in the form of frames.

Nlb.exe A command-line tool used to control operation of a cluster.

Non-paged memory Memory that is always resident in physical RAM and cannot swap out to the pagefile.

Nslookup A command-line utility that can be used to test the DNS domain namespace.

Out-of-band management Using a separate port of a network device that cannot be accessed through the network, such as a TTY port instead of an Ethernet port. See also in-band management.

Paged memory Memory that can swap out of physical RAM to the pagefile to make more room in RAM for other processes and data.

Password Authentication Protocol (PAP) A simple authentication protocol that transmits the user's name and password over a dial-up connection to a RRAS server.

Pathping A utility that combines the features of the Ping and the Tracert commands.

Performance console A tool that captures information similar to that captured by Task Manager, plus data such as the total number of bytes sent and received per second, how many packets were received and then discarded due to errors, and so on.

Performance Logs and Alerts Snap-in for the Performance console that is used to store performance data in log files and to create alerts.

Perimeter network See Demilitarized Zone (DMZ).

PERT Program Evaluation Review Technique applies statistical analysis to the probability associated with task schedules to determine the most likely completion date.

Physical network diagram a diagram representing the physical network connections and their characteristics, network attached devices, and servers along with their function and IP address.

Pilot plan Defines the scope and objectives of the pilot implementation test, including participants and the test location.

Ping (Packet Internet Groper) A command used to test connectivity in IP-based networks.

PKI (Public Key Infrastructure) A set of services that supports the use of cryptography. Includes rules, policies, standards, and software that manage certificates and public/private keys to authenticate the validity of each party involved in a transaction.

Planning phase The second phase in the MSF process model during which design documents are refined, specifics are added, technology is validated and risks are managed.

P-Node Peer-to-Peer, or Point-to-Point nodes query a WINS server.

Port Address Translation (PAT) An Internet standard that enables one or more external addresses to represent internal hosts by mapping specified ports on the external interface of a NAT device to a port on an internal host.

PPTP (Point-to-Point Tunneling Protocol) A TCP/IP protocol that provides an internal address configuration to the remote client; used in virtual private networks (VPNs).

Primary DNS server A DNS name server in a zone that stores the primary zone database file; also called the primary name server.

Primary zone The zone in which all updates for records belonging to a zone are made. See also secondary zone.

Private network A network that is intended to be accessed by persons only within an organization.

Process model Defines the different processes that are involved in producing a successful IT solution when using MSF.

Product mindset Identifying what the key deliverable is for a project and focusing on the successful delivery of that objective as the primary task of all team members rather than focusing on the individual activities that are required.

Program Evaluation Review Technique (PERT) Performing statistical analysis on project data to determine the most likely completion date for the project.

Project scope All of the work that will be required to deliver the desired solution; Completion Criteria.

Protocol A well-defined rule that specifies exactly how one computer, application, or network interface can send and receive information with another.

Proxy server A server, such as Microsoft ISA server, that enables hosts on a private network to connect to the Internet through a single public IP address. A proxy server receives a request from a client, de-encapsulates that request by stripping off all headers added by each protocol, and then rebuilds a new packet. It then encapsulates the received data with new headers for each protocol used on the destination network.

Pull partner A WINS server that requests to receive changes from its partner after a specific period of time has elapsed. If the pull interval is set to ten, the pull partner will attempt to retrieve changes every ten minutes, regardless of whether any changes have occurred.

Push partner A WINS server that sends replication data to its partner after a specific number of changes. If the interval for push replication is set to 10, the push partner will push replication data every time ten or more changes occur.

Registry The area of the Windows operating system that contains critical configuration data for the operating system and applications, and therefore must be protected from manual modifications by unauthorized users.

Reliable Multicast Protocol A protocol developed to support the dependable transmission of multicast data streams rather than using User Datagram Protocol (UDP), which provides no guarantee that data packets will reach their destination. PGM (Pragmatic General Multicast) is the reliable multicast protocol supported by Windows Server 2003.

Remote access server Provides remote connectivity for dial-up and Virtual Private Network (VPN) clients, as well as routed network connections to other locations. Routed connections can also have NAT enabled to allow a single external address to provide connectivity for a number of internal hosts.

Remote Assistance Utility based on Terminal Services that is used to allow a trusted party such as a help desk support person or network technician to remotely access your system. This expert can be allowed to either just view your system or to both view and interact with your system.

Remote Authentication Dial-In User Service (RADIUS) An industry-standard protocol that provides authentication, authorization, and accounting services for dial-up networking.

Remote Desktop for Administration and Remote Assistance Used to manage a computer from nearly any other computer on the same network, enabling a trusted party to access a computer for observation and repair.

Remote Desktop Protocol (RDP) Handles communication between a Terminal Services client and the Terminal Server. Designed to handle transmission of graphical data, RDP supports automatic disconnection, remote configuration, and three levels of session encryption.

Reset Occurs when a frame fails to reach its destination.

Resource Record Contains all information on a specific DNS resource.

Reverse Lookup Zone DNS zone used to resolve IP addresses to host names.

Risk Any uncertainty that could affect the successful completion of the solution.

Rogue DHCP server An unauthorized server on a network that hands out IP addresses to DHCP-enabled clients. Use the *ipconfig /all* command to review DHCP configuration information on a client.

Role Clusters One or more people with the necessary functional skills to fulfill the requirements and responsibilities of a specified role.

Root Domain The domain at the top of the DNS namespace.

Root Zone A DNS zone authoritative for the root domain.

Route A command used to modify the local routing table.

Routed protocol A protocol which, like Internet Protocol, carries actual network communications. Contrast with routing protocol.

Routing and Remote Access Services (RRAS) A multiprotocol routing service that enables routing of data traffic on IP, IPX, and AppleTalk networks, as well as providing remote access capabilities. Use RRAS to connect remote clients working from remote locations to a network.

Routing protocol A protocol which, unlike Internet Protocol, does not carry actual network communications. Contrast with routed protocol.

RRAS See Routing and Remote Access Services.

SAP An acronym for Server Access Point.

Scope A definition of the features or deliverables that a solution will provide.

Secondary DNS server Stores copies of the primary zone database file; also called the secondary name server.

Secondary zone Represented by a read-only copy of the primary zone.

Second-level domain The subdomain of a top-level domain, which in turn is the subdomain of the root domain.

Security Log An event log where access and security data is recorded. Audited events are stored here. Also referred to as a Security event log.

Security template Allows administrators to set a wide range of security settings on computers.

Server farm A group of computers configured to provide a common service through Network Load Balancing.

Shared project vision Each team member has a clear and consistent understanding of what the goals and objectives are for the project.

Shiva Password Authentication Protocol (SPAP) A protocol used for compatibility with remote access hardware devices manufactured by a company called Shiva.

Solution scope Specifies what features of the shared vision the solution will deliver.

Stakeholder An individual or group that has interests at stake in the outcome of a project.

Stakeholder map A diagram that indicates the relationship between stakeholders from a political perspective.

Start of Authority (SOA) Record The first record in a DNS zone that indicates the zone's principal nameserver.

Stub zone Resembles a delegated zone, but it caches the SOA, NS, and core A records for the zone to reduce query time slightly. Stub zones do not participate in zone transfers.

Supernetting The process of modifying the subnet mask to include multiple, contiguous address spaces.

SUS (Microsoft Software Update Services) Used to manage the delivery of software security updates to the server and desktop computers.

System Log A component of Event Viewer that logs system events; enables you to obtain detailed information about related events recorded during DHCP audit logging.

System Monitor A tool that provides real-time monitoring that can provide insight as to how processes are progressing using the process, memory, and disk input/output on the server; used to observe and record system activity for specified objects and counters.

Task Manager A tool that provides real-time quantitative feedback on network use, the number of unicasts and non-unicasts sent, and the media speed for each network adapter.

Team model Under MSF, teams share responsibilities and work together as peers toward a common shared vision.

Terminal Services Administration tool used to administer remote clients. It is Windows Server 2003's implementation of a centralized computing architecture that enables users to execute Windows-based applications on a remote server.

Test environment One or several test labs, including test plans describing what you will test and the test cases describing how you will test each component of new server deployment.

Test lab A controlled environment for learning about and then testing and validating a proposed infrastructure.

Test plan A description of what you will test in a proposed network infrastructure, including test cases describing how you will test each component. Used to ensure that a proposed infrastructure will work properly and cause the shortest downtime during an infrastructure startup or update.

Throughput The results of the quantity of Utilization minus Collisions multiplied by Line Speed times Efficiency. That is, (Utilization - Collisions) * Line Speed * Efficiency.

Top-level domain A subdomain of the root domain.

Tracert A command-line utility used to search the route taken when data is transferred between communicating devices and to discover the point at which communication has failed. It displays the FQDN and IP address of each gateway along the route to a remote host.

Trade-offs Compromises and adjustments made to the resources, schedule, and the feature set in order to deliver a successful solution that provides the components that the customer agrees have the highest priority.

Transmission Control Protocol/Internet Protocol (TCP/IP) A protocol suite that enables computers to communicate with each other across a network. TCP/IP is the core set of protocols used by the Internet. You can use it on both large and small networks to transfer data between computers using different operating systems and widely varying hardware platforms.

Transport Mode The default mode for IPSec that protects the data over the entire path between two computers.

TTL The Time To Live for a DNS record entry.

Tunnel Mode Under IPSec, a mode that protects data between two endpoints (typically routers/gateways). Traffic behind the routers/gateways remains unencrypted.

Utilization The percentage of time that media on a network is busy transferring frames.

Variable Length Subnet Mask (VLSM) A method of changing subnetting by removing the requirement that all subnets be of equal size. VLSM allows you to break up an IP address into its largest subnets and then subnet the subnets.

Virtual LAN (VLAN) A local area network on network switches that requires a subnet for its hosts; used to create additional broadcast domains.

Virtual Memory Manager (VMM) A core service for Windows Server 2003 that manages memory and pagefile usage.

Virtual Private Network (VPN) A virtual network that can provide a secure connection between a user on an external network, such as the Internet, and an internal corporate network.

Windows Internet Naming Service (WINS) A Microsoft Windows feature that translates NetBIOS names into IP addresses. Using a WINS server enables NetBIOS name resolution to proceed in situations where broadcasts do not function, as when multiple networks are interconnected by routers.

WINS Replication Enables a WINS server to resolve NetBIOS names of another WINS server because the database is replicated from one server to another.

WINS server Resolves NetBIOS name queries into the corresponding IP address.

Wired Equivalency Privacy (WEP) The method of encryption defined by the IEEE 802.11b standard, and used to protect data from wireless eavesdropping.

Work Breakdown Structure An outline of the tasks needed to produce the required deliverables. The WBS also tracks tasks to solution requirements and can assist in time estimation.

Zero-Defect mindset A commitment by each team member to deliver components of a solution with the highest possible quality.

Zone A subdivision of the DNS structure that defines a scope of names that are served by a particular DNS name server.

Zone file Contains all resource records for a particular DNS zone. Also called the zone database file.

Zone of Authority The part of the DNS namespace for which a zone is responsible.

Zone transfer The replication of DNS zone files from a primary server to other DNS servers.

Index

A

account policies, default security configuration, **5.6**
Active Directory default security configuration, **5.6**
Active Directory-integrated zones, **4.12, 4.15**
Add Counters dialog box, **4.25, 8.23**
Add IP Filter dialog box, **6.7**
Add Objects dialog box, **3.39**
.adr files, **8.12**
addressing
    broadcast addresses, 3.12-3.13
    class-based addressing, 3.8-3.9
    IP addressing. *See* IP addressing
    name resolution. *See* name resolution
    Network Address Translation. *See* NAT
administration (remote)
    remote assistance, 7.14-7.17
    Remote Desktop for Administration, 7.10-7.13
    Terminal Services, 7.4-7.9
Advanced Schedule Options dialog box, **9.13**
Advanced TCP/IP Settings dialog box
    troubleshooting client configurations, 10.26-10.27
    WINS tab, 10.9
AFXR (complete zone transfers), **4.16**
AH (Authentication Header), **6.22-6.23**
analyzing network data
    DNS Debug and Event logs, 8.18-8.23
    Network Monitor
        Capture Filter dialog box, 8.16-8.17
        Network Monitor Capture window, 8.10-8.11
APIPA (Automatic Private IP Addressing), **3.16-3.17**
AppleTalk, **3.4-3.5**
application directory partitions, **4.18-4.19**
application logs, monitoring security, **5.20-5.21**
application server security settings, **5.10**
archive attribute/archive bit, **9.4-9.5.** *See also* backups
ASCII display of captured network data
  (Network Monitor)
    Capture Filter dialog box, 8.12-8.13
    Network Monitor Capture window, 8.10-8.11
ASR (Automated System Recovery) backup sets, **9.18**
assigning subnet masks, **3.14-3.15**
audit policies
    default security configuration, 5.8-5.9
    monitoring RRAS server log on events, 10.25
auditing, **5.4-5.5**
    RRAS server log on events, 10.24-10.25
authoritative restores, **9.14-9.15**
Automated System Recovery (ASR) backup sets, **9.18**

Automatic Private IP Addressing (APIPA), **3.16-3.17**
authentication, **5.4-5.5**
    Kerberos v5, 2.6
    remote access, 6.4
        authentication methods, 6.10-6.13
        troubleshooting, 10.22-10.25
    wireless RADIUS authentication, 6.28-6.29
Authentication Header (AH), **6.22-6.23**
Authentication Methods dialog box, **6.13**
Authentication-Type dialog box, **6.13**
authoritative servers, **4.6**
authorization, **5.4-5.5**
    remote access, 6.4
availability planning, **2.22-2.27**

B

B-node (Broadcast node), **4.27**
Backup Job Information dialog box, **9.7**
Backup or Restore Wizard, **9.7.** *See also* backups
    restoring system data, 9.16-9.17
Backup Progress dialog box, **9.9**
Backup Wizard, **9.10-9.13**
backups, **9.2-9.9**
    archive attribute/archive bit, 9.4-9.5
    Automated System Recovery (ASR) backup sets, 9.18
    Backup log, 9.9
    performing backups, 9.6-9.9
    permissions, 9.4
    restoring data, 9.8, 9.14-9.19
    scheduling, 9.10-9.13
    storage media, 9.5
    System State data, 9.10-9.13
    types of backups, 9.5-9.6
    viewing scheduled jobs, 9.13
    Volume Shadow Copy Service (VSS), 9.18
bandwidth, **3.32**
    example Internet bandwidth usage analysis,
      11.16-11.17
    multicasting, 3.48-3.49
    Terminal Services requirements, 7.6-7.7
baselines, **1.8**
    baseline server security, 5.6-5.9
    creating, 2.16-2.21, 3.38-3.39
    Microsoft Baseline Security Analyzer (MBSA),
      5.24-5.25
BGP (Border Gateway Protocol), redundant Internet
  connectivity, **3.46**
BOOTP relay agents, **2.8**

The Prentice Hall Certification Series features a building-block approach that organizes the material into a series of skills that students master one at a time. We adopted a two-page spread featuring a highly graphical approach with hundreds of screenshots that shows students how and why Windows Server 2003/Windows 2000/Windows XP works, rather than forcing them to memorize rote software procedures.

Windows Server 2003 Core Exam Texts

Exam 70-290: Microsoft Windows Server 2003: Managing and Maintaining

Text: 0-13-144743-2
Project Lab Manual: 0-13-144974-5
Interactive Solution CD-ROM: 0-13-144974-5

Exam 70-291: Microsoft Windows Server 2003: Network Infrastructure: Implementing, Managing and Maintaining

Text: 0-13-145600-8
Project Lab Manual: 0-13-145603-2
Interactive Solution CD-ROM: 0-13-145604-0

Exam 70-293: Microsoft Windows Server 2003: Network Infrastructure: Planning and Maintaining

Text: 0-13-189306-8
Project Lab Manual: 0-13-189307-6
Interactive Solution CD-ROM: 0-13-189308-4

Exam 70-294: Microsoft Windows Server 2003: Active Directory Infrastructure: Planning, Implementing, and Maintaining

Text: 0-13-189312-2
Project Lab Manual: 0-13-189314-9
Interactive Solution CD-ROM: ISBN TBD

Exam 70-297: Designing a Microsoft Windows Server 2003 Active Directory and Network Infrastructure

Text: 0-13-189316-5
Project Lab Manual: 0-13-189320-3
Interactive Solution CD-ROM: ISBN TBD

Exam 70-298: Designing Security for a Microsoft Windows Server 2003 Network

Text: 0-13-117670-6
Project Lab Manual: 0-13-146684-4
Interactive Solution CD-ROM: ISBN TBD

Value Pack Options Available

Series Features

The ONLY academic series developed by instructors for instructors that correlates to the MCSE and MCSA exam objectives.

4-color, 2-page layout
- Improves student retention through clear, easy-to-follow, step-by-step instructions.

Skills-Based Systematic Approach
- Uses integrated components: Main text, Project Lab Manual, Interactive Solution CD-ROM, and Web site with online quizzes.

Hands-on projects and problem-solving projects at the end of each lesson
- Help students better understand the material being taught.

Learning Aids
- Include Test Your Skills, On Your Own Projects, and Problem-Solving Cases at the end of each lesson.

Instructor's Resource CD
- PowerPoint slides containing all text graphics and lecture bullet points.
- Instructor's Manual that includes sample syllabus, teaching objectives, answers to exercises, and review questions.
- Test Bank with 40+ questions per lesson based on the text. Not generic MCSE questions.

Windows Server 2003 Enterprise 180 day evaluation software included in every text.

Project Lab Manuals

The Project Lab Manuals are designed as an additional tool that allow students to implement the concepts and practice the skills they have read about in the textbooks and CD-ROMs. With more hands-on projects and concept review, the Project Lab Manuals enable students to learn more about Windows 2003/2000/XP in real-world settings, practice the skills needed to prepare for the MCSE/MCSA exams, and prepare for a career as a network administrator.

The Project Lab Manual features:
- An overview of the task to be completed tied directly to the MCSA/MCSE Exam Objectives.
- 4-6 projects per lesson directly associated with the MCSA/MCSA Exam Objectives.
- Specific hardware requirements necessary to complete each lab.
- Step-by-step, hands-on instruction—it's like having an MCSE right by your side.
- Tips and Cautions elements designed to ease the learning process.
- Suggested completion times for each lab.

Interactive Solutions CD-ROMs

The Interactive Solutions CD-ROM was designed to directly support the Prentice Hall Certification Series texts by giving students a number of ways to enhance their studies.

The Interactive Solutions CD-ROM provides a simulated Windows 2003/2000/XP environment where students can learn and practice their skills without actually installing Windows 2003/2000/XP.

The learning modules are organized according to Microsoft knowledge domains and objectives. Conceptual overview sessions provide concise, animated descriptions of key networking concepts. Three types of interactive sessions (Play, Practice, and Assessment) provide students with hands-on experience with Windows Server 2003 and a realistic, challenging assessment environment.

Prentice Hall Certification Series for Windows 2000/Windows XP

Exam 70-210: Microsoft Windows 2000 Professional: Installing, Configuring, and Administering; Text: 0-13-142209-X; Lab Manual: 0-13-142257-X; Interactive Solutions CD-ROM: 0-13-142260-X

Exam 70-215: Microsoft Windows 2000 Server: Installing, Configuring, and Administering; Text: 0-13-142211-1; Lab Manual: 0-13-142281-2; Interactive Solutions CD-ROM: 0-13-142284-7

Exam 70-216: Microsoft Windows 2000 Network Infrastructure: Implementing and Administering; Text: 0-13-142210-3; Lab Manual: 0-13-142278-2; Interactive Solutions CD-ROM: 0-13-142277-4

Exam 70-217: Microsoft Windows 2000 Active Directory: Implementing and Administering; Text: 0-13-142208-1; Lab Manual: 0-13-142252-9; Interactive Solutions CD-ROM: 0-13-142254-5

Exam 70-218: Managing Microsoft Windows 2000 Network Environment; Text: 0-13-144744-0; Lab Manual: 0-13-144813-7; Interactive Solutions CD-ROM: 0-13-144812-9

Exam 70-270: Microsoft Windows XP Professional; Text: 0-13-144132-9; Lab Manual: 0-13-144450-6; Interactive Solutions CD-ROM: 0-13-144449-2

Test with Pearson VUE and Save 50%!

Get Certified Through the Microsoft Authorized Academic Testing Center (AATC) Program:

You invested in your future with the purchase of this textbook from Prentice Hall. Now, take the opportunity to get the recognition your skills deserve. Certification increases your credibility in the marketplace and is tangible evidence that you have what it takes to provide top-notch support to your employer.

Save 50% On Microsoft Exams!

Take advantage of this money-saving offer now. The cost of taking the exam is $60.00 with this offer.

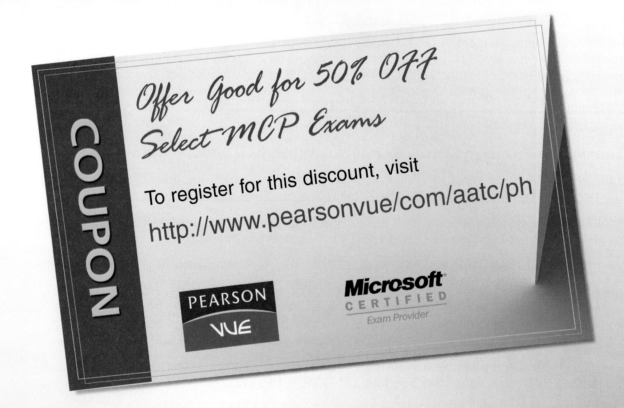

COUPON

Offer Good for 50% Off Select MCP Exams

To register for this discount, visit
http://www.pearsonvue/com/aatc/ph

PEARSON VUE

Microsoft CERTIFIED
Exam Provider

Select Microsoft exams, including the full suite of MCSA exams, are available at the discounted price to students and instructors who attend, or are employed by, academic institutions. Students and instructors can take advantage of this offer via the URL below.

MCSA on Microsoft Windows Server 2003 Certification Requirements for Students

Core Exams: Networking System (2 Exams Required)

72-290 Managing and Maintaining a Microsoft Windows Server 2003 Environment

72-291 Implementing, Managing, and Maintaining a Microsoft Windows Server 2003 Network Infrastructure

Core Exams: Client Operating System (1 Exam Required)

72-270 Installing, Configuring, and Administering Microsoft Windows XP Professional

72-210 Installing, Configuring, and Administering Microsoft Windows 2000 Professional

Elective Exams (1 Exam Required)

72-086 Implementing and Supporting Microsoft Systems Management Server 2.0

72-227 Installing, Configuring, and Administering Microsoft Internet Security and Acceleration (ISA) Server 2000, Enterprise Edition

72-228 Installing, Configuring, and Administering Microsoft SQL Server™ 2000 Enterprise Edition

72-284 Implementing and Managing Microsoft Exchange Server 2003

72-299 Implementing and Administering Security in a Microsoft Windows Server 2003 Network

Upgrade Exam for an MCSA on Windows 2000

An MCSA on Windows 2000 has the option to take Exam 70-292 instead of the two core network exams. No additional core or elective exams are required for an MCSA on Windows 2000 who passes Exam 70-292.

Upgrade Exam for an MCSA on Windows 2000 (1 Exam Required)

72-292 Managing and Maintaining a Microsoft Windows Server 2003 Environment for an MCSA Certified on Windows 2000

Offer also good on selected Windows 2000 exams.

For more information on Prentice Hall textbooks for MCSA and MCAD, *visit* www.prenhall.com/certification

Take advantage of this great offer! Go to www.pearsonvue.com/aatc/ph for complete details and to schedule a discounted exam at an AATC near you!